Metropolis in the Making

Metropolis
in the Making

Los Angeles in the 1920s

EDITED BY

Tom Sitton

AND

William Deverell

UNIVERSITY OF CALIFORNIA PRESS

Berkeley   Los Angeles   London

"Mulholland Highway and the Engineering Culture of Los Angeles," by Matthew W. Roth, first appeared in *Technology and Culture,* vol. 40, no. 3 (July 1999), pp. 545–575. © 1999 by the Society for the History of Technology.

"Sunshine and the Open Shop," by Mike Davis, first appeared in *Antipode,* vol.29, no. 4 (October 1997), pp. 356–382. © Editorial Board of *Antipode.*

Portions of "Did the Ruling Class Rule at City Hall in 1920s Los Angeles?" by Tom Sitton, first appeared in Tom Sitton, "The 'Boss' Without a Machine: Kent K. Parrot and Los Angeles Politics in the 1920s," *Southern California Quarterly* 65 (Winter 1985), pp. 365–387.

University of California Press
Berkeley and Los Angeles, California

University of California Press, Ltd.
London, England

Library of Congress Cataloging-in-Publication Data

Metropolis in the making: Los Angeles in the 1920s / edited by Tom Sitton and William Deverell.
    p.   cm.
Includes bibliographical references and index.
ISBN 0-520-22626-7 (cloth : alk. paper) — ISBN 0-520-22627-5 (pbk. : alk. paper)
    1. Los Angeles (Calif.)—History—20th century.   2. Los Angeles (Calif.)—Social conditions—20th century. 3. Los Angeles (Calif.)—Economic conditions—20th century. 4. City planning—California—Los Angeles—History—20th century.
5. Nineteen twenties. I. Sitton, Tom, 1949– II. Deverell, William Francis.

F869.L857 M48 2001
979.4′94052—dc21

                         00-057715

Printed in the United States of America

08 07 06 05 04 03 02 01
10 9 8 7 6 5 4 3 2 1

For Karen and Jenny

CONTENTS

ILLUSTRATIONS

PREFACE

This book has its origin in conversations that we have been having for more than a dozen years. Following in the tradition of an earlier collaborative effort, *California Progressivism Revisited* (University of California Press, 1994), we have assembled here a collection of original essays exploring a topic of scholarly interest and dynamism. Investigations of the history of early twentieth-century Los Angeles have, in recent years, reinvigorated such fields as California history, urban history, and western American studies. In this volume, inquiries into the critical decade of the 1920s are carried further and explored in greater depth than most monographic treatments allow.

The essays are the work of a group of talented historians, including established scholars as well as those just embarking on careers. We expect that the volume will be an important addition to the scholarly literature addressing the rise of one of the world's most important cities.

As with our earlier jointly edited book, we have accumulated numerous debts along the way. First of all, we would like to thank all our authors for their patience in working with us as we brought the volume to publication. We thank the editor of *Technology and Culture* for allowing us to reprint Matthew Roth's essay, which was recently awarded the Usher prize as the best article in that journal over the last three years; and we thank the editor of *Antipode* for permission to reprint a revision of the essay by Mike Davis. In addition, the editor of *Southern California Quarterly* allowed us to reprint portions of an essay by Tom Sitton. We enjoyed remarkable cooperation and help from curators and archivists in acquiring photographs for this volume. We'd especially like to thank the incomparable Dace Taube at the USC Regional History Center; Jennifer A. Watts and Erin W. Chase of the Huntington Library; Kate McGinn of Fuller Theological Seminary; Carolyn Kozo Cole of the Los Angeles Public Library; Victoria Seas at Caltech; and John

Cahoon at the Seaver Center for Western History Research. Anonymous reviewers of the volume helped strengthen its content, and we are grateful for their insights. At the University of California Press, Marilyn Schwartz and David Gill helped us prepare the manuscript for publication, as did copyeditor Kay Scheuer. Also at UC Press, Monica McCormick shepherded the project with care and attention, and we are continually grateful for her support and counsel.

INTRODUCTION

Metropolis in the Making

Los Angeles in the 1920s

Jules Tygiel

Carey McWilliams, the patron saint of Los Angeles history, first arrived in the City of Angels at the dawn of the great boom of the 1920s. He had departed his native Colorado in the midst of a snowstorm, but stepped off his train, not unlike Dorothy landing in Oz, into a land of bright colors, flowers, and perpetual sunshine. "The extraordinary green of the lawns and hillsides" dazzled McWilliams. But, he perceived, "it was the kind of green that seemed as though it might rub off on your hands; a theatrical green, a green that was not quite real." Like most migrants to Los Angeles, McWilliams was unprepared for the scenes that he witnessed. In the teeming downtown district, he observed unsettling crowds, the "aimless restless movement of armies of people with nothing much to do who were not going anyplace in particular."[1] McWilliams also discovered a "vicious economic underworld" of "two bit predators out to con the ignorant and fleece the innocent." On the outskirts of the city, he saw prosperous orchards, citrus groves, and produce fields making way for "unplanned and often jerry-built subdivisions."[2]

McWilliams developed an instant loathing for this "strange new city that was changing every hour." He "quickly got the feeling that, sociologically speaking, Los Angeles was a very strange community," a mushroom civilization in which "the surface was bright and pleasing, but the nether side was often dark and ugly."[3] Los Angeles, he complained, "lacked form and identity; there was no center." Gradually, however, the seemingly perverse charm of the region began to grow on McWilliams. "For an informal but revealing 'education' in the ways of laissez-faire capitalism, I had come to the right place at precisely the right time," he concluded. "Here the American people were erupting, like lava from a volcano; here was the place for me—a ringside seat at the circus." Los Angeles, McWilliams came to believe, would

I

become America's "great city of the Pacific, the most fantastic city in the world."[4]

Indeed, Los Angeles assumed much of its modern form in the 1920s. Not only did the city's population more than double, from 577,000 to 1.24 million, but much of what we would now recognize as Los Angeles—the vast sprawl, its reliance on the automobile, its predominance as a western business and financial center, the allure of Hollywood—took shape during the twenties. In 1919 Los Angeles had been physically smaller, anchored by a downtown and central district that housed more than half the population, the vast majority of whom came from white Anglo-Saxon Protestant stock. The Big Red Cars of Pacific Electric, the nation's largest electric streetcar system, connected the downtown and its hinterland. Most of the surrounding communities were unincorporated and sparsely developed. The hills remained barren of settlement. The city presented, according to McWilliams, "the curious spectacle of a large metropolitan area without an industrial base."[5] Los Angeles ranked behind seventeen other cities as a manufacturing center, its labor force disproportionately concentrated in service and tourist-based enterprises. The region remained a relatively minor player in the nation's petroleum industry, and Goodyear Tire had just become the first significant national company to open a branch plant in the area. The city's most famous industry, motion pictures, on the other hand, had already established itself in Hollywood, producing over 80 percent of the world's movies. Seventy independent companies turned out a multitude of silent movies featuring diverse themes and a variety of political agendas.

By 1929, however, on the eve of the Great Depression, Los Angeles had experienced a dramatic transformation. A combination of rapid in-migration and aggressive expansion had added 80 square miles and almost 600,000 residents to create a new metropolis. During the 1920s Los Angeles annexed 45 adjacent communities, spreading out northward into the San Fernando Valley and southward toward the harbor at San Pedro. By the end of the decade less than a third of the population lived in the downtown, East Los Angeles, Hollywood, and Wilshire districts,[6] with residents increasingly relying on the automobile, rather than the Big Red Cars for transportation. Real estate developments like Bel-Air and Hollywoodland began to open up the hillsides to settlement. The population remained overwhelmingly Caucasian and Protestant, but the decade had also witnessed the beginnings of two "great migrations": of Mexicans uprooted by the Mexican Revolution and of African Americans leaving the South. Combined with a growing Japanese population, they gave Los Angeles the second-highest percentage of nonwhites of any major city in the nation (after Baltimore). Substantial communities of Jews, Slavs, Italians, Russians, and Armenians had also taken shape.

The most striking change had occurred in the industrial realm. Spectacular oil discoveries just south of the city in Huntington Beach, Long Beach, and Santa Fe Springs had made the Los Angeles basin into one of the world's great petroleum-producing areas. The development of a rapidly growing Central Manufacturing District had attracted myriad corporations to locate branch plants in the region, generating a veritable industrial revolution. By 1930, Los Angeles ranked not only first in the nation in movie production, but second in the making of automobile tires, and it was rapidly rising in a host of other areas. The city had emerged as the aviation capital of the United States, with a third of the nation's air traffic centered in the region. More than a quarter of its workers were now engaged in manufacturing, and the city had leaped to ninth place among the nation's industrial centers. Large corporate employers had increasingly replaced smaller enterprises as the dominant economic players. In Hollywood, for example, the Big Eight companies now produced 90 percent of all major movies, controlling not just the making of films but, through ownership of theater chains, their distribution and exhibition as well.

"The history of Los Angeles," McWilliams would write, "is the history of its booms." Indeed, he commented, from 1870 on there had been "one continuous boom, punctuated at intervals by major explosions." Even within this context, however, the boom of the 1920s stood out to McWilliams as a "truly bonanza affair . . . one long drunken orgy, one protracted debauch," that would undermine the community's social structure, "warping and twisting its institutions."[7] *Saturday Evening Post* correspondent Albert Atwood commented in 1923 on the "extraordinary and almost unprecedented pouring of population, money and prosperity into one section of the country and more particularly into one city," and the "insistent element of speculation [that] permeates all walks of life."[8] Local journalist Guy Finney described a city "particularly ripe for heedless financial adventure."[9] This runaway growth occurred against a backdrop of constant spectacle: the foibles and scandals of affluent Hollywood, the oil stock promotion schemes of colorful confidence artists like C. C. Julian, and the boisterous religious revivalism of Aimee Semple McPherson.

In 1946, McWilliams recorded his impressions of his adopted homeland in his engaging classic, *Southern California: An Island on the Land.* In it he disavowed "the well worn path of most books about Southern California," and attempted instead to unearth what he called "the region's cultural landscape."[10] Several themes underscored his interpretation. To McWilliams Southern California was a paradoxical region, both in its physical realities ("a desert that faces an ocean") and in a political and cultural sense. "Almost every aspect of life in Southern California possessed a delightful novelty," he wrote. "Sociologically detached from the rest of the country," the section existed "as a kind of sovereign empire by the western shore."[11] Furthermore, "Southern California is man-made, a gigantic improvisation," into which "virtually everything has been imported . . . an artificial region, a product of forced growth and rapid change." Los Angeles itself was a "city based on improvisation, words, propaganda, boosterism," a "series of connecting villages . . . lacking traditional, ties, associations, and restraints."[12] Perhaps most significantly, McWilliams attributed the area's eccentricities not to its "fabled climate," but to its incessant growth. The "volume and velocity of migration" had created a "sociology of the boom," that had reshaped the contours of the American dream in Southern California and Los Angeles.[13]

Borrowing heavily from 1920s magazine journalists like Sarah Comstock, McWilliams portrayed Los Angeles as "the melting pot for the peoples of the United States."[14] Although he acknowledged the presence of other racial and ethnic groups, the overwhelming predominance of white migrants from the Midwest attracted most of his attention. Anticipating historians like James Gregory[15] by almost half a century, McWilliams treated these new arrivals from the heartland not as simply transplanted citizens, but as immigrants in their own right, undergoing a "process of cultural adaptation." To combat the loneliness created by migration, they patronized cafeterias and formed state societies where they might meet people from home. Like European transplants, they developed an "alien patrimony," an identification with their home states, which they romanticized with qualities they could not find in their strange new surroundings.[16]

The never-ending influx of new arrivals, according to McWilliams, determined virtually every aspect of life in California, from its "confused arboreal pattern" to its religious eccentricities and its "curious lack of social continuity." The boom cycle had given Los Angeles its "sprawling centrifugal form," and made it "a city without a center . . . a collection of suburbs in search of a city." Migration had made Los Angeles a haven for evangelical sects, cults, and "freak religions" and rendered it a "vast drama of maladjustment," with soaring rates of divorce, suicide, and addiction. Repeated "avalanches of population" had "corrupted the civic virtue of the body politic" and disrupted political reform movements. The succession of booms had encouraged "a rather easy code of commercial ethics" and a toleration of business practices that "would be abhorrent in a more stable community." Even Hollywood benefited from "the kind of community where a circus industry could take root . . . a frontier town forever booming; a community kept currently typical-American by constant migration."[17]

As a result, Southern Californians suffered from what McWilliams called a "slight case of cultural confusion."[18] Long before the pioneering writings of historian Herbert Gutman in the 1970s,[19] McWilliams, recognized that a continuous influx of newcomers meant that each wave of migrants would be "compelled to discover the region afresh." Migrants repeatedly "came bearing a load of previously acquired notions, customs, practices, and concepts which they stubbornly insisted could be applied in Southern California." They engaged in a massive environmental facelift, decimating the native live oaks and burning the indigenous chaparral, introducing flowers, trees, and shrubs from "the far corners of the earth." They introduced modes of architecture more characteristic of eastern climes. The unplanned mixing of regional styles gave Southern California an "unreal appearance," but it also made the region a "great laboratory of experimentation," and a proving ground for imported ideas, practices, and customs.[20]

Southern California: An Island on the Land became to generations of Los Angeles historians what W. J. Cash's *Mind of the South* was to scholars of the American South—a seminal work that inspired others to examine the region and sharply influenced their ultimate interpretations.[21] McWilliams's lively writing and provocative insights, however, obscured the book's shortcomings. At times, as in his overwrought retelling of the Owens Valley "tragedy," McWilliams substituted local folklore for sound history. He also exaggerated the uniqueness of Los Angeles. His assumptions about other American cities were based more on speculation than research, and he underestimated the unsettled nature of other urban areas. The work of Stephan Thernstrom and others would demonstrate the common volatility of cities in the United States and render the Los Angeles experience less exceptional than McWilliams indicated.[22] In addition, McWilliams overstated the isolation of Los Angeles from national influences. He argued that political developments elsewhere had "virtually no repercussions here," and that the region was "sociologically detached from the rest of the country."[23] But Los Angeles largely followed the patterns of national politics—Progressive reform, reaction in the 1920s, and a swing to the New Deal in the 1930s—and responded to the effects of national economic swings. Much of the sense of excitement and recklessness in the 1920s came not only from the local boom, but from the greater accessibility of spectacle created nationally by the advent of radio, newsreels, and tabloid newspapers and the speculative frenzy that gripped the nation as a whole. Los Angeles might arguably have sailed toward the extreme ends of the spectrum at various moments in its history, but it rarely, if ever, drifted entirely out of the American mainstream.

More surprising, given McWilliams's leftist politics, is the mildness of his critique of the Los Angeles political and economic establishments. McWilliams, to be sure, ardently exposes the repressive nature of the city's antiunion, open shop, and antiradical crusades. The *Los Angeles Times,* the Merchants and Manufacturers Association, and other allies, in their ardor to make Los Angeles the "white spot" of the nation, ruled Southern California with "an iron hand," charges McWilliams. The Better America Federation and like-minded groups employed a "host of spies, stool pigeons and informers to disrupt trade unions, to provoke violence, and to ferret out the reds." The Red Squad of the Los Angeles Police Department "made a mockery of the right of free speech," creating a "background of terrorism and police brutality."[24]

But beyond his revealing commentary on Los Angeles business leaders as boosters, McWilliams delves little into the nonlabor activities of the city's economic elites. Harry Chandler, the powerful publisher of the *Times,* godfather to a myriad of Los Angeles business ventures, and in popular mythology the éminence grise of the city's economic successes and excesses, makes but a few token appearances. Influential bankers like Henry M. Robinson and Joseph F. Sartori merit a single mention. Nor does McWilliams comment on the planning initiatives underwriting the creation of the innovative Central Manufacturing District and other industrial districts. Local political elections and issues never enter McWilliams's narrative.

Southern California, however, remains a formidable achievement. More than half a century after its publication, it still dominates the historiographical landscape as a starting point for most research on Los Angeles. In part this is true because of the relative dearth of other studies until recent years. The city's history became the grist for scores of mystery novels and motion pictures. However, with the exception of *The Fragmented Metropolis: Los Angeles, 1850–1930* by Robert Fogelson, *Thinking Big: The Story of the Los Angeles Times, Its Publishers and Their Influence on Southern California* by Robert Gottlieb and Irene Wolt, and books about the movie industry or the quest for water, few book-length scholarly explorations of the city's history surfaced before 1990.[25] In that year, two significant new volumes—Mike Davis's *City of Quartz* and Kevin Starr's *Material Dreams: Southern California through the 1920s*—appeared.[26] Their publication indicated a shifting of the tide. A new generation of scholars turned their attention to the history of Los Angeles and began to create a richer, more detailed analytical tableau of the city's past.[27]

The essays in this volume present some of the best of this work. In some instances they reinforce McWilliams's interpretations, in others they critique his conclusions, and often they delve into areas that he barely touched upon. McWilliams portrayed Los Angeles as a largely unplanned product, cobbled together by the whims of new arrivals and the excesses of mindless boosterism. Greg Hise and Mike Davis, on the other hand, show how elites, entrepreneurs, and planners consciously guided the manufacturing growth in the region, according to Hise, fixing "the coordinates for an industrial Los Angeles that has structured the pattern of city building and urban life from that time forward." Matthew W. Roth unveils the role of city engineers, emboldened by the success of the Owens Valley water project, in the construction of Mulholland Highway.

Even more than McWilliams, the current authors stress the extraordinary variety of the Los Angeles experience. As Michael E. Engh comments in his article "Practically Every Religion Being Represented," Angelenos in the 1920s became "pioneers of religious diversity in the United States" in this century, seeking to "articulate a new model beyond that of the melting pot" to accommodate a society more multicultural than that in other American cities. While McWilliams stressed the more flamboyant religious leaders like Aimee Semple McPherson, Philip Goff looks at the career of fundamentalist minister Charles E. Fuller of the Bible Institute of Los Angeles. Fuller, more measured and understated than McPherson, became "the most popular radio preacher in history" and laid the foundation for the fundamentalist resurgence of the late twentieth century. William Deverell resurrects the alternative religious career of Garfield Bromley Oxnam, preacher of the Social Gospel, who ran afoul of the city's conservative watchdogs when he entered the political arena in 1923.

Like McWilliams, many of these articles address the process of resettlement and redefinition, but the drama here is more often one of healthy adaptation rather than social maladjustment. Douglas Monroy describes the efforts of Mexican immigrants to create a *México de afuera,* or "Mexico away," in their new homeland, re-creating a more familiar landscape through theater, sports, and religion. Douglas Flamming captures the African American community struggling to achieve not just a local, but a national identity, culminating in the establishment of one of the country's most active branches of the National Association for the Advancement of Colored People and the successful staging of the 1928 NAACP convention. David Charles Sloane, in a revealing essay on Forest Lawn, shows how Hubert Eaton, recognizing the needs of a transplanted populace, "reinvented the cemetery as a memorial park . . . a place of life, not death," an eternal resting place more in keeping with the values of twentieth-century consumer society.

Throughout the Los Angeles basin, new arrivals, even those with modest means, became home owners and established substantive communities. Becky Nicolaides depicts families like the Smiths of South Gate who acquired a patch of land, built their own home, and, through a combination of industrial employment and subsistence farming, "devised a pre-modern solution to the problems posed by industrial capitalism." Even amid the burgeoning oilfields, as Nancy Qwam-Wickham demonstrates, workers formed communities of single-family homes and maintained an anti-urban ethos, at the very time they were becoming engulfed by the oil rigs and refineries of the expanding metropolis. Throughout the working-class suburbs, laborers took advantage of Pacific Ready Cut Bungalow kits and low property prices to acquire a foothold, and as Nicolaides argues, turn "their residential environment into a source of economic security."

For many, however, as Mike Davis notes, the need to meet house payments and to maintain these homes bred fear and uncertainty, particularly in the harsh anti-union, low-wage environment. The Los Angeles of these essays remains an often grim, repressive universe. The creation of the Central Manufacturing District in Vernon, according to Davis, offered businessmen "a scientifically planned, intensified industrial district," a community devoid of residences and occupied almost exclusively by factories, where entrepreneurs could be free of political opposition from workers and labor unions. Clark Davis portrays "legions of white-collar employees working in crowded downtown offices," receiving blue-collar-level wages. Beneath the glitter of Hollywood, Laurie Pintar discovers a world of low pay and poor working conditions.

The oppressive politics of the open shop reinforced this reality. "Militant anti-unionism, together with scientific factory planning, low taxes, abundant electric power, warm weather, mass-produced bungalows, and a racially selected labor force made Los Angeles a paradise of the open shop," writes Mike Davis. Pintar describes how movie moguls crushed the strikes of studio unions. Steven Ross argues that the rise of the studio system and theater chains allowed the conservative leaders of the industry to purge mentions of class conflict, labor unions, and radicalism, all staples of independent moviemaking in the 1910s, from the mass market feature films of the 1920s. Deverell reveals the "powerful shrill voice of reaction," represented by conservative groups like the Better America Federation, which stridently combated not only labor unions and radical activists, but liberal Progressive political and school reforms.

Los Angeles was also a land of harsh discrimination. The Ku Klux Klan found a ready following in 1920s Southern California. Employers in many industries, especially the expanding white-collar sector, as Clark Davis illustrates, sought to hire only "red-blooded Americans." According to Hise, the "imaginative geographies" envisioned by local leaders and planners stressed whites-only policies, and zoning in towns like Torrance specifically barred non-Caucasians. Restrictive housing covenants in most sections of the region prevented nonwhites from moving in. The Legal Committee of the NAACP, writes Flamming, found ample work warding off police brutality against minorities and segregation in housing and public swimming pools. Exclusion persisted even in death. At Forest Lawn, notes Sloane, "only people of Caucasian descent were welcome to purchase lots."

McWilliams ignored local politics, but Deverell and Tom Sitton flesh out the dynamics of electoral contests in the city. Sitton explores the limitations of the economic oligarchy and alleged political boss Kent Parrot in enforcing their respective agendas on local voters. Sitton contends that the entrepreneurial elite was "not as dominant in municipal politics as its contemporary opponents and some later observers have claimed." Rival forces consistently and often successfully challenged its hegemony. Alternatively, Deverell demonstrates the considerable power that the local political establishment, led by the *Los Angeles Times* and the Better America Federation, could muster when challenged in a school board race by a liberal outsider like Reverend Oxnam.

Although these essays do not always coincide with his interpretations, Carey McWilliams no doubt would have enjoyed this volume. McWilliams viewed Southern California as "an archipelago of social and ethnic islands, economically interrelated but culturally disparate."[28] These articles traverse these isles at a deeper level, exposing their distinctiveness as well as their interconnections. To McWilliams Los Angeles was "not merely a testing ground," but "also a forcing ground, a place where ideas, practices, and customs must prove their worth or be discarded."[29] The same may be said of the city's history. The writers assembled here have tested *Southern California* and other earlier chronicles, accepting what remains viable and discarding what no longer rings true, while inevitably casting their own ideas into the forcing ground of history.

NOTES

1. Carey McWilliams, *Southern California: An Island on the Land* (1946; Santa Barbara: Peregrine Smith, Inc., 1973), ix.

2. Carey McWilliams, *The Education of Carey McWilliams* (New York: Simon and Schuster, 1978, 1979), 42–45.

3. McWilliams, *Southern California*, x; McWilliams, *Education*, 44.

4. McWilliams, *Education*, 45, 42; McWilliams, *Southern California*, 376–77.

5. McWilliams, *Southern California*, 238.

6. David Brodsly, *L.A. Freeway: An Appreciative Essay* (Berkeley and Los Angeles: University of California Press, 1981), 91.

7. McWilliams, *Southern California*, 114, 136.

8. Albert W. Atwood, "Money from Everywhere," *Saturday Evening Post*, May 12, 1923, 10.

9. Guy W. Finney, *The Great Los Angeles Bubble: A Present Day Story of Colossal Financial Jugglery and of Penalties Paid* (Los Angeles: Milton Forbes, 1929), 9.

10. McWilliams, *Southern California*, xiii, 138.

11. Ibid., 6, 104, 313.

12. Ibid., 13, 293, 169, 303.

13. Ibid., 227.

14. Ibid., 232. See also Sarah Comstock, "The Great American Mirror: Reflections from Los Angeles," *Harper's Monthly*, May 1928, 715–23.

15. James Gregory, *American Exodus: The Dust Bowl Migration and Okie Culture in California* (New York: Oxford University Press, 1989).

16. McWilliams, *Southern California*, 350, 166–70.

17. Ibid., 232–49, 342.

18. Ibid., 350.

19. Herbert Gutman, *Work, Culture, and Society in Industrializing America: Essays in American Working-Class and Social History* (New York: Vintage Books, 1977).

20. McWilliams, *Southern California,* 350–70.

21. W. J. Cash, *The Mind of the South* (New York: A. A. Knopf, 1941).

22. See, for example, Stephan Thernstrom, *The Other Bostonians: Poverty and Progress in the American Metropolis, 1880–1970* (Cambridge: Harvard University Press, 1973).

23. McWilliams, *Southern California,* 313.

24. Ibid., 290–92.

25. Robert Fogelson, *The Fragmented Metropolis: Los Angeles, 1850–1930* (Cambridge: Harvard University Press, 1967); Robert Gottlieb and Irene Wolt, *Thinking Big: The Story of the Los Angeles Times* (New York: G.P. Putnam's Sons, 1977). Other earlier books include Scott L. Bottles, *Los Angeles and the Automobile: The Making of the Modern City* (Berkeley and Los Angeles: University of California Press, 1987); Louis Perry and Richard Perry, *A History of the Los Angeles Labor Movement, 1911–1941* (Berkeley and Los Angeles: University of California Press, 1963); Ricardo Romo, *East Los Angeles: History of a Barrio* (Austin: University of Texas Press, 1983); John Modell, *The Economics and Politics of Racial Accommodation: The Japanese in Los Angeles, 1900–1942* (Urbana: University of Illinois Press, 1977); Gregory H. Singleton, *Religion in the City of Angels: American Protestant Culture and Urbanization, 1850–1930* (Ann Arbor: UMI Research Press, 1979). In addition to these books, several significant doctoral dissertations appeared. On the 1920s see especially James C. Findlay, "The Economic Boom of Los Angeles in the 1920s" (Ph. D. dissertation, Claremont Graduate School, 1958); and Leonard Leader, "Los Angeles and the Great Depression" (Ph. D. dissertation, University of California, Los Angeles, 1972). There is also a rich body of articles in scholarly journals and collections.

26. Mike Davis, *City of Quartz: Excavating the Future in Los Angeles* (New York: Verso, 1990); Kevin Starr, *Material Dreams: Southern California through the 1920s* (New York: Oxford University Press, 1990).

27. The new generation of books includes Edith Blumhofer, *Aimee Semple McPherson: Everybody's Sister* (Grand Rapids, Mich.: William B. Eerdmans, 1993); Brian Masaru Hayashi, *'For the Sake of Our Japanese Brethren': Assimilation, Nationalism and Protestantism among the Japanese of Los Angeles, 1895–1942* (Stanford: Stanford University Press, 1995); Douglas Monroy, *Rebirth: Mexican Los Angeles from the Great Migration to the Great Depression* (Berkeley and Los Angeles: University of California Press, 1999); Deborah Dash Moore, *To the Golden Cities: Pursuing the American Jewish Dream in Miami and Los Angeles* (New York: Free Press, 1994); Steven J. Ross, *Working-Class Hollywood: Silent Film and the Shaping of Class in America* (Princeton: Princeton University Press, 1998); George Sanchez, *Becoming Mexican American: Ethnicity, Culture, and Identity in Chicano Los Angeles, 1900–1945* (New York: Oxford University Press, 1993); Tom Sitton, *John Randolph Haynes: California Progressive* (Stanford: Stanford University Press, 1992); Raphael J. Sonenshein, *Politics in Black and White: Race and Power in Los Angeles* (Princeton: Princeton University Press, 1993); Jules Tygiel, *The Great Los Angeles Swindle: Oil, Stocks, and Scandal during the Roaring Twenties* (New York: Oxford University Press, 1994).

28. McWilliams, *Southern California,* 314.

29. Ibid., 370.

PART ONE

Metropolitan Spaces

LOS ANGELES IN the 1920s was at once a city of rigid social space and a place of dynamic movement. As these five essays demonstrate, the city's spatial complexities offer much for the historian to ponder. Greg Hise's investigation of occupational landscapes reminds us of the often neglected industrial past of Los Angeles. Matthew Roth's essay on the construction of a major transportation artery explores the city's growth patterns and offers a glimpse into the region's critically important engineering culture. Becky Nicolaides, Mike Davis, and Nancy Quam-Wickam, each in different ways, examine the residential geography of 1920s Los Angeles from the perspective of the city's workers. Often hidden from view, like the industries they worked in, working-class communities of Los Angeles were the product both of the external forces that shaped them and of the aspirations of their residents.

CHAPTER ONE

Industry and
Imaginative Geographies

Greg Hise

"The City of the Angels," so attractive to the tourists because of climate and natural beauty, is fast becoming a great industrial center. The Panama Canal will bring the ships of the world to its own harbor. The awakening of the nations across the Pacific will create demands for goods manufactured in coast cities. Oil fuel is at hand, transportation is assured, and a vast market is being opened. Capital will quickly respond, and soon the loom and furnace will furnish products for a new world of commerce. Already great industrial plants are busy day and night satisfying the demands of an ever-widening district.

DANA BARTLETT, 1907

In the domain of city growth Southern California finds itself reversing the ordinary processes of municipalization. The attractiveness of life in this community draws, as with a magnet, thousands upon thousands each year who beg for a chance to make a living in this nature favored spot. Many specialize in intensive agriculture. Others try to pry their way into industry. . . . The problem of Southern California thus becomes the difficulty of providing an economic foundation for its rapidly accumulating population. The people continue to come. How shall they be cared for?

CLARENCE DYKSTRA, C. 1930

In a 1907 reform tract, *The Better City*, Dana Bartlett, a Protestant cleric and urban progressive, waxed euphoric about the promise of Los Angeles. From its church-centered founding to the beneficent climate and increasing civic "patriotism," Bartlett cast his eyes upon an "American city," where the foreign-born "vied with his neighbor in devotion to high ideals," a city poised for greatness and, if residents heeded the social gospel, goodness. In its setting and its development to date, Los Angeles had avoided the blight Bartlett saw in Chicago, New York, and other eastern cities. "Ugliness," he wrote, "has no commercial or ethical value. The crowded tenement and rookery, a city's ill-kept streets and yards, are not incentives to higher living." Los Angeles, by contrast, was a "city of homes, without slums." There might be "slum people," Bartlett confessed, but "no slums in the sense of vicious, congested districts." Here the "poor live in single cottages, with dividing fences

13

and flowers in the front yard, and oftentimes with vegetables in the back yard." The notable exception, cited to prove the rule, was the house courts along Utah Street, east of the Los Angeles River, occupied by laborers "brought in from Mexico to work on the trolley."[1]

Bartlett lavished considerable praise on the river itself, a site, as he envisioned it, for promenades, ornamental bridges, and the coming together of diverse culture groups and classes. Although recently, and lamentably, given over to base uses, the river still possessed its "ancient possibilities," and Bartlett's initial plan was to hide existing warehouses and factories behind a "wealth of climbing vines and roses," clear the area north of First Street to Elysian Park as a playground for the children of the "congested districts," and construct public baths, gymnasia, and civic centers along the river banks.[2]

Whether hidden by flowers or open to view, those factories posed a considerable challenge; in Bartlett's lifetime, the "call of the factory whistle [had become] louder and more insistent than the sweet music of the mission bells." Quite rapidly, it seemed, the City of Angels as a "city of homes" was giving way to a great industrial center. This was particularly true for a zone lying between Alameda Street and the Los Angeles River from Ninth Street north to Elysian Park, which came to be known as the East Side Industrial District. In many ways this moniker was a misnomer. Although there were a number of manufacturing concerns in this district it was, in fact, a polyglot landscape of the type most urbanists associate with the teeming central area in cities like Chicago and New York. In Los Angeles, this mixed zone housed an extraordinary degree of diversity in terms of land uses and activities as well as of the people who lived and worked there.

Walking along North Main from Alameda to Sotello Streets Bartlett would have passed by foundries, boilerworks, patternmakers' shops, and both Llewellyn and Western iron works. Interspersed among these firms were a Salvation Army store, two groceries, and a number of restaurants and saloons, as well as residences ranging from single-family dwellings to apartments and furnished rooms. Writing in 1919, following a survey of this district, the California Commission on Immigration and Housing deduced that "surely life can not be normal in an area so much given over to industry, where there must of necessity be noise, grime, confusion, unpleasant odors, and nothing restful or beautiful to look upon." True to his politics and position, Bartlett imagined this mix of uses and people as a problem to be overcome. He shared the progressive vision, advanced by public health professionals, social workers, and advocates of urban improvement and city planning, that the proper solution to this problem was a parsing out of land uses, people, and activities to create a more orderly, rational, efficient city.[3]

Bartlett feared the prospect that Los Angeles might come to resemble eastern cities: "As factories increase in size and number, aliens will be attracted, tenements and house courts will become congested, causing an increase in sickness and crime." Salvation would be assured if industrialists took up the cause; they could become architects of the better city. "No modern industrial movement," Bartlett wrote, "means more for the welfare of the working people than the transfer of manufacturing plants from the crowded city to the country where, with better housing conditions, better sanitation, fresh air, greater freedom from temptation, and with flowers and parks and bright work rooms, life seems worth the living."[4] Supporters of this kind of urban improvement believed the rational, orderly dispersion of jobs and people would benefit the majority of Angelenos, if not all. In his 1907 tract Bartlett evoked an imaginative geography that would inform city building in Los Angeles for decades, a vision of manufacturing facilities and working-class residences moving out from the city center and into the surrounding country.

Bartlett was not a prophet; Los Angeles, and other American cities, did not expand along the lines he envisioned. He was prescient, however, and rather than dismiss his account outright, it is worth considering the ways in which industry has shaped, and continues to shape, Los Angeles and Southern California. The 1920s was a generative period when civic elites, entrepreneurs, and workers fixed the coordinates for an industrial Los Angeles that has structured the pattern of city building and urban life from that time forward. For this line of inquiry, the primary concern is locational with an eye toward understanding the ways industrialists, in concert with developers, design professionals, and other city builders, helped shape the precise nature of urban expansion in the region. This essay features two factors that are absent in most narratives about Los Angeles: an investigation of the connection between residential development and industrial development—what geographers call the workplace-residence link—and the role that planning, broadly defined, played in this process. To put it more concretely, my first concern is city building, the creation of industrial Los Angeles as a material artifact, with its particular production landscapes and social patterns.

At the same time, I am interested in a concomitant creation, the construction of industrial Los Angeles in narratives about Southern California. At first glance this may appear an unlikely topic of investigation, one that could offer insights into culture, perhaps, but might not provide much explanatory power for questions of lived experience or policy. As recent scholarship has shown, however, cultural practices like the plotting and dissemination of stories about manufacturing prowess and the spatial reach of local capital are not simply fabrications or passive reflections. Often these narratives serve as instruments that people leverage as a means for acting on the

Figure 1.1. View from Sunset Boulevard looking north toward the Southern Pacific Railroad yard and Elysian Park, c. 1929. North Broadway is on the left, Alameda Street is on the right. In between is the so-called congested district, a zone of mixed land uses and diverse population that Dana Bartlett and other social reformers intended to rationalize by encouraging working-class residents to move to housing tracts in the emerging eastside. Prominent manufacturing firms and commercial interests in this image include Brunswig Drug Co., Lincoln Fireproof Storage Co., and Llewellyn Iron Works (immediately adjacent to the railyard). *Hearst Collection, Department of Special Collections, University of Southern California Library*

world. For this line of inquiry we might ask, simply, Who told what stories when and with what effect or effects? [5]

On a similar, or somewhat higher, level of abstraction, a study of industrial Los Angeles during the 1920s should be situated within the expanding literature on the history of the western United States. One aspect of this investigation would contribute to a general reinterpretation of the relationship between financial interests in East Coast and midwestern cities and urban development in the intermountain area and along the Pacific slope. As was the case in the nineteenth century, investments by Chicagoans, New Yorkers, and capitalists in other cities provided the financial wherewithal mandatory for controlling land, creating infrastructure, constructing manufacturing plants, and commanding labor. Just as critically, however, the story of industrial Los Angeles is a regional one. Over time, civic elites, businesspeople, and residents in western and West Coast cities transformed these settlements from mercantile centers dependent on outsiders for goods and the means of exchange to command and control centers with Los Angeles, for example, playing an increasingly important role in international trade and production networks through the twentieth century.

If we return to Bartlett's tract with these themes in mind, we find that his assessment generates as many questions as it might possibly answer. There are the obvious contradictions; Los Angeles is a city without tenements and slums poised to be overrun by "aliens," who will then congest the tenements and house courts. His language and terminology raise questions as well. What, precisely, would it mean to have a "city" freed of production and manufacturing located in the "country"? Finally there is an imaginative and idealized coupling of industry and nature; factories with bright work rooms and fresh air surrounded by parks and humble yet uplifting cottages, the latter housing workers and their families who are invited to inhale the "golden smoke" of industry.[6]

But the vision that aroused Bartlett's imagination can be described summarily. He believed in a spatial fix, an extensive pruning and thinning out in the congested districts intended to alleviate unhealthy physical conditions such as overcrowding. Out in less densely settled sections of the city, workers could construct single-family dwellings surrounded by open space, light, and air. Here, according to Bartlett, even though the "walls may be only the thickness of a single board, [a worker's house] covered in vines and flowers equals in comfort an Eastern palace."[7] We recognize this as part of an Americanization project, acculturating immigrants through industrial employment and a normative standard of living. During the subsequent decade, sociologists, health professionals, and housing reformers would offer alternative assessments of conditions in the congested districts, but their prescriptions for change remained consistent with Bartlett's vision.

Of course, any chance of realizing some version of Bartlett's vision hinged on the interests of industrialists, particularly their locational decisions, and on a continued expansion of industry in the region. The latter became increasingly critical during the 1920s since over the course of the decade more and more people chose to move to greater Los Angeles. Given this, it is important to consider the magnitude of industrial expansion in the region and then situate this change in a national context. Contemporary accounts featured quantitative assessments with associated charts and graphs. Both plotted an ascending trajectory and implied that continued expansion was expected, if not inevitable.[8]

This accounting of industrial progress, to use a phrase that boosters trotted out routinely, can never convey the nature and texture of change in Los Angeles during the 1920s. However, the acres of land developed for manufacturing, the increasing number of firms setting up plants in the region, the rising employment in industrial production, the innovation in products and production processes, the enhanced array of goods available from local suppliers, as well as less positive, and therefore less often noted, changes such as growing pollution and an increase in physical and social congestion were important factors that shaped the city, and it is instructive to review the numbers.

During the decade total land area increased by approximately 80 square miles through 45 separate annexations, and the population grew from 577,000 to almost 1.24 million. Population in the county increased 140 percent, from just over 900,000 residents in 1920 to over 2.2 million in 1930; the latter translates into an average of 350 newcomers a day for ten years.[9] During these years civic elites noted with escalating concern that it would require more than tourism, land speculation, and services to provide employment for all the new residents streaming into the southland. By 1930, the promotion of industrial expansion as a means to meet this perceived shortfall between wage earners and jobs—a call the Los Angeles Area Chamber of Commerce (LAACC or Chamber) first issued in the 1910s as a novel adjunct to the standard litany of year-round sunshine, recreation, and an expropriated Spanish culture—had become the equivalent of a civic mantra.[10]

As Robert Fogelson has shown, the plea to wean the regional economy from the "tourist crop" and real estate speculation and reorient it toward industry was advanced with an ever-increasing measure of urgency.[11] A *Los Angeles Times* editorial, "Balanced Progress," published on Sunday, November 18, 1923, articulates this particular vantage on existing conditions and advances one vision of the region's future. Los Angeles, the editors declared, "stands at the dawn of a golden tomorrow." But even though they gazed out upon a city "glittering" with promise and opportunity, the future was "fraught with great problems" because population growth routinely "staggered all power of anticipation." (Keep in mind that this statement was crafted at the beginning of the even greater increases of the 1920s.) It was time

> for us to see to it that the various forces that go to make up this terrific expansion are kept working in even and balanced effort . . . new industries must be established to provide a stable means for the largest possible number of

people to make their living. . . . This vast hegira of people who are rushing into Los Angeles must find a way to work and make their living. They can't go on indefinitely supporting themselves by building each other houses and selling lots. As roofs are built to cover their heads, big industries must be developed to give them means to earn money. Whenever population outruns industry, stagnation follows. The principal industry of this city at the present time is building new houses. Other industries of more stable and permanent character must be planted and encouraged.[12]

What would it take to achieve this objective? The *Times* identified a series of needs. The majority can be categorized as urban infrastructure—water and power, an expanded harbor, solutions for traffic congestion, police protection, schools and parks. But it also required "men with a large enough vision, prophetic instinct, and practical unselfishness to make these dreams come true." To turn dreams into reality, entrepreneurs would have to reach "further into the back country," where they could control the coal, iron, wool, and cotton necessary "to feed the industries which will grow."[13] I will consider much of this inventory but want to underscore the call for territorial expansion, a project of annexation, whether political, economic, or cultural, that would dominate the agenda of movers and shakers in Los Angeles throughout the decade.

For a comparative, statistical assessment of change over the course of the decade we can turn to a special report produced by the Industrial Department of the Los Angeles Area Chamber of Commerce for Henry M. Robinson, chairman of the board of Security-First National Bank. This accounting shows that in eight years, 1919–27, industrial output in the county had increased from just over $400 million to almost $1 billion, an advance of more than 140 percent. Comparable records for the city showed an increase of almost 500 percent, from $103 million in 1914 to just over $610 million in 1927. In 1929, Los Angeles County, which began the decade as the twenty-eighth leading manufacturing center in the nation, had moved to ninth. Between 1925 and 1927, the county was second only to Flint, Michigan, in the percentage increase in value added, fourth behind New York, Flint, and Milwaukee in terms of dollar value of output, and fifth in value added by manufacturing wage earner.[14]

When the Chamber's industrial committee handed over its report, the county led the nation in motion picture production, was second in the manufacture of automobile tires and tubes, and led "all cities west of Chicago" in the production of bakery products, canned fish, machine-shop products, furniture, ice cream, printing and publishing, pumps, structural and ornamental iron work, wall plaster and wall board, and window shades and coverings. Notably absent in this account is any explicit analysis and interpretation of how this change came about. Readers are left to assume that the Chamber's efforts to set industrial development on a "firm foundation" had resulted in the construction of urban infrastructure, the attraction, training, and retention of skilled workers and salaried employees, and the appearance of investment capital in amounts adequate to finance development of this magnitude.[15]

A third source provides a timeline that allows us to put the decade of the 1920s in longitudinal perspective. In 1937, a New Deal agency, the Federal Housing Administration (FHA), undertook a housing market analysis of the city and Los Angeles County. The administration's Division of Economics and Statistics produced a three-volume report, a dense statistical portrait of regional development that included an assessment of why Los Angeles had grown so dramatically during the 1920s. The authors attributed the "upswing" to seven factors: a westward drift of population; good marketing; climate and soils conducive for specialized agriculture; tourism and retirees; oil, oil refining, and associated industries; the motion picture industry; and the "rapid expansion of manufacturing industries."[16] FHA surveyors mined the U.S. Department of Commerce's bi-decennial census of manufacturing for text, graphics, and statistical abstracts that chart the emergence of Los Angeles as an industrial center.

On one hand, their findings situate the Chamber's brief for Robinson, using data for the city reaching back to 1899. At that time, the "economic interests of the city were largely centered upon growing fruit and raising cattle," the eponymic growers and grazers, and the total value of manufactured products recorded for that year amounted to just over $15 million. Over the next five years, that figure increased to almost $35 million (+130 percent) with meat packing alone adding $4 million in value and significant output in printing, foundry and machine shops, flour and grist milling, and planing mill products. A decade later (1914) output from the city's industries topped $100 million for the first time; by 1919 it had increased to $300 million.[17]

The FHA enumerators situated this expansion in industry and output in a state and national context. Data for 1919 and 1929 show a significant increase for the Los Angeles industrial area (the same as Los Angeles County) relative to the remainder of California. We find this in terms of the number of wage earners employed (up from 25 percent of the state total in 1919 to 37 percent in 1929), the percentage of the total number of manufacturing establishments in the state (from 29 percent to 40 percent), and the value of product (21 percent to 40 percent). Included in the regional market analysis were annual compendia of "important, nationally-known manufacturers" that established branch factories in Los Angeles. The list for 1929 featured American Brake Shoe & Foundry Co. (Chicago), Bethlehem Steel Corp. (N.Y.), the Joslyn Company (Chicago), National Lead Co. (N.Y.), Procter & Gamble (Cincinnati), U.S. Steel Corp. (N.Y.), and Willard Storage Battery Co. (Cleveland). The FHA timeline also quantified the effects of the Depression downturn on Southern California concerns and the relatively rapid return, in most sectors by 1934–35, to the heights first achieved in the late 1920s. In fact, by 1935, Los Angeles had advanced from ninth to seventh in the national rankings of industrial areas.[18]

What did this statistical evidence of an emergent manufacturing prowess mean for industrial workers? First, during the decade their numbers, countywide, grew from just over 61,000 to almost 106,000.[19] Second, by 1930, 28 percent of Los Angeles workers received their paychecks from manufacturing, the greatest percentage of any occupational classification.[20] Third, over the course of the decade a number of these workers enjoyed an increase in hourly wages. A comparison of city-level aggregate data reported in the 1919 and 1929 census of manufactures shows that on average, workers in some of the more significant industrial sectors such as meat packing and foundry and machine-shop products saw hourly wages rise on the order of 50 and 75 percent respectively.[21]

A study conducted by Helen Liggett, a special agent for the Department of Labor's Bureau of Labor Statistics, provides precise data on wages and hours worked in select industries from 1915 to 1920. Her findings reveal a wage increase of over 75 percent on average, with a notable advance in the skilled trades (+87.5 percent). In 1915, steamfitters, for example, worked 44 hours a week and received $29 in exchange. Five years later they received $45 on average for the same hours of labor. While these gains are impressive, they must be considered in light of an even more robust 107 percent growth in the cost of living. If we compare the wages Liggett recorded for 1919 with those the Chamber provided Robinson in 1930, the figures point to a slight rise in the hourly wages paid to skilled tradespeople such as machinists, welders, molders, and structural steel workers as well as carpenters, cement finishers, hod carriers, plumbers, and other members of the building trades. There is a notable lack of advance in the wages paid to day laborers and unskilled laborers. Although Liggett did not distinguish differing salary levels among laborers, the Chamber quoted one rate for "unskilled labor, American" (50 to 60 cents an hour) and another, lower, wage for "unskilled labor, Mexican" (45 to 50 cents an hour). As for the cost of living at the end of the decade, when the Works Progress Administration (WPA) quantified values for 59 cities in 1935 based on family expenditures for food, clothing, housing, and household operation, Los Angeles ranked tenth, behind New York, Chicago, Detroit, Boston, Cleveland, and San Francisco.[22]

Although verifiably true, these statistical accounts concealed as much as they revealed. As the Dykstra epigraph reminds us, it seemed, at the time, that no matter how many new firms set up shop in the region and regardless of how many times existing plants expanded, there apparently would never be enough industry to provide jobs for all the newcomers streaming into Southern California.[23] Also missing in these presentations of industrial progress were the working poor engaged in pursuits which, if they were factored in at all, showed up as "all others" or "all other types" on the surveyors' decimally correct charts and graphs, as well as those workers who by definition were unemployed or unemployable, and the undocumented and therefore uncounted. Many Angelenos absent in the manufacturing censuses and housing market surveys worked for the railroad and traction companies, in brickyards, in lumber and cement yards, as teamsters and day laborers. These workers, many of them recent immigrants or "foreigners" in the contemporary parlance, were counted and their activities analyzed in a series of reports, articles, and theses examining the "foreign districts" and living conditions in the East Side Industrial District, the zone along the Los Angeles River that Bartlett first focused on in 1907.[24]

In his report of a 1920 survey of Mexicans in Los Angeles sponsored by the Interchurch World Movement of North America, the cleric and reformer Bromley Oxnam projected a "possible shift in Mexican population" if, or when, the city selected the downtown Plaza site for a Union Passenger Terminal. "This means that between five and ten thousand Mexicans will have to move to other sections of the city. He noted that some of the displaced would move to Palo Verde or cross the river and locate around Stephenson Avenue. "Still another group will seek the new Industrial District just south of the city limits. It will therefore be necessary for the church to look toward [these] sections for possible fields of community development." Oxnam shared the reformers' and social scientists' perception of Mexican "sections" and a Mexican problem. However, fifteen years after sociologist Bessie Stoddard first called attention to the house courts and thirteen years after Bartlett first proposed a move out from the congested districts to the country, Oxnam renewed this call with a proposal for the "unplanned yet orderly dispersion" of manufacturing and working-class housing from the center city to surrounding zones, a demonstration of the persistence of the spatial fix and a particular imaginative geography.[25]

The "all others" also appear, somewhat obliquely, in a 1926 survey of Negro workers that Charles S. Johnson conducted for the National Urban League. (I include the term "Negro" for historical accuracy whenever the reference is directly to the contemporary text.) Johnson, a sociologist who trained at the University of Chicago, was director of the League's Department of Research and Investigations. He found that many of the racialized attributes ascribed to Mexicans, Mexican Americans, southern Europeans, and African Americans through the biased assessments of dwellings and surrounding spaces were also prevalent at the workplace. Johnson's transcripts of interviews with business owners and plant managers reveal how these unfounded "racial beliefs" and "racial theories" determined not only who might enter plants but also the nature of participation on the shop floor and in the yard and the general physical and social relationships among white workers and their racialized counterparts.[26]

Johnson surveyed 456 industrial firms employing 75,754 workers and found that roughly 3 percent of the workers (or 2,239) were African American men. For observation and extended interviews he selected 104 firms. Fifty-four of these had Negro workers, fifty had none. The former included the majority of firms in Los Angeles with more than ten African American employees. Johnson's findings subverted long-held stereotypes. For example, he found a distinct lack of specialization—"Whatever is elsewhere evident of the special use of Negroes for special things, the plants which employ them [in Los Angeles] found them adaptable over a rather wide range"—and did not find a significant differential in the wages paid African Americans and whites for similar occupations. However, he uncovered a remarkable variance in perception, policies, and practices regarding "racial contacts in industry." Popularly held "race theories" were diametrically opposed; some proprietors believed Mexicans were white and white workers accepted them, others held that Mexicans were colored and white workers objected to Mexicans but accepted Negroes. As Johnson put it: "Plants of the same type in the same city declare precisely opposite facts as inherent in Negro nature."[27]

Johnson concluded that plant policies designed to address questions of race mixing were based on unsubstantiated beliefs, a majority of which could be traced to plant owners. However, the standard practice was to limit race mixing, and plants were divided spatially through the institution of overt and covert policies designed to enforce segregation. These policies, and the imaginative geographies that informed them, meant that most African Americans who worked in industry during the 1920s were employed as members of work crews with discrete tasks and well-defined boundaries that delimited the workplace into zones where they were permitted and those where they were denied.

Now that we have an understanding of how reformers and social scientists envisioned industry, urban expansion, and social patterns in 1920s Los Angeles and a quantitative overview of industrial development during the decade, we need to consider questions of location and city building. Where was this industrial activity taking place? What kinds of firms were establishing plants in the Los Angeles industrial area? How had industrial development contributed to city building? And what kind of city had emerged?

If we turn our attention to city boosters, developers, and planners we find imaginative geographies distinct from those advanced by clerics and social workers. There were, however, considerable overlaps and at least two salient points of intersection. First, both groups, broadly defined, shared a belief that industry should be zoned for discrete segments of the city and segregated by type. Second, both encouraged development that surrounded these production landscapes with a complement of residences, services, and community institutions. However, most developers and boosters joined industrialists in articulating boundaries between the races, and their advertisements and sales activities promoted ownership for white workers.

The minutes of a January 1922 meeting of the Los Angeles Area Chamber of Commerce records these property holders and boosters engaged in a rancorous debate regarding the relative merits of "opening up" San Pedro Street to industry, a move, they duly noted, guaranteed to antagonize voters on Boyle Heights. On one level, this was a debate concerning where Westinghouse should build its first Los Angeles facility. No one in attendance was opposed to the move. On the contrary, the entire board congratulated A. G. Arnoll, who had been working for six months to persuade Westinghouse to set up shop in their city rather than in Oakland. The only question was where the firm should locate. The proposal before the board called for a site at the corner of Ninth Street and San Pedro. Embedded in the resolution was an implicit proposal to transform San Pedro into a "wholesale district"; as Chamber president Sylvester Weaver noted, "all those who do not believe in it as a wholesale section and who do not want [the construction of additional] grade crossings will be in opposition." The opposition, directors Shannon Crandall, John Fredericks, and A. F. Osterloh, argued for a Vernon location, where there is "plenty of vacant ground served by three railroads only twenty minutes from 7th and Broadway."[28]

It was an inflammatory session with directors opposed to a downtown adjacent siting making unsavory comparisons to New York, Pittsburgh, and St. Louis, and President Weaver arguing that he was all for "giving Los Angeles the advantages those cities have." Though united in principle, these antagonists were drawing precise distinctions among different types of industry, the exact needs of particular firms, the appropriate location for various manufacturing activities, and, most critically, the optimal pattern of land uses in Los Angeles. The geography of industry, as the majority defined it, had retail and offices in the Central Business District (CBD), surrounded by warehouses and jobbers serving this downtown core, and production segregated in outlying districts such as Vernon, the Union Pacific's Metropolitan Warehouse and Industrial District, or the Southern Pacific's tracts in present-day Commerce.[29]

In *The Fragmented Metropolis*, Robert Fogelson documented the Chamber's efforts to set growth in the city and region on a firm industrial foundation. This assessment, and similar arguments, derive their explanatory power from the stated or implied imposition of external financing and business control.[30] In one sense, the Chamber's Industrial Department had followed a proven strategy, cajoling eastern and midwestern industrialists to Southern California, a process similar to the successful appeal for residents to migrate from these regions. One sector, rubber and tire production, can provide some sense of the scale and rapidity of change. In 1919, when Goodyear decided to build a southland plant, only a few independent firms were in operation, producing less than 1 percent of the national output. A decade later, after Firestone, Goodrich, and U.S. Rubber—the nation's number two, three, and four producers—had followed suit, the region's share had grown to 6 percent, which translated into 35,000 tires and 40,000 tubes a day. During that time, employment went from a few hundred workers to over 5,000, almost 7 percent of the industry total, and annual output reached a value of $56 million. Los Angeles's location and transit infrastructure were critical factors in terms of raw materials and sales for finished goods. Goodyear's and Firestone's subsidiaries supplied the intermountain and Pacific states including Alaska and Hawaii.[31]

But as the Chamber exchange reveals, the creation of industrial Los Angeles was just as much a local initiative. As Goodyear and Firestone executives were divvying up the continent into what economist Frank Kidner labeled "branch plant empires," Los Angeles entrepreneurs and civic elites were turning their spatial imaginations to the creation of a "back country" empire.[32] Over time, the spatial reach of this branch plant network meant that Los Angeles assumed a new position in the nation's urban system. In other words, the formation of branch plant empires, an endeavor that combined external coordination with local capital and initiative, was part of a dynamic process through which Southern Californian business leaders recast the city and region to their advantage.

In "Los Angeles, A Miracle City" (1926), Edgar Lloyd Hampton imagined the city and its hinterlands in terms of raw materials and resource extraction. "The West," he wrote, "is largely composed of these commodities [and] Los Angeles is especially fortunate." He drew his map of this imaginative geography to include Mexico and all the states on the arid side of the Rocky Mountains where "almost every known basic metal is on a downgrade haul to Los Angeles harbor." Immodest and imperial, Hampton's vision was nonetheless consistent with the principles and strategies that had shaped development in the American West. The novelty was that now Southern California would assume the role of entrepôt, usurping East Coast and midwestern cities, and become the control center for western resources and products.[33] Bromley Oxnam envisioned the city's emergent status and asserted it succinctly in a diary entry following his visit to the 1922 Pageant of Progress at Exposition Park. "From the moment one enters . . . to the last, after miles and miles of exhibits, the bewildering progress of manufacturing Los Angeles is before the eyes. A generation ago we bought everything from the East. Today we make our stuff and control the West."[34]

This shift in perception and changing practice signaled the emergence of Los Angeles as the epicenter of a city-centered region whose entrepreneurs and financiers would exercise influence over dependent territories.

It represented enhanced material and symbolic connections in national and international systems of trade and culture as well as an extension of local authority. And like their counterparts in Chicago and New York, Los Angeles entrepreneurs sought to control the hinterlands in two ways, by making the city a center for processing and converting resources but also by making it a center for shaping ideas and marketing culture to mold preferences for consumer goods and exchange.[35]

The historical record suggests that residents also perceived the city dichotomously. In 1924, George Law stated boldly in the *Los Angeles Times* that in order to understand Los Angeles it was necessary to motor south through the manufacturing district. "The rest of the city, from the winsome foothills to the glittering beaches, when viewed alone does not convey an adequate idea of the true situation." A drive from the eastside southward would bring into view what Law imagined as a stage for the newest and biggest act in the great L.A. drama. "The air," he continued, "is filled with industrial haze and queer smells, huge trucks trundle along paved thoroughfares. Here then is the new city; it is not amusements or tourists, it is industrial production."[36]

Five years later, when the Samson Tyre Company broke ground for its new $8 million plant on Telegraph Road in the Union Pacific industrial tract, J. A. Owen, editor of the Huntington Park *Daily Signal,* proclaimed: "Without industry the development of the region would be greatly limited. Thousands would not be able to enjoy the beaches, mountains, and other peerless advantages which California offers its residents were it not for the industries which make it possible for them to gain a livelihood. Back of the beautiful residential development of the county's west side is the industry of the east side."[37] Here we find a similar shaping of the city into discrete zones with the river as a great divide between landscapes of production and landscapes of leisure.

We can extend this interpretation through a consideration of two factors neglected in most studies of urban growth and city building in Southern California, the workplace-residence link and planning. In Los Angeles, as elsewhere, industrialists, investors, planners, and wage earners envisioned a tight and desirable link between the workplace, residence, and local institutions. And design professionals and real estate interests, often acting in concert, devised policy and adopted practices that promoted and supported this form of development. I will use the area east of the Los Angeles River and the Central Manufacturing District (now part of Vernon) to illustrate these points.

In 1925, the Chicago-based engineering firm Kelker, De Leuw & Co. presented a report to the Los Angeles City Council and the County Board of Supervisors with recommendations for a comprehensive rapid transit plan. In the appendices, four diagrams fix the distribution of residences and the place of work for persons employed in the Central Business District

Figure 1.2. View from the southwest of Samson Tyre and Rubber Co. plant (later United States Rubber) at 5675 Telegraph Road, c. 1930. At the groundbreaking for this $8 million facility, located in the Union Pacific Railroad's industrial district, Los Angeles mayor George Cryer proclaimed: "It seems only the other day that we drove out Whittier Boulevard and this was a dairy district. Now there are 160,000 people living here." Initial daily capacity was 6,000 tires and 10,000 tubes. To the north of the plant is J. B. Ransom's "Montebello Park," a residential tract straddling the boundary between Montebello and East Los Angeles. The oil wells in the far distance are in the Montebello field. *Hearst Collection, Department of Special Collections, University of Southern California Library*

(27,022 total), the East Side Industrial District (11,080), the Vernon Industrial District (2,507), and the North Side Industrial District (2,184). Contrary to the received wisdom regarding traction, residential dispersion, and sprawl (generally presented as the alpha and omega of a Los Angeles growth machine), a significant percentage of workers employed in the East Side and North Side Industrial Districts in 1925 lived within walking distance of their work. Between one-fifth and one-third of all workers employed in the North Main, East Side, and Vernon Districts lived less than two miles from their place of employment. This is the equivalent of the standard distance urbanists accept as a metric for the preindustrial walking city. If we extend our compass to the three-mile circle, it includes over one-third of workers in North Main, one-half of those employed in Vernon, and three-fifths of East Side workers.[38]

For some workers, economic considerations determined the choice of residence and the relative proximity to work. In many cases, restrictions on employment opportunities, the place of residence, or both determined the physical and social parameters of everyday life in Los Angeles. Whether legal or extralegal, these restrictions delineated and configured urban space in the 1920s. It is useful, in this case, to consider a set of legal regulations that spelled out where manufacturing could occur within city boundaries. In 1904, the Los Angeles City Council approved an ordinance restricting certain industrial uses in a residential area. This was followed by statutes, passed in 1908 and 1909, that divided the city into two residential and seven industrial districts. The next year, a January ordinance designated as residential all city land not falling within the industrial districts. Although designed to protect single-family housing, this legislation promoted dispersed industrial clusters, which in turn encouraged manufacturers and developers of these tracts to plan for working-class housing and services in close proximity to employment.[39]

We find this pattern of development in a wedge-shaped segment of the county east of the Los Angeles River. The zone between Whittier Boulevard and Gage Avenue extending out to Montebello and then south along the Rio Hondo encompasses parts of Boyle Heights, East Los Angeles, Commerce, Vernon, and Bell. During the 1920s, it was the site of intensive development. Within these boundaries industrial realtors like W. H. Daum leased or sold property to B. F. Goodrich, Samson Tyre and Rubber, Union Iron Works, Truscon Steel, O'keefe and Merritt, Illinois Glass, and Angelus Furniture. Daum began his career as an industrial agent for the Atchison, Topeka, and Santa Fe Railroad and opened his own Los Angeles firm in 1913. Over the next four decades he helped set the pattern for industrial dispersion in the region. Through a series of holding companies he managed property in the East Side Industrial District between Central Avenue and the river. At the same time, he was developing sections of Vernon and property along Slauson Avenue. In some cases Daum leased land in these new industrial tracts to firms such as the Pacific Coast Planing Company that were moving from parcels he held in the East Side District. All this activity was in addition to his position with the Sunset Park Land Company, developers of residential property west of downtown and in Hollywood.[40]

Concomitant with Daum's and other realtors' industrial programs, firms such as the Janss Investment Company, J. B. Ransom Corporation, Walter H. Leimert and Co., and Carlin G. Smith were promoting Belvedere Gardens, Samson Park, Bandini, Montebello Park, City Terrace, and Eastmont. Smith noted that Eastmont, his first subdivision on the eastside, was "neighbor to a mighty payroll . . . facing a destined city of factories. The amazing development of the great East Side—teeming with its expanses of moderate priced homes—has become almost overnight one of the most startling features of the city's growth." The Janss Company, better known for Westwood, Holmby Hills, and other exclusive westside projects, had been developing

Belvedere Heights and then Belvedere Gardens, now part of Boyle Heights, since 1905. The former tract ran along First Street and was intended for the "workingman with limited capital." By 1922 the firm was concentrating on parcels adjacent to the Hostetter Tract, site of Sears-Roebuck's regional distribution center and department store, and adding its voice to calls for street widenings to provide for the anticipated 25,000 new residents "who will make their homes in Belvedere Gardens owing to the great industrial program inaugurated for this section."[41]

Walter H. Leimert began his career as a land subdivider in the San Francisco East Bay cities Oakland and Piedmont. He timed his move to Los Angeles in 1923 to coincide with the upswing in development and building. Leimert coordinated a series of industrial and residential ventures. Although he was best known for Leimert Park (1927), near Baldwin Hills, his first projects in the region were on the eastside, specifically City Industrial Tract along Alhambra Avenue and the adjacent residential district, City Terrace, a "veritable city of working men's homes." Here Leimert's partners included financiers Joseph Sartori, William Gibbs McAdoo, Irving Hellman, and Charles Toll. Their sales strategy included a "build your own home campaign" with a single price for lot and lumber. Advertisements for the district alerted potential buyers to another option, setting up a tent or other impermanent structure until the time and means for a permanent dwelling could be secured. The J. B. Ransom Corporation's Bandini tract, "The 'Miracle City' of the East Side," and Montebello Park offered lots and houses to workers who wanted to "live in pleasant surroundings, near their work, and yet close to down-town Los Angeles." The Bandini community package included a grade school and proximity to two high schools and the commercial development anticipated along Washington and Atlantic Boulevards.[42]

Over time, the development process varied, and districts took different forms. For the eponymic Torrance, Jared Sidney Torrance coordinated the program, financing, and construction of a comprehensive industrial satellite. In this 1911 project he consolidated residential, commercial, civic, and industrial uses and brought them under the control of a single organization. Torrance made his fortune in railroads, real estate, and oil (the Southern California trinity) before announcing plans for an industrial city. The timing, relative to the bombings at the *Los Angeles Times* and Llewellyn Iron Works and Socialist Job Harriman's mayoral bid, was not incidental. Torrance incorporated the Dominguez Land Corporation with financier Joseph F. Sartori (Security Pacific Bank), purchased 2,800 acres in southwest Los Angeles, and hired F. L. Olmsted Jr. and Irving Gill as designers. Olmsted's site plan centered on a transit gateway; visitors and residents disembarked into a civic center with theater, public library, and linear park leading to small, detached, workingmen's cottages. Industrial development was piecemeal even though contemporary accounts lauded the application of protective zoning which attracted "non-speculative ownership in large tracts." In 1916, Dominguez Land donated a 125-acre parcel to the Pacific Electric Railway for its construction and repair yard, a predictable gambit in the internecine politics of urban growth. Union Tool Company, a 25 percent stakeholder in the investment, remained the largest employer into the 1920s. During this decade a number of other firms, including Columbia Steel Corporation, Western Sheet Glass, Llewellyn Iron Works, Pacific Metal Products, and Hendrie Rubber, established plants in Torrance.[43]

Promotional materials and publicity photographs for the eastside residential tracts and Torrance's model community depict houses under construction on apparently vacant land. Like other frontiers, the crabgrass frontier on the eastside and in southwest Los Angeles required the imagined and, in some cases, actual removal of previous groups of residents. Advertisements for the small, working-class cottages that took the place of self-built or "makeshift" quarters made it clear that industrialists and land developers envisioned these new miracle cities as Anglo-only enclaves. In Vernon, for example, the creation of the Central Manufacturing District followed the displacement of residents in a "Mexican village" and the tearing down of this "colonia." Occupants of stand-alone dwellings along Twenty-sixth Street suffered a similar fate. In Torrance, zoning excluded "non-caucasians," who were required to live outside the city proper in areas designated "special quarters" on land-use maps.[44]

Goodyear constructed a $6 million branch plant on Central Avenue in 1919. The "most momentous industrial announcement ever made in the city," as the *Los Angeles Times* described it, provides another variant of the coupling of manufacturing and housing. A *Times* follow-up, "Will Build Model Village," described the firm's plans for Goodyear Park, an 800-unit "industrial residential district" sited immediately adjacent to the plant. Here the company drew lessons from Goodyear company president Frank Sieberling's response to the 1913 strike in Ohio called by Akron rubber workers. Although the company did not build its model community in Los Angeles, it did take credit for the creation of a satellite industrial district. Goodyear published images showing "Yesterday" and "Today," taken in 1920 and 1928, to illustrate "how the surrounding territory had built up and filled in" and "how industrial development affects city growth."[45]

Other nationally prominent firms including Swift & Company, Phelps-Dodge, U.S. Steel, Willys-Overland, and Liquid Carbonic established branch plants in Los Angeles during the 1920s. Swift & Company joined local firms such as Deshell Laboratory, Reo Motor, and Sperry Soap in a 300-acre development planned, constructed, and managed by Chicagoans John Spoor, A. G. Leonard, and Halsey Poronto, prominent members of the syndicate responsible for that city's Central Manufacturing District. In Los Angeles these entrepreneurs purchased part of the Arcadia Bandini estate, rancho land that had been held in trust and leased for cattle grazing and farming until 1922, and recast the site for modern industry with large, single-story, fireproof buildings, top-of-the-line services and amenities, and low taxes. Like their Chicago venture, the first phase of development centered on a 100-acre livestock market and the construction of a central administration building, a terminal warehouse, and a manufacturers' building with leasable production and storage space for small firms. They subdivided the remaining acreage into 125 parcels with switch track connections for sale or lease to manufacturing firms. The syndicate offered prospective lessees and buyers financing and construction assistance; infrastructure improvements including parkways, landscaping, and ornamental street lighting; and the Los Angeles Junction Railway, a beltline with direct connection to all trunk lines entering the city.[46]

Vernon annexed the CMD in 1925. Then in 1929, the Chicago syndicate sold out to the Atchison, Topeka and Santa Fe Railroad, which purchased the remaining 2,000 acres in the Bandini estate and extended track and industry west into the remainder of Vernon and east into Commerce. Workers resided in Maywood, Huntington Park, and Bell. The last, "an island of homes in a sea of industry," was an unincorporated community of 9,000 with direct bus service to the CMD.[47] By 1930, this configuration had become such a standard that Thomas Coombs, an engineer with the Los Angeles City Planning Commission, could state simply: "The work shops of the city, the industrial and manufacturing district, should be selected with great care. . . . [F]ar enough from the residential section . . . but not so located as to make traveling between the two a disadvantage. These areas should be large [with] a small part reserved for a local business center. Before it is possible to intelligently subdivide a city, all these subjects should be given careful consideration and well planned."[48]

How, we might ask, did contemporaries perceive and comprehend this reconfiguration of urban space? In 1922 the Los Angeles County Board of Supervisors sponsored a conference on regional planning. A diagram in the published proceedings offers yet another imaginative geography. These engineers, elected officials, and design professionals found the "whole district crystallizing around natural centers and subcenters. The nucleus is the business center of Los Angeles. Beyond the five or six mile circle we find subcenters developing, each with its own individual character and identity." What they envisioned, in effect, was a network of villages connected by transit forming a dispersed but coherent region. More concretely, in Los Angeles they could claim an empirical basis for advancing these objectives. They viewed Bandini, Inglewood, Hollywood, and Pasadena, to cite examples from each sector, as discrete satellites within a comprehensive and comprehensible metropolitan orbit.[49]

If participants at the conference had chosen to extend their study and plot the location of firms in the movie and aircraft industries, the map they produced would have coincided with the idealized diagram of a regional metropolis. Although the initial movie colony settled in Hollywood, by 1915 the Chamber of Commerce's directory of manufacturers recorded a considerable degree of dispersal. Firms could be found in Long Beach, Santa Monica, Mount Washington, and multiple districts in between. There were also significant secondary concentrations. That same year Thomas Ince established a studio in Harry Culver's new community on the former Rancho Ballona eight miles west of city hall. Within five years, Goldwyn Pictures, the Henry Lehrman Studios, Sanborn Laboratories, and the Maurice Tourneur Film Company had joined the Ince studio in Culver City, making it the "greatest producer of pictures in the world" after Hollywood.[50]

Industrial location for aircraft and parts, a critical sector for understanding industry and urban expansion in Southern California, fits within this model as well. The origins of Southern California's vaunted aircraft (later aerospace) industry can be traced to small, undercapitalized companies renting space for office and plant in warehouses and loft buildings in the East Side Industrial District before acquiring more suitable sites along the then urban fringe. Glenn L. Martin founded the first Los Angeles firm in 1912. Previously a crew of mechanics under his direction had been assembling biplanes in a Methodist church and later a cannery in Santa Ana. The company relocated its plant into a brick loft building, formerly a bedding and upholstery shop, with a first-floor storefront at 943 South Los Angeles Street.[51]

Donald Douglas, an engineer and Martin vice president, opened his own firm, the Douglas-Davis Company, in June 1920, renting the back room of a barber shop at 8817 Pico Boulevard south of Beverly Hills. Five former Martin employees crafted one-off components for a transcontinental plane in a second-floor loft space at Koll Planing Mill, a woodworking shop ten miles east at 421 Colyton, near Alameda and Fourth Streets. Finished parts were lowered down an elevator shaft and trucked to the Goodyear Blimp hanger in south-central Los Angeles for final assembly. After securing a contract for three experimental torpedo planes Douglas, with financial support from Harry Chandler, incorporated as the Douglas Company in July 1921. The following year forty-two employees relocated to a movie studio on Wilshire Boulevard in Santa Monica. The site was chosen for its adjacent field, which, however, proved inadequate for test flights; completed aircraft were towed to Clover Field. Between 1922 and 1928 Douglas produced 375 units. In the latter year, the company moved its entire operations to Clover Field, which the city of Santa Monica had purchased two years before. Municipal ownership assured continuity of operation, the requisite zoning, and eminent domain for expansion. In 1928 the firm opened a subsidiary adjacent to Mines Field, an airstrip the city of Los Angeles had recently leased for a municipal airport. By the time the city purchased the property in 1937, the district had become a center for prime airframe contractors, subassemblers, and parts and component manufacturers.[52]

During World War II, homebuilders anticipating an influx of defense workers drawn by these employment centers selected sites in close proximity for community projects. In just three years, four sets of developers converted a five-square-mile parcel owned and master planned by Security Bank into a district for 10,000 residents. A map accompanying advertisements for Westchester in the *Los Angeles Herald and Express* plotted prime contractors and eleven ancillary industries. The copy underscored the district's proximity to a "wide variety of employment." Broadsides enticed potential buyers who could "live within walking distance to scores of production plants."[53]

When Carey McWilliams surveyed Southern California's immediate postwar landscape for *Harper's Magazine* he began by asking rhetorically why the influx of three million people during the war years did not result in sheer chaos; his answer revealed the degree to which the decisions and actions industrialists, planners, and engineers took during the 1920s had informed future patterns. If Los Angeles, he wrote, "had been a compact, centralized city, the migration would have had a devastating impact." Instead, the region's spread-out character "resulted in a natural, and highly desirable, dispersion of population. Industries are widely scattered in Los Angeles. For the most part growth has taken place round the edge. . . . By an accident, therefore, Los Angeles has become the first modern, widely decentralized industrial city in America."[54]

McWilliams's perceptive account, in many ways an upbeat update of Bartlett's 1907 vision, was exceptional; most observers did not view the pace and pattern of wartime development in Los Angeles as "natural" or "highly desirable." However, his exceptionalist explanation—Los Angeles as the "first modern . . . industrial city"—missed the mark. First, the city's industrial districts had been highly planned, in terms of location, internal organization, external connections, and ancillary development such as housing. More critically, he neglected the implications of this "natural" dispersion of population for the city's social landscape. A map produced for the Haynes Foundation, published in a 1949 study of social areas in Los Angeles by Eshref Shevky and Marilyn Williams, identifies 146 census tracts with high indexes of racial segregation, and plots these as a series of dots in relation to industrial areas delineated in cross-hatching. It is not surprising to find the majority of dots clustered tightly alongside the industrial districts lining the river and extending south and east into Vernon, Montebello, and the more recently incorporated city of Commerce. The remaining dots have a close graphic affinity with dispersed industrial zones of the type outlined in this essay. The rate of coincidence, even if anticipated, is striking and demands attention.[55]

We can find a partial explanation for the residential segregation Shevky and Williams recorded if we return to the numbers. The FHA's housing market analysis is presented as a straightforward exercise in the manner of academic social science. It is intended to be read as a recitation of facts; the text sections are secondary to charts, graphs, and tables. Of course the numbers were not neutral: they were marshaled to achieve specific ends. Congress endorsed the FHA in 1934 as a means for mitigating the crisis in foreclosures that had plagued the mortgage industry even during the 1920s boom and then threatened to shut down savings and loans and other segments of the financial markets after 1929. Shoring up these institutions was the agency's initial mandate. Within a few years' time, however, FHA administrators had identified a more proactive and interventionist strategy, and staff began formulating policies and sponsoring programs designed to increase home ownership and extend its perceived benefits to wage earners and workers previously priced out of the market.

In intention and effect these programs advanced the social and environmental reformers' earlier efforts to alleviate conditions in the congested, mixed-use districts along the river in Los Angeles, southwest of the Loop in Chicago, and on the Lower East Side of Manhattan: districts the Chicago School sociologists characterized as "zones of emergence." From the 1910s to the 1930s, and beyond, elected officials, civic elites, philanthropists, and a considerable percentage of citizens viewed owning your own home, to paraphrase the title of a popular publication and the moniker of a national organization devoted to this cause, as an essential means and criterion for self-improvement, the creation and maintenance of a proper, child-based family setting, and true citizenship.[56]

There are critical distinctions among the goals of these various groups, however, and these have had enormous consequence. Whereas the social reformers, in Los Angeles and elsewhere, viewed home ownership as one aspect of an Americanization project, a means for acculturating immigrants into shared norms and practices, the FHA followed a course closer to the one Los Angeles industrialists and developers had set in terms of distinctions and preferences predicated on race and ethnicity. These objectives were articulated and achieved through explicit instruments and practices that were presented and defended as scientific and race-neutral but veiled so thinly that even the untutored could see them for what they were. These included an active promotion of restrictive covenants for the creation and enhancement of property value, visible in crystalline form in the survey maps the Home Owners' Loan Corporation (HOLC) drew for major cities. HOLC maps record the population, structures, real estate activity, mortgage financing, and "description and character" of residential districts in American cities. Population, in this case, refers to a quasi-quantitative accounting of class and occupation, the number of "foreign families," nationalities, "negro," and "shifting or infiltration." Description and character is a catch-all for everything from terrain and land use to family types and property maintenance.

HOLC surveyors produced one such map for the area between Hawthorne and Torrance in 1939. From the inside looking out, Jared Torrance, industrialists, and residents viewed their city favorably, as orderly and uplifting. On the other hand, HOLC surveyors fixed on the outlying area, an outlier in the imaginative geography of Torrance residents. This "suburban farming district" had a "residential character begun less than twenty years ago." Here land use was controlled by "sketchy zoning" and subject to frequent change. "Under these circumstances it is not surprising that population, improvements and maintenance are extremely heterogeneous. Many Japanese gardeners and Mexican farm laborers are found in the outlying districts. Oil well and tank farms occupy adjacent territory to the west. The area is assigned a 'medial red' grade." As damning as the entire assessment was, it is the last sentence that fixed this district's fate. The red pencil and a "Security Grade: 4th" rating meant that the green of capital investment, directed in large measure by the federal government's issuance or withholding of mortgage guarantees, would not venture into this and other similar heterogeneous, industrial, and primarily working-class districts in Los Angeles.[57]

At the same time, it is interesting to compare the FHA's mid-1930s assessment of industrial Los Angeles with the accounts of the social reformers and the Los Angeles Chamber of Commerce in the 1910s and 1920s respectively. Despite the unmistakable advances in the number of firms, the number of wage earners and salaried employees, the payroll these workers commanded, and the value of output—all of these data quantified and packaged in extraordinary detail—there remains an explicit, pressing, almost nagging concern. In the FHA's eyes, industry in Southern California remained dependent on tourism and services, the manufacturing that was in place was producing overwhelmingly for a local market, these plants were predominantly branch facilities of national firms, and, most generally, production was almost exclusively of "light industry" and consumer goods rather than the long-desired heavy industry for "capital goods."[58]

Although the authors noted grudgingly that Los Angeles was "not a one-industry city" and that the Los Angeles industrial area "possessed an extremely high degree of industrial diversification," in their estimation it was the focus on consumer goods that explained why the region had recovered relatively quickly from the Depression. When advancing this case, the authors pointed to the rubber tire and tubes industry, which was ranked fourth at the time in terms of value of product (just over $34 million) and percentage of the area total (3.4) and sixth in the number of wage earners employed (3,588) and percentage of the area total (3.5). Adopting a line from the Chamber of Commerce, the FHA pointed out that in fifteen years (1919–34), Los Angeles had risen from a position as one of many local centers for vulcanizing and small-scale tire production to become the second leading center in the country behind Akron, Ohio.

At the groundbreaking for Samson Tyre and Rubber's new eastside plant in 1929, company president Adolf Schleicher claimed that now Los Angeles was the "Akron of the West" and that "soon Akron will be known as the Los Angeles of the East." This was a bold and imaginative reworking of the nation's industrial geography. The FHA knew better. Despite the fact that automobile tire and tube production was critical for industrial Los Angeles, the agency put this in perspective when it noted simply that the second-place ranking should not be seen as an indicator "that Los Angeles in any way compares with Akron as a rubber center." Statistics from the census of manufactures supported this claim. Los Angeles branch plants employed less than 10 percent of the total number of wage earners in the industry, these workers earned less than 10 percent of the aggregate wages paid their counterparts in Akron, and they produced approximately 10 percent of the value of product.[59]

Organized as an analysis of housing, and intended as an assessment of the housing market, the FHA survey offers researchers a rich statistical abstract of Los Angeles at a particularly critical moment in the city's history. The longitudinal data on mortgages and financing, construction costs, subdivision, building, and real estate activity are packaged with a quantitative accounting of the city and county in terms of population, migration, employment and wages, and the region's "economic background and structure." It is as if the FHA's Division of Economics and Statistics gave itself the task of taking the city's pulse precisely when manufacturing, commerce, homebuilding, and other business interests had regained the momentum that characterized regional advance during the 1920s and had achieved or almost achieved the seemingly dizzying heights of employment and output first reached in 1927, 1928, and 1929.

What the FHA enumerators could not have known, however, was that achieving that kind of milestone, well in advance of other industrial areas in the nation, was actually a first step into a new era. In hindsight, the Depression downturn appears merely as a pause in the long-range trajectory of manufacturing and city building in industrial Los Angeles. The mid 1930s saw the beginning of a new transformation, one that would prove just as dynamic as the changes that occurred during the 1920s. This transformation was precipitated by different factors and furthered by different agents and agencies. The FHA played a central role. It was one of a number of New Deal agencies whose policies—for water and power, roadbuilding, aviation, and other infrastructure—laid the groundwork for increased industrial expansion and the emergence in Southern California of the kind of high capital, basic, and export-oriented manufacturing that promoters had longed to put into place for decades.[60]

Homebuilders in the 1930s capitalized on the FHA's mortgage guarantee program to secure financing for projects with increasing numbers of units. The FHA also endorsed and institutionalized a set of building practices and planning principles that Southern California homebuilders had hammered out during the 1920s. Housing developments that met these standards, codified loosely as modern community planning, received an FHA stamp of approval which opened up an array of attractive financing options to an expanded pool of potential homebuyers.[61] This was but a single aspect of one of the most intensive and comprehensive episodes in the long history of federal intervention in the West and California.

These New Deal policies and programs for infrastructure and housing were put into service almost immediately with the escalation of armed conflict in Europe and Asia and the eventual entry of the United States into World War II. The New Deal, the war, and the defense emergency ushered in a qualitatively different moment for Los Angeles and Southern California as the federal government provided the capital, capacity, and demand mandatory for southland industrialists and entrepreneurs to create an industrial region comparable to that of metropolitan areas in the East and Midwest. Elements of this development were similar to the type of expansion that had occurred during the 1920s and as the region emerged from the Depression in 1934 and 1935. But much of it was qualitatively and quantitatively different.[62] Put most simply, the creation of the post–World War II city began in the mid 1930s, but that is a story for a different essay in a subsequent volume.

NOTES

1. I borrowed the concept and title, "imaginative geographies," from Kay Anderson, "The Idea of Chinatown: The Power of Place and Institutional Practice in the Making of a Racial Category," *Annals of the Association of American Geographers* 77 (December 1987): 580–98. Dana W. Bartlett, *The Better City: A Sociological Study of a Modern City* (Los Angeles: The Neuner Company Press, 1907), quotes on 14, 27, 71–72. Los Angeles as a "slumless" city was the subject of numerous stories in newspapers as well as in the booster and popular press. At a dedication for the North Broadway Bridge in October 1909, President Taft asked, "Have you no slum districts?" Note that Taft was less than one-half mile from the Ann Street district which reformers cast as a zone of immigrant "peons or peasants" and a site for disease and disorder. See Gladys Patric, "A Study of the Housing and Social Conditions in the Ann Street District of Los Angeles" (Los Angeles: The Society for the Study and Preven-

tion of Tuberculosis, c. 1917). In "Yes, we have no smokestacks, and likewise no tenements—latest figures about the factories in our big garden community," *Southern California Business* 11 (August 1932): 12–13, R. D. Sangster, manager of the Chamber of Commerce's Industrial Department, presented a city with an "utter absence of tenements . . . workman's homes are almost entirely single-family on large lots." The Los Angeles newspapers reported a lack of slums, poverty, and the poor as the product, reputedly, of a predominantly American population and their passion for home ownership.

2. Bartlett, *Better City,* 33–34.

3. Los Angeles City Directory Co., *Los Angeles City Directory, 1905;* California Commission of Immigration and Housing, "A Community Survey Made in Los Angeles" (San Francisco: The Commission, 1919), 23.

4. Bartlett, *Better City,* 191.

5. Robert A. Beauregard, *Voices of Decline: The Postwar Fate of American Cities* (Cambridge: Blackwell, 1993); J. M. Blaut, *The Colonizer's Model of the World: Geographical Diffusionism and Eurocentric History* (New York: Guilford Press, 1993); William Cronon, "A Place for Stories," *Journal of American History* 78 (March 1992): 1347–76; Alan Mayne, *The Imagined Slum: Newspaper Representation in Three Cities, 1870–1914* (Leicester: Leicester University Press, 1993); Denis Wood, *The Power of Maps* (New York: Guilford Press, 1992).

6. The promotional literature is rife with these tropes; see especially the "Real Estate, Industrial, and Development" section in the Sunday *Los Angeles Times.* I will address this topic in a forthcoming book, *Nature's Workshop: Industry and Urban Theory in Twentieth-Century Los Angeles.* For an introduction see William Cronon, ed., *Uncommon Ground: Rethinking the Human Place in Nature* (New York: Norton, 1995).

7. Bartlett, *Better City,* 19–20.

8. Publications, broadsides, and advertisements trumpeting the southland's industries and emergent industrial prowess are voluminous. Indicative are articles such as "5,100 Factories Now Los Angeles Total; 900 New This Year," *Illustrated Daily News,* December 15, 1923. For similar presentations see issues of the *Los Angeles Times,* especially the Sunday real estate section, as well as the Los Angeles Area Chamber of Commerce (LAACC) publications *Industrial Los Angeles County* and *Southern California Business.*

9. Population and annexation from Robert M. Fogelson, *The Fragmented Metropolis: Los Angeles, 1850–1930,* rpt. ed. (Berkeley: University of California Press, 1993), table 4, 78, and table 24, 226–27, respectively. The LAACC Research Department noted the change in the census bureau's accounting for the metropolitan district in a January 1932 news release: in 1920, the "area extended further to the west [out to Ventura County], today [1930] it omits this western section and extends farther toward the east and southeast to include thickly settled communities, regardless of county boundary lines." Census enumerators noted an increase of 165 percent for this ten-year period in the reconfigured metropolitan area. Report in County of Los Angeles, *Regional Planning Notes,* vol. 2, 1931–32 (Los Angeles: Regional Planning Commission, 1933).

10. See, for example, the various Chamber publications, especially its annual directories of manufacturing, as well as the *Los Angeles Times,* which featured industry weekly and in the January "Mid-Winter Annual." Other sources include the *Los An-*

geles Realtor, Southwest Builder and Contractor, local papers such as the Huntington Park *Daily Signal,* and city biographies such as Carson B. Hubbard, *History of Huntington Park, in 2 parts* (Huntington Park: A. H. Cawston, 1935). For a contemporary overview see Robert Glass Cleland and Osgood Hardy, *March of Industry* (Los Angeles: Powell, 1929). This promotion continued beyond 1930 and saw a considerable flourish as the World War II defense effort wound down. For an indicative study see Industrial Department, Los Angeles County Chamber of Commerce, "An Industrial Development Plan for Los Angeles" (n.d./c. 1945).

11. Fogelson, *Fragmented Metropolis,* esp. 123–29.

12. *Los Angeles Times,* November 18, 1923, section 2, 4.

13. Ibid.

14. Industrial Department, Los Angeles Area Chamber of Commerce, *Special Report to Henry M. Robinson, Chairman of the Board, Security-First National Bank of Los Angeles, California,* 2 vols. (Los Angeles: Industrial Department, 1930).

15. Ibid. The economists Eberle and Riggleman challenged the Chamber's standard glowing assessments in their weekly summary of business conditions. A September 21, 1925, article, "Some Consideration of the Los Angeles Industrial Situation," outlined eight points of concern ranging from the lack of careful planning and the detriments of dispersion to excessive intraregional competition and the low operating efficiencies of established plants. *Eberle & Riggleman Economic Service,* vol. 11, 1925.

16. Federal Housing Administration, Division of Economics and Statistics, *Housing Market Analysis, Los Angeles, California as of December 1, 1937,* two parts and statistical appendix (Washington, D.C.: Government Printing Office, 1938), 3.

17. Ibid., chart 43, 251.

18. The U.S. Bureau of the Census introduced the designation "industrial area" in 1929. The state comparisons are from FHA, *Housing Market Analysis,* table 68, 588; the national rankings can be found in table 70, 590. Aggregate data for the Los Angeles industrial area were reported twice. The first report excluded motion pictures; the second included an estimate for this industry. Census enumerators instituted this accounting procedure because the film industry leased rather than sold its product; therefore actual value could not be calculated in a manner consistent with that of other sectors. The latter figures included cost of production; see ibid., 262, for an explanation.

19. Ibid., table 68, 588.

20. Ibid., 321. The percentage in manufacturing was followed closely by workers in the trades (25.4%). No other city with more than 500,000 population had a similar distribution across sectors. See chart 53, 322. In 1930, the FHA estimated there were 84,565 unemployed persons in the county and set the number of "gainful workers" at 964,436. Ibid., 341.

21. United States Department of Commerce, Bureau of the Census, *Fourteenth Census of the United States, Manufactures: 1919* (Washington, D.C.: Government Printing Office, 1922), "Cities of 50,000 Inhabitants or More—All Industries Combined and Specified Industries, Los Angeles," 44–49, and ibid., *Fifteenth Census of the United States, Manufactures, 1929: State Series, California* (Washington, D.C.: Government Printing Office, 1932), "General Statistics for Important Cities, by Industries: 1929," 17–18.

22. Helen M. Liggett, "The Relation of Wages to the Cost of Living in Los Angeles, 1915 to 1920," *Studies in Sociology,* Monograph No. 19, 5 (March 1921), table 12, 8 and 11. LAACC, "Special Report," in WPA, "Inter-City Differences in the Cost of Living," reported in FHA, *Housing Market Analysis,* table 92, 621–22.

23. Clarence Dykstra, "The Boulder Dam Project" (n.d.), in Dykstra Collection, box 2, folder "Addresses or Articles Prior to 1930," Department of Special Collections, UCLA.

24. John Emmanuel Kienle, "Housing Conditions among the Mexican Population of Los Angeles" (M.A. thesis, Department of Sociology, University of Southern California, 1912); William Wilson McEuen, "A Survey of the Mexicans in Los Angeles" (M.A. thesis, Department of Economics and Sociology, USC, 1914); Patric, "A Study of the Housing and Social Conditions in the Ann Street District"; Emory S. Bogardus, "The House-Court Problem," *American Journal of Sociology* 22 (November 1919): 391–99; California Commission of Immigration and Housing, "A Community Survey Made in Los Angeles"; Elizabeth Fuller, "The Mexican Housing Problem in Los Angeles," *Studies in Sociology,* Monograph No. 17, 5 (November 1920); G. Bromley Oxnam, "The Mexican in Los Angeles: Los Angeles City Survey" (Los Angeles: Interchurch World Movement of North America, 1920).

25. Oxnam, "The Mexican in Los Angeles," 23. Stoddard's study of house courts, "The Courts of Sonoratown," appeared in *Charities and the Commons,* December 2, 1905: 295–99.

26. Charles S. Johnson, "Industrial Survey of the Negro Population of Los Angeles, California, Made by the Department of Research and Investigations of the National Urban League" (1926), and idem, "Negro Workers in Los Angeles Industries," *Opportunity: A Journal of Negro Life* 6 (August 1928): 234–40.

27. Johnson, "Negro Workers," 234–37. Of course industrialists were not the only ones who gave credence to theories of "racial traditions" as intrinsic social divides. See, for example, USC sociologist Emory S. Bogardus's primer *Introduction to Social Research* (Los Angeles: Suttonhouse, 1936) for a discussion of "racial traditions" as "natural barriers" separating people into "compatibles and incompatibles."

28. "Manufacturing Committee—Westinghouse Track Connections," in Los Angeles Area Chamber of Commerce, *Stenographer's Notes, Board of Directors Meetings, 1922,* 2–5, Chamber of Commerce Collection, box 18, Regional History Center, USC.

29. Ibid.

30. Fogelson, *Fragmented Metropolis,* esp. chapter 6, "Commercial and Industrial Progress."

31. Hugh Allen, *The House of Goodyear* (Akron, Ohio: Superior Printing, 1936); Goodyear Tire and Rubber Company of California, *Three Dynamic Decades in the Golden State, 1920–1950,* a pamphlet published to commemorate the firm's thirtieth anniversary, in *Los Angeles Examiner* Collection, photo folder "Goodyear," Regional History Center, USC; Paul Rhode, "California's Emergence as the Second Industrial Belt: The Pacific Coast Tire and Automobile Industries" (unpublished paper, Department of Economics, University of North Carolina, Chapel Hill, September 1994); "Civic Heads, U. Officials Aid Ceremony, Los Angeles May Outstrip Akron Soon," *Los Angeles Examiner,* January 24, 1929: 1; "Tire Manufacture a Major

Industry Here," *Industrial Los Angeles County,* vol. 2 (May 1930): 4; "Rubber Industry—Los Angeles County," editorial in *Industrial Los Angeles County,* vol. 2 (May 1930).

32. Frank L. Kidner and Philip Neff, *An Economic Survey of the Los Angeles Area,* Haynes Foundation Monograph Series 7 (Los Angeles: Haynes Foundation, 1945).

33. Edgar Lloyd Hampton, "Los Angeles, A Miracle City," *Current History* 24 (April 1926): 35–42. See *Los Angeles Today,* May 1, 1916: 24, and "Los Angeles, The Hub of a Great Empire," *Los Angeles Times,* January 1, 1926: 15, for similar presentations.

34. Oxnam diary entry, August 30, 1922, in Oxnam Papers, box 32, Library of Congress.

35. Here I am applying an interpretation drawn from Deryck W. Holdsworth's assessment of Chicago in "The Invisible Skyline," *Antipode* 26 (April 1994): 141–46.

36. Law quoted in Perley Poore Sheehan, *Hollywood as a World Center* (Hollywood: Hollywood Citizen Press, 1924), 20–21.

37. Editorial, Huntington Park *Daily Signal,* January 24, 1929.

38. Plates 14–17 bound as an appendix to *Report and Recommendations on a Comprehensive Rapid Transit Plan for the City and County of Los Angeles* (Chicago: Kelker, De Leuw & Co., 1925).

39. The history of zoning in Los Angeles, and the effect of these regulations for zoning in other cities and national guidelines, has yet to be written. For a contemporary assessment see Lawrence Veiller, "City Planning in Los Angeles," *The Survey* July 22, 1911: 599–600. For the district boundaries see Ordinance N.17135 (new series, 1908), Ordinance N.17136 (new series, 1908), and Ordinance N.19500 (new series, 1909), Los Angeles City Records Center.

40. Author interview with William Daum Jr., June 19, 1996, and clippings in scrapbooks at the Daum office, 123 South Figueroa, Los Angeles.

41. "The Cat's Out of the Bag," six-column advertisement in the *Los Angeles Times,* September 10, 1922; "Mr. Workingman and Mr. Wage-Earner," tract brochure for Belvedere Gardens, reproduced in Bruce Henstell, *Sunshine and Wealth: Los Angeles in the Twenties and Thirties* (San Francisco: Chronicle Books, 1984); "Bandini: The Model Community on the *New* East Side" (1926), Ephemera Collection, F21–B11, Huntington Library.

42. "City Industrial Tract," Report for A. G. Arnoll (Los Angeles Chamber of Commerce) by H. A. Lafler, Sales Agent, Walter H. Leimert Co. (c. 1923), in LAACC Collection, box 74, Department of Special Collections, USC; John R. Boyd, "Looking Ahead Industrially," *Southern California Business* (August 1924): 14; J. B. Ransom Corporation, "Montebello Park—The Model Community of the New East Side," (Los Angeles: J. B. Ransom, 1925).

43. "Torrance, The Model Industrial City," California Ephemera Collection, box 103, folder "Torrance," Department of Special Collections, UCLA.

44. For Vernon see the photographs available through the Bancroft Library's webpage at http://sunsite.berkeley.edu:38008/ead/calher/bubonic/5141. This was an ongoing process. For a post–World War II account see "Farewell to 'Manana': Hicks Camp Prepares to Abandon Old Ways," *Los Angeles Times,* May 13, 1949, which describes how an enclave of approximately 150 farmworker families living in "El

Monte's bit of old Mexico which has lain sleepily under the California sun for years" were being forced out by a new property owner, Harvey Youngblood, who planned to develop the land as an industrial park for light manufacturing.

45. "Rubber Company to Build Great Factory at Ascot Park," *Los Angeles Times,* June 24, 1919; "Will Build Model Village, Eight Hundred Fine Houses for Workers to Rise at Ascot Park," ibid. For Akron and a company history see Allen, *The House of Goodyear.* For the images see "Los Angeles—'Queen of Homelands,'" *Industrial Los Angeles County,* vol. 2 (May 1930) and Goodyear Tire and Rubber Company of California, "Three Dynamic Decades in the Golden State."

46. Central Manufacturing District, Inc., "Central Manufacturing District of Los Angeles: A Book of Descriptive Text, Photographs and Testimonial Letters About the Central Manufacturing District of Los Angeles—'The Great Western Market'" (August 1923), LAACC Collection, Department of Special Collections, USC; "Great Industrial City Here Being Created by the Central Manufacturing District," *Los Angeles Times,* July 15, 1923; "Cabbage Patch to Industrial Paradise," *Santa Fe Magazine* (November 1929): 21–25; H. E. Poronto, "How Chicago Came to Los Angeles Told by Head of Central Manufacturing Dist.," *Southwest Builder and Contractor,* July 13, 1923: 34. For an outsider's vantage presented as a photo-essay see Richard Neutra, *Amerika: Die Stilbundung des neven bauens in den Vereinigten Stacten; mit 260 abbiblungen* (Vienna: A. Schroll, 1930).

47. On the sale see "Los Angeles Holdings Go to Rich Group," March 7, 1928, and "Santa Fe Buys Industrial Hub for $15,000,000," April 11, 1929, both in the *Los Angeles Examiner.* For city biographies of Bell and other incorporated communities see Los Angeles Chamber of Commerce, Industrial Department, *Industrial Communities of Los Angeles Metropolitan Area* (Los Angeles: The Chamber, 1925) and *California Real Estate Magazine* 10 (June 1930), a special issue devoted to "Growth and Progress of the Golden West."

48. "Subdividing of Land" in Los Angeles Board of City Planning Commissioners, *Annual Report, 1929–1930* (Los Angeles: The Board, 1930), 49.

49. County of Los Angeles, "Proceedings of the First Regional Planning Conference of Los Angeles County" (Los Angeles: The Regional Planning Commission, 1922), 6.

50. For firm locations see the Los Angeles Chamber of Commerce, Industrial Bureau publication *Manufacturers' Directory and Commodity Index.* I consulted the second (1915) and fifth (1920) editions. On Harry H. Culver see a biography ("as of Sept. 1, 1929") in the *Examiner* Collection, Department of Special Collections, USC, and the clippings files in that collection. Culver City was a Better Homes in America site in 1926, and the brochure for that event is in the Seaver Center, Los Angeles County Museum of Natural History. When enumerators employed by the Works Progress Administration conducted a comprehensive survey of county residents, structures, and land uses, their findings underscored the diversity of manufacturing and its reach. Coded data cards report the tenancy, occupation, place of and journey to work, and mode of transit for each household in the county. A summary noted small industrial districts in "almost every municipal and geographic division of Los Angeles as well as in outlying satellite centers." Los Angeles Regional Planning Commission and the Works Progress Administration, *Land Use Analysis: Final Report* (Los Angeles: RPC, 1941).

51. This section is drawn from Greg Hise, *Magnetic Los Angeles: Planning the Twentieth Century Metropolis* (Baltimore: Johns Hopkins University Press, 1997), chapter 4, "The Airplane and the Garden City."

52. Don Hansen (McDonnell Douglas, Long Beach) letter to author, June 3, 1994. See also Frank Cunningham, *Skymaster: The Story of Donald Douglas* (Philadelphia: Dorrance, 1943), and Crosby Maynard, *Flight Plan for Tomorrow: The Douglas Story, A Condensed History* (Santa Monica: Douglas Aircraft Co., 1962).

53. "Finest Community Development in 20 Years" and "Typical Homes in Westchester District," *Los Angeles Evening Herald and Express,* March 28, 1942. See also "City Planners Flock to Study Westchester," *Los Angeles Daily News,* May 8, 1942, 27, and the low-altitude oblique aerials of this development in the Spence and Fairchild Aerial Photo Collections in the Department of Geography at the University of California, Los Angeles.

54. Carey McWilliams, "Look What's Happened to California," *Harper's Magazine,* October 1949: 21–29, quote on 28.

55. Eshref Shevky and Marilyn Williams, *The Social Areas of Los Angeles: Analysis and Typology,* published for the John Randolph Haynes and Dora Haynes Foundation (Berkeley and Los Angeles: University of California Press, 1949), figure 18, opposite 56.

56. Robert E. Park and Ernest W. Burgess, *The City: Suggestions for Investigation of Human Behavior in the Urban Environment* (Chicago: University of Chicago Press, 1925), especially the Burgess essay "The Growth of the City: An Introduction to a Research Project"; United States Department of Commerce, *How to Own Your Home: A Handbook for Prospective Home Owners,* prepared by John M. Gries and James S. Taylor (Washington, D.C.: Government Printing Office, 1923).

57. "Southern Hawthorne and Suburbs, Area No. D-44," March 17, 1939, HOLC city survey files, National Archives, Record Group 195. Richard Harris (McMaster University) brought these documents to my attention. On the HOLC, restrictive covenants, and redlining see Kenneth T. Jackson, "Race, Ethnicity, and Real Estate Appraisal: The Home Owners' Loan Corporation and the Federal Housing Administration," *Journal of Urban History* 6 (August 1980): 419–52.

58. FHA, *Housing Market Analysis,* 331. The authors considered aviation an emergent sector with the potential to become an export industry capable of generating ancillary capital goods manufacturing, thereby setting the region firmly on a foundation of industrial progress. Ibid., 252–57.

59. Ibid., 270–71; "Civic Heads, U. Officials Aid Ceremony, Los Angeles May Outstrip Akron Soon," *Los Angeles Examiner,* January 24, 1929.

60. The obvious example is Kaiser's steel plant in Fontana, but during the World War II defense buildup, industrialists and entrepreneurs, with financial and material assistance from the federal government, coordinated the development of an extraordinary complex of chemical, power, and technology concerns that became the basis for postwar advances in aviation and other sectors. The government invested more than $800 million in over 5,000 industrial plants in the region between 1940 and 1943. See Hise, *Magnetic Los Angeles,* as well as Carey McWilliams, *Southern California: An Island on the Land* (1946; Salt Lake City: Peregrine Smith Books, 1990), especially the "Epilogue," where McWilliams states that during the war Los Angeles became an important industrial area "overnight . . . preoccupied not with

tourists and climate alone, but with such problems as 'smog' and 'smoke' and 'strikes'" (371).

61. For the FHA's role in transforming homebuilding and homebuying during the 1930s in Los Angeles and the rise of modern community planning see Hise, *Magnetic Los Angeles,* chapters 1, 2, and 4. On the FHA generally see Gertrude Fish, ed., *The Story of Housing* (New York: Macmillan, 1979), and Nathaniel S. Keith, *Politics and the Housing Crisis since 1930* (New York: Universe Books, 1979).

62. Industrial Department, LAACC, "Statistical Record of Los Angeles County Industrial Development: Summary, on an Annual Basis, for Years 1929–44" (1945).

CHAPTER TWO

Mulholland Highway and the Engineering Culture of Los Angeles in the 1920s

Matthew W. Roth

Mulholland Highway, a twisting 22-mile roadway along the ridgetops of the Hollywood Hills (fig. 2.1), meant different things to the real estate investors who first promoted it, to the engineers who designed it and supervised its construction, and to the property owners who encountered the environmental effects of its completion.[1] "The property in the district is owned by a small group of capitalists who expect to be rewarded for their enterprise by the subdivision of the frontage on the highway into building sites," wrote the trade journal for the region's construction industry.[2] But Mulholland Highway did not raise property values and development opportunities in the hills and the adjacent San Fernando Valley until a generation later than anticipated, when its original advocates were no longer in a position to benefit. The reasons are apparent in retrospect: the highway created a cul-de-sac rather than a connection with the principal roads of the growing city, and the threat of fire and landslide in the chaparral environment of the hills discouraged development and settlement. Despite the known fire threat and the city's established practice of integrating the construction of highways and underground utilities, the roadbuilding project did not incorporate provision for water mains. The fire hazard surfaced in the proceedings only when the city engineering staff sought a pretext for accelerated administrative procedures, and it still did not cause modification of the design or construction.

The disjunction between the expectations of its promoters and what the engineers produced was so extreme that the promoters petitioned to close the road barely five years after raising a million dollars to complete it.[3] This disparity cannot be explained away as unanticipated consequences because, for one thing, the engineers knew the consequences even as they conducted the work. For another, they pursued the project with uncommon fervor,

45

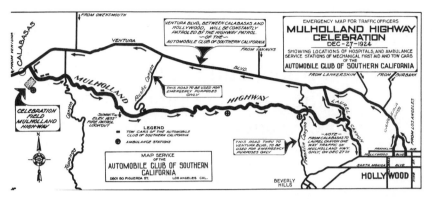

Figure 2.1. For the motorcade celebrating the opening of Mulholland Highway, the participants traveled from the western terminus to Laurel Canyon. The highway extended further east from there, but because it dead-ended at a cliff the celebrants were diverted to Laurel Canyon. *Automobile Club of Southern California Archives*

even making successful requests for dispensation from standard administrative practices. What did the engineers want? If they were not simply compliant technicians leashed to the aims of business and political elites, how did they decide what to build? During the approval process and the construction itself, the city engineers left a record of their aspirations in testimony to the city council, in departmental reports, and in naming the highway after William Mulholland, the principal figure in the construction of the Los Angeles Aqueduct and the founder of municipal engineering practice in the city. As John A. Griffin, head of the city's engineering department, wrote: "It is named as a tribute and to be built as a monument to a great engineer, 'Our Bill,' Bill Mulholland, the builder of the Los Angeles Aqueduct and the one man among all others who put our beloved City of Los Angeles on the map."[4] They also left the record of the road itself, an expressive if not articulated statement by engineers who, for the most part, spoke with their shovels.

To the city engineering department, Mulholland Highway was a massive reordering of the natural environment that followed in several ways the pattern of the engineers' greatest triumph, the Los Angeles (or Owens Valley) Aqueduct, which opened in 1913 and carried water 233 miles to the city from the eastern Sierras. The highway accorded with the engineers' sense of beauty in the landscape, an aspect of engineering that historian David Nye has described as the "technological sublime."[5] Its construction engineer, Dewitt Reaburn, described one aspect of this aesthetic when he extolled the vantage points that the road would afford: "In driving over the completed portion of the highway, one is charmed and amazed at the wonderful view of the surrounding country, which is continually changing as the vision sweeps from one side of the summit to the other. The Mulholland Highway is destined to be the heaviest traveled and one of the best known scenic roads in the United States."[6] Creating vistas for scenic motoring was a conscious goal in much of the parkway construction throughout the nation in the 1920s and 1930s. As their name implied, however, parkways also were thorough, polished designs in their own right, with picturesque light fixtures and railings as well as fully thought-out landscaping along the roadside.[7] Mulholland Highway lacked all such amenities. It was a simple graded cut through the hills that afforded pleasant views but was not part of them. The road itself and the act of building it through mountainous terrain satisfied what landscape historian John Brinckerhoff Jackson identified as the engineer's deep appreciation for flow, or the successful application of the engineer's skill in conveying energy and material from one place to another.[8]

William Mulholland, the principal figure in the construction of the Owens Valley Aqueduct, had nothing to do with the planning or construction of Mulholland Highway, but the engineers' symbolic association of him with this road indicates the importance of the aqueduct in shaping their sense of mission and their desire for an autonomous administrative structure. The significance of the naming cut both ways: they chose this particular construction project to venerate the aqueduct builder (fig. 2.2). The highway through the hills was a most appropriate shrine because it enabled the engineers to act on their vision of beauty as transformed landscapes of movement and flow, and because it was an opportunity to transfer crucial aspects of their aqueduct achievement to the arena of their greatest disappointment, broad-scaled road systems. Mulholland Highway offered a chance to build without opposition and to devise a model for project administration that could ease subsequent undertakings. The engineers consciously sought to reproduce the aqueduct experience, even hiring aqueduct veterans when they could.

The first task of this essay, then, is to fill in the background of disappointment and canceled road projects that conditioned the engineers' response to the Mulholland Highway proposal. That effort takes us through the literature on transportation in twentieth-century Los Angeles, which furnishes only a minimally useful framework for comprehending Mulholland Highway. The historiography of transportation in Los Angeles (and many other cities, too) dwells on systemic struggles between the street railways and the automobile infrastructure.[9] But policy debates waged by politicians and community leaders did not necessarily determine what was built. Participants in such debates were not above distorting the extent of their support, and their pronouncements must be carefully interpreted.

Figure 2.2. Tributes to Mulholland were not confined to engineers. At the ribbon-cutting ceremony on December 27, 1924, Mulholland, appearing somewhat embarrassed at center, is surrounded by "motion picture and theatrical stars and artists" including Natalie Kingston, who performed her "famous Peacock Dance," and Betty Blythe, who did her "Baghdad Number, Magical Carpet of Love" (City Council file #8470 [1924]). *Hearst Collection, Department of Special Collections, University of Southern California Library*

Moreover, if engineers spoke with their shovels, policy proponents favored words, and exclusive reliance on documentary sources can privilege the role of those who produced the documents, perhaps beyond their ability to shape events.

The extant explanations of Los Angeles transportation omit any formative role for the city engineers in their role as engineers rather than as participants in policy debates. The engineers had their own notions about what should be built. They were able to act on those preferences outside the broad policy considerations that have occupied the existing interpretations, and in ways that did not necessarily fulfill the intentions of those who funded the work. Thus the second major task of this essay is to explain how a massive project such as Mulholland Highway could get built within a climate of resistance to broad-scaled road schemes. By scrutinizing the Mulholland project, I try to demonstrate how the municipal engineers carved out a role as brokers between private economic interests and the political authority of the city council, enabling them to hijack such a project for their own ends. To them, the road was its own justification: an artery, a vantage point, the technological transformation of nature to a sublime engineered landscape, and a monument to the revered forefather.

This effort to clarify the role of the city engineers touches on the work of other scholars concerned with the course of engineering in American society. Bruce Seely's research on the Bureau of Public Roads has shown how federal engineers advanced expertise as a political value and formulated transportation policy out of the public view. In the realm of construction, rather than policy, Jameson Doig and David Billington explain how engineers concerned with a single transportation project could mediate among political and economic interests to serve their own ends, an interpretation that is germane to Mulholland Highway. Doig and Billington probe deeply within tight geographical limits, thus converging with Bruce Sinclair's call for the exploration of localism as a factor in twentieth-century engineering. It is my hope that this essay also contributes to that undertaking proposed by Sinclair, as well as to his proposition that emotionalism demands further inquiry as a factor in engineering practice.[10]

The following account of Mulholland Highway is divided into four sections. The first provides the political context of roadbuilding in 1920s Los Angeles. The second tracks the machinations of the real estate sector that provided the initial impetus for the roadway. The third follows the city engineers on the job, and the fourth recounts the difficulties attending the early years of the highway's operation. Concluding remarks reflect on how the highly contingent and rapidly shifting meanings of Mulholland Highway might help unlock some of the apparent paradoxes in the history of transportation in Los Angeles. These engineers' ability to conceive and construct substantial portions of the city according to their own values, and outside of systemic policy considerations, can suggest a more nuanced understanding of the roads and freeways that constitute the largest human-built component of the region's metropolitan landscape.

BOULEVARDING THE CITY

The existing interpretations of Los Angeles's transportation development offer a choice between two universalizing concepts: corporate malfeasance or representative democracy. The noir fantasy of a General Motors–led conspiracy that killed the street railways in favor of the automobile has been exposed as a fable by Scott Bottles and other scholars.[11] Constructed counter to the conspiracy theory is the equally fabulous picture of the roads and freeways as the result of an unrealistically pure democratic impulse: the people of Los Angeles enthusiastically endorsed rebuilding the city to accommodate the automobile. Bottles, David Brodsly, and Mark Foster paint a picture of dissatisfaction with the street railways and connect the adoption of automotive transportation with Progressive animus against the monopolistic Southern Pacific Railroad and the Huntington interests, which dominated the region's rail transit. "By jumping in their cars," according to Bottles, "urban denizens thumbed their noses at their long-standing antagonist—the railway executive. But however individualistic this reaction may have been in the beginning, it soon evolved into a collective effort to facilitate automobile transit within America's urban areas."[12]

This view of behavior does not consider that during the first third of the twentieth century people acquired automobiles for a host of other reasons that had nothing to do with anti-streetcar sentiment, and that such purchase did not necessarily carry deliberate policy implications regarding transportation infrastructure. Individuals bought and used automobiles for basic convenience, in the pursuit of social status, and as a manifestation of gender anxieties, not to mention the exhilaration and fascination that has long been recognized as a factor in technological change and the adoption of new technologies.[13] To comprehend the automobile as an inherently "democratic technology" or "a democratic alternative to the inadequacy of public transportation" strangely echoes the tactics of advertisers at the time, who sought to conflate consumption and democracy as a means of selling goods.[14] This approach to marketing encouraged the notion that freedom of choice should "be perceived as an act more significantly exercised in the marketplace than in the political arena," as Roland Marchand has put it.[15] But to grasp the political dimensions of the "effort to facilitate automobile transit," we need not interpret automobile purchase as a proxy vote for the tax-funded provision of road systems. A more direct path to political meaning is to examine political acts, such as elections, public hearings, and lawsuits over municipal construction ventures. Far from a "collective effort," these actions show that accommodating the automobile was highly contested during this period.

The argument of consensus in favor of the automobile draws pivotal support from the operation of assessment districts to fund road projects in the years between 1910 and 1930, but a closer look reveals a different picture. Under the assessment-district process, property owners voted to accept or reject increased property taxes to pay for infrastructure work.[16] Unlike recent interpretations, however, the city engineers took pains to disaggregate major road projects from more routine urban construction. The approval process generally went smoothly for streetlights, sidewalks, curbs, and the initial paving of existing streets.[17] In contrast, opening new streets or widening existing ones caused extensive protest. The most frequently specified complaints were the taking of land for public rights-of-way; cost, which was always higher in projects that included right-of-way acquisition; and various impacts on the character of the immediate locale, such as increased traffic or increase (or decrease) of commercial use. Every year between 1912 and 1932 majority protests forced abandonment of proposals for opening or widening through-traffic streets after years of planning and design; the city engineers estimated that citizens rejected more than half of such projects in all.[18]

From a legal and institutional standpoint, the assessment-district process made a poor setting for consensus in favor of road construction. As Robin Einhorn has demonstrated with reference to nineteenth-century Chicago, assessment districts provided a means to limit public expenditure and to fund infrastructure without any redistributive economic impact. For California, Terrence McDonald has shown that the state legislature's stipulations for assessment districts followed the preferences of the San Francisco delegation. Acting out of a "poisonous anti-state atmosphere" that sought to minimize taxes by constraining the ability of city government to fund infrastructure, the San Franciscans in the state assembly elevated property-owner protest over centralized authority in planning and spending for infrastructure. Protests and abandoned projects did not violate the intent of the assessment-district process, but fulfilled it.[19]

As early as 1915, the city's engineer for street design, H. Z. Osborne Jr., grew frustrated with the difficulty of building through highways in Los Angeles and called for a city charter amendment to ease the process. Since 1912 he had spearheaded the department's plans for "boulevarding the entire city" with a vast grid of wide, arterial thoroughfares, only to encounter such widespread resistance that within a year a majority of the opening and widening proposals were stalled in court.[20] The immediate cause for the amendment recommendation was Osborne's attempt to improve a dirt path in the Silver Lake district to a 60-foot-wide boulevard. When the abutting property owners sued the city to prevent that, he anticipated (correctly) losing the case and launched his attempt to circumvent the established approval process.[21] But the city council could not amend state law, so Osborne turned to other political channels and formed an alliance with the Chamber of Commerce to lobby at the city, county, and state levels on behalf of centralized authority for highway construction.[22] These efforts led directly to the formation in 1921 of the Traffic Commission of the City and County of Los Angeles, a private, nonprofit organization, and Osborne left city employ to become its executive chairman and chief engineer. Dedicated to the promotion of street construction and traffic regulation, the traffic commission included representatives from city and county planning and engineering departments, as well as from the Chamber of Commerce, the Automobile Club of Southern California, and other civic groups.[23]

The commission's principal accomplishment was the Major Traffic Street Plan of 1924, produced by a team of three nationally prominent planning consultants. This plan essentially reproduced Osborne's grid of boulevards covering the Los Angeles basin, wrapped it in the authority of hired experts, and introduced it with accompanying fanfare from the *Los Angeles Times,* whose owner, Harry Chandler, served on the traffic commission's board.[24] That fall, the voters of Los Angeles approved a $5 million bond issue to build the Major Traffic Street Plan, which vote has been interpreted as consensus in favor of highways.[25] But, since $5 million could not complete more than 10 percent of that program, residents would still have to form assessment districts and accept land-taking and tax increments to carry it out. Many did, especially for paving existing streets. Through arteries, however, required assent from landowners along extended corridors, which did not materialize despite the traffic commission's reports of highly positive response.[26] The city engineering department admitted as much when it compared progress on the plan to more conventional kinds of work: "A great deal more difficulty is experienced in getting the major traffic projects past the protest stage."[27]

The largest single component of the plan, Tenth Street (later known as Olympic Boulevard), offers a vivid illustration of the difference between the rhetoric surrounding the plan and the actual construction that occurred. Even before the traffic commission hired its consultants, the city engineers had embraced the proposal for a 100-foot-wide boulevard extending between the east and west boundaries of the city. Beyond the need for a "great cross-town boulevard," the engineers envisioned a regional artery that would extend "on the west to the Pacific Ocean and on the east by way of Telegraph Road and Whittier Boulevard to San Diego and the Imperial Valley." They persuaded the city council to make the highly unusual commitment of direct funding to upgrade Tenth Street, in the amount of $1.5 million, or a quarter of the projected cost. The traffic commission's consultants duly incorporated an upgraded Tenth Street into the Major Traffic Street Plan.[28]

By far the most extensive and costly highway proposal in the city, the Tenth Street project involved some eleven thousand property owners in the assessment district that the engineers mapped out. Many of them objected, but the size of the district posed a considerable organizing challenge to opponents. When the council opened public hearings in June 1923, the opposition represented the largest road protest the city had seen, but barely 17 percent of the affected properties. Most of the objections concerned the scope of the project and the use of assessments to benefit other parts of the city, though with no agreement on where those beneficiaries might be; some protestors thought the project would benefit downtown retailers, while others believed that outlying districts would gain disproportionate advantage from the work. A group of property owners sued to stop the project on procedural grounds, claiming that in drawing up the proposal the engineers did not reveal the precise route or full extent of the work. The case ultimately reached the state supreme court, which upheld the protestors in April 1926. The biggest through-highway project in the city was stopped, never to be completed.[29]

In its next annual report following the supreme court decision, the traffic commission claimed that none of its recommended road improvements had been blocked by a majority protest.[30] That was technically correct: the 17 percent who protested the Tenth Street project did not constitute a majority. But the road was not completed or under construction at the time of that report, and a subsequent effort to win approval for an amended version of Tenth Street went down to defeat by majority protest.[31] The implication that the Major Traffic Street Plan enjoyed public support verging on unanimity was more hopeful, or polemical, than it was an accurate reflection of reality. The traffic commission sought to mold consensus in favor of the automobile, and the bombast surrounding the Major Traffic Street Plan was a means to that end. When Bottles, planner Martin Wachs, and historian Robert Fishman point to the Major Traffic Street Plan as a watershed in the city's transportation history, they may have mistaken the promotional agenda for the reality of grading roadbeds and pouring concrete.[32] The difference matters, as no amount of rhetoric could, by itself, reshape the everyday experience of Angelenos plying the streets in their automobiles, or provide the engineers with the authority to complete arterial highways according to design. Fragmentary fulfillment meant thorough ruin for the plan. Removing an element from the grid disrupted the carefully drawn circulation patterns, and a through highway that choked down to fewer lanes at certain locations could not carry its intended traffic load.

The city engineers accommodated their work to the incrementalist disposition of a citizenry that liked their motorcars but offered no consensus toward comprehensive reconstruction of the city to ease their movement. The office's responsibilities for a range of engineering functions enabled the engineers to upgrade highways by attaching the work to diverse projects and resources. At the intersection of Sunset Boulevard and Myra Avenue, a culvert with inadequate capacity resulted in flooding each rainy season. Charged with alleviating the water problem, the engineering office submitted a plan for an 80-foot-wide bridge that would not only carry the culvert but also separate the grades and widen the constricted Sunset right-of-way to the dimensions called for in the Major Traffic Street Plan.[33] In the most spectacular highway reconstruction project of the 1920s, the city engineers produced a series of monumental bridges across the Los Angeles River, largely through the financial support of the Southern Pacific and Santa Fe railroads. The bridges also spanned the tracks that ran along both sides of the river, and the railroads saw the advantage of separating their grades from road traffic in that busy industrial corridor.[34]

Those bridges reveal values embodied in the construction of Mulholland

Highway operative in other work by the engineering office. The impulse to reflexive memorialization imbued the river bridges with impressive art deco finishes. Unlike the monumental and decorative structures associated with the City Beautiful movement in other cities, these bridges stood in a gritty landscape of factories, railyards, and warehouses rather than institutional and cultural districts. The Los Angeles engineers did not mind presenting such gestures to a limited audience, consisting significantly of themselves. Viewing scenery from highways (not formal parkways) was also a long-standing concern in their work. When cooperative subdividers had earlier approved tax increments to open a 3-mile-long segment of Pico Boulevard through undeveloped land on the west side of Los Angeles, the street engineers extolled the views of open fields and low hills that the new roadway would provide for the passing motorist.[35]

Nonetheless, the engineers' more typical experience with major highways was less satisfying. As Los Angeles's population almost tripled during the 1920s, the city engineering office undertook scores of road projects, as well as providing sewers and water service, sidewalks, streetlights, and a host of other urban amenities. Arterial highways, however, loomed as the most significant category of proposed but unrealized work. When venturesome real estate promoters concocted the plan to open a vast new territory for development by running a highway atop the Hollywood Hills, the engineers saw an opportunity to express what was important to them: to build a major highway without opposition, to create an uninterrupted corridor, to honor their own work and those associated with it, and to frame nature with artifice. These ideas had developed during the construction of the Los Angeles Aqueduct, pervasively influenced the engineers afterward, and blossomed during the Mulholland project. The ideal of transportation efficiency, which dominated the contemporary policy debates as well as the later interpretations of the city's transportation history, had little effect on Mulholland Highway. The story now turns to the real estate developers who furnished that golden opportunity.

A SMALL GROUP OF CAPITALISTS

The subdivision and development that transformed the landscape of the Los Angeles basin in the 1920s also created an imbalance that threatened to end the prospects for further profitable speculation. The basin was completely subdivided by 1924, even though much of the property stood vacant as subdivisions that existed only in legal, rather than physical, form.[36] To the north, in the San Fernando Valley, a different kind of problem disrupted the plans of subdividers. Almost two decades earlier, Harry Chandler, H. J. Whitley, Moses Sherman, and other real estate moguls had projected the San Fernando Valley as the ultimate suburban frontier. In the transactions central to that stratagem, they optioned almost 50,000 acres of valley land and profited handsomely by reselling after the aqueduct brought water to the valley. The lucrative proceeds from this scheme were the gains of the speculator who sold to other investors, not of the subdivider who bought land by the acre at wholesale and sold it by the lot, at retail, to homeowners. These machinations pushed up the price of the land, which made development more difficult by increasing the price of entry for those who would attempt it. William Mulholland complained in 1912 that "The capitalists have stolen the unearned increment for the next 20 years."[37] In the early 1920s, much of the valley land just north of the hills was still identified by section nomenclature rather than lot numbers or street addresses, a sure sign of stalled development.[38]

Constrained by thorough exploitation in the basin and an oversupply of valley land that was overpriced and still distant from the built-up part of the city, real estate investors in the 1920s turned their attention to the Hollywood Hills, which stood between the basin and the valley.[39] The imposingly steep topography had delayed the advance of development into the hills and left them relatively undisturbed in comparison to the feverish speculation on either side. Reporting in 1924 on residential development in the hills, John R. Prince, who headed the city engineering department's street design unit, commented that "a tract located in the hills implies irregular lots and curved streets, wherein the grades afford many problems."[40] Prince agreed to relax the street-width requirements to enable development in the hills. "Subdivision streets," he had reported a year earlier, "may be [as little as] 50 feet in width, and in rare instances 40 feet will be allowed. Hillside streets, 26 to 30 feet."[41]

Winning cooperation from the city engineers posed less of an obstacle than overcoming the reluctance of home buyers to consider dwellings on precarious sites subject to brush fires. Hillside charm was not yet a salable commodity, especially when so many other home sites were available in the flats. Extravagant advertising and promotion accompanied most subdivisions in this period, but those in the hill sections set new standards for flamboyance and creativity. W. H. Woodruff's daring lunge into the hills, with his Beachwood Canyon development of 1922–23, occasioned the construction of an enormous sign atop Mount Lee, proclaiming the new subdivision's name of Hollywoodland.[42] Alphonzo Bell's scheme for Bel-Air, started in 1923, differed in two significant ways from the hundreds of subdivision applications filed for flat land in the basin that year. The hilly, rugged land was expensive to build on, and Bell sought to overcome this limitation by establishing an aura of elegance and exclusivity, including imposing, if nonfunctional, gates. Bell also donated prime property for the creation of the Bel-Air Country Club, and his landscape architect laid out bridle trails for the residents.[43]

The difficulties of developing the hills were already evident to a group of property owners who convened at the Hollywood Country Club in December 1922. Their goal was to promote construction of a road traversing the top of the hills, running west for some 22 miles from Cahuenga Pass to Calabasas, in the valley. They formed two organizations that day, the Hollywood Foothills Improvement Association, which was the umbrella group for promotion, and Municipal Improvement District Number 22, which was the legal entity for the payment of property tax increments to finance the project.[44]

There was more to their vision than building homes in the hills. The 431 members of the municipal improvement district controlled virtually all the land between Sunset Boulevard and the valley's Ventura Boulevard, more than 50,000 acres in all.[45] Besides advancing development in the hills, these promoters wanted to start the process of connecting the basin and the valley in order to bring the valley more fully into the profitable orbit of the city's real estate market. "The proposed route," reported Prince, "will intersect many beautiful canyons, among which are mentioned Laurel, Benedict, Sepulveda, Franklin, Coldwater and Mandeville, through which roads will eventually be opened from the San Fernando Valley to Los Angeles."[46]

Harry H. Merrick, a partner in the real estate firm of Merrick and Ruddick, served as president of the Hollywood Foothills Improvement Association. He represented more substantial stakeholders: real estate speculators such as Victor Girard, W. F. Holt, the Whitley family, Thomas C. Bundy, Alvaro Pratt, and Louis Evans; movie-business moguls Sid Graumann, Thomas Ince, and Edgar Rice Burroughs; bankers Marco Hellman and Willis Longyear; and representatives from the powerful Title Insurance and Trust Company. The roster was also sprinkled with city officials who owned land in the hills or the valley, including those connected with the city's work on the project, such as John Shaw, from the city engineer's office, and Clarence Dykstra, who served on the Board of Public Works that oversaw the city engineer.[47]

The formation of Municipal Improvement District Number 22 only started the process of securing funding for the project. Merrick had to collect signatures on a petition from the landholders in the district, which took eight months.[48] Merrick's group also retained engineer Dewitt Reaburn, an aqueduct veteran with a close relationship to Prince and his colleagues, to survey the assessment-district boundaries. With the boundary certified, the city clerk needed only a week to check the names on the petition against the voter rolls, an uncommonly short interval for that process.[49] Then the city council scheduled the minimum public-notice period and set the bond issue referendum for 9 October 1923. The property owners approved the bond issue by a 2 to 1 margin.[50]

The petition and the referendum gave the city council the assurances it needed to allow the project to proceed. The council acted in much the way that Einhorn has described the elected officials in Chicago behaving: if property owners wanted to pledge property tax increments to pay for the work, the council would not stand in the way. Certainly the scheme also fit the picture of booster-led development of Los Angeles in the 1920s, but the congenial setting afforded by the council depended fundamentally on the lack of expenditure from public funds. None of the members offered opinions on the Mulholland plans, but merely voted the necessary authorizations to proceed. During construction they would also approve the municipal engineers' requests for accelerated operating procedures. All the votes on Mulholland Highway carried unanimously.

After the referendum passed, the city attorney advertised for bids to underwrite $1 million in bonds and received a single submission, from a consortium of seven banks and securities brokers.[51] The council voted to accept the bid, then on advice of the city attorney contracted for outside counsel to review the procedures. The firm of Henry O'Melveny, a founder of Title Insurance and Trust and a well-known member of the city's economic elite, got the job. O'Melveny's firm would receive $2,000 for its opinion "in the event same is favorable and $1,200 in case said attorneys are unable to give an approving opinion."[52] There was no delay. The bonds went on sale in January 1924 and yielded a million dollars to build Mulholland Highway. For the next 40 years, until 1963, landowners in the improvement district would carry a special increment on their property taxes to reimburse the city for the principal and interest that the city paid to the bondholders.[53]

Merrick and his colleagues eagerly consented to higher taxes because they expected to pass them on to the people who bought house lots in the hills and in the adjacent section of the San Fernando Valley. Their fondest dreams, however, were not fulfilled in their lifetimes. The hilltop highway did not become the spine for main roads linking the basin and the valley, in part because of topography and in part because commercial-property developers from central Hollywood had another plan. While Merrick was circulating the petition, landowners in the Hollywood business district sought to reinforce the natural advantages of Cahuenga Pass by widening and paving the road through the pass and similarly improving the roads at the southern outlet of the pass: Wilcox, Cahuenga, Ivar, Vine, and Yucca. Though it took nearly a decade to complete, this "Five Finger Plan" captured the bulk of traffic between the basin and the valley.[54] Moreover, even as Prince dutifully reported the intention that Mulholland Highway would serve as a meaningful link in the surface transportation system, he and Reaburn knew that it would not make the crucial connection with Cahuenga Pass. It would indeed be an uninterrupted artery for 22 miles through the hills, but an isolated one leading nowhere.

Not until the real estate boom of the 1950s would dense settlement extend throughout the San Fernando Valley. Before World War II, despite the completion of tract homes in the southern sections of Van Nuys and Lankershim/North Hollywood, much of the subdivided land on the valley side of Improvement District Number 22 remained unimproved. During the Depression, the city planning commission noted that to avoid taxes that would be higher on house lots than on undivided parcels, subdividers filed to have their holdings "reverted to acreage." The planners envisioned a landscape of small farms in the San Fernando Valley, as previously approved subdivisions were consolidated back into larger tracts.[55] The largest landholder in the improvement district, Girard's Boulevard Land Company, went bankrupt without selling its valley acreage as house lots.[56]

By the end of the 1930s, slope-clinging dwellings in the lower reaches of the Hollywood Hills had entered into the representations of Los Angeles. But images of Douglas Fairbanks and Mary Pickford's estate on Summit Drive say more about the reputation of the place than its reality on the ground. The success of Hollywoodland was more exception than rule. In Bel-Air, sales were only modest during the 1920s and fell off sharply in the 1930s. By 1947, when Alphonzo Bell died, the disappointing results had contributed to his insuperable financial predicament. Similarly, H. J. Whitley's opening of Whitley Terrace, and the completion of several prototype hillside houses, did not prevent the financial debacle that marked the end of his long, successful career as a developer. Only after World War II was the attraction of a house in the hills finally marketed more broadly to a well-to-do clientele.[57]

The term of the bonds for Mulholland Highway turned out to be prophetic: it took most of those 40 years to fulfill the pecuniary ambitions of the people who first proposed building it, and many of them missed out on the payoff. However, the money they devoted and the political influence they applied had another, more immediate impact, by enabling the city engineers to create one of the transformed landscapes that they relished so deeply.

A MONUMENT TO "OUR BILL"

The overt association with William Mulholland came only after Merrick's group formulated its proposal for the highway. A year and a half after the establishment of the improvement district, Dewitt Reaburn put forward his version of an appropriate history: "The idea of constructing a scenic highway along the crest of the Santa Monica Mountains westward from Cahuenga Pass [*sic*] originated some ten or fifteen years ago with Chief Engineer William Mulholland of the City Water Department."[58] Whether that was true or not, it was certainly not part of Merrick's petition. The only change between the petition language and the text of the referendum was the insertion of the phrase "commonly known as Mulholland Highway."[59]

The city engineers' verbal identification of the road with the leader of the aqueduct project corresponded to the characteristics of the work that they most fervently wished to reinforce. Both projects drew proponents from among the same civic leaders and real estate speculators; both projects followed a vision of metropolitan growth stimulated by constructing extensive works of civil engineering; both received overwhelming endorsement in bond-issue referenda that allowed the engineers to prosecute the work without further concern over funding; and both entailed the construction of linear-flow systems through inhospitable terrain.[60]

In contrast to the contested character of most large road projects, William Mulholland had acted with extraordinary independence in building the aqueduct. The bond funding approved by referenda in 1905 and 1907 played a critical role in that, but the administrative structure contributed as well. The city council formed the water department in 1903 specifically to assume the responsibilities of the private company that had controlled the local water supply and its distribution. The Board of Water Commissioners governed the department with broad authority to hire and fire personnel, enter into contracts, determine the department's budget, and set water rates and sell bonds to defray that budget. With a strong chief such as Mulholland framing the deliberations of the board, the water department offered a compelling model of a public agency run by engineers.[61] Under that authority Mulholland set up a structure for administering the aqueduct project that served as its own government, with internal departments for accounting, supply, engineering, legal affairs, and construction.[62]

Mulholland and his staff also derived satisfaction from the character of the work. Rearranging the hydrology of California was no small task, but beyond the immensity of the construction work, living in wilderness camps and withstanding harsh conditions contributed to the conscious sense of re-engineering nature. Civil engineering of that magnitude commonly took its practitioners to environments that contrasted with any notion of urban civility, and the aqueduct was a radical example, as it spanned both the Sierra Nevada and the Mojave Desert. The exhilaration of outdoor life was not diminished by altering nature with dynamite and Caterpillar tractors. The "natural sublime intertwined with technological conquest," as David Nye has put it. Civil engineering work was seen not so much as subduing nature as setting nature off with the "dramatic contrast" of human achievement.[63]

The work was an adventure in the landscape, a camping expedition with a purpose. The aqueduct project employed as many as four thousand workers at a time along the route, and the provision of shelter and food was a considerable portion of the cost. Mulholland did not entirely delegate the responsibility of setting up and running the construction camps, and kept a close eye on the off-hours practices of the crews. These matters deserved attention, as the largest disruptions of the work came when workers at two of the camps rioted over the quality of the food. Mulholland did not mind that the conditions fostered a hard-edged male comraderie that was often expressed in drinking and gambling. Many years later, a surveyor recalled: "Bill Mulholland, the Aqueduct's chief engineer, used to say that it was whiskey that built the Aqueduct. Pressed for an enlightening word, Mulholland declared that no man would do the hard, hazard-filled work of driving tunnels or skinning mules through the canyons, while putting up with blistering heat, biting cold, dust storms and indifferent food, if whiskey didn't keep him broke."[64] Perhaps Mulholland appreciated the harsh ethos of the construction camp because he associated it with boldness in the face of dangerous working conditions, or because the control he could exercise in the camps was far greater than could be applied over a commuting workforce. For all these reasons, the veterans of the aqueduct included construction camps in their conception of subsequent landscape-altering engineering projects.[65]

Completion of the aqueduct was barely a decade in the past when Merrick began circulating the petition for a roadway in the Santa Monica Mountains. Veterans of the aqueduct worked throughout the ranks of the city engineering department, and included two men, A. C. Hansen and Homer Hamlin, who would go on to lead the department.[66] The engineers understood what the bond issue represented and set to work to reproduce their aqueduct experience, free from the irksome necessities of public hearings, court cases, and appropriation requests to the city council.

In February 1923, six months before Merrick filed the petition and almost a year before the sale of the bonds, surveys and exploratory excavation had already begun. The Hollywood Foothills Improvement Association hired on its own account engineer Dewitt Reaburn, who was well known to the city staff from his service on the aqueduct. The city would later reimburse the improvement association out of the bond proceeds for the fees paid to Reaburn and the crews he hired.[67]

With the active cooperation of the city street engineer, John Prince, Reaburn established the basic design of the roadway: maximum grade of 6 percent, minimum curve radius of 100 feet, and width of 30 feet.[68] Driving there today, it is hard to imagine that the engineers worried about the difficulties of negotiating some of the narrow, steep, and sharply curved sections of the road in an automobile. It seems more like a pipeline or electrical transmission line right-of-way, fit for the movement of liquids or current, but perversely troublesome for a human in an automobile. The project's ironies go beyond the tortuous roadbed. Development in the area required water mains, and providing a pipeline right-of-way might have been an appropriate criterion in setting the course and shape of the road, but water service had no place in the original design. Reaburn and Prince did not perform the centerline survey that would have provided the fundamental data necessary to integrate the road with below-grade utilities. That survey was under way two years after highway construction was completed.[69] Not convenient to drive, and not based on utility service, the design of Mulholland Highway reflected aesthetic considerations more than anything else. Insofar as the pragmatic concerns associated with engineering practice entered the project, they were directed toward resource utilization: finish as fast as possible.

During this preliminary stage of the work, in 1923, the engineers began articulating the association with William Mulholland and pressed the city to name the road in his honor. The scenic character of the new highway also entered the discourse, at the same time that the engineers specifically ruled out the immediate possibility that the road would fill any role in the larger transportation network. Prince and Reaburn noted that Mulholland Highway would not connect with anything at its eastern terminus near Cahuenga Pass. It ended at an elevation high above the pass, requiring a bridge or causeway to bring it to level grade, which the bond issue could not pay for.[70] Scenic enjoyment was also construed quite narrowly. When the Bridle Path Association asked that the design allow for horseback riding along the side of the road, the city council filed the request with no action, on the advice of the engineering department.[71] Mulholland Highway was not to be a transportation link but neither was it to be a sylvan setting for active recreation. Its beauty would be appreciated in the making of it, or perhaps through a windshield, or not at all.

Reaburn and Prince applied the aqueduct model in highly practical terms when they recommended that the city set up the Mulholland Highway Department as part of the city engineering office. Reaburn would supervise the work for an annual salary of $10,000 from the city. When the engineers presented this plan to the city council in December 1923 they justified the extraordinary setup with a line of reasoning not previously applied toward the project: "Owing to the fact that the supply of water from the Municipal System to a large section of the territory in the western part of the city, particularly that part known as Laurel Canyon Section, is dependent on the construction of said highway; and, having in view the necessity of such a supply of water, both for domestic purposes and for the purpose of protection from fire, it appears to this Board that the earliest possible construction of said highway is of great public importance."[72] The city engineering establishment yearned to build the road but could not claim any transportation necessity and obviously could not justify a special operating department on the basis of providing a scenic amenity or the desire to enrich some subdividers. They understood the volatility of the chaparral environment, however, and, presciently, fastened on that as the rationale for extraordinary operating procedures.[73]

The council not only consented to set up the department under Reaburn, but also agreed to lend it $25,000 from reserve funds in order to start heavy construction before the city received the bond proceeds. Two days later Reaburn submitted his staffing plan, a total of 411 people. Besides 200 laborers and 50 skilled workers of unspecified trades, he asked for a full complement of steam-shovel operators, mechanics, blacksmiths, drivers, teamsters, surveying crews, clerks, and a supervisory staff of assistant engineers, foremen, and shift bosses. Lest heroic engineering plans chafe under the reins of bureaucracy, Reaburn made a further unusual request: "In order to get this work started at the earliest possible date, and to push it through to completion within the prescribed period of one year, it is very important that all of these employees be exempt from Civil Service rules." The council approved unanimously.[74]

Completing the picture of a small-scale revival of the aqueduct project, over the next month Reaburn and the city engineering staff submitted plans for a series of construction camps. It was true that the project area was generally inaccessible to vehicles, and that getting crews to and from the work sites would consume time and resources better spent on blasting rock and bulldozing soil. However, one of the camps stood on the grounds of the Hollywood Country Club, a genteel and easily accessible location. The engineers' idea of heroic construction included camps, whether or not they were required by the conditions of the work. Reaburn paid particular attention to the food. He recruited a commissary superintendent "of wide experience in handling mess houses, having been [a] Division Superintendent for the Mess Contractor during the Aqueduct construction," presumably one of the divisions where the workers had not rioted over the meals.[75]

Accelerated operating procedures continued throughout the project. The council granted all of Reaburn's frequent requests for exemption from civil service rules when he made adjustments in staffing.[76] The project routinely benefited as well from waiver of the bidding provisions that governed city purchases, obtained by claiming that the project fell "under the emergency provisions of the city charter." The city council provided retroactive ratification after the project staff came to terms with vendors for rental of construction equipment and purchase of explosives and vehicles. These were no small expenditures; the blasting powder order filled five rail cars.[77]

Most of the massive earthmoving was completed by April 1924, when monthly expenditures peaked at $149,000. For every square foot of road-

Figure 2.3. The steam shovel on Caterpillar treads was the principal earthmoving tool in the construction of Mulholland Highway. Two weeks before the opening of the highway, the crew staged this shot for a newspaper photographer. The identity of the couple aloft is not known. *Hearst Collection, Department of Special Collections, University of Southern California Library*

way, the crews had to scrape away or otherwise reconfigure some 9 cubic feet of soil (fig. 2.3). By July much of the skilled work was in place, notably a concrete retaining wall along a curving section of road near the eastern terminus. After that, the outlays ran between $50,000 and $70,000 per month, until December. With the opening ceremonies just two weeks away, completion of the gravel surface required an extra fifty dump trucks working around the clock.[78]

They did finish on time (fig. 2.4), and for the first three months of 1925 the city assigned traffic checkers to measure the use of the new highway. They counted 750 cars a day, fewer than the streets in the built-up areas saw in an hour and about 5 percent of the traffic that plied an outlying highway such as Long Beach Boulevard.[79] The sparse use did not disappoint the city

Figure 2.4. The opening motorcade approaches a series of switchbacks. *Hearst Collection, Department of Special Collections, University of Southern California Library*

engineers, who never intended Mulholland Highway to carry traffic in any great capacity. After all, its eastern terminus dead-ended on a cliff. Its importance to them sprang from the chance to indulge their passion for complementing nature with construction. Generations of motorists who have enjoyed the view from Mulholland would testify to the engineers' success, although the turnouts that enable safe contemplation of the vistas were not part of the original design of the road.[80]

The engineers also viewed the project as an opportunity to install a construction regime that could approximate the autonomy of the aqueduct enterprise. It succeeded in that goal too, at least when designated tax increments provided a modicum of funding. Six months after the project ended, Reaburn and the Mulholland Highway Department were still in business, building Beverly Boulevard.[81] The Mulholland Highway Department later worked on the Cahuenga Pass road and several smaller projects, until the city auditors caught on to the arrangement. In August 1928, the staff of the council's Personnel and Efficiency Committee called for disbanding the Mulholland Highway Department, and the council had no choice but to accede.[82]

At that particular moment, association with William Mulholland had turned into a liability, which might also have been connected with the department's termination. In March 1928, a dam of his design in Ventura County had failed, causing hundreds of deaths and irrevocably staining his reputation. No longer could the aura of the aqueduct builder contribute to the administrative objectives of the city engineers.[83]

FIRE IN THE HILLS

The connection between roadbuilding and the provision of water mains for fire suppression had been commonplace in municipal engineering since the 1880s, and the Los Angeles city engineering office had a special committee to coordinate road construction with installation of sewer and water service.[84] Reaburn clearly understood the environmental implications of planting settlement in the hills and, when submitting his construction plan in late 1923, used the fire hazard as a means to win emergency status that would loosen the administrative requirements for the project. He did not mention then that the water mains would come later, and at considerable additional cost.

The real estate speculators who petitioned for the highway must have been aware of the fires that periodically consumed the brush in the hill sections. As suggested above, this condition might have accounted in part for the delay in exploiting the hills, and for the particular attention given to promotion and image-building to counter that negative reputation by establishing fashionable cachet for the area. If such observations are necessarily speculative, it is nonetheless certain that the developers, like Reaburn, expressed abundant awareness and concern once construction was under way.

In July 1924, when the last rain had fallen months earlier and the summer sun parched the chaparral into so much dry kindling, Merrick alerted the city council to the urgent matter of "prevention of fires in the hills during this most hazardous season." The project itself had heightened the problem by depositing "cut brush along the Mulholland Highway." Merrick did not confine his apprehension to the vicinity of the road construction but also asked for help in "cutting new fire breaks in the hills." He recommended assigning convicts from the city jail, which the council agreed to do.[85]

The fire breaks did not help at all when fire raged through the mountains in September. On 2 October the Board of Public Works reported that

"A very serious fire has just been extinguished after the most strenuous efforts on the part of the fire department and the employees of the Board in
the Mulholland Highway [Department]." The fire department asked the
council to establish two new fire companies along Mulholland Highway and
to authorize surveys and construction to lay temporary water mains, install
communication lines, and cut more fire breaks. "I believe that the late experience with fire in these mountains," wrote the fire department's chief
engineer, "will be sufficient argument for the establishment of these companies without any further statement from me."[86]

The fire department's urgent request reflected the recognition of a new
situation. Brush fires in the hills did not concern them when the area was
uninhabited, but the highway was intended to stimulate development. The
fires also had the paradoxical effect of accelerating the urbanization of the
region. Before the embers had cooled, the investors who owned the land in
Benedict Canyon donated a right-of-way through their property: "In order
to provide that the City of Los Angeles may lay a water pipeline from Mulholland [Highway] to the territory within Benedict Canyon and south of
same, [we] have provided for a road which will extend from the end of the
present road in Benedict Canyon to Mulholland." They had not intended
to open the road for "some years," but desired the "benefit of protection,"
and even offered to pay half the cost.[87]

Mudslides also afflicted the hill regions, particularly after fires had
cleared the slopes of the vegetation that helped to retain the soil. Two years
after the highway opened, in December 1926, a flood obliterated 17 of its
22 miles. Part of the problem was that Reaburn had stinted on drains to conduct runoff under the roadway. Silt had clogged the minimal drains that did
exist, forcing mud and debris to cascade over the road, where much of it remained when an inspection team from the city engineering department was
finally able to survey the damage. The council had to appropriate money
for repair from the city's share of motor-vehicle registration fees, because
the remaining money from the bond funds was earmarked for the centerline survey so that water mains could be installed along the route.[88]

The city and the landowners struggled with the issues of fire and mudslides through the rest of the 1920s. The engineering department estimated
the water-main installation at $2.5 million and wanted to assess the prop-
erty owners for the cost.[89] Opposing the assessment, the Mulholland Highway Committee of the Ventura Boulevard Chamber of Commerce (which
had Merrick on its board) proposed instead "that the closing of the Highway will minimize the fire hazard in this hill area." They asked the city to
gate the highway and supply keys to those "certain property owners who
find it necessary to use the highway occasionally."[90] John Shaw, who had become the head of the city engineering department, countered that the en-

tire project would be lost if it were not maintained as a public right-of-way: "Whenever heavy rainfalls occur it is necessary to spend several thousand dollars to make it passable, and I do not believe that the city would be justified in closing the road and still keep it in passable repair. If this road is not kept in a certain degree of repair, much of it will be lost, and I do not think that it would be a good thing to close Mulholland Highway."[91] In this beguiling statement Shaw proposed to save the property owners "several thousand dollars" in repairs by keeping the road open as a city-owned right-of-way. The property owners sought to avoid a $2.5 million assessment by closing the road. Despite the apparent mismatch in the arguments, Shaw's recommendation prevailed and the highway remained open.

While the different agendas of the property owners and the city engineers had reinforced each other during the initial construction, they did not provide the basis for any long-term alliance. In 1929, the Board of Public Works proposed paving Mulholland Highway with concrete in order to facilitate the bulldozing of debris off the road after mudslides. The property owners saw the need for the work but balked at pledging more tax increments to be spent at the discretion of the city engineers. They mustered the votes to defeat the ordinance and decided to contract for the paving themselves.[92]

CONCLUSION

When advocates such as Osborne, Chandler, and the traffic commission achieved a measure of success for their highway proposals, they proclaimed the wisdom of a populace dedicated to the attainment of the greatest good for the greatest number of Angelenos. In the late 1920s, when it could no longer deny that the Major Traffic Street Plan would fail to achieve its objectives, the commission shifted its emphasis from asserting consensus to castigating those who would oppose its program and thereby frustrate the wishes of the majority. As the struggle over Tenth Street/Olympic Boulevard wound into the 1930s, the *Los Angeles Times* stepped up its efforts to demonize highway opponents and approvingly reported condemnation suits brought by the city against recalcitrant landowners and taxpayers.[93] Comparing the pronouncements about the Major Traffic Street Plan with the progress of its actual construction indicates that the rhetoric changed more drastically than did citizens' willingness to support the program. That support was conditional and limited from the start. When a comprehensive road system with smooth-flowing traffic continued to be elusive despite dramatic increases in miles paved and dollars spent, highway advocates rationalized the contradiction by employing the narrative of the public will rising up and then being thwarted. Their rendering of the public will was a rhetorical device enlisted to mobilize opinion. Later interpretations that reify such a conception are bound to obscure as much as they reveal about the processes that produced the automotive infrastructure.

Mulholland Highway and the events surrounding it can help to recover some of the contradictions at the core of the transportation system and to demystify the narrative abstractions of the public will and its denial. The provision of automotive infrastructure in Los Angeles always grappled with a range of views contingent on localized and temporal circumstances, and could reflect aesthetic, emotional, or political considerations that had nothing to do with the nominal purpose of building a road. It was possible, even probable, that people could like their automobiles but not approve the allocation of resources to build highways. It was possible, too, that major road projects could go forward without any basis in transportation efficiency and without widespread public support.

In Mulholland Highway, the engineers exploited the possibilities for action that resided in these tensions. They built a road that connected to nothing, that was not part of the comprehensive strategy of the Major Traffic Street Plan, and that spent an amount equal to 20 percent of the direct funding for that much heralded plan. It did not enrich the promoters who funded it, nor did it fulfill the engineers' hope for a long-term method to circumvent citizens' ability to impede ambitious road projects. Mulholland Highway did not result from rational, comprehensive planning but from a fragmentary process, a collection of goals representing a wider array of interests than have been recognized. Chief among these unacknowledged interests were the city engineers, whose goals were clearly separate from, if at times congruent with, those of the speculators. Mulholland Highway and the events surrounding it suggest that the city's transportation system resulted not from conspiracy and not from consensus but from temporary convergences of diverse and sometimes impractical agendas.

Today, in the early twenty-first century, the freeways of Los Angeles haunt any discussion of the city's transportation development, and recent experience is also redolent with contradiction: most people use the freeways but few people like them.[94] If we try to follow this dissatisfaction back toward some time when consensus might have flowered, it is conceivable that a disjunction occurred, that recent discontent represents a pendulum swing from acceptance to rejection when unanticipated outcomes arose or when the city's ferocious growth overwhelmed rational plans. The evidence from the 1920s of highly contested infrastructure development and roadbuilding that did not accord with systemic planning provides the basis for another reading. Is it possible that the roads and freeways of Los Angeles, and of other metropolitan regions as well, did not create the contradictions of the twentieth century but arose from those very contradictions? What, if any, are the connections between the contradictions of the recent past and those of that earlier time? Further exploration of the relationships between the rhetoric of transportation development and the record of actual practices should help answer those questions.

NOTES

I thank Philip Ethington, Lois Banner, William Deverell, Tom Sitton, Judith McGaw, John Staudenmaier, the *Technology and Culture* referees, Robert Post, Jonathan Spaulding, Susan LaTempa, Donald Jackson, Jeffrey Chusid, the students in Professor Banner's History 601 seminar at the University of Southern California, and Professor Ethington's Los Angeles history research group for comment and criticism.

1. The name of the road was changed from Mulholland Highway to Mulholland Drive in 1939; Los Angeles City Council Minutes (hereinafter Council Minutes), 286:21 (1939) and 286:600 (1939). City of Los Angeles documents cited in this essay may be found in the city archives, Records Center, Piper Technical Center.

2. "Progress of Work on Mulholland Highway Reviewed in Report of City Engineer," *Southwest Builder and Contractor,* 1 August 1924.

3. Joseph Tanner, managing director, Ventura Boulevard Chamber of Commerce, to Los Angeles City Council, 18 May 1927, Council File #3776 (1927).

4. Los Angeles City Engineer (hereinafter City Engineer), *Annual Report,* 1922–23, 49.

5. David Nye, *American Technological Sublime* (Cambridge, Mass., 1994), esp. 86–87, 126.

6. City Engineer, *Annual Report,* 1923–24, 23.

7. Clay McShane, *Down the Asphalt Path: The Automobile and the American City* (New York, 1994), 21–40; Bruce Radde, *The Merritt Parkway* (New Haven, Conn., 1993).

8. Jackson described this functionalist aesthetic on the part of engineers in "A Puritan Looks at the Landscape," in *Discovering the Vernacular Landscape* (New Haven, Conn., 1984), 57–64. In an assessment of engineering similar to Jackson's, Eugene S. Ferguson agreed with a statement made in 1828 by a British engineer who emphasized that a sense of dynamism ("directing the great sources of power in nature") characterized engineering practice more fundamentally than any association with certain types of objects or structures; see Ferguson, *Engineering and the Mind's Eye* (Cambridge, Mass., 1992), 1.

9. Paul Barrett, *The Automobile and Urban Transit: The Formation of Public Policy in Chicago* (Philadelphia, 1983); Glenn Yago, *The Decline of Transit: Urban Transportation in German and U.S. Cities* (New York, 1984); David St. Clair, *The Motorization of American Cities* (New York, 1986).

10. Bruce Seely, *Building the American Highway System: Engineers as Policy Makers* (Philadelphia, 1987); Jameson W. Doig and David P. Billington, "Ammann's First Bridge: A Study in Engineering, Politics and Entrepreneurial Behavior," *Technology and Culture* 35 (1994): 537–70; Bruce Sinclair, "Local History and National Culture: Notions on Engineering Professionalism in America," in *The Engineer in America: A Historical Anthology from Technology and Culture,* ed. Terry S. Reynolds (Chicago, 1991), 249–59.

11. Scott Bottles, *Los Angeles and the Automobile* (Berkeley, Calif., 1987), esp. 2–6

and 236–48. Also see Robert C. Post, "Images of the Pacific Electric: Why Memories Matter," *Railroad History* 179 (autumn 1998): 31–68; Sy Adler, "The Transformation of the Pacific Electric Railway: Bradford Snell, Roger Rabbit and the Politics of Transportation in Los Angeles," *Urban Affairs Quarterly* 27 (September 1991): 51–87; and Jonathan Richmond, "Transport of Delight: The Mythical Conception of Rail Transit in Los Angeles" (Ph.D. diss., Massachusetts Institute of Technology, 1991). For a thorough explanation of the operational and financial problems that afflicted the Pacific Electric interurban system, and that raise questions about the continued viability of the system after the artificial surge of ridership during World War II, see Lawrence R. Veysey, "The Pacific Electric Railway Company: A Study in the Operations of Economic, Social and Political Forces upon American Local Transportation," typescript seminar paper, 1953, Yale University (copy in the MTA Library, Los Angeles), 102–65, 267–322. For an analogous case study from another city, see Martha J. Bianco, "Private Profit versus Public Service: Competing Demands in Urban Transportation History and Policy, Portland, Oregon, 1872–1970" (Ph.D. diss., Portland State University, 1994).

12. Bottles, 22–51, 54 (quotation); David Brodsly, *LA Freeway: An Appreciative Essay* (Berkeley, Calif., 1981), 89–96; Mark Foster, *From Streetcar to Superhighway: American Planners and Urban Transportation* (Philadelphia, 1981), also characterizes the automobile as a tool in the Progressive response to perceived urban ills.

13. McShane (n. 7 above), 125–71; Virginia Scharff, *Taking the Wheel: Women and the Coming of the Motor Age* (New York, 1991); James J. Flink, *The Automobile Age* (Cambridge, Mass., 1988), 1–14; Robert C. Post, *High Performance: The Culture and Technology of Drag Racing* (Baltimore, 1994), x–xi and 349 n. 3.

14. Bottles, 15, 56–57, 88.

15. Roland Marchand, *Advertising the American Dream: Making Way for Modernity, 1920–1940* (Berkeley, Calif., 1985), 222.

16. Bottles, 117–18, 247–49; Brodsly, 5, 149. Property owners would first petition the city council to create an improvement district, within which the properties would be assessed a special tax increment to pay for specified construction. The city engineering office then surveyed the boundaries and confirmed the petitioners' status as owners within those boundaries. The city council called an election of all property owners in the district, with a majority prevailing. A description of the process can be found in Appendix B of Frederick Law Olmsted [Jr.], Harland Bartholomew, and Charles Henry Cheney, *A Major Traffic Street Plan for Los Angeles* (Los Angeles, 1924), 55–56.

17. City Engineer, *Annual Report,* 1922–23, 12.

18. See multiyear tabular summary and accompanying commentary in City Engineer, "Annual Report," 1931–32, chap. 6, p. 5, typescript, Los Angeles City Archives (paginated by chapter). A detailed summary for the years up through 1925 is also provided in "List of Projects Abandoned Through Litigation or Protest," Council Minutes, 171:647 (1926). Among the major arteries where opening or widening failed to gain approval were Broadway, Vermont Avenue, Long Beach Avenue, Silver Lake Boulevard, Pico Boulevard, Overland Boulevard, and Venice Boulevard.

19. Robin Einhorn, *Property Rules: Political Economy in Chicago, 1833–1872* (Chi-

cago, 1991), 14–19; Terrence McDonald, *The Parameters of Urban Fiscal Policy: Socio-economic Change and Political Culture in San Francisco, 1860–1906* (Berkeley, Calif., 1986), quotation on 281. The state legislature established the basic process opera-tive during this period in 1903, when it accorded cities the right to acquire property for public works and to charge additional property tax to the parcels judged to benefit, subject to majority vote of the property owners. In 1911, another state statute enabled cities to overcome majority protest by four-fifths vote of the city council, but only for right-of-way acquisition, not for construction costs; see Olm-sted, Bartholomew, and Cheney, 55–56. These statutes governed until 1939, when the legislature allowed the state Transportation Commission to accomplish urban right-of-way acquisition through eminent domain; see *Statues and Amendments to the Codes*, 53rd sess., chap. 687 (Sacramento, Calif., 1939), 2203–4.

20. City Engineer, *Annual Report*, 1912–13, 19.

21. City Engineer, *Annual Report*, 1914–15, 39.

22. City Engineer, *Annual Report*, 1915–16, 35; *Annual Report*, 1919–20, 81–82.

23. Paul G. Hoffman, "Untangling Our Traffic," *Touring Topics*, December 1923, 16–17, 42–43; William A. Spalding, *History of Los Angeles City and County* (Los An-geles, 1932), 3:113–16.

24. Olmsted, Bartholomew, and Cheney (n. 16 above); *Los Angeles Times*, 17 Au-gust 1924, 7 October 1924, 26 October 1924.

25. Bottles (n. 11 above), 113–18; Brodsly (n. 12 above), 89.

26. Traffic Commission of the City and County of Los Angeles (hereinafter Traffic Commission), *Annual Report*, 1927, 19–35.

27. City Engineer, *Annual Report*, 1925–26, 75. Comparison between the through highways in the plan and the streets as they exist today yields unequivocal evidence that the Major Traffic Street Plan was not fulfilled. Narrower-than-specified rights-of-way in proposed arterials include Fairfax north of Pico and La-Brea south of Pico. Failure to resolve offset intersections—one of the main recom-mendations in the plan—also compromised the performance of arterials, resulting in such tortuous and notorious corridors as La Cienega as it crosses Venice, Adams, and Washington Boulevards within some two thousand feet. More widespread ob-jection caused reduction in designs, e.g., Sunset was never built out to the specified ten lanes along its entire length.

28. City Engineer, *Annual Report*, 1921–22, 39; City Engineer, *Annual Report*, 1922–23, 47; Council Minutes, 137:208 (1923); Olmsted, Bartholomew, and Che-ney (n. 16 above), 40 and unpaginated maps.

29. Council Minutes, 137:78–87, 90–159, 179–210 (1923). *Viola Bogue et al. v The City of Los Angeles, Report of Cases Determined by the Supreme Court of the State of Cali-fornia*, vol. 198 (San Francisco, 1926), 327–28; City Engineer, *Annual Report*, 1924–25, 82; and Council Minutes, 167:549 (1926). After the adverse court decision, the engineering department redrew the route and the assessment-district boundary in order to continue the project without defying the court. Considerable tinkering with the maps ensued, in large part to avoid the locations of most vociferous objection. This process consumed six years, which gave opponents ample opportunity to orga-nize their resistance efforts, and when the project came up for a vote in 1932 the property owners rejected it by a 64 to 36 margin. Much of the work was eventually

performed under new funding authority enacted to provide work relief during the Depression, but the plan for Tenth Street was never completed in such critical locations as the blocks east of Figueroa Street, just south of downtown. See Council Minutes, 237:233 (1932), 237:340–44 (1932); and City Engineer, "Annual Report," typescript, 1932–33, 79.

30. Traffic Commission, *Annual Report,* 1927, 19–35; Bottles, 117.

31. See n. 29.

32. Martin Wachs, "The Evolution of Transportation Policy in Los Angeles: Images of Past Policies and Future Prospects," in *The City: Los Angeles and Urban Theory at the End of the Twentieth Century,* ed. Allen J. Scott and Edward W. Soja (Berkeley, Calif., 1996); Robert Fishman, "Re-Imagining Los Angeles," in *Rethinking Los Angeles,* ed. Michael J. Dear, H. Eric Schockman, and Greg Hise (Thousand Oaks, Calif., 1996).

33. Council Minutes, 176:771 (1927); *Los Angeles Examiner,* 19 April 1928. The flooding was a long-standing problem that had demanded attention at least as early as 1913; see Council Minutes, 91:420 (1913).

34. City Engineer, *Annual Report,* 1923–24, 33; Stephen D. Mikesell, "The Los Angeles River Bridges: A Study in the Bridge as a Civic Monument," *Southern California Quarterly* 68 (winter 1986): 365–86.

35. Mikesell. On Pico, see *Touring Topics,* January 1916, 17.

36. City Engineer, *Annual Report,* 1923–24, 58.

37. Abraham Hoffman, *Vision or Villainy: Origins of the Owens Valley–Los Angeles Water Controversy* (College Station, Tex., 1981), 157–70, quotation on 161; Catherine Mulholland, *The Owensmouth Baby: The Making of a San Fernando Valley Town* (Northridge, Calif., 1987), 73, 81, 89, 96, 104, 132; W. W. Robinson, *History of the San Fernando Valley* (Los Angeles, 1961), 37–40.

38. See petition for Municipal Improvement District No. 22, Council File #4536 (1923). Section nomenclature described multiacre parcels, whereas a street address or lot number usually identified a property of 5,000 square feet, the most common lot size in Los Angeles. "R 16 W Sec 25," meaning Range 16 West Section 25, is a typical section designation from this petition. The range designation itself dates from the initial Public Land Survey of California under United States jurisdiction, which was mandated by Congress in 1853. For Southern California, the surveyor general for the state laid out a grid of squares, six miles on a side, from the datum of Mount San Bernardino. East-west divisions were called "ranges" and north-south divisions "townships." Each square was in turn divided into 36 sections. Thus, at the time of the Mulholland petition, the legal description for much of the San Fernando Valley still reflected the Public Land Survey undertaken in the 1850s; the petition lacked "township" designation because the entire area fell into one north-south unit but extended across three east-west "range" units. See W. W. Robinson, *Land in California: The Story of Mission Lands, Ranchos, Squatters, Mining Claims, Railroad Grants, Land Scrip, Homesteads* (1948; reprint, Berkeley, Calif., 1979), esp. 208–11.

39. The contemporary documents use Hollywood Hills and Santa Monica Mountains more or less interchangeably to describe this feature that divides the basin from the valley. In current usage, the Sepulveda Pass generally separates the Hollywood Hills to the east and the Santa Monica Mountains to the west.

40. City Engineer, *Annual Report,* 1923–24, 58.

41. City Engineer, *Annual Report,* 1922–23, 53.

42. Edwin O. Palmer, *History of Hollywood* (Hollywood, 1937), 1:223.

43. John O. Pohlmann, "Alphonzo E. Bell: A Biography," part 2, *Southern California Quarterly* 46 (December 1964): 325–26; Joseph K. Horton, *A Brief History of Bel-Air* (Los Angeles, 1982). Thanks to Janet R. Fireman for pointing out that the gates do not function and that even if they were closed they would not reach far enough across the road to prevent traffic from passing through.

44. Improvement District No. 22 petition (n. 38 above); City Engineer, *Annual Report,* 1923–24, 20.

45. City Engineer to Los Angeles City Council, 23 January 1928, Council File #3776 (1927); also see petition for Improvement District No. 22.

46. Improvement District No. 22 petition; City Engineer, *Annual Report,* 1922–23, 48.

47. Except for the communications with the city council, the records of the Hollywood Foothills Improvement Association were privately held, probably by Merrick, and have not been found to survive in any repository. The membership of the group has been reconstructed to the extent possible from various correspondence and transactions in the city records: easement deeds transmitted to city, 18 March 1924, in Council Minutes, 143:597–98 (1924); petition regarding Benedict Canyon, Council Minutes, 149:444 (1924) and Council File #6378 (1924); petition regarding fire breaks, 26 July 1924, Council Minutes, 47:463 (1924) and Council File #4908 (1924); petition to reduce right-of-way, 11 December 1929, Council Minutes, 212:510 (1929). The improvement district petition (n. 38 above) gives the names of 431 property owners, but the improvement association was a smaller, more select group. Occupations and affiliations of participants from *Los Angeles City Directory,* 1920–30.

48. Council Minutes, 138:602 (1923).

49. Council Minutes, 138:647 (1923). The petition was filed on 17 August and the city clerk validated it on 22 August.

50. Council Minutes, 139:449 (1923), 139:647–48 (1923). Only property owners in the improvement district voted in the referendum.

51. Council Minutes, 140:310–11, 140:404–5, 140:507–8, 140:548 (1923), and city clerk report in Council File #6096 (1923).

52. Council Minutes, 140:242–43 (1923), 140:559 (1923).

53. Ordinance for bond issue in Report of City Attorney, Council File #218 (1924) and Council Minutes, 142:13 (1924).

54. Palmer (n. 42 above), 224–26; *Los Angeles Examiner,* 18 May 1929.

55. City Planning Commissioners, *Annual Report,* 1932–33, 18.

56. Milton Breivogel, principal planner for City of Los Angeles (retired), interview #339, transcript, Department of Special Collections, University of California at Los Angeles, 88.

57. Pohlmann (n. 43 above); Mulholland (n. 37 above), 94–100; *Los Angeles Times,* 9 November 1928; Reyner Banham, "Ecology II: Foothills," in *Los Angeles: The Architecture of Four Ecologies* (1971; reprint, London, 1990), 95–109.

58. Dewitt L. Reaburn, "Report on Mulholland Highway," in City Engineer, *An-*

nual Report, 1923–24, 20. William Mulholland was alive and active during the construction of Mulholland Highway, working on the continued elaboration of the city water supply system.

59. Council Minutes, 138:647 (1923).

60. The Owens Valley Aqueduct was certainly not without controversies, but those centered on the contention between the region from which the water came and the one that appropriated it, and on the question of unethical behavior on the part of J. B. Lippincott during the securing of the Owens Valley water rights. Among the citizens who approved the aqueduct bond issues by more than 10 to 1 margins, and the city employees and elected officials responsible for the work, the aqueduct benefited from overwhelming support. See Hoffman (n. 37 above), 91–99, 141–45.

61. Stanley K. Schultz and Clay McShane, "To Engineer the Metropolis: Sewers, Sanitation, and City Planning in Late Nineteenth-Century America," in *The Making of Urban America,* ed. Raymond A. Mohl (Wilmington, Del., 1988), 81–98, traces the institutional model of political autonomy by municipal engineers in the industrial cities of the Northeast and Midwest. My concern is not to establish that the Los Angeles experience set any precedent in the Progressive-era phenomenon of the agency led by experts, but rather to discern how the engineers exercised that expertise in building parts of the city.

62. Burton L. Hunter, *Evolution of Municipal Organization and Administrative Practice in the City of Los Angeles* (Los Angeles, 1933), s.v. "Board of Water Commissioners" and "Board of Water and Power Commissioners"; Hoffman (n. 37 above), 35–46, 146–47.

63. Nye (n. 5 above), 76.

64. Frederick C. Cross, "My Days on the Jawbone," *Westways,* May 1968, 3–8, quotation on 6–7. The Jawbone was one of the most onerous stretches of the work, in Kern County north of the town of Mojave. Cross also noted that the crew members' preferred headgear, derby hats, went by the name of "dice boxes," in keeping with the practice of storing dice in them.

65. Hoffman (n. 37 above), 150–51; Los Angeles Board of Public Service Commissioners, *Complete Report on Construction of the Los Angeles Aqueduct* (Los Angeles, 1916), 256; Remi Nadeau, *The Water Seekers* (1950; rev. ed., Salt Lake City, 1974), 41–43.

66. Hoffman (n. 37 above), 250.

67. Hollywood Foothills Improvement Association to Los Angeles City Council, Council File #4908 (1924); the improvement association also gave Reaburn a seat on its board. Reaburn described his aqueduct experience in testimony to the city council, 20 December 1923, Council Minutes 141:408–9 (1923). Reaburn was a principal in the consulting engineering firm of Reaburn and Bowen; *Los Angeles City Directory,* 1924, p. 1868. Reimbursement to improvement association in Council Minutes, 147:252 and 147:356–57 (1924); the amount of reimbursement was $17,596.

68. City Engineer, *Annual Report,* 1922–23, 48; 1923–24, 20–21.

69. Council Minutes, 175:387–88 (1926).

70. City Engineer, *Annual Report,* 1923–24, 20–21. Two years later the city engineers tacked onto the language for another bond issue, which had the primary

purpose of erecting bridges over the Los Angeles River, the inadequate amount of $50,000 for a bridge to carry Mulholland over the pass, then ended up raiding the Mulholland money to complete the other projects; see Council Minutes, 164:214–16 (1926). The bridge that finally carried Mulholland Highway across Cahuenga Pass was built in 1940 as part of the project to build a freeway through the pass, with 45 percent of the cost contributed by the federal government; see Spencer V. Cortelyou, "Cahuenga Freeway Unit Opened," *California Highways and Public Works,* July 1940, 2–3, 17.

71. Council Minutes, 141:167 (1923).

72. Report of Board of Public Works, 5 December 1923, Council Minutes, 141:55–56 (1923).

73. Once established, the Mulholland Highway Department proved a useful precedent; over the next two years the engineers cited it as justification to set up four more special departments for specific road projects.

74. Report of Board of Public Works, 5 December 1923, Council Minutes, 141:55–56 (1923); Report of Dewitt Reaburn to the Board of Public Works (quotation), submitted to city council on 7 December 1923, Council Minutes 141:141–42 (1923).

75. Council Minutes, 141:408–9 (1923), quotation, and 142:311 (1924); City Engineer, *Annual Report,* 1923–24, 21.

76. Council Minutes, 141:681, 142:5, 143:193–94, 143:323, 144:150, 144:584, 144:783, 146:226, 146:353, 146:506 (1924).

77. Quotation in Council Minutes, 141:157–58 (1923); equipment rental in Council Minutes, 149:521 (1924); vehicle purchase in Council Minutes, 141:586 (1923); blasting powder in Council Minutes, 147:54–55 (1924).

78. Monthly expenditures in Council Minutes, 144:260, 149:522, 150:543, 151:326, all 1924; retaining wall in Council Minutes, 147:741 (1924); extra dump trucks in Council Minutes, 151:610 (1924). Excavation statistics in Dewitt Reaburn, Report to the Board of Public Works on the Mulholland Highway Department, 24 June 1925, Council File #4003 (1925); Reaburn reported an aggregate excavation figure of 70,000 cubic yards per mile, and unit calculations were made by the author.

79. Traffic-count comparisons from Olmsted, Bartholomew, and Cheney (n. 16 above), 19.

80. Council Minutes, 286:21 and 286:600 (1939).

81. Dewitt Reaburn, Report to the Board of Public Works on the Mulholland Highway Department, 24 June 1925, Council File #4003 (1925).

82. Council Minutes, 209:256 (1928).

83. Doyce B. Nunis, ed., *The St. Francis Dam Disaster Revisited* (Los Angeles, 1995). The other four special operating departments for specific road projects were also abolished under the same ordinance.

84. Improved roads were a prerequisite for the installation of underground systems because the level pavement provided the necessary baseline for setting vertical placement. See McShane (n. 7 above), 66–67; City Engineer, *Annual Report,* 1925–26, 7.

85. Harry Merrick to Los Angeles City Council, 26 July 1924, and instruction to

city attorney to draft ordinance for convict labor, 30 July 1924, both in Council File #4908 (1924); Council Minutes, 147:463, 147:553 (1924). Fire breaks are swaths cleared of all brush and vegetation that, in theory, arrest the spread of fire.

86. Report of Board of Public Works (first quotation) and letter from R. J. Scott (second quotation), both to city council on 2 October 1924, Council File #6302 (1924); Council Minutes, 149:368, 149:370, 149:583 (1924).

87. Thomas Ince, Sid Graumann, and Joseph Schenck to Los Angeles City Council, 6 October 1924, Council File #6378 (1924); Council Minutes, 149:444 (1924). Mike Davis, "The Case for Letting Malibu Burn," in *Ecology of Fear: Los Angeles and the Imagination of Disaster* (New York, 1998), 93–147, uses the city's history of fire suppression as an incisive case study to analyze the capture of public resources for the benefit of elite residential districts.

88. Council Minutes, 175:360 and 175:387–88 (1926).

89. Letter from the Mulholland Highway Committee of the Ventura Boulevard and Hollywood Chambers of Commerce, reported to city council on 3 November 1926, in Council Minutes, 174:201 (1926). This organization succeeded the Hollywood Foothills Improvement Association.

90. Mulholland Highway Committee of the Ventura Boulevard Chamber of Commerce to Los Angeles City Council, 18 May 1927, Council File #3776 (1927).

91. Report of Shaw to Los Angeles City Council, 23 January 1928, Council File #3776 (1927).

92. Council Minutes, 212:543 (1929), 218:584 (1930), 224:6 (1931); *Los Angeles Examiner,* 2 December 1930.

93. Traffic Commission, *Annual Report,* 1929, 15; Bottles (n. 11 above), 118; *Los Angeles Times,* 16 January, 17 January, and 19 April, 1936.

94. For a summary of freeway utilization see the (unpaginated) maps and discussion of District 7 (Los Angeles and Ventura Counties) in California Department of Transportation, Operational Systems Branch, *Statewide Highway Congestion Monitoring Program, 1993 Report* (Sacramento, 1994). For data collection and analysis regarding public opinion on freeways in Los Angeles see Elham Shirazi, Stuart Anderson, and John Stresney, *Commuters' Attitudes toward Traffic Information Systems and Route Diversion* (Washington, D.C., 1988).

CHAPTER THREE

The Quest for Independence
Workers in the Suburbs

Becky M. Nicolaides

"Southgate Twilight"

Southgate Gardens is an ideal place,
Where "Home Sweet Home" rings true;
Where the sun at last drops the day that is past
From a cloudland of azure and blue . . .
The hands that are weary from labor and toil,
Contentedly "rest on their oars."
One listens in peace as night's murmurs increase
Borne in from the ocean-washed shores.
'Tis a dear spot of land where one meets the glad hand
Of friendship from friends who are true,
While the moon and the stars greet the sunset bars,
I want to live there, don't you?

Southgate Gardener, *August 1918*

Along with its sunshine and cinema, 1920s Los Angeles was known for a far more insidious quality: its brazen hostility to labor unions. The city gained a reputation as a citadel of the open shop under the leadership of a powerful business elite that included the likes of *Los Angeles Times* publisher Harry Chandler and, before him, his father-in-law Harrison Gray Otis. These leaders pressed down hard and furiously on organized labor by mandating the open shop, persecuting labor leaders and activists, and wielding the powers of the state to maintain this condition. So harsh was their action, it prompted Pasadena resident Upton Sinclair to label this elite "the Black Hand." While recent studies have found evidence of union persistence and successes during the decade, most Los Angeles workers lived in a world dominated by an aggressively open shop ethos.[1]

How did workers cope in this environment? How did they protect their interests, ensure their security, and look after their needs in a metropolitan milieu that offered them few avenues to assert power in the workplace?

77

In Los Angeles, they moved to the suburbs, specifically, the working-class suburbs. These affordable, rough-hewn communities enabled working-class families to carve out a niche of economic security for themselves. In the realm of residential life, working people found ways to shape their environment to meet their own class-based needs. The very nature of these communities allowed them to do this. The working-class suburb, dramatically distinct from the affluent suburbs of the upper and middle classes, offered working people the chance to maximize the use of their domestic property in a number of critical ways.

This essay tells the story of these working-class suburbs in Los Angeles during the 1920s, focusing particularly on those communities inhabited by native-born whites in southern Los Angeles, a key industrial center of the metropolis. We begin by looking briefly at the city's broader economic geography to clarify why these communities sprouted where they did. Then we move into a case study analysis of South Gate, located about seven miles south of downtown in the heart of the industrial district. South Gate was subdivided in 1917 and incorporated as an independent municipality in 1923. The detail afforded by a "case study" approach enables us to appreciate what these communities meant to their inhabitants in terms of the gritty realities and concerns of everyday life. I argue that in the blue-collar suburbs of Los Angeles, workers turned their residential environment into a source of economic security, a place where they devised and pursued strategies for surviving in a maturing capitalist world. By so doing, they found ways to cope in the hostile, open shop climate of Los Angeles.

The significance of this story becomes clearer if we briefly contextualize it. How representative were these working-class suburbs? Were they flukes of Los Angeles, or were they typical of broader urban developments? The nascent scholarship on the topic, although small, strongly suggests that blue-collar suburbs were surprisingly prevalent in cities across North America during the first half of the twentieth century. Geographer Richard Harris, who has done seminal work in this field, argues they were at least as widespread as the middle- and upper-class suburbs that have monopolized scholarly attention. In Toronto, for example, the social composition of the fringe areas shifted from predominantly middle class in 1900 to working class by 1920. In the United States during the 1920s, at least 20 percent of homes were owner-built, an emblem of working-class suburbia. By 1940, the suburbs had proportionately more working-class residents than the inner city in three of the six largest American cities. Other scholarship has identified suburbs for African American working people as an important part of the pre–World War II urban landscape in the United States; they shared certain traits of white working-class suburbs.[2] Beyond North America, various renditions of working-class suburbs have appeared in cities across space and time. Indeed, by far the most prevalent social patterning in cities around the world finds the wealthy at the city core and the poor on the outskirts. In urban areas from South America to Africa to Europe, lower-income workers have dominated the suburbs, while the old city center has been the preserve of the affluent. This has been the historic pattern.[3] Placed in this broader context, the story of a suburb like South Gate takes on greater significance for shedding light on a residential experience not untypical for many working people.

THE INDUSTRIAL LANDSCAPE OF LOS ANGELES

How did South Gate fit into the broader social and economic geography of Los Angeles? How were industry and working-class suburbs patterned in the metropolis? Almost from its beginnings, Los Angeles developed according to the suburban paradigm. Influenced by a domineering aesthetic of "country living," advanced transportation technology, geography, and ambitious leaders and developers who favored expansive residential districts to preserve the region's natural physical beauty, the metropolis decentralized from the outset.[4] The ubiquity of suburbia in Los Angeles strongly suggests that industrial dispersal and working-class suburbs were widespread, if only by default.

Both economic and aesthetic factors shaped this pattern, which had begun increasingly to characterize the entire nation after the turn of the century. Particularly for the "automobile cities" of the twentieth century, decentralization became possible with the emergence of auto and truck transportation to move goods. Dense industrial concentrations near downtown areas, typical of older eastern cities, made little sense for a city like Los Angeles, where the harbor was located 20 miles from the central business district. Furthermore, the production processes dominant by the twentieth century, particularly economies of scale and assembly lines, meant factories expanded horizontally and sought locations on the urban periphery where land was cheap and plentiful. In some cases, large developers favored industrial dispersal as a strategy to weaken the labor movement. Henry E. Huntington was the prime example. A staunch open shop advocate whose interwoven business ventures in trolleys, electric power, and real estate gave him power to shape the urban landscape, he believed that spatial dispersal thwarted labor's efforts to organize unions. Finally, an aesthetic shared by the city's early planners promoted industrial sprawl. The planners' goal was to keep Los Angeles exceptional, to build a city not with the industrial congestion of eastern cities, but rather one that looked beautiful, natural, and pristine, where industry would be out of sight and out of mind. This ideal encouraged industrial dispersal, freeing the city center from dirty smokestacks and poor working people, making it instead the urban centerpiece of an idyllic region, ringed by mountains, lush trees, and the soft aroma of orange blossoms. Suburbia became a logical destination for the factory.[5]

In the 1920s, industry began creeping southward toward the harbor. Although there was substantial industrial clustering near downtown by 1925, even then a southward sprawl was evident. Manufacturing plants sprang up in the Vernon and Florence areas, particularly around the Central Manufacturing District (CMD). By the end of the 1920s, industry emerged around the harbor, the central business district, and the southern suburbs in between.[6]

The suburbs of southern Los Angeles became a key industrial hub for several reasons. First, transportation advances, especially the development of major truck highways and a consolidated harbor railroad system, facilitated the movement of materials from these suburbs to San Pedro/Long Beach Harbor. The proximity of the southern suburbs to the port helped seal their industrial future, since it would be cheaper to move manufactured goods for export from these sites. South Gate was particularly well situated in this transportation matrix, bordering on three freight railroad lines and traversed by two major port-bound truck highways established in the mid 1920s—Alameda Avenue and Long Beach Boulevard. These routes assumed critical importance as trucking became the most common way to move goods into and out of Los Angeles. A second factor was the natural geography of oil reserves. A line of oil fields swept across southern Los Angeles, with a heavy clustering around the Dominguez, Torrance, and Brea areas. Working-class residential and industrial suburbanization followed this geography. Whittier, Brea, Fullerton, and El Segundo housed the refineries as well as the families of oil workers, while purely residential working-class suburbs, like La Habra, sprang up in adjacent areas. In this way, both industrial and residential suburbanization followed the extractive industry, in some cases before the arrival of the streetcar. A third factor was zoning. In 1908, Los Angeles passed the first major land-use zoning law in the United States, eight years before the more famous New York City measure. This law created seven industrial districts, mainly along the Los Angeles River and the railroad lines that traversed the central, eastern, and southern suburbs. It reserved western Los Angeles to "higher class residential areas." City leaders believed such a plan would allow Los Angeles to avoid the urban congestion typical of older industrial cities, maximize accessibility for workers, and minimize fire hazards. Despite numerous zoning variances granted by the city in the western residential section, this plan established a general schema that guaranteed an industrial future for southern Los Angeles.[7]

Boosters of southeastern Los Angeles also helped define the area as a future industrial hub. While the Los Angeles Chamber of Commerce promoted the industrial potentials of the entire metropolitan region, local boosters mobilized particularly strongly to attract industry to the southeastern suburbs. To spearhead their efforts and consolidate their power, they formed the East Side Improvement Organization, the Harbor District Chamber of Commerce, and the Southeast Realty Board. The Greater East Los Angeles Chamber of Commerce, formed in 1925, was composed of community leaders from the small blue-collar suburbs of Home Gardens, Cudahy, Bell, and adjacent subdivisions. Many of these modest suburbs supported the balanced growth of industries, residences, and business. Apparently they had few qualms about the possible side effects of factories located near homes. Industry, they believed, was the key to local prosperity.[8]

Shoulder to shoulder with industrial dispersal, working-class suburbs stretched across the Los Angeles landscape in the 1920s. They tended to cluster near factories and oil reserves, giving labor and industry easy access to each other. Incorporated suburbs like South Gate, Compton, Torrance, Maywood, Signal Hill, La Verne, Pomona, Chino, Azusa, El Segundo, San Fernando, and Hawthorne fit the working-class mold. Some workers also found their way into larger, wealthy suburbs like Pasadena. In this old-money town, Mexican and African American domestic workers who serviced the town's wealthy households formed their own modest enclaves. Within the city borders of Los Angeles, pockets of working-class suburbia existed in areas like Boyle Heights, Watts, Venice, West Los Angeles, Mar Vista, Belvedere, El Sereno, Lincoln Heights, and Highland Park. It was in unincorporated territory, however, that working-class suburbia flourished most profusely, following the typical pattern in North America. If we use housing data as the gauge, it is possible to classify nearly 79 percent of unincorporated Los Angeles as working-class suburbia by 1940.[9] Thus, although blue-collar suburbs concentrated heavily in southern Los Angeles, in fact they existed all over the metropolis. They represented a critical, palpable presence in the metropolis, a place where working people would pursue their version of the American Dream.

"WHERE THE WORKING MAN IS WELCOMED": A PROFILE OF SOUTH GATE

Juanita Smith was 13 years old in 1925 when her family decided to pull up its Tennessee roots and head west.[10] It was not an easy decision, but rather one motivated by a series of misfortunes. The first struck in 1922. Juanita's parents, Daniel and Jessie Smith, ran the only hotel in Pond Switch, Tennessee, a tiny rural railroad junction 40 miles west of Nashville. They were hard-working, upstanding citizens, always willing to lend a hand to a neighbor. On a cold January day, life changed for the Smiths. A little boy boarding in the hotel sneaked a box of matches into an upstairs closet and began playing with them. Sparks flew, setting off a fire and sending the hotel up in flames. The fire destroyed the livelihood of the Smiths. When the insurance company took a year to pay the meager settlement, the family grew desperate and made the tough decision to leave Pond Switch. Juanita, her parents, and her three sisters moved to suburban Nashville to begin anew. Daniel was a carpenter, and he immediately built the family a small house. But it wasn't long before ill fortune struck again. A year after the Smiths arrived in Nashville, the doctors diagnosed Daniel with tuberculosis and warned him that the cold Tennessee winters were only worsening his condition.[11]

As if in answer to the family's prayers, Juanita's Uncle Walter appeared on the scene with a plan. A career soldier and world traveler, Uncle Walter had recently visited Southern California and was so impressed by the region's climate that he had bought multiple lots in a new suburban tract called Home Gardens, about seven miles south of downtown Los Angeles. (Home Gardens would be annexed to South Gate in 1927.) He immediately urged the Smiths to move west for the sake of Daniel's health. And he offered his relatives the gift of land—along with the promise of a better life. Local realtors soon sent the Smiths picture postcards of the new development, showing a beautiful lake surrounded by palm trees and flowers. It was enough to convince the family to leave Tennessee and begin a new life in California.

After selling the Nashville house and their larger furniture, the Smiths packed up their belongings in two Ford Model Ts—a sedan and a truck purchased by Uncle Walter—and headed west. They beat a path for families of the Dust Bowl exodus, who would follow a decade later. Like the fictional Joads of *The Grapes of Wrath*, the Smiths pitched a tent along the way. Although campgrounds with showers and cooking facilities were few and far between, Jessie cooked resourcefully wherever she could. And Daniel insisted that the family rest on the Sabbath, telling them: "Sunday is the Lord's day, and we're not going to drive."

When they finally reached their destination after a long, tiring month on the road, Juanita's heart dropped at the sight of Home Gardens. She looked in vain for the lake, flowers, and palm trees. All she saw were vacant lots overgrown with weeds, dirt roads, curbs, and sidewalks—the skeleton of a suburb. A few tiny houses—call them shacks—were scattered here and there, but mostly there was empty space.

As the Smiths began to unpack their belongings, it was their ideological baggage they brought out first: independence, resourcefulness, frugality. Rather than rent a place downtown while their house was constructed, they pitched a tent right on their vacant lot. Then they began the long, exhausting process of securing permanent shelter. They did this not by opening savings accounts and visiting mortgage lenders, but rather by spending their spare cash on lumber, nails, and other building materials, then rolling up their sleeves. In this way, they entered the ranks of suburban home owners. Daniel built the house with the aid of Jessie and the children. The garage was the first to go up, a small structure barely big enough to accommodate two cars. The family of six immediately moved into this meager space. Daniel installed a gas main so Jessie could cook, and he hung mattresses from the ceiling as beds for Juanita and her sisters. A small table was their principal piece of furniture. They lived in that garage for several months as they continued to build. When the family finally moved into the house, it was still unfinished—lacking a roof—and Daniel carried on construction even as they occupied it.

It soon became clear that the house represented a financial anchor for the Smiths, a source of sustenance in dire times, especially as other resources disappeared. Just months after the family arrived in Los Angeles, Uncle Walter died suddenly, sadly never attaining his dream of retiring in Home Gardens alongside his relatives. No longer could the Smiths rely on this prosperous, generous relative for help. And with Daniel's health failing, he could no longer take on full-time work. Instead, he took a job as a night watchman downtown, which paid little but allowed him to lie down and rest during his shift. With sources of cash weak and unpredictable, the suburban home became their most reliable financial resource, providing much more than shelter. Jessie tapped the full potential of their property, raising vegetables, poultry, rabbits, and even a goat that ate its way through the vacant lots of Home Gardens. She sold chickens to a small poultry business on Central Avenue. She bartered vegetables with neighbors, saving money for her family when they couldn't spare the extra penny to buy from the local grocer. If Daniel was out of work for a stretch, Jessie's bartering kept the family afloat. By turning their property into a modest suburban homestead, the Smiths devised a premodern solution to the problems posed by industrial capitalism.

The Smiths lived in an era of increased market dependency, an economic life of wage work, market fluctuations, layoffs—with a deep chasm of poverty looming beneath them and no safety net of state-based welfare. In the face of these forces, their key goal was to maintain some semblance of economic security by minimizing their dependence on cash assets and wages. This followed a long historic tradition in America, the valuing of family security over profit maximization.[12] For the Smiths, like many working-class Americans, the last rope to grasp before falling from autonomy was their home in the suburb. These broad functions of home ownership realized their fullest fruition in the blue-collar suburbs of North America during the first half of the twentieth century.

Several key traits characterized the working-class suburb, all effectively illustrated by a close look at South Gate and neighboring Home Gardens. First, property was cheap. Indeed, the nature and terms of property sales in South Gate helped to keep costs down. The sale of empty lots opened the suburb to diligent residents—short on cash but long on energy—who intended to build for themselves. In 1918, 40- x 130-foot lots in the better part of town started at $490, a sum less than half of the average annual income of a wage earner in manufacturing or construction in 1920—or roughly the value of a good car. Lots in Home Gardens, the poorest part of town, sold for $295. The terms of sales also made property affordable. In 1924, a person could buy a lot in Home Gardens for $20 down and $10 per month, much less than rent in most parts of Los Angeles ($20–$37 per month for a "moderately priced house" in 1920). For buyers with a bit more cash, cheap homes were available. One seller offered to exchange a house and lot for either a "small auto" or $950. In 1924, a two-room house and garage on a 60- x 130-foot lot was listed for $1,200, at $300 down and $25 per month.[13]

Second, the suburb imposed few building regulations. This allowed working-class families to build their own homes as best they could. And it meant residents could rely upon sweat—rather than cash—equity to achieve home ownership. As a result, owner-building proliferated. Although exact numbers are elusive, various sources suggests the practice was fairly widespread in South Gate. Sanborn fire insurance maps offer one clue. They strongly suggest the presence of owner-building, particularly in Home Gardens, by revealing an erratic pattern of dwelling placement on the lots: some at the front, some in the middle, some at the back. In contrast, homes built by developers tended to sit in the same position on the lot. Oral histories and building permits also disclose frequent self-building in South Gate. One study of neighboring Bell Gardens, similar to South Gate in terms of class and physical appearance, found that nearly three-quarters of the homes there were self-built. A final, comically poignant bit of evidence about the jerry-built nature of local housing was a common mortgage clause in South Gate. It stipulated that homes worth less than $1,500 had to sit at the back of the lot, a sheepish admission that cheap homes were allowed as long as they were not too conspicuous.[14]

Self-building was an arduous process that consumed the spare time of wage earners, who put in an hour or two on the house in the evenings, and more on weekends. The finished products were often little more than shack-like bungalows, with one or two bedrooms, a kitchen, living room, and bathroom. As one observer of South Gate in the 1920s recalled:

> More than half built them themselves [laughs]. But what did they build? 600 square feet, maybe. Little tiny places. They lived in tents a lot of people. . . . It was as common as dirt. . . . Those old houses that those jackknife carpenters

built, a guy built for himself 500 to 600 square feet. They'd build a little garage that they slept in and cooked out of doors. That was common. We were delivering milk here, and got stiffed for a few milk bills here, I'll tell you that. They were really poor. . . . But [out here] you had a chance, even the working people had a chance because land was cheap, they could scrounge around and buy a lot. . . . [A]nd they'd buy a little bit of lumber every month and put in a foundation, mix it by hand. I saw hundreds of them do that.[15]

The home ownership rates in South Gate reached nearly 90 percent in the late 1920s, testifying to the importance of the home in the lives of these workers.[16]

A third quality of the suburb was few regulations on land use. This flexibility allowed residents to use their property in ways that enabled them to pursue economic security. Suburban land thus became highly valued as a site of domestic production. City ordinances allowed residents to raise chickens, ducks, geese, other fowl, and rabbits in backyards, as long as they were kept at least twenty feet from their closest neighbors. Up to fifty chickens were permissible. Rabbit hutches and chicken pens were common sights; milk goats were not unusual. Even the local doctor's family raised a home garden and rabbits, critical during lean times when cash was scarce and patients couldn't pay their bills. These practices gave South Gate a distinctly rural atmosphere. "Chickens and other poultry . . . entering my Home Gardens properties," warned one resident in 1924, "will provide excellent short-range practice for me with my new Winchester repeating shot gun." Residents either consumed, bartered, or sold their produce. Testifying to the economic importance of these practices, Juanita (Smith) Hammon recalled, "Sometimes residents would trade vegetables, they would exchange produce if someone had a big crop of this or that. Instead of money, like bartering. There was all that land around. I remember one lady saying, 'Why do they bother growing produce when it's so cheap anyway?' Well they were cheap according to her. She was buying vegetables for a penny a bunch. But when they're a penny a bunch and you don't have the penny, they're expensive."[17] In this way, small-scale provisioning enabled residents to insulate themselves from dependence on cash income.[18]

A fourth characteristic was a lack of municipal services, which kept tax rates low. The result was a shabby suburb. Unpaved roads, cesspools, and kerosene lamps all substituted for normal urban amenities. But residents preferred doing without these services, rather than pay the taxes to finance them. One astute realtor recognized this in 1925: "What brought all these people here . . . [was] the terms on which they could get their homes and be able to get a start without too much interference." Interference meant taxes. The importance of this issue emerged in a series of political battles during the 1920s, which found working-class residents vociferously resist-

ing efforts by local merchants to develop the infrastructure of South Gate —
and thus raise taxes. A commitment against taxation ultimately became a
key element in the political self-identity of local residents, who were struggling hard to maintain their foothold in suburbia.[19]

A fifth trait was that industries were situated either in or directly adjacent
to the suburb. From the outset, the subdividers envisioned industry as critical to South Gate's prosperity. As early as 1924, city promoters spoke enthusiastically of a $4 million "industrial program" of plant construction for
South Gate, destined to make it "one of the most important [communities]
in Southern California." In their efforts to attract industry, city leaders emphasized convenient access to transportation, a dependable labor supply,
low rates for water, electricity, and gas, and cheap land and tax rates, particularly in the unincorporated areas just outside the suburb's borders. Industries responded to the call almost immediately. In 1922, Bell Foundry
became the first plant to locate in South Gate, followed two years later by
the A. R. Maas Chemical Company, which produced chemicals for the film
industry. In 1928, South Gate scored a major coup with the arrival of Firestone Tire and Rubber, which soon became one of the largest employers
in the area. By the late 1920s, 14 major industries had established plants in
and adjacent to South Gate, producing such goods as iron products and
castings, concrete pipes, paper goods, and electric products. In 1928, the
value of manufactured products in South Gate topped $24 million, with
$4.7 million paid in wages.[20]

Perhaps more than any other quality, the presence of industry set South
Gate apart from the typical middle-class "bedroom" suburb. Residents often had to cope with noxious odors, noise, and other nuisances caused by
local factories, which were sometimes nestled among the homes. By 1930,
for example, three blocks of Otis Street in northeast South Gate housed
Weiser Manufacturing, Long Beach Steel Foundry, and the National Paper
Products Company. Western State Chemical had had a plant there a few
years earlier. Along the same three blocks were 32 houses. In some cases,
homes were actually next door to the plants. On other streets, factories sat
adjacent to backyards, separated only by a narrow alley. Because the poorer
homes were at the back of their lots, it was not uncommon for them to sit
right up against a factory. This proximity sometimes caused friction. In
1927, Otis Street residents complained to City Hall about the "parking of
cars and litter thrown on the streets" by workers at the National Paper Products Company. The following year, 43 householders on San Vicente Street
signed a petition complaining about the noise caused by a trip-hammer or
riveting machine at a local boiler works. The very framework of a working-
class suburb like South Gate, which mixed residences and industries, virtually ensured that problems like this would arise from time to time.[21]

Figure 3.1. The sprawling Firestone Tire and Rubber factory, just outside of South Gate, 1931. Factories like this were welcomed in working-class suburbs, which balanced homes, industry, and business. *Hearst Collection, Department of Special Collections, University of Southern California Library*

The final defining trait was that South Gate was pitched squarely at white working people. Home Gardens, annexed in 1927, did this most strikingly. From the days of its earliest subdivision in 1922, Home Gardens touted itself as "the workingman's ideal home town." Local promoters described Home Gardens as "situated conveniently to scores of factories in different industrial centers, and with property values and terms within the reach of every honest workingman." In 1925, the local booster-editor asserted, "Home Gardens is a town of, by and for workingmen—and we want hundreds more of them. The only restrictions are racial—the white race only may own property here." By 1927, Home Gardens called itself the place "where the working man is welcomed and given an even break." Most residents would agree with one booster's claim that South Gate was the "ideal residence for people of moderate means."[22]

Figure 3.2. Bill Ziegler, resident of Home Gardens, stands proudly in front of a local home in the 1920s. Homes represented a critical source of economic security for working-class suburbanites. *Glenn T. Seaborg*

FINDING MEANING IN THE WORKING-CLASS
SUBURBS OF LOS ANGELES

Nestled on the border between rural and urban life, working-class suburbs fused elements from both realms to fill the particular needs of their inhabitants. In contrast to more affluent suburbs that melded rural and urban elements to create an aesthetic of romantic pastoralism, the working-class suburb combined these milieus for the more prosaic purpose of economic survival in the modern industrial metropolis. These suburbs enabled families to secure the basic necessities of shelter and food cheaply and efficiently. Especially in cities like the Los Angeles of the early twentieth century, when land was cheap, abundant, and often vacant, such suburbs fulfilled these functions effectively and frequently.

If the developers erected a scaffolding for the suburb, the residents built the structure itself—often literally. In the process, they imprinted their own vision of suburbia upon South Gate. Theirs was an image shaped by class needs, motivated by the desire for family security, and driven by an intensive need to economize. Molded by these concerns and pressures, South Gate became a rough-and-tumble suburb where homes were humble, yards were productive, streets were dusty, and families made do. The pastoral ideal extolled in elite suburbs gave way to the squawks of chickens, the shaky wails of goats, and the sharp crack of hammers driving nails into solid wood.

It is no coincidence that migrants to California in the early twentieth century were labeled "homeseekers." The quest for homes reflected several important impulses within the homeseekers themselves that extended beyond the ideology and controlling influences of the land developers and real estate industry. It is true that developers controlled the housing options of many; yet we need to look beyond these forces "from above" to understand how and why Americans embraced home ownership so fervently. Particularly the perspective of the poor, for whom home ownership served a very distinct purpose, is critical for understanding this vital twentieth-century phenomenon. To the worker in 1920s Los Angeles, a home represented independence, a goal highly valued in both American and immigrant traditions.

For American workers living on the edge of poverty, particularly in the period before state-based welfare, security and autonomy were the pressing goals. They pursued these goals in many ways: some through workplace actions such as unionization and demands for job security, others in realms beyond the wage-based economy, such as neighborhoods, popular culture, and public spaces. As workplace autonomy became more elusive with the maturing of industrial capitalism in the late nineteenth century, the spheres beyond the factory gates took on even greater significance. As Ira Katznelson has written, "Paradoxically, just at the moment when the development of industrial capitalism undercut the skill levels and control over work that artisans had exercised, the working class became capable of developing and controlling the institutions of daily neighborhood life."[23]

Housing represented a crucial aspect of this quest for independence. To working-class residents of suburbs like South Gate, individual housing production and ownership became a viable route to family security in the context of an unpredictable job market, where sources of cash income were often fleeting. Longtime South Gate resident John Sheehy explained that home ownership "meant nobody could evict you. Security for your family.

When you're raising five kids you pretty much think you need to own a place. . . . It was tragic if you couldn't buy a house. You really were at the bottom . . . floundering around, trying to survive. There was no such thing in those years as a real stability in employment that we came to have later." Family security, via home ownership, was the key aspiration of South Gate's citizenry. With home ownership such a central goal for local residents, it follows that their status as "home owner" profoundly shaped their social and political identity, as the total history of South Gate reveals.[24]

The meaning of home ownership for working-class Americans takes on added significance if seen in light of the movement toward welfare capitalism during the 1920s. In the wake of Progressivism, it was widely acknowledged that industrial capitalism required a social "safety net" for working Americans living on the edge, those most vulnerable to the unpredictable swings of the economy. In the era before state-based welfare, sickness, old age, or simply bad luck could spell doom and poverty for an otherwise hardworking family. Business-led welfare capitalism was proffered as one solution to stabilize life for working Americans, and in the process to counteract simmering radical tendencies.[25] Another solution was suburbanization and single-family home ownership. To many working Americans, this alternative promised more autonomy and a deeper sense of palpable security in the soil they could call their own. Under welfare capitalism, employees paid the price of flagrant dependency on their employers in exchange for "security." As suburban dwellers and home owners, they perceived themselves as more independent and insulated from an unpredictable marketplace, particularly important to Los Angeles workers, who lacked an alternative in a strong labor movement.

In many ways, working-class families in suburbia had more options for achieving family security than their urban counterparts. For example, in cities, wage reductions or price increases forced families to seek solutions within the market economy, such as sending children to work. In New York City, housewives responded to rising food costs by organizing and protesting politically since they had few ways to produce their own food.[26] In suburbs like South Gate, however, residents responded to similar crises by self-provisioning on their own land. It was a more individualized solution, but it was an equally viable one.

The South Gate story thus suggests that working-class aspirations for security defined the very meaning of suburban living for these people. In most cases, residents favored the "use value" over the "commodity value" of their homes. In their quest for independence, residents set the community off in a direction that would best meet their needs. South Gate's working-class residents ironically had more control over their environment than the typical middle-class suburbanite. Since they couldn't afford a well-developed community, it was up to them to create community for themselves. In their quest to make a secure place for themselves in a world of advancing industrial capitalism, working-class families ended up shaping the very process of suburbanization in Los Angeles.

NOTES

1. Robert Gottlieb and Irene Wolt, *Thinking Big: The Story of the Los Angeles Times, Its Publishers and Their Influence on Southern California* (New York: Putnam, 1977); Louis Perry and Richard Perry, *A History of the Los Angeles Labor Movement, 1911–1941* (Berkeley: Institute of Industrial Relations, 1963); Upton Sinclair, *The Goslings* (Pasadena: published by the author, 1924); Nancy Quam-Wickham, "Petroleocrats and Proletarians: Work, Class, and Politics in the California Oil Industry, 1917–1925" (Ph.D. dissertation, University of California, Berkeley, 1994).

2. Richard Harris, *Unplanned Suburbs: Toronto's American Tragedy, 1900–1950* (Baltimore: Johns Hopkins University Press, 1996); Richard Harris, "Working-Class Home Ownership in the American Metropolis," *Journal of Urban History* 17, 1 (November 1990): 46–69; Richard Harris, "Self-Building and the Social Geography of Toronto, 1901–1913: A Challenge for Urban Theory," *Transactions of the Institute of British Geographers* 15 (1990): 387–402; Richard Harris, "'Canada's All Right': The Lives and Loyalties of Immigrant Families in a Toronto Suburb, 1900–1945," *Canadian Geographer* 36 (1992): 15; Richard Harris, "The Impact of Building Controls on Residential Development in Toronto, 1900–40," *Planning Perspectives* 6 (1991): 269–96; Richard Harris, "The Unplanned Working-Class Suburb in Its Heyday, 1900–1940" (paper presented at the Organization of American Historians meeting, Chicago, 1992); Andrew Wiese, "Places of Our Own: Suburban Black Towns before 1960," *Journal of Urban History* 19, 3 (May 1993): 30–54; Andrew Wiese, "The Other Suburbanites: African American Suburbanization in the North before 1950," *Journal of American History* 85 (March 1999): 1495–1524.

3. For international comparisons, see Kenneth T. Jackson, *Crabgrass Frontier: The Suburbanization of the United States* (New York: Oxford University Press, 1985): 8–10; John M. Merriman, *The Margins of City Life: Explorations on the French Urban Frontier, 1815–1851* (New York: Oxford University Press, 1991), chapter 1; Tyler Stovall, *The Rise of the Paris Red Belt* (Berkeley and Los Angeles: University of California Press, 1990). In developing countries over the past few decades, uncontrolled peripheral settlements have grown explosively. See D. Conway, "Self-help Housing, the Commodity Nature of Housing and Amelioration of the Housing Deficit: Continuing the Turner-Burgess Debate," *Antipode* 14 (1983): 40–46. Further research is needed to examine these international comparisons more closely.

4. The key works that examine patterns of metropolitan development in Los Angeles are Robert Fogelson, *The Fragmented Metropolis: Los Angeles, 1850–1930* (Cambridge: Harvard University Press, 1967); Fred Viehe, "Black Gold Suburbs: The Influence of the Extractive Industry on the Suburbanization of Los Angeles, 1890–1930," *Journal of Urban History* 8 (November 1981): 3–26; Mark S. Foster, "The Model-T, the Hard Sell, and Los Angeles's Urban Growth: The Decentralization of Los Angeles during the 1920s," *Pacific Historical Review* 44 (November 1975): 459–84; Stephan Thernstrom, "The Growth of Los Angeles in Historical Perspective:

Myth and Reality," in *Los Angeles: Viability and Prospects for Metropolitan Leadership*, ed. Werner Z. Hirsch (New York: Praeger, 1971), 3–19; Carey McWilliams, *Southern California Country: An Island on the Land* (New York: Duell, Sloan & Pearce, 1946); Scott L. Bottles, *Los Angeles and the Automobile: The Making of the Modern City* (Berkeley: University of California Press, 1987); Greg Hise, *Magnetic Los Angeles: Planning the Twentieth Century Metropolis* (Baltimore: Johns Hopkins University Press, 1997); Greg Hise, "Home Building and Industrial Decentralization in Los Angeles: The Roots of the Postwar Urban Region," *Journal of Urban History* 19 (February 1993): 95–125.

5. Richard Harris, "Pioneering the Jungle Suburbs: Owner-building in North American Cities, 1900–1950" (unpublished manuscript, September 1991, in author's possession), 26; Allan R. Pred, "The Intrametropolitan Location of American Manufacturing," *Annals of the Association of American Geographers* 54 (June 1964): 178–79; William B. Friedricks, "Capital and Labor in Los Angeles: Henry E. Huntington vs. Organized Labor, 1900–1920," *Pacific Historical Review* 59 (February 1990): 375–95; Edward Soja, Rebecca Morales, and Goetz Wolff, "Urban Restructuring: An Analysis of Social and Spatial Change in Los Angeles," *Economic Geography* 59 (1983): 197–98, 207; Marc Weiss, *The Rise of the Community Builders* (New York: Columbia University Press, 1987), chapter 4; Hise, "Home Building."

Marxist urban theorists have argued that labor militancy in the late nineteenth century encouraged capital to disperse its operations, thus diffusing the power of labor. These theorists, particularly Ernest Mandel (*Long Waves of Capitalist Development: The Marxist Interpretation* [Cambridge: Cambridge University Press, 1980]), have developed an explanation for urban restructuring that links the spatial reorganization of production—and, thus, urban form—to capitalist crises and needs. In the late nineteenth century, when Los Angeles was emerging as a city, the restructuring of capital and the urban form occurred in response to militant working-class unrest and protest. As Soja, Morales, and Wolff described it, "In part as a means of escaping agglomerated working class militancy, industrial production decentralized into the formerly residential inner rings and to satellite centers. . . . Among other advantages to expanding capitalist accumulation, this allowed employers more effectively to escape union pressures, isolate and segment the workforce" ("Urban Restructuring," 197).

6. Kelker, De Leuw & Co., *Report and Recommendations on a Comprehensive Rapid Transit Plan for the City and County of Los Angeles* (Chicago: Kelker, De Leuw & Co., 1925), plate no. 9, and see 32–34; (Los Angeles County) Regional Planning Commission, *Comprehensive Report on the Regional Plan of Highways. Section 4. Long Beach–Redondo Area* (Los Angeles, 1931); Myrna Cherkoss Donahoe, "Workers' Response to Plant Closures: The Cases of Steel and Auto in Southeast Los Angeles, 1935–1986" (Ph.D. dissertation, University of California, Irvine, 1987), 67. On Vernon, see Mike Davis, "The Empty Quarter," in *Sex, Death and God in L.A.*, ed. David Reid (New York: Pantheon, 1992), 60.

7. George Eastman, "Industrial Development in Southern California," *Southern California Business* 7 (July 1928): 10; Fogelson, *Fragmented Metropolis*, 115–19, 144–54; Frank L. Kidner and Philip Neff, *An Economic Survey of the Los Angeles Area* (Los Angeles: Haynes Foundation, 1945), 3; John Sheehy, Oral History with author, May 1, June 19, June 21, June 26, 1990, South Gate, Calif., transcript of tape-

recorded interview; *Home Gardens Press,* July 10, 1925 (from Weber field notes, Federal Writers Project collection, Special Collections, University Research Library, University of California, Los Angeles [hereafter FWP collection, UCLA]); George W. Robbins, "Transport: The Movement of Commodities," in *Los Angeles: Preface to a Master Plan,* ed. George W. Robbins and L. Deming Tilton (Los Angeles: Pacific Southwest Academy, 1941), 121; Viehe, "Black Gold Suburbs"; Weiss, *Rise of the Community Builders,* 83–85; G. Gordon Whitnall, "Industrial Analysis of Los Angeles," *Los Angeles Realtor* (February 1922): 4–5.

8. Fogelson, *Fragmented Metropolis,* 127; *South Gate Tribune,* December 25, 1924; *Home Gardens Press,* July 22, 1927, January 30, 1925 (from Weber field notes, June 20, 1941, FWP collection, UCLA). The small suburbs of Bell, Bell Gardens, Cudahy, and Maywood were exceptions to the rule of including industries within their borders. They allocated no space to manufacturing and, accordingly, lacked the tax revenue from these sources. These were primarily residential suburbs, although they routinely touted the advantages of their *proximity* to many industries (Mike Davis, Tour of Industrial Los Angeles, November, 26, 1996).

9. Becky Nicolaides, "'Where the Working Man Is Welcomed': Working-class Suburbs in Los Angeles, 1900–1940," *Pacific Historical Review* 68 (November 1999): 517–59.

10. The story of the Smith family is from Juanita (Smith) Hammon, Oral History with author, July 5, 1990, South Gate, Calif., transcript of tape-recorded interview.

11. In the late nineteenth and early twentieth centuries, physicians commonly recommended clean, fresh air and a mild climate that allowed outdoor exercise as treatment for tuberculosis. Southern California thus became a favorite destination of tuberculosis patients. See Barbara Bates, *Bargaining for Life: A Social History of Tuberculosis, 1876–1938* (Philadelphia: University of Pennsylvania Press, 1992), 29; Fogelson, *Fragmented Metropolis,* 64; John E. Baur, *The Health Seekers of Southern California, 1870–1900* (San Marino: Huntington Library, 1959).

12. For examples of uses of the home to support this purpose, see Richard Bushman, "Family Security in the Transition from Farm to City, 1750–1850," *Journal of Family History* 6 (Fall 1981): 248–49; Virginia Yans-McLaughlin, *Family and Community: Italian Immigrants in Buffalo, 1880–1930* (Urbana: University of Illinois Press, 1982).

13. Charles Hopper, *Through My Window at Southgate* (Southgate Gardens, 1918); *Los Angeles Times,* March 1, 1918; U.S. Bureau of the Census, *Historical Statistics of the United States, Colonial Times to 1970* (Washington, D.C.: Government Printing Office, 1975), 166; Glenn T. Seaborg, "Journal of Glenn T. Seaborg, January 1, 1927 to August 10, 1934," unpublished typewritten manuscript in author's possession, ii–iii; *Home Gardens Booster,* February 15, 1924, March 7, 1924; *Home Gardens Press,* December 12, 1924, December 18, 1925; Hazal Liggett, "The Relation of Wages to the Cost of Living in Los Angeles, 1915 to 1920," *Studies in Sociology* 5 (March 1921): 5–6.

14. Sanborn Map Company, "Insurance Maps of Los Angeles, California," vols. 28, 30–31 (Sanborn Map Company of New York, 1927, 1929); Virgil Collins, Oral History with author, August 20, 1991, UAW Retirees Headquarters, Artesia, Calif., August 25 and September 15, 1991, Laguna Hills, Calif., transcript of tape-recorded

interview, 2; Ruth (Barrett) Lampmann, Oral History with author, February 13, 1991, South Gate, Calif., transcript of tape-recorded interview, 1, 11; Wallace McFadden, "Biography of Wallace McFadden," interview by Sandy McFadden, June 12, 1971, Oral History 1029, transcript of tape-recorded interview, California State University, Fullerton Oral History Project, Fullerton, 5; John Sheehy, Oral History, 1, 14, 20; Charles Spaulding, "The Development of Organization and Disorganization in the Social Life of a Rapidly Growing Working-Class Suburb within a Metropolitan District" (Ph.D. dissertation, University of Southern California, 1939), 127–28; South Gate Bicentennial Heritage Committee, *South Gate 1776–1976* (South Gate: South Gate Press, 1976), 31; *South Gate Daily Signal,* January 19, 1973; South Gate City Council Minutes, November 3, 1926 (vol. 4: 694).

On methods for determining owner-building rates, see Richard Harris, "Self-Building in the Urban Housing Market," *Economic Geography* 67, 1 (January 1991): 1–21.

15. John Sheehy, Oral History, 14, 20.

16. Local home ownership rates are from *Los Angeles Times,* February 13, 1927, and an analysis of the South Gate City Directory for 1929.

17. Juanita (Smith) Hammon, Oral History, 13.

18. *Home Gardens Booster,* April 18, 1924; "Ordinance No. 4" (1923) and "Ordinance No. 86" (1926), City Clerk's Office, South Gate; Juanita (Smith) Hammon, Oral History; Ruth (Barrett) Lampmann, Oral History. The *Southgate Gardener* and *Hopper Tour Topics* (1918–22), both early local papers, ran frequent articles on vegetable and small livestock raising, particularly rabbits and poultry. Such articles continued well into the 1920s, testifying to the persistence of this practice.

19. *Home Gardens Press,* March 27, 1925; see Becky Nicolaides, "In Search of the Good Life: Community and Politics in Working-Class Los Angeles, 1920–1955" (Ph.D. dissertation, Columbia University, 1993), chapter 6.

20. Quote from *South Gate Tribune,* September 12, 1924; *Home Gardens Press,* June 10, 1927; *South Gate Press,* December 14, 1928; Los Angeles Chamber of Commerce, "South Gate edition" (from Weber field notes, May 11, 1941, June 6, 13, 20, 1941, Weber and Thienes field notes, FWP collection, UCLA).

21. *City and Telephone Directory of South Gate, 1926* (South Gate: Tribune-News, 1926); *City and Telephone Directory of Greater South Gate, 1930* (South Gate: Tribune-News Publishing, 1930); and for National Paper Products Co., see *Home Gardens Press,* September 17, 1926 (Weber field notes, June 20, 1941, FWP collection, UCLA); Sanborn Map Company, "Insurance Maps of Los Angeles, California: Map of South Gate," vols. 28, 30–31; South Gate City Council Minutes, May 3, 1927 (vol. 5: 789), April 17, 1928 (vol. 6: 1031).

22. *Home Gardens Press,* October 9, 1925, August 7, 1925, March 1927 (masthead). For similar statements touting Home Gardens as a working-class suburb, see *Home Gardens Press,* August 7 and 21, 1925, March 11, 1927.

23. Ira Katznelson, *City Trenches* (Chicago: University of Chicago Press, 1981), 52.

24. John Sheehy, Oral History, 14; Nicolaides, "In Search of the Good Life," passim. The meaning of home ownership is a subject of much debate among historians. One school of thought sees the proliferation of home ownership as the legitimate, self-directed action of Americans seeking a particular lifestyle. Another school sees

the home ownership movement as a way that capital diffused the independence and class consciousness of working-class Americans, by tying them to a near-strangling financial commitment, thus vesting their loyalty in the protection of property. For a range of interpretations, see Matthew Edel, Elliott D. Sclar, and Daniel Luria, *Shaky Palaces: Homeownership and Social Mobility in Boston's Suburbanization* (New York: Columbia University Press, 1984); Constance Perrin, *Everything in Its Place* (Princeton: Princeton University Press, 1977); Gwendolyn Wright, *Building the Dream* (Cambridge: MIT Press, 1983); Jackson, *Crabgrass Frontier;* Bushman, "Family Security"; and Harris, "Working-Class Home Ownership."

25. The seminal discussion of welfare capitalism is in David Brody, *Workers in Industrial America* (New York: Oxford University Press, 1980), 48–81.

26. Michael R. Haines, "Poverty, Economic Stress, and the Family in a Late Nineteenth-Century American City: Whites in Philadelphia, 1880," and Claudia Goldin, "Family Strategies and the Family Economy in the Late Nineteenth Century: The Role of Secondary Workers," both in *Philadelphia: Work, Space, Family, and Group Experience in the Nineteenth Century,* ed. Theodore Hershberg (New York: Oxford University Press, 1981); Yans-McLaughlin, *Family and Community,* 164–77; Dana Frank, "Housewives, Socialists, and the Politics of Food: The 1917 New York Cost-of-Living Protests," *Feminist Studies* 11 (Summer 1985): 255–85.

CHAPTER FOUR

Sunshine and the Open Shop

Ford and Darwin in 1920s Los Angeles

Mike Davis

At the turn of the twentieth century, Los Angeles had plenty of sunshine and oranges, but few of William Blake's despised "Satanic mills." All far-sighted local leaders agreed that prosperity was unbalanced by the absence of significant industrial output. Thus, in his otherwise triumphal history of the Los Angeles Chamber of Commerce, Charles Dwight Willard (1899: 171–80) complained that the region, despite its explosive growth, lacked any manufactures worthy of the name. A burgeoning real estate and tourism economy rested precariously upon an attenuated industrial base (see Table 4.1) of a brewery, a few foundries, the Southern Pacific machine shops and several big planing mills.

In the past, Los Angeles' industrial backwardness had been blamed on a vicious circle of natural and market constraints: the lack of an improved harbor, the high cost of imported coal, discriminatory railroad tariffs, and the absence of a populated hinterland. No major region of the United States was more peripheral to the national industrial economy or less obviously endowed to become a manufacturing center. Yet the Chamber's executive secretary was optimistic that this "most difficult question" would soon be resolved as federally subsidised port construction and newly discovered oil fields, together with population growth and the rise of a rich citrus hinterland, created a sunnier climate for industrial investment (Willard, 1899).

Over the next generation, Willard's bullishness was dramatically vindicated. Miracles occurred on both the supply and demand sides of the industrial equation. Thus the energy-impoverished Los Angeles basin became the largest and most productive oil field in the world during the 1920s, while new engineering marvels—the Panama Canal, the municipal harbor at San Pedro, and a burgeoning highway system—reduced historical freight differentials (Williams, 1996). In addition to the aqueduct that brought

TABLE 4.1.   Industrial employment
in Los Angeles—1905

metal works	2,000
lumber works	2,050
furniture	400
confections	343
pipe	334
leather	300
flour mills	210
olive mills	200
misc.	1,039
total	6,876

SOURCE: From an industrial survey conducted for the Los Angeles County Board of Supervisors by John O. Lowe and summarized in the *Los Angeles Express,* November 22, 1905.[1]

pilfered water from the Sierras, Los Angeles was also irrigated by the life-savings of hundreds of thousands of middle-class immigrants from the American heartland. The 1900–1919 period was the peak of Midwest farm prosperity, and a significant fraction of this agricultural boom was transmuted into Southern California bungalows, orange groves and small businesses.

In response, the local manufacturing workforce grew tenfold, from 6,876 in 1905 to 66,536 reported by the Census of Manufactures in 1927. (Despite the Depression, Los Angeles' factory working class continued to grow: doubling by 1939, then again by 1943.) Industrial output, only 51% of San Francisco's in 1890, surpassed the latter in 1921, and was 42% higher in 1927 (see Table 4.2). The city that produced negligible manufactured exports in 1905 became the country's eighth largest manufacturing center in 1924, and nearly half of its industrial workforce was employed in the production of such high-value exports or durable goods as motion pictures, aircraft and refined oil products.[2]

Although manufacturing still lagged far behind the growth of population, income and services (making 1920s Los Angeles the precocious forerunner of Daniel Bell's 1960s "post-industrial society"),[3] the adolescent metropolis boasted the nation's most modern and rapidly growing manufacturing district. Indeed, its business elites, under the leadership of Harry Chandler of the *Los Angeles Times,* claimed that 1920s Southern California was a new kind of industrial society where Ford and Darwin, engineering and nature, were combined in a eugenic formula that eliminated the root causes of class conflict and inefficient production. Militant anti-unionism,

TABLE 4.2. Population and manufacturing
growth in major West Coast cities

(1) population (1,000s)

	a. 1890	b. 1930	b/a
Los Angeles	50	1,238	24.76
San Francisco	229	634	2.12
Seattle	43	366	8.51
Portland	46	302	6.57

(2) manufacturing value added ($ millions)

	a. 1890	b. 1927	b/a
Los Angeles	68	610	8.97
San Francisco	133	430	3.23
Seattle	51	60	3.16
Portland	47	147	3.13

(3) ratio of manufacturing to population growth

Los Angeles	.36
San Francisco	1.52
Seattle	.37
Portland	.47

SOURCES: Census of Population (1890, 1930); Census of Manufactures (1927).

together with scientific factory planning, low taxes, abundant electric power, warm weather, mass-produced bungalows, and a racially selected labor force made Los Angeles a paradise of the open shop. Or, as the Chamber of Commerce put it, "a land of smokeless, sunlit factories, surrounded by residences of contented, efficient workers" (cf. Sanger, 1927; Los Angeles Chamber of Commerce, 1927: 10).

Like other contemporary assertions of L.A. exceptionalism, the Chamber's extravagant claims deserve skepticism. Yet there is little doubt that the industrial geography of Los Angeles by 1931 was highly distinctive. As Figure 4.1 and Table 4.3 illustrate, manufacturing in Los Angeles was informally zoned in a pattern that correlated with surprising fidelity to firm size, market orientation, capitalization, and dominant labor process.

Thus the industries producing for a national market—motion pictures, oil refining and (after 1940) aircraft, together with local-market rock products producers—formed distinctive archipelagos of very large plants, enclaved within Los Angeles' agricultural/suburban periphery. In many cases,

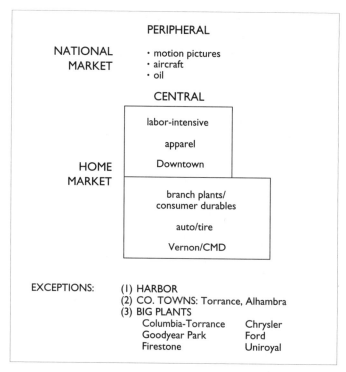

PERIPHERAL

NATIONAL
MARKET
- motion pictures
- aircraft
- oil

CENTRAL

labor-intensive

apparel

Downtown

HOME
MARKET

branch plants/
consumer durables

auto/tire

Vernon/CMD

EXCEPTIONS: (1) HARBOR
                (2) CO. TOWNS: Torrance, Alhambra
                (3) BIG PLANTS
                    Columbia-Torrance   Chrysler
                    Goodyear Park   Ford
                    Firestone   Uniroyal

Figure 4.1. Industrial geography of Los Angeles (1929).

these enclaves were de facto company towns, like MGM in Culver City or Standard Oil in El Segundo, or their functional equivalents, like Universal Studios in its unincorporated "county hole" of Universal City.[4]

Home-market production, on the other hand, was still centralized around Downtown. This industrial core, however, was divided into two distinct subregions. Locally owned, labor-intensive manufactures like apparel, food-processing and furniture tended to be concentrated in the city's original industrial district east of Alameda, between North Broadway and Ninth Street. More capital-intensive branch plants of major corporations, including the West's largest concentration of auto and tire factories, were located southeast of Downtown in the Central Manufacturing District (CMD—which after 1929 included the huge Bandini estate), in adjacent parts of the "exclusively industrial" City of Vernon (incorporated in 1905), or in the nearby Union Pacific Industrial District (see Figure 4.2).

In the jargon of labor-process theory, the suburban enclaves were favored locations for the extraordinarily large assemblages of craft labor— "flexible manufacturing"—intrinsic to motion pictures and airframe manu-

TABLE 4.3.   Location of plants with
more than 500 workers (1931)

	(a) suburban[§]	(b) central
1. studios	10	0
2. aircraft	5	0
3. refineries	5	3
4. steel	1	3
5. railroad	0	5
6. food-related	2	10
7. branch plants	1	9
8. other	2	5
total	26	35

SOURCES: "Factories Over 500 Employees—1931" (typescript),
Chamber of Commerce archive, Southern California Regional History Center, University of Southern California. Locations from business directories.
[§]Includes Los Angeles Harbor district

facture. The old industrial section of Downtown, on the other hand, preserved sweatshop manufactures, while Vernon/CMD was the hub for
"Fordist" mass-production of consumer durables and capital goods.[5]

Peripheral industrialization in Los Angeles, and the stimuli it provided
to blue-collar suburbanization, have been the subjects of notable recent
monographs by Fred Viehe (1981) and Greg Hise (1994). Indeed there
probably has been a tendency in studies of the modern Los Angeles region
to treat industrial decentralization as the dominant and defining trend. Yet
the dispersion of certain manufacturing sectors, like oil, aircraft and motion
pictures, was clearly counterbalanced by centrifugal forces that concentrated other sectors, like apparel, food-processing, and metal-working, in
the core. The rise of the highly centralized Vernon/CMD district, moreover, was the paramount achievement of the 1920s "crusade for industry":
that decade's counterpart to the construction of a water-and-power infrastructure in the 1910s or the wartime expansion of the aircraft industry
during the 1940s.

Branch-plant industrialization, as I will show, depended upon a dense
railroad infrastructure and a central location in the metropolitan network.
Institutionally, it required the complex coordination of initiatives by national manufacturers, regional business elites, railroads, utilities, industrial
land developers, and residential subdividers. In turn, the new industries
provided an engine for the Chamber of Commerce's vision of an urban regime of accumulation that rationalized control of every major variable af-

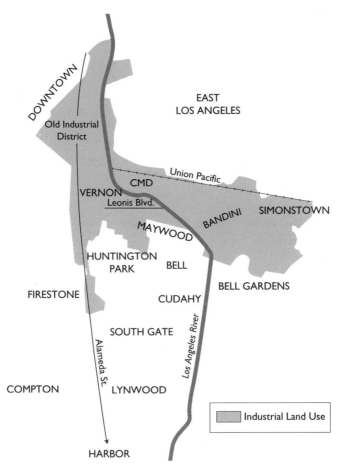

Figure 4.2. The industrial core.

fecting production (a "eugenics of industry"). In its contemporary context, open shop Los Angeles of the 1920s was as hubristic and implicitly totalitarian as Henry Ford's company welfare states in Highland Park and Detroit, and, ultimately, just as short-lived.

THE CRUSADE FOR INDUSTRY

In its 45th special midwinter issue (Jan. 1, 1930), the *Times* looked back upon the long crusade to bring industry to Los Angeles. "This city begins with almost no national advantages to industry; the cities of the north with nearly every one of importance. Apart from these, the only difference between Los Angeles industry and that of the north—the one great difference which has outweighed all natural handicaps and has made this city one of the first manufacturing centers of the country—is the fact that, from its beginnings, Los Angeles industry has been maintained under the open shop as against union rule in San Francisco, in Portland and in Seattle."[6]

By 1930, of course, the open shop was no longer a Los Angeles monopoly, as unionism had been crushed along the Pacific Slope during the violent maritime and general strikes of 1919–21. Yet from the *Times'* point of view, the keystone of industrial prosperity was the Merchants and Manufacturers Association (M&M), established in 1896, and since the bombing of the *Times* in 1910 devoted entirely to the struggle against trade unionism. The culminating battle in the "Forty Year War for the Open Shop" was the defeat of militant longshoremen, sailors and oil workers in the Los Angeles Harbor in 1921–23. The M&M and maritime employers used California's draconian criminal syndicalism legislation to imprison 27 key strike leaders (members of the IWW) while the infamous Red Squad of the Los Angeles Police Department and the Ku Klux Klan terrorized rank-and-file supporters. As the United States Commission on Industrial Relations had observed as early as 1914, "freedom [for workers in Los Angeles] does not exist either politically, industrially or socially" (cf. Perry and Perry, 1963, esp. pp. 163–211; Merchants and Manufacturers Assn., 1986:20–23; U.S. Senate Commission on Industrial Relations, 1916: 87).

When the M&M abdicated its regional promotion work in 1910 to concentrate on union-busting, the campaign for industrial development reverted to the Chamber of Commerce. Since the 1890s the Chamber's Committee for Home Manufactures had been sponsoring public exhibits to advertise Los Angeles' industrial potential, and in 1908 it established "Prosperity Week," including a parade with floats, to make the case for home production and import substitution. The wartime transportation emergency in 1918 provided a patriotic excuse for the Los Angeles City Council of National Defense to officially promote the consumption of home products.[7]

Yet there were major divisions within the Chamber of Commerce over the best strategy for encouraging industrial growth. The "home industries" wing was led by W. T. Bishop, a prominent candy-maker and chairman of the Chamber's committee on manufactures. His chief allies were other food and confectionery makers, and the two major local iron works—all of whom stood to lose from branch investments by their national competitors.[8]

On the other side, many of the region's major bankers and land developers, led by Chamber pioneer Frank Wiggins and W. J. Washburn of Security–First National Bank, were critical of this parochial focus on local products, particularly in commodities where local capital was doomed to be defeated in competition with national monopolies. Citing an optimistic study of Los Angeles' industrial resource and market potentials that had been prepared by the War Industries Board, they instead advocated an aggressive campaign for "Balanced Prosperity" that targeted Eastern manufacturers who might be encouraged to open branch plants in Los Angeles' expanding market.[9]

In 1919, Henry Ford and Harvey Firestone, both visiting Pasadena, accepted the Chamber's invitation to discuss Los Angeles' industrial prospects. They assured Washburn and other local leaders, including Harry Chandler of the *Times,* that the booming automobile market in Southern California was making the region increasingly attractive as an auto-assembly and tire-building center. In the same year, Goodyear became the first Eastern corporation to open a major Los Angeles plant; in this case, a textile fabric mill and rubber factory just west of Vernon in south-central Los Angeles, using cotton from the nearby Imperial Valley. The tire maker soon added an 800-home "company neighborhood," Goodyear Park, that replicated its namesake in Akron (*Los Angeles Times,* Dec. 21, 1920).

To capitalize on this burgeoning Eastern interest in the Los Angeles market, the Chamber brought A. G. Arnold from the East in 1921 to general the "Balanced Prosperity" campaign. His mandate was to make Los Angeles, already the most rapidly and densely automobilized city in the world, the "Akron and Detroit of the West." To this end he was given a large budget to staff a new Industrial Department (headed by R. Sangster) with nationally recognized experts on manufacturing like automotive engineer H. Crites and traffic engineer H. Brasheer. Their capital-recruiting expeditions to the East were often joined by Chamber leader Frank Coates, acting as an official industrial commissioner for Los Angeles County.[10]

During the 1920s the Industrial Department, working in alliance with the transcontinental railroads, as well as the Los Angeles Department of Water and Power,[11] sold Los Angeles' manufacturing potential with the same zeal with which the Chamber had previously sold sunshine and oranges. "Mr. Sangster lays down a veritable barrage of facts in a particular group of industries, and then sends his engineers afield to do the 'hand-to-hand' fighting for Los Angeles' industrial supremacy."[12] More than 5,000 Eastern industrialists were provided with detailed information about the market opportunities in Southern California. Interested companies then received valuable business and engineering assistance in establishing branch operations in Los Angeles.[13]

By 1930, both Henry Ford and Harvey Firestone had made good on their promised investments, and Los Angeles had become the world's second largest center of tire production. (Arnold's other goal would be achieved in the late 1940s when it became second only to Detroit in auto assembly.) In the last eighteen months of the fatally superheated Wall Street boom, there was a particularly dramatic surge of industrial investment (27% gain in number of plants) and output (35% increase in value added) in Southern California. The newcomers included Willys-Overland, Goodrich Rubber, Procter and Gamble, Continental Can, Pittsburgh Plate Glass, Willard Storage Battery, American Maize Products, U.S. Steel and Bethlehem Steel.[14]

The Industrial Department could triumphantly boast that "more than 177 nationally known concerns now have factories within the Los Angeles area—bona fide manufacturing establishments, as distinguished from branch stocks and sales offices." By 1930 diversified manufacturing investment exceeded one billion dollars and had created nearly 50,000 new jobs. Although most people still failed to associate Los Angeles with manufacturing, the branch-plant sector had equivalent weight in the regional economy to the glamorous motion picture industry. Moreover, the Industrial Department, acting in tandem with the Chamber's Domestic Trade Department, claimed to target only noncompetitive investments that reinforced rather than harmed local industry and agriculture. As an example of such a virtuous circle, auto assembly was often cited: the factories opened by Ford in 1927 and Willys-Overland in 1928 attracted Willard Storage Battery in 1929 which, in turn, stimulated local lead refining.[15]

This concept of branch-plant industrialization inducing downstream and upstream investment will be familiar to any student of modern developmental economics. Los Angeles in the 1920s not only pioneered the kind of regional industrial policy that was widely adopted by Sunbelt localities in the 1950s and 1960s, but it also anticipated the "assembly-platform" strategy of national economic modernization that was embraced by countries and areas like Ireland, Taiwan, Puerto Rico and Yugoslavia in the 1960s and 1970s. Just as historians have recognized the seminal role of Southern California's fruit-marketing cooperatives, like Sunkist, in influencing models of business self-regulation (including the National Recovery Administration), the Industrial Department of the Chamber of Commerce deserves attention as an early prototype of scientific management applied to "place promotion."

THE PRIVATE INDUSTRIAL CITY

Historians have curiously neglected the central roles of industrial land developers, as well as utilities and railroads, in facilitating regional development. Industrial land is itself a complex manufactured product. Los Angeles' crusade for manufactures, moreover, coincided with a revolution in the technological foundations of industry. The success of the Industrial Department's branch-plant strategy depended upon the ability of the local market to supply cheap land in central locations that met the space requirements of the new, "horizontalized" mass-production processes. Equally it assumed abundant electric power and water, as well as a dense network of trackage and modern roads.[16]

A major stumbling block was the inability of the city's original industrial belt in the crowded floodplain of the Los Angeles River to satisfy the basic requirements of modern factory planning. Pioneer zoning ordinances in 1908 had drawn a red circle around the area between Main Street and the palisades of Boyle Heights as the city's official industrial district, but this had little impact on the actual chaos of land usage. Two-fifths of the private land area of the district was owned by three transcontinental railroads, and most of their property was intensively dedicated to marshaling yards, freight and commercial depots, and trackage. The rest of the district was a checkerboard of intermingled residential and industrial development (California Railroad Commission, 1920:474–75; Los Angeles Department of City Planning, 1964:3).

In a 1906 survey of Los Angeles' "proletarian wards," W. A. Corey, a local Socialist leader, estimated that the sixth, seventh and eighth wards— bounded by the Fremont gates of Elysian Park (north), Main Street (west), the Los Angeles River (east), and Vernon Avenue (south)—contained 80,000 people (Corey, 1906).[17] Although the comprehensive subdivision of south-central and east Los Angeles after 1920 siphoned off the majority of this population, a WPA survey found 916 households persisting in the area between Alameda and the river as late as 1940. Mateo Street, the last of these old Alameda corridor neighborhoods, was not torn down until the end of the Korean War. In short, it took landowners and the railroads, supported by city planners and housing reformers, nearly forty years to establish uniformity of industrial land use.[18]

Although some large parcels were assembled and put on the market during the 1920s, these sites suffered from the conflict of automobile, streetcar and train right-of-ways that produced the worst downtown traffic congestion of the twentieth century. The competition of intensive industrial and commercial uses, moreover, raised land values and made the old industrial district increasingly unattractive to factories, lumber-yards, oil firms, and other industries that required large acreages.[19]

Finally the area continued to carry the political stigma of being the city's "Red Belt." If trade unionism was in steep decline after 1912, Los Angeles' labor left—rooted in the Downtown and eastside industrial neighborhoods—retained surprising electoral strength. Carpenters' leader Fred Wheeler, supported with massive majorities from the three wards that straddled the Downtown industrial district, became the first Socialist to attain office in a major American city when he won an at-large seat on the City Council in 1913. Defeated in 1917, he was reelected during the turbulent strike year of 1919 and remained on the Council, skirmishing with the M&M and the *Times,* preaching municipal ownership and progressive taxation, until his retirement in 1925.[20]

For all these reasons, the Chamber of Commerce endorsed a shift of new branch-plant investment away from Downtown. Specifically, they opposed the addition of railroad trackage that would undermine their campaign against Downtown gridlock. The area east of Alameda, in their opinion, was best suited for non-railroad-dependent loft manufacturing, especially apparel. New factories, on the other hand, should be sited in planned, railroad-served industrial districts to the immediate south and southeast of the city center where greenfield land prices and taxes were less than half of Downtown values.[21]

Eventually, a number of powerful actors, led by the railroads' industrial departments, emerged in this competition to provide cheap, centrally located manufacturing space for national corporations. Suburban communities, including the unincorporated areas represented by the East Side Organization, also competed to attract the new factories.[22] But it was a group of tax-phobic hog ranchers, led by the French Basque immigrant John Leonis, who made the decisive move.

In 1905, they incorporated the eastern portion of the farm township of Vernondale, much of it land recently reclaimed from the floodplain of the Los Angeles River, as the City of Vernon.[23] The controversial incorporation campaign, launched in 1902, was Leonis and company's militant response to annexation efforts by Los Angeles, which acquired the western portion of Vernondale in 1893, as well as a shrewd preemption of transit magnate Henry Huntington's plan to incorporate the area into his new city of Huntington Park.[24] Located immediately southeast of Downtown, adjacent to new spurs of the Southern Pacific's harbor line, Vernon, like the state of Nevada, possessed one priceless resource: sovereignty.[25]

From the beginning, Leonis and his partners, the Furlong brothers, envisioned a unique proprietary municipality, "exclusively industrial" (city motto) and tightly controlled by its principal landowners. To safeguard this private industrial plantation, they adopted at the very outset a policy of negative population growth by refusing to issue new residential building permits and systematically condemning or buying up the existing housing stock, occupied by a largely disenfranchised population of Mexican farm and factory workers. Starting with nearly 5,000 inhabitants in 1905, Vernon had fewer than 100 residents, almost all city employees, in 1980.[26]

With a captive electorate and a single slate of candidates, usually unanimously endorsed, Vernon unilaterally abolished democratic politics and its occasional turmoil. Instead, as a conservative family business, it offered investors the guarantee of a stable environment with no political or industrial strife. As Leonis' awed hagiographer notes, "with but few exceptions— and these due to death or removal of legal residence—there had been no changes in the personnel of the administrative departments or City Council since the city was founded until the 1950s." To maximize the city's attraction to industry, moreover, Leonis decided to minimize taxation, and in its early years, Vernon was financed exclusively by business license fees (Kilty, 1963:49; *Times,* Aug. 8, 1917).

This attracted a handful of refugee firms from Downtown (led by Los Angeles Storage Company in 1905), but most manufacturers were dissuaded by the tax-less city's inability to finance paved streets or sewers, as well as by the area's punitively high electrical rates. It was liquor, sports and vice— hounded from Los Angeles by the Methodists and blue laws—that took immediate advantage of Vernon's anomalous sovereignty. Until 1920, the little city, with its baseball stadium, world-championship boxing arena, nightclubs, slot-machines, and working women, was a Las Vegas *avant l'lettre,* as Leonis and the Furlongs shared the spoils with the era's most colorful gamblers and sports promoters.

But Vernon's proprietors never lost sight of the larger prize of industrial investment. In 1912, they annexed the neighboring Santa Fe Railroad classification yards, establishing a partnership with the giant corporation that became the city's leading landowner and industrial developer. They also used some of their sporting profits to build a new viaduct across the Los Angeles River and to pave Santa Fe Avenue (Kilty, 1963:49; Nelson, 1952: 180). At the same time, Pacific Light and Power constructed a huge new transformer station that brought Vernon cheap power from the Big Creek project, while General Petroleum completed a natural gas pipeline from the Midway Field in the San Joaquin Valley. With paved roads and cheap power, the city's raw acreage—most of it still in hogs or cauliflower—began to attract some of Downtown's largest and most claustrophobic firms, like Union Iron Works (200 workers), which moved from Mateo Street in 1914, and Pinney and Boyle (150 workers), which moved from Santa Fe and Palmetto Streets the same year (*Times,* June 14, 1914).

The migration accelerated during the First World War, with oil companies, metal works, lumber yards and building-material manufacturers in the forefront. The City of Los Angeles, in the middle of a massive annexation campaign based on its monopoly of Owens Valley water, seemed relatively indifferent to the future fiscal costs of losing so many important firms. Although advocates of unionism were regularly accused by the *Times* of betraying Los Angeles' competitive interests, no sanction was invoked against the Chamber of Commerce's efforts to site new industry outside the city limits. Vernon, meanwhile, completed flood control works in 1919, while replenishing its supply of developable land with the strategic annexation of the 500-acre Fruitland Association tract in November 1920 (*Times,* Dec. 20, 1914; Pollard, 1928:46–47).

CHICAGO COMES TO LOS ANGELES

Despite these improvements, Vernon and other greenfield industrial areas along the edge of Downtown remained in a primitive state of development in the early 1920s. With local investment tied up in oil speculations and residential construction, industrial land was still poorly capitalized. Site planning was rudimentary, and there was an acute shortage of railroad spurs and connecting trackage. Local companies could compensate by using motor trucks, but branch plants were strictly dependent upon the rail shipment of parts and raw materials from the East. They were also burdened with the high charges of switching freight between three competing transcontinental railroads.

Moreover, neither Vernon nor adjacent districts possessed the experience or ranking to finance infrastructure development through large-scale public debt. And few national manufacturers were willing to undertake the scale of infrastructure and residential investment represented by Goodyear Park (literally a company town within the urban fabric). As a result, the shortage of improved industrial land threatened to become a fatal bottleneck in the Chamber of Commerce's crusade for manufactures.

The *deus ex machina* in this case was massive investment by Chicago capitalists. As far back as the 1880s, Los Angeles' neighbor Pasadena had become the favorite winter resort and, eventually, second home for such Midwestern dynasts as Wrigley, Gamble, Cudahy, Markham, etc. Intimate familiarity with the region and its commercial prospects gradually led to the purchase of latifundian estates like Catalina Island (Wrigley in 1919) and the Cudahy Ranch, as well as strategic investments in meat-packing and manufacture that aimed to integrate Southern California into Chicago's vast sphere of influence.[27] The watershed was the arrival of the Union Stockyard investment group in 1922.

The previous year, the Chamber of Commerce had invited the Union Stockyard management to develop a Los Angeles stockyard district along Chicago lines. After taking a firsthand look at the Southern California situation, the Stockyard's president Arthur Leonard and board chairman J. Spoor approved the purchase of 300 acres of cauliflower fields along the Los Angeles River, just east of Vernon. One-third of the area was dedicated to the Los Angeles Union Stockyards Company, while the rest was subdivided into 125 large industrial lots provided with spurs to the new Los Angeles Junction Railroad (completed in 1923), an independent "beltline" that eliminated switching charges between the three transcontinental railroads. The industrial real-estate operations were managed by the Los Angeles Central Manufacturing District, headquartered in 1924 in an impressive Mission-revival terminal building, designed by architect Frank D. Chase, that also provided warehousing space for 150 Eastern manufacturers.[28]

"Centralization," claimed J. A. McNaughton, the new general manager of the Los Angeles Union Stockyards, "is the keynote to industrial progress in any metropolitan area." Cloned from the parent Central Manufacturing District in Chicago, the L.A. CMD was the nation's second "scientifically planned, intensified industrial district." The original District, a fruit of the Burnham and Olmsted "White City" ideal so powerfully expressed in Chicago's World Columbian Exposition, had been developed by the Union Stockyards group in 1902–05. It married American scientific management and German city-planning in an ambitious attempt to impose order upon an anarchic industrial real-estate market that lacked uniform standards of land use, subdivision and street design.[29]

In both Chicago and Los Angeles, the CMD assembled and subdivided land according to a flexible master-plan, with detailed specifications for rights-of-ways, setbacks, site coverage, building lines, and so on. Acting like private municipalities, the CMDs also provided manufacturers with the Junction Railroads ("America's most efficient freight-handling system"), street maintenance, and the District Police. In addition, they sometimes financed the sale of sites (Boley, 1962:39–43; see also *Times,* July 15 and 22, 1923).

In the Los Angeles case, the high up-front costs of District development were designed to be amortized by the income generated for the Los Angeles Junction Railroad. The District's owners were at pains to distance themselves from the bad odor of previous industrial land speculations. In an interview with the *Times,* they explained that land prices were kept low to encourage growth, but that they accepted only tenants, like national branch plants, "with good prospects for increasing freight shipments." Manufacturers, they claimed, would benefit from the lower freight costs that resulted from the economy of scale produced by the vast volume of stockyard traffic. Demand for industrial space, moreover, was so great that they predicted the District would grow by a new corporate tenant each week. As factory output in Los Angeles increased by an incredible 41% in 1924, the CMD easily achieved its ambitious goal.[30]

This profit strategy, which conceived of the District primarily as an incubator of railroad tonnage, suggested to local journalists that a major railroad probably had a stake which it disguised for anti-trust reasons. Suspicion only increased in 1927 when the District's new produce terminal declared war on the Southern Pacific's Union Terminal downtown. (The Southern Pacific eventually won.) The *Times* alluded to a "persistent theory that the Union Pacific was in a sort of godfather position for the CMD." But it was the Santa Fe (also Chicago-based) that stepped out of the shadows in

1928 to purchase the District, including the Stockyards and the Junction Railroad, after it briefly passed into the hands of millionaire Eugene Thayer. (Again the *Times* speculated that he was only a front man for the Santa Fe, which probably acquired control as early as 1926.) [31]

The strategic calculations behind the purchase were revealed by the Santa Fe's president, William Storey, during the 1931 hearings of the Interstate Commerce Commission in Los Angeles. The I.C.C. was investigating charges made by the Southern Pacific and Union Pacific that Santa Fe's acquisition of the 31-mile Junction Railroad had resulted in discrimination against other carriers. In defense, Storey testified that the Santa Fe, lacking suitable factory real estate of its own, was merely responding to the Union Pacific's promotion of its new industrial district next to its classification yard along Mines Avenue. "We looked to the Central Manufacturing District as territory for location of industries in competition with the lands served exclusively by the Union Pacific." The I.C.C. eventually allowed the Santa Fe Railroad to keep the Junction Railroad.[32]

The railroad corporation's superior capital resources maintained the pace of industrial land development through even the darkest years of the Depression. In the first of a half dozen major expansions that would eventually extend all the way into Orange County, and make the CMD the largest centrally planned industrial district in the world, the Santa Fe quintupled its size in 1929 by purchasing the Bandini Estate Company east of Vernon. The Junction Railroad simultaneously expanded its trackage into the Bandini and Laguna areas, as well as the new Leonis Industrial Tract.[33] Meanwhile, Vernon had already annexed the original core of the District in an election that became the butt of local vaudeville humor:

> The annexation of the Central Manufacturing District, a triangular piece of land of about 300 acres, was unanimously voted yesterday by Mr. and Mrs. A. J. Olsen, 4318 S. Downey Road, the only two legal voters in the district.
>
> The polls, located in the Olsen house, were kept open the legal number of hours, and the two voters were also the election officials. Vernon acquired 28 individual units, adding an assessed valuation of app. $8 million. The principal loser will be the Maywood Grammar School, for years one of the richest in California. (*CMD Magazine,* January 10, 1926)

Thus the District kept one foot in Vernon and one foot out, a pattern of overlapping, essentially private sovereignties that would grow even more complicated in the 1960s with the incorporation of the CMD's Bandini district as the special-use City of Commerce. However anomalous its political geography, Vernon/CMD in the 1920s constituted an evolutionary advance in the separation of the industrial from the residential city. In 1929 more than 300 firms, with a commuter workforce of approximately 16,000, were located in Vernon/CMD This was a minimum ratio of 50 commuter workers for each resident voter. (This ratio would eventually reach 500:1 in the late 1960s.) Less than 5% of the city's surface area was dedicated to residential uses; a ratio that would decline to just 0.3% by 1950.[34]

SLAVES OF THE BUNGALOW?

With land uses so rigorously segregated, where, and how, would workers live in the ideal open shop society? The Chamber of Commerce and the M&M had long touted the California bungalow subdivision as a chief pillar of "industrial freedom." Indeed, Felix Zeehandelaar, the secretary of the M&M, began his testimony before the U.S. Senate's Commission on Industrial Relations in 1914 by showing commissioners photographs of craftsman bungalows on broad palm-lined streets. "I believe we are unique in this city and that a majority of the wage earners, or at least a vast proportion, own their own homes; and that is a condition typical to Los Angeles. . . . On behalf of our association I would strongly urge the commission to take a ride in the auto we will furnish, or as many as you want, to look for yourself at the character of the homes that are occupied at the present time, and have been for years past, by the wage earners who own their homes" (CIR, 1916:5501).

Local trade unionists responded with their own show-and-tell. Curley Grow, a prominent metal-trades organizer, submitted to the Commission an idyllic postcard of West Lake Park that was captioned: "Aren't you coming to California this Spring? The Golden state was never more beautiful, prosperous, attractive in every way, than it is this year. Big agricultural and industrial opportunities are awaiting the arrival of folks like you." The card, millions of which reputedly had been circulated by the Southern Pacific Railroad, listed occupations—some of them on strike—that were waiting for eager immigrants. Grow explained that the railroads, in collaboration with the Chamber of Commerce and the M&M, were using postcard landscapes of Southern California to attract a labor reserve army to lower wages and break strikes (pp. 5550–51).

Other trade unionists told bitter stories about Los Angeles–sponsored land shows that lured Chicago workers westward with false images of cheap homes and bountiful employment. (Their wives were even promised that "through the absence of wet and stormy weather and mud and slush in the streets, clothes last longer and retain their color and shape.") Katherine Edson of the State Industrial Welfare Commission complained about the railroad-subsidized "homeseekers" excursions that every October brought thirty to forty thousand eager pilgrims to the Land of Sunshine. "Now, these are not people of means. They are not this limited class who come here to die. They are the people, the working people. . . . They come out here with a little money expecting to get work. And they say they can save enough money back East to get here, but they have great difficulty in saving enough money here to get back" (pp. 5645, 5687).

While a parade of local capitalists reassured the Commission that home ownership was nurturing a contented labor force, trade unionists stressed the fear and insecurity of families struggling to meet their monthly house payments. Edson pointed to the unusually large number of married women working outside the home. "The fearfulness with which these women—under which these women work—is great. They are so afraid that they are not going to meet the payments on their homes." Mrs. Noel of the National Women's Trade Union League agreed: "I know myself quite a number of women who have for the past seven or eight years worked at any price in order to meet the installment plan payments that result in buying a home." Home ownership as a result sapped the will of workers to fight for higher wages and better working conditions. "The mode of housing in Los Angeles," Mrs. Noel concluded, "while in itself ideal, has produced more out and out slaves in the labor world than perhaps any other condition we have had in Los Angeles" (pp. 5686, 5718, 5721).

Confronted with such polarized views of the housing situation, the Commission solicited testimony from the two leading developers of blue-collar tracts in the fast-growing areas of south-central and east Los Angeles. Avery McCarthy, who had subdivided 29 tracts in the Vernon-Central district south of Downtown since 1905, explained the operation of the installment plan system that was so excoriated by labor leaders. In order to purchase the $2,000, five-room bungalow that was considered the regional housing standard, workers paid $100 down and $12–$25 per month. The financing was carried by the developer without a mortgage, and McCarthy admitted that his gross profit, including 7.5% interest charges, was $1,500 or 75% per unit (pp. 5857–62).

The $2,000 bungalow, however, was far beyond the reach of the "$2 a day men" who composed the majority of Los Angeles' unskilled labor force. To meet their needs, Edwin Janss (whose Janss Investment Company would later be identified with such prestigious developments as Westwood Village and Holmby Hills) was subdividing thousands of lots in Ramona Acres and Belvedere Heights, a half-hour east of Downtown by streetcar. His cheapest model, a two-room shack without a bathroom, sold for $625 on a tiny lot. For $10 per month, however, an enterprising family could purchase a larger lot suitable for growing vegetables or raising chickens. They might live in a tent or temporary shack while accumulating the extra income to build a house, perhaps from a prefabricated kit. In a typical Janss or McCarthy tract, residents had the option of buying a bungalow from the developer/builder or constructing it themselves (pp. 5826–31, 5858).

Although neither Janss nor Zeehandelaar could furnish the Commission with any proof that a majority of workers were actually owner-occupiers, low-end house prices were significantly cheaper in Los Angeles than in most eastern industrial cities.[35] In part, this was a dispensation of the mild climate that allowed construction with thin lath-and-plaster walls. But it was also the result of the M&M's relentless war on the unionized building trades that kept carpenters' wages 25% below the San Francisco standard. After 1919, however, land inflation, stoked by the huge population influx, began to erode Los Angeles' comparative advantage in building costs. At the same time, there was a growing disjuncture between the movement of new industry to the Vernon/CMD area and the location of blue-collar housing. A survey of several major Vernon factories revealed that fully half of the employees spent more than 96 minutes—20% of the working day—commuting to and from work.[36]

The boldest solution to this incipient housing crisis—and most fully in keeping with Los Angeles' claim to be inventing a new social/industrial order—was provided by a local firm, Pacific Ready-Cut Homes. Founded in 1909 by William Butte and Francis Barker as Pacific Portable Construction Company, the firm grew rich prefabricating bunkhouses and mess halls for the crews building the great aqueduct from Owens Valley. At the end of World War I, the re-christened company moved from Downtown to a huge factory on a 24-acre site along the Vernon/Huntington Park border. Employing more than 1,000 workers on a series of assembly lines, Pacific Ready-Cut could produce a complete bungalow kit (containing pre-cut lumber, nails, paint, plumbing and electrical hardware, and roofing) in 20 minutes, or 25 homes per day. The kits were usually shipped to buyers via Pacific Electric "red cars" (which carried freight as well as passengers) and took merely two days for a small crew (provided by Ready-Cut or hired by the home owner) to assemble (Flynn, 1986: 11–15, 49–55).

Pacific Ready-Cut's motto was "Henry Ford's Principle—large production/low price—Applied to Home-building," and the firm boasted of producing the quality of a Lincoln with the economy of a Ford. Butte and Barker achieved dramatic economies through buying huge quantities of lumber off-season and by abolishing the role of skilled carpenters in the construction process. In 1924, when the average single-family home in Los Angeles was valued at $3,224, the most popular Pacific model, a basic bungalow with a Spanish stucco exterior, cost only $2,750 assembled. Unlike the mass-built ranch-style home of the 1940s, the 1920s bungalows allowed a certain spectrum of individual customization. "There were approximately fifteen basic designs upon which Pacific expanded to produce hundreds of floor plans. Rarely, though, were two models offered with identical plans." In a typical subdivision, Zorro (Spanish-colonial facade) lived next door to Robin Hood (English-Tudor facade) or Hansel and Gretel (Alpine facade).[37]

Where lots were large enough, families grew fruits and vegetables to the delight of Chamber of Commerce propagandists who boasted that home gardens reduced the cost of living and therefore wages. As one recruiting pamphlet for industrial investment put it, "the real secret of the efficiency of the workers in Southern California may be found in their home life. . . . For a little effort on his part, [the worker] can have the fruits and vegetables known in the East, at much less cost, his living expenses can be sharply reduced and his family supplied with luxuries from his own backyard" (Chamber of Commerce, 1927:2).

Although Pacific, the third largest factory homebuilder in the nation (after Sears and Aladdin), exported bungalow kits throughout the Southwest and even Latin America, their greatest concentration was in the arc of new subdivisions around the Central Manufacturing District. A Huntington Park firm, Metzger and Kaler, financed and assembled thousands of Ready-Cut homes in the cities of Bell, Maywood, Huntington Park, South Gate, and the unincorporated Bandini and Florence districts. By the 1940 census, 32,000 production workers—nearly half of Los Angeles County's manufacturing workforce outside of aircraft and motion pictures—were living in 1920s-era subdivisions, south and southeast of Vernon/CMD.[38]

The political configuration of this region became an important variable in the overall balance of class power. If the residential ideal of the open shop order was defined by the extension of de-skilling Fordism to home construction, as exemplified by the Ready-Cut bungalow, then the political ideal was represented by the contrast of the planned factory district, with its central management and formidable political clout, to the political balkanization of the new blue-collar suburbs.

Los Angeles in this regard followed the centrifugal model pioneered by Chicago, whose suburban industrial belt was already splintered into tiny, competitive municipalities (see Harris, 1994). The singularity in the Los Angeles case was that so many subdivisions, undoubtedly seduced by the low tax environment of the county, resisted incorporation. When they did incorporate, as in the cases of Bell and Maywood in the 1920s, or Bell Gardens and Cudahy in the 1960s, it was only to escape annexation by a larger municipality. (Significantly all four of these Lilliputian cities are only a mile square and lack significant industrial or commercial land use.) This "pathological" fragmentation of civic life gave residents little leverage in future struggles against such powerful and centralized interests as the Leonis dynasty or the Santa Fe railroad.

URBAN EUGENICS

For Los Angeles' industrial boosters of the 1920s, the planned factory district and the mass-produced bungalow were pillars of the open shop strategy, but Nature was its chief ally. In its promotional literature, the Chamber of Commerce, at times sounding like a businessmen's franchise of the Sierra Club, constantly invoked the city's natural setting as a prime reason for investment. Los Angeles, it promised, offered the Eastern manufacturer, burdened "with labor difficulties, inefficient workers and a constantly rising labor cost . . . a real opportunity to operate WHERE NATURE HELPS INDUSTRY MOST."[39]

As we have seen, Southern California's Mediterranean environment did give various gifts to the capitalist. In the first place, the climate lowered traditional overhead costs of lighting, heating, and insulation, as well as allowing lighter, cheaper materials to be used in plant construction. There was also less production lost to bad weather and seasonal illness. Secondly, as trade unionists continued to complain throughout the 1930s, the region's real and imagined charms kept labor markets overstocked with new immigrants ready to work under open shop conditions. And, finally, nature tranquilized the working class—or so the Chamber of Commerce claimed—through myriad opportunities for health and leisure. "There is no need for the manufacturer in Southern California to think of expenditures for recreational purposes. Nature provides such for him free of expense. . . . Consequently the worker finds rest and refreshment for his daily tasks."

The open shop, by aggressively capitalizing climate and landscape as productive forces, was establishing new competitive advantages in what Los Angeles elites had long conceived as a fundamentally Darwinian competition between urban centers. More precisely, the Chamber of Commerce and the M&M claimed that they were engineering natural selection to attract the most efficient workers from all over the country. Indeed, the very act of moving to militantly anti-union Los Angeles was characterized as a liberation of individual energy from the stifling collectivism of the East. "Hundreds of thousands of families have migrated to Los Angeles and Southern California from the east, cutting loose from their old associations, and in their new homes have sought new employment. Having once broken the old associations, in Los Angeles they seek employment, bringing into our industrial structure employees of a very high standard of efficiency."

Los Angeles' gain, moreover, was other regions' loss in a zero-sum competition for the moral and biological aristocracy of the working class. "If the best American types are attracted to municipalities where the 'American Plan' prevails," said a *Wall Street Journal* editorial widely quoted by the Chamber of Commerce, "it follows that the process of selection set up diminishes the grade of citizenry in closed shop cities and an indirect relationship is established between unionism and the tax rate." An inverse relationship was thus assumed between the "grade of citizenry" or "quotient of Americanism" and the proportion of foreign-born and potentially radical workers from eastern and southern Europe. Contemporary academic eugenicists openly worried about the "dysgenic environment" being created by the large families of Catholic immigrants, Jews, and hillbillies. ("The city's greatest evil," complained Chicago School sociologist Roswell Johnson, is "the subfecundity of its superiors.")[40] Los Angeles, by deliberate intervention, was reversing biological and cultural degeneration. As the premier American Plan metropolis, with the smallest percentage of European new immigrants, it envisioned itself as the racial antipode to San Francisco, Chicago, Cleveland and New York with their teeming Irish, Italian, Polish and Jewish populations.

Los Angeles, indeed, had long distinguished itself as a national, even world center of "Aryan Revival" in opposition to the immigrant-dominated industrial cities of the East. As Charles Fletcher Lummis had boasted years before, "the ignorant, hopelessly un-American type of foreigner which infests and largely controls Eastern cities is almost unknown here" (quoted in Starr, 1985:89). In the 1920s the most prestigious apostle of the Chamber of Commerce's vulgar Darwinist ideology was Nobel laureate Robert Millikan from the California Institute of Technology, who toured the country promoting industrial investment in the Los Angeles area. In a set speech echoing Lummis, he declared that Southern California was "as England two hundred years ago, the westernmost outpost of Nordic civilization." The region, moreover, had the "exceptional opportunity" of having a "population which is twice as Anglo-Saxon as that existing in New York, Chicago or any of the other great cities of this country."[41]

Southern California, in other words, was a Mediterranean land without any pesty Mediterranean immigrants to cause discontent. This good fortune, however, could be preserved only through vigilant weeding and pruning in the garden. Joseph Widney, the former president of the University of Southern California and an ardent Aryanist, called upon Los Angeles' captains of industry to become "the first Captains in the race war" (Kay, 1993: 61). Racial-selectionist ideology, of course, was in perfect resonance with open shop philosophy, and it was no accident, as Lily Kay has pointed out, that Los Angeles in the 1920s was the world capital of the eugenics movement. "The grip of conservative Republican politics and its nativist fervor juxtaposed against rising social disorder fostered in Southern California an extreme form of negative eugenics" (Kay, 1993:63).

Although some local industrialists supported Paul Popenoe and his Pasadena-based Human Betterment Foundation, which advocated mass sterilization of the unfit (and provided an inspiration to Germany's National Socialists),[42] the real vogue in Chamber of Commerce circles was "positive eugenics" or "euthenics": the purported science of "promoting the reproduction of superior human stock." Just as local citrus growers grafted from only the most fertile fruit-bearing trees, so did Los Angeles' business leaders hope to graft only the most loyal and efficient "American qualities" onto their workforce. There was considerable conceptual overlap, moreover, be-

TABLE 4.4.   Official descriptions of community labor markets

Bell:	Nine thousand people—no Negroes and very few Mexican and Chinese.
Bellflower:	Ample supply of good labor, of the open shop type . . . much of the necessary food supply is provided from the people's own small gardens.
Compton:	Conditions are good, since workers may live close to their work in inexpensive homes of individuality, where flowers and gardens may be grown the year around. White help prevails.
Huntington Park:	This population is 100% American of the White race.
Lynnwood:	. . . being restricted to the white races can furnish ample labor of the better class.
South Gate:	Abundant supply of skilled and unskilled white labor . . . no foreign population.

Collated from various 1920s Industrial Department publications.

tween positive eugenics and the contemporary passion for "human engineering" as pioneered by the welfare departments of major industrial corporations.[43] What Ford was doing on a corporate level, however, the Chamber of Commerce proposed to implement on an urban scale.

Trade groups and suburban chambers of commerce, along with realtors and landlords, all played important roles in the struggle to maintain "Anglo-Saxon" hegemony in the workforce. For their part, Los Angeles' industrial employers, especially in the metal trades and the lumber industry, relied on extensive blacklists, regularly updated by private detective agencies, to exclude job applicants with union backgrounds.[44] Presumably employers also discriminated against immigrant ethnicities that failed to meet open shop standards of ideal American labor. In addition, subdivision covenants universally restricted occupancy to whites or gentiles only, and informal discrimination by landlords and realtors against southern and eastern Europeans may also have been quite common.

Indeed, the new blue-collar suburbs that surrounded the Central Manufacturing District on three sides—many of them dominated by the Ku Klux Klan during the 1920s—were proud to proclaim their ethnic cleanness. Table 4.4 quotes from official community descriptions, prepared by local chambers of commerce, that were circulated throughout the United States by the Industrial Department of the Los Angeles Chamber.

Not all factory workers, however, lived in idyllic bungalows or punched time clocks in modern branch plants. To accommodate employers' demands for a flexible supply of low-wage labor, the Chamber of Commerce made a dramatic exception to its general opposition to foreign-born workers. "We have a Mexican population in this section in excess of 50,000

people and these people make excellent workers, the men as common laborers in different crafts and the women make splendid workers in textile
plants, wearing apparel plants and in other plants where skilled female labor is desired." Indeed the Chamber was ecstatic about the genetic aptitude
of Mexicanas for garment work: "these women come from a race who have
been workers in textiles, laces and embroideries for centuries and are naturally adept with their fingers" (Chamber of Commerce, 1927).

A dual labor market, integral to Los Angeles' manufacturing economy,
was thus defined on the basis of a racial hierarchicalization of efficient
Anglo-Saxons and obedient Mexicans. Unlike the new immigrant nationalities of the East, who were infected with the deadly virus of Bolshevism, Los
Angeles' Mexicans were depicted by the Chamber of Commerce as a good,
simple-hearted peasantry. Apart from their central role in Los Angeles' fast-
growing sportswear industry (10,000 workers in 1930), and their traditional
niche in railroad construction, Mexican workers during the 1920s also became the backbone of the construction materials and furniture industries.
Their wage levels were largely determined by prevailing rates in the geographically overlapping markets for agricultural labor, and thousands of
workers cycled annually between citrus and industry. In the last instance,
the conditions of their labor were established, not by the invisible hand, but
by "extra-economic coercion": direct use of force or the threat of deporta-
tion. Mexicans, in addition, were excluded from most of the new bungalow
subdivisions, and their *colonias* usually grew out of existing ranch or railroad
camps scattered in the interstices of the emergent industrial-suburban grid
of the 1920s: Vernondale, Simonstown, Laguna, Watts, Hicks Camp, Bandini, and so on.

Thus the geography of caste—literally, industrial peonage—completed
the map of Los Angeles' central industrial belt. The sleek Art Deco exteri-
ors of the new branch plants in Vernon and Bandini dissimulated the
threatened and real violence, coordinated by the M&M, that undergirded
the idyll of "Nature's Workshop" (official Chamber of Commerce slogan).
Despite the Chamber's eugenic fantasy of a racially elite, contented working
class, Los Angeles was no more immunized against industrial revolt than
Seattle or Detroit. The golden age of the open shop, as defined by the *Times*,
lasted barely longer than the 1920s boom. After the final hoopla of the 1932
Olympic Games, the sunshine began visibly to dim in Southern California.
As banks closed and breadlines grew, it was increasingly difficult to mask
social conditions with postcard clichés of palm trees and bungalows. With
the arrival of the CIO in 1937, rebel workers in the new tire, auto and steel
plants, together with their Mexican counterparts in the garment and furniture sweatshops, began to reshape industrial Los Angeles in their own militant image.

NOTES

1. The figure for metal works is Lowe's conjecture since machine shop and iron works employers refused to cooperate with the survey.

2. See story headlined, "City Looms as Seventh in Nation's Industry," *Los Angeles Times,* Dec. 20, 1924.

3. The industrial boom was diluted by the more rapid growth of the entire workforce. Thus manufacturing employment actually declined as a percentage of the labor force from 1920 (28.3%) to 1930 (22.5%). Los Angeles, moreover, had the highest percentage of tertiary employment (57.8% in 1930) of any major city (Coons and Miller, 1941:7, Table 1).

4. The dispersed motion picture and oil industries, however, depended upon specialized clusters of support services. Hollywood, for example, concentrated post-production services, casual labor, and marginal, "poverty row" studios. The oil tool industry was likewise concentrated in Huntington Park and Compton.

5. A major exception was Ford's big assembly plant at Los Angeles Harbor. Here, however, location was dictated by the overseas export orientation (to Australia and South America).

6. "An Open Shop Milestone," *Los Angeles Times,* Jan. 1, 1930.

7. Cf. articles in *Los Angeles Times* on home products, Jan. 5 and March 25, 1919.

8. On Bishop, as well as the War Industries Board report, see *Los Angeles Times,* Feb. 9, 1919.

9. On Chamber infighting, see "Campaign Justified," Los Angeles Chamber of Commerce, *Bulletin,* May 23, 1927. Washburn had made his views known as early as 1909; see Los Angeles Chamber of Commerce, *Members Annual-1909,* pp. 54–56; also his obituary, *Los Angeles Times,* Feb. 5, 1935.

10. Los Angeles Chamber of Commerce, *Bulletin,* Feb. 25, 1925; Apr. 18, May 16, 1927; Feb. 14, 1937 (recalling Firestone and Ford visit); and Chamber, stenographic minutes (Box 84), Jan. 12, 1933 (history of industrial crusade and role of A. Arnold).

11. On the DWP's central role in 1920s Los Angeles, see Erie, 1994.

12. From Chamber of Commerce *Bulletin,* May 23, 1927.

13. Industrial Department, Los Angeles Chamber of Commerce, *General Industrial Report of Los Angeles County, California and Surrounding Communities,* typescript master, Los Angeles, 1930, n.p. (hereafter *Industrial Report*); and Chamber, *Bulletin,* Dec. 12, 1938 (on history of solicitation efforts).

14. See the *Industrial Report,* 1930.

15. From *Industrial Report* and Chamber *Bulletin,* June 29, 1927.

16. Branch plants crucially depended upon rail for shipment of parts and materials from the East. The very largest plants, like Firestone, Goodyear, or later Chevrolet, chose sites along main lines to the harbor. Most, however, found it preferable to locate in the Vernon/CMD complex with its established infrastructure and heavy density of rail spurs.

17. This was an installment in Corey's fascinating series on working-class life in Edwardian Los Angeles.

18. WPA (Works Progress Administration) 1940, calculated from block data maps.

19. See Eberle and Riggleman Economic Service, *Weekly Letter* (Los Angeles) for Sept. 21, 1925, and Feb. 15, 1926.

20. In addition to his obituary file in the Los Angeles Municipal Library, Wheeler's career can be reconstructed from extant issues of *Common Sense* and *Western Comrade*—two Socialist periodicals from Southern California. Analysis of the records of election returns, Los Angeles City Archives, shows that the sixth, seventh and eighth wards also provided large Socialist majorities for Job Harriman in the December 5, 1911, and June 3, 1913, mayoral elections.

21. Board of Directors, Los Angeles Chamber of Commerce, stenographic minutes, January 11, 1922; and Eberle and Riggleman, Feb. 15, 1926 (on comparative taxes and land values).

22. The East Side Organization, under the leadership of George Baker, an employee of the Bandini Land Company, crusaded for infrastructure improvements east of the river and was a significant developmental force in the 1920s. See, for example, Baker's speech to the Central Manufacturing District in *Los Angeles Times,* July 26, 1926.

23. The river once ran through the center of Vernon, but its diked banks were shifted eastward at the beginning of the century after a bitter battle between landowners on opposing banks. See Pollard, 1928:20.

24. In 1902 Huntington routed the Pacific Electric through eponymous Huntington Park and the new tract of Bell. The actual development of the area was undertaken by two of his close associates, A. Burbank and E. Baker. (For background, see Huntington Park, *Daily Signal,* Aug. 13, 1923.)

25. On the origin of Vernon, cf. Kilty, 1963:16–23 and 44; *Los Angeles Times,* Feb. 7, 1904, and Aug. 8, 1917 (retrospective); Nelson, 1952:187–88; and Pollard, 1928:21–23.

26. 1980 Census of Population.

27. See *Los Angeles Times,* Feb. 13, 1919, on Wrigley investments.

28. H. Poronto (President of the Central Manufacturing District), "Why Chicago Came to Los Angeles," Chamber of Commerce *Bulletin,* Jan. 1922. See also *Los Angeles Times,* Jan. 1, June 17, July 15, 1923.

29. McNaughton speaking to the Huntington Park Chamber of Commerce, *Los Angeles Times,* Mar. 21, 1923.

30. See "The Development of a New Manufacturing District," *Los Angeles Times,* Feb. 15, 1925, pp. 20–23.

31. See *Los Angeles Times,* Mar. 17, 1928, on produce war and purchase of CMD.

32. See *Los Angeles Times,* June 17, 1923, and March 28, 1931 (on Interstate Commerce Commission hearings).

33. Boley, 1962:41; *CMD Magazine,* Jan.–Feb. 1966, p. 18; *Santa Fe Magazine,* Nov. 1929, pp. 21–25; and *Times,* May 25, 1930. Bandini retained ownership of the 10,000-acre Laguna parcel for residential development.

34. City of Vernon, *Fact Sheet,* 1929; *Times,* May 25, 1930 ("Vernon Sees Epochal Industrial Growth"); and Nelson, 1952:180. See different estimates in Pollard, 1928:62 and Kilty, 1963:49.

35. Los Angeles had the highest home ownership rate in the nation (41.2%). Contrast to San Francisco (28.2%), Chicago (26.1%) or New York (12.2%). (Los Angeles Chamber of Commerce, *Bulletin,* May 1925, p. 21.)

36. Perry and Perry, 1963:27–31; Eberle and Riggleman, *Weekly Letter* for Feb. 15, 1926.

37. Flynn, 1986. Ready-Cut's low-end competitor was Redimade Building Company, located at 6310 South Park Ave., which sold a one-bedroom "economy home" for only $524. For a typical ad, see Los Angeles *Record,* April 3, 1926.

38. Chamber of Commerce (1927); *1940 Census;* and Huntington Park *Signal,* May 20, 1926.

39. Cf. Arthur Kinney (Industrial Commissioner), "Southland Climate Big Manufacturing Factor," *Los Angeles Times,* Jan. 27, 1918; and Chamber of Commerce, *Facts About Contented Los Angeles* (n.d.), p. 10 ("The Home of Contented Labor"), the source of all quotations attributed to the Chamber in the discussion that follows.

40. Johnson, 1925.

41. See Millikan Archive, box 37, California Institute of Technology, Pasadena.

42. See Kay, 1993:39. German eugenicists publicly acknowledged their "great debt" to California's forced sterilization program, the most sweeping in the world before 1930. See Kevles, 1985:118.

43. See the discussion of eugenics as mainstream scientific management culture in Trent (1994:135–44).

44. The 1938–39 La Follette Committee hearings in Los Angeles used Senate subpoena power to pry open a window into the inner workings of the open shop, from blacklisting to company spies. See *Violations of Free Speech and the Rights of Labor,* Hearings before a Subcommittee of the Senate Committee on Education and Labor, 76th Congress, 3rd Session, Parts 8, 14–D, 52–75. Washington, D.C., 1940.

REFERENCES

Boley, R. (1962) *Industrial Districts: Principles in Practice.* Washington, D.C.: Urban Land Institute.

California Railroad Commission, Engineering Department (1920) *Report on Railroad Grade Crossing Elimination and Passenger and Freight Terminals in Los Angeles.* Sacramento.

Coons, A., and A. Miller (1941) *An Economic and Industrial Survey of the Los Angeles and San Diego Areas.* Sacramento: California State Planning Board.

Corey, W. A. (1906) "The proletarian wards of Los Angeles." *Common Sense,* May 26.

Erie, S. (1994) "How the urban west was won: The local state and economic growth in Los Angeles, 1880–1932." Manuscript.

Flynn, C. (1986) "Pacific Ready-Cut Homes: Mass-Produced Bungalows in Los Angeles, 1908–1942." Unpublished MA thesis, Urban Planning, University of California, Los Angeles.

Harris, R. (1994) "Chicago's other suburbs." *The Geographical Review* 84:394–410.

Hise, G. (1994) "The Minimum Ideal: Mass-Housing, Working-Class Home Ownership, and the Blue-Collar Suburb in California, 1935–1950." Unpublished Ph.D. dissertation, Geography, University of California, Berkeley.

Johnson, R. (1925) "The eugenics of the city," in Ernest Burgess (ed.), *The Urban Community.* Chicago: University of Chicago Press.

Kay, L. (1993) *The Molecular Vision of Life: Caltech, the Rockefeller Foundation and the Rise of the New Biology.* Oxford: Oxford University Press.

Kevles, D. (1985) *In the Name of Eugenics.* Cambridge, MA: Harvard University Press.

Kilty, J. (1963) *Leonis of Vernon.* New York: privately published.

Los Angeles Chamber of Commerce (n.d) *Facts About Contented Los Angeles.* Los Angeles.

Los Angeles Chamber of Commerce (1927) *Facts About Industrial Los Angeles: Nature's Workshop.* Los Angeles.

Los Angeles Department of City Planning (1964) *City Planning in Los Angeles — A History* (typescript), Municipal Library, Los Angeles.

Merchants and Manufacturers Association (1986) *Celebrating 90 Years of Service.* Los Angeles.

Nelson, H. (1952) "The Vernon Area, California—A study of the political factor in urban geography." *Annals of the Association of American Geographers* 42.

Perry, L., and R. Perry (1963) *A History of the Los Angeles Labor Movement, 1911–1941.* Berkeley: University of California Press.

Pollard, G. (1928) "Recent Developments in Commerce and Industry in Southern California Using Vernon as a Type." Unpublished MA thesis, History, University of Southern California.

Sanger, R. D. (1927) "How industry came to Los Angeles County." Los Angeles Chamber of Commerce *Bulletin,* June 22.

Starr, K. (1985) *Inventing the Dream: California through the Progressive Era.* Oxford: Oxford University Press.

Trent, J. (1994) *Inventing the Feeble Mind.* Berkeley: University of California Press.

U.S. Senate, Commission on Industrial Relations (1916) *Final Report and Testimony Submitted to Congress by the Commission on Industrial Relations,* 64th Congress, 1st session. Senate Document 415, Volume VI, Washington, D.C.

Viehe, F. (1981) "Black gold suburbs: The influence of the extractive industry on the suburbanization of Los Angeles, 1890–1930." *Journal of Urban History* 8.

Willard, C. D. (1899) *A History of the Chamber of Commerce of Los Angeles, California.* Los Angeles: Kingsley-Barnes & Neuner Company.

Williams, J. (1996) "Fuel at last: Oil and gas for California, 1860s–1940s." *California History* 75(2):114–27.

Works Progress Administration (1940) *Housing Survey Covering Portions of the City of Los Angeles,* Vol. III. Los Angeles.

CHAPTER FIVE

"Another World"

Work, Home, and Autonomy in Blue-Collar Suburbs

Nancy Quam-Wickham

In 1922, Mr. and Mrs. John East ventured into downtown Los Angeles to purchase some camping equipment at a large sporting goods emporium. When they arrived outside the store, John East left his wife, Lorecia, and their three small children in the car, parked at curbside, while he ran inside to make the family's purchases. Unfortunately for the Easts, it was rush hour in downtown Los Angeles, parking was prohibited, and within moments one of Los Angeles's finest arrived to order Mrs. East to move her vehicle. Only intending to move the car as far as the nearest legal parking space, Lorecia East soon found herself on a frightening adventure that lasted more than two hours. After driving several blocks, Mrs. East pulled into one of the city's new private parking lots, parked her car, and instructed her three children (ages 3, 4, and 6) to wait for her. After assuring the lot attendant that she would return in just a few minutes, Mrs. East dashed off in search of her husband.

But Mrs. East promptly got hopelessly lost. Frantic, confused by Los Angeles's wide streets and cosmopolitan nature, she became even more disoriented. Meanwhile, after the just-a-few minutes had lapsed into more than an hour, the parking lot attendant also panicked. Convinced that Mrs. East had abandoned her children in his lot, he called the police, who soon arrived to take charge of them. Back outside the store, John East became alarmed when he could find no trace of his wife or children. Thinking they had been abducted, he, too, called the police. Finally, some time later, Mrs. East regained the presence of mind to approach a local traffic cop who helped reunite her with her—by this time—very anxious and very unhappy family.[1]

A few years later, in 1927, Dyer Bennett had an encounter with Los Angeles, too. But Bennett's venture was much shorter than Mrs. East's. Arriving in the city, he got off the train, walked to the curb at the front of Union

Pacific's terminal, took one look around at "all these people, these wagons, and horses and mules hauling stuff, and these Model T's and Model A's running around, and the trolley streetcars clanging by," then abruptly turned around, strode back into the terminal, and boarded a train going back home. Some 60 years later, Bennett, a boilermaker who later nearly lost his life in an industrial accident, recalled that he had never seen anything that "scared me as much in my life" as that initial encounter with Los Angeles.[2]

At first glance, these two encounters with 1920s Los Angeles would seem to be standard tales of urban-rural tension, of the dismay and social alienation that countryfolk routinely experienced once they landed in the big city. Yet these stories have an unusual twist, for both "victims" were residents of greater metropolitan Los Angeles: the Easts were from Long Beach, fewer than 30 miles south of downtown Los Angeles, while Bennett was from Brea, about 20 miles southeast of the city. At one level, we can attribute their experiences to their backgrounds as residents of the small towns that dotted the Southern California landscape of the 1920s. But at another level, their experiences demonstrate a different social reality: the strong sense of separation, of isolation and independence from the metropolis that was shared by many working-class residents of Los Angeles's blue-collar suburbs. Both John East and Dyer Bennett were oil workers: East was a driller in the Signal Hill oil field, while Bennett was a boilermaker in the Brea-Olinda oil field in northern Orange County. Indeed, John Royal, who was born and raised in San Pedro and became a union fisherman, called Los Angeles "another world," noting that none of his friends—all from working-class families—ventured into the city before they were 20 or so years of age. "Los Angeles was where the rich and middle-class people lived, not us."[3] "We didn't have any of the social life of the city," longshoreman Bill Ward later recalled about San Pedro residents. He went on to say that the working-class community was all anti-L.A.[4] Newspapers in working-class towns derisively referred to Los Angeles as "that tax-imposing place fifteen miles down the road," or, more commonly, simply as "Louse Angeles."[5]

Only recently have historians of the region's urbanization acknowledged the class dimensions of population dispersal in Los Angeles. Instead, most standard works have tended to see the suburb as a monolithic entity, varying little over time or space.[6] Emphasis has been placed on the horizontal spread of middle-class suburbs as places of consumption, brought about first by the interurban rail system and later by the automobile and the region's extensive freeways. Yet blue-collar towns proliferated throughout the region, especially in the suburban ring south of the Los Angeles city limits. This essay is indebted to the pioneering work of urban historian Fred Viehe, who has noted that many of these new blue-collar suburbs arose in the 1920s, as the Southern California oil boom spurred industrial development and suburban growth.[7] While acknowledging Viehe's revision of the suburbanization model, I argue two points here. First, whatever their state of development prior to 1921, the residents of Los Angeles's suburbs seldom hesitated to embrace industrial development once the oil boom began in the early 1920s. Communities that had once prided themselves on being rural towns for home folks now rushed to get a piece of the oil and industrial action, in the process casting off any claims to the rustic ideal of the archetypal Los Angeles suburb. The decisions these towns made during the 1920s and 1930s set metropolitan development on the track toward creating Los Angeles as we know it today.[8]

Second, given the overwhelming industrial identity of many of these blue-collar suburbs, especially the close proximity of basic industrial sites—primarily factories, oil fields, and transportation complexes—to housing, there was little spatial or cultural separation between work and home. Work, as much as consumption, structured the lives of blue-collar suburbanites: men, women, and children. People saw themselves first as workers (or families of workers), then as residents of a particular town, but rarely as Los Angelenos. Most of this discussion will focus on life in the region's oil and harbor towns, where an estimated 70,000 workers labored during the 1920s. The extension of the argument to other industries in the region is based on a work-in-progress that suggests that the experience of industrial town residents was not at all anomalous or unusual.[9]

In the decade of the 1920s, the Eden-like landscape of Los Angeles would become the most intensive oil field development in history.[10] Oil production, refining, and transportation were central elements in the economic transformation of Southern California in this period. Southern California's tremendous petroleum industry accounted for about 20 percent of the world's output of crude oil during part of the 1920s.[11]

The oil industry dramatically transformed Southern California's landscape. Located within the country's fastest growing metropolitan area, the oil industry accelerated changes in urban form by altering existing land-use patterns, contributing to speculation in real estate, and—most important for this discussion—encouraging industrialization and suburbanization. The example of the small working-class suburb of Lomita illustrates how profoundly oil development changed the social and cultural character of southland communities. On the eve of oil development in the early 1920s, Lomita was a small community with a population of approximately 4,000 people, located just north of the San Pedro harbor and near the industrial town of Torrance. And before oil drilling commenced, Lomita was a typical Los Angeles suburb, in the ways that historians have come to define Southern California's suburbs: it was located at some distance from the center of the metropolis, Los Angeles; it was a community of single-family homes; and its residents shared, in historian Robert Fogelson's words, an anti-urban ethos.[12]

Figure 5.1. Looking south toward beach, from above the McMillan Oil Company refinery on Walnut Avenue in Signal Hill, a major oil-producing area in Southern California, August 1928. Note the well-established residential neighborhoods, a school building, and other business establishments in background. *Historical Society of Long Beach*

Yet however typical Lomita may have been, it did not conform to the predominant cultural view of an early twentieth-century Los Angeles suburb: it did not represent the triumph of middle-class residential uniformity, materialistic Puritanism, and political conservatism. At the beginning of 1922, like many other blue-collar suburbs in the region, Lomita was an unincorporated area. People could still buy acreage cheap in a community of "chicken corralls [*sic*], alfalfa patches, small dairies," where Issei-run truck gardens were commonplace. The local newspaper, the Lomita *News-Letter*, reported that many of the community's streets were nothing more than "cow trails." The town had no street lights or gas service, and most residents still heated their homes with and cooked on wood- or kerosene-burning stoves. The newspaper prided itself on being "a home paper for home folks," and featured weekly columns on local church activities, county farm bureau

doings, and cottage gardening methods. According to one prominent resident, Lomita was "but a thrifty little community of home people."[13]

The pace and nature of life in Lomita, as elsewhere, changed dramatically once oil was discovered in the southland. In 1922, oil development work began in nearby Torrance; by June of that year, the Lomita newspaper reported that the Torrance field's discovery well was flowing at 1,000 barrels per day. "Wells may yet be pumping oil from our own back yards," the paper predicted hopefully. By July 1922, newspaper headlines proclaimed that Lomita was within the proven "oil belt," although the town would not see its first derrick erected until months later.[14]

Industrial development abounded in the region. Property values skyrocketed as companies relocating their operations to Los Angeles sought prime industrial land. One company planned to build a gasoline refinery in

Torrance. In May 1922, the Santa Fe Railroad, itself a large oil concern, proposed a new line from the refining center of El Segundo (northwest of Lomita) through the town, then southward to Union Oil's export wharves at the harbor in Wilmington. During the late spring and summer of 1922, the Union Tool Company compelled its Torrance steelworkers and machinists, many of whom lived in Lomita, to work overtime just to keep up with the rush of orders for oil field equipment. Some 3,000 men worked in Torrance's oil tool supply manufacturing firms, most of them at the huge Union shops.[15] Drilling companies spudded in exploration wells in Gardena, and in Watts and Compton, to the north and northeast of Lomita.[16] Derricks went up just to the west of Lomita, and, in a northwesterly direction, just outside the city of Redondo Beach.[17]

In many cases, these blue-collar towns rapidly shed any remnants of their pastoral suburban identity, instead rushing to celebrate heavy industrial development. Press reports of oil development were downright giddy. Consider one account of Torrance:

> Thousands of oil workers are toiling relentlessly day and night in the local fields. . . . The concert of sounds made by the ponderous machinery, gushing steam from exhaust pipes and the steady drive of powerful engines tells the story of immense doings. . . . It is becoming more wonderful as the carpenters, who are the vanguards, put up a derrick almost in a day, to be followed by giant truck loads of machinery and oil rigging apparatus. Thus the field grows with magnetic power. . . . With every well a success where will the end be?[18]

By December, one booster remarked, "Lomita has much to be thankful for in addition to her many beautiful homes, orchards, and chicken ranches." Indeed, new derricks were "springing up in most every direction, as well-paid, happy workers are piercing the bowels of old Mother Earth" for oil, "that wonderful liquid gold." Ironically, oil had not yet been discovered in Lomita.[19] A month later, in January 1923, one writer reported that "Lomita [is] in the throes of an oil boom," where the turmoil and excitement of oil development had supplanted the "peace and quietness" of the town. By the end of the month, the local paper had replaced the regular column on horticultural techniques, "The Cottage Gardener," with a new column, "In the Grease: Notes Gleaned While the Oil Editor Bumps Around Proven Territory."[20] Coverage of local oil developments dominated the front page of every issue of the *News-Letter* for the next eighteen months.

Oil profoundly changed the social life and cultural identity of residents in the Los Angeles basin during the 1920s. In 1921, before oil was discovered in its environs, Lomita was a town of peace-loving homemakers, the type of people who were then flocking into Southern California on every train and steamship coming west and south.[21] Less than two years later, in the midst of unabated activity in the local oil fields, Lomita's newspaper recorded with pride how oil development was changing the town: the population was increasing rapidly owing to the desire of oil crews to live near their work. Housing was in critically short supply. The Republic Supply Company (a large oil tool manufacturing concern), several oil equipment firms, a handful of retail businesses, several machine shops, two new restaurants, and several rooming and boarding houses all set up operations in Lomita. Local real estate men, the paper reported, received daily inquiries for locations to be utilized by institutions affiliated with the oil industry. One real estate developer explicitly linked the decentralization of the region to the growth of industrial and blue-collar suburbs, many of which came in the wake of oil.[22] By the end of the decade, residents of Torrance hoped to make it the best factory district in the West, while Lomita prided itself on being the residential community of the harbor district.[23]

The southern half of the Los Angeles basin was transformed from a semi-rural region of garden cities to an expansive manufacturing district interspersed with oil fields, railroad and trucking yards, the giant harbor complex, working-class suburbs, and the occasional agricultural tract. Any lingering anti-urban, pastoral, or suburban identity was betrayed by the rapidity and zeal with which these various suburbs of the southland embraced industrialization. However ironic its name, blue-collar Gardena welcomed oil and industrial development, calling the oil industry the hope of its future, advising local residents that "a progressive epoch is opening."[24] Blue-collar towns vied with each other to attract oil refineries, storage and transportation facilities, and factories of all descriptions. Directly related to the increase in oil production in the 1920s was the growth of other industries. Between 1922 and 1926, the period of greatest petroleum production, 29 of 37 new steel fabrication plants were devoted entirely to the manufacture of oil tools, pipelines, and refinery components. Some of these firms, like Emsco Steel, Ideco Steel, and Baker Tools, quickly ranked among the nation's largest of such firms. This area along the industrial corridors of Slauson and Santa Fe Avenues near Huntington Park was called Steeltown by local residents. Other steel fabrication plants both converted to oil tool manufacture and significantly enlarged their operations. Further south, in the harbor area, the town of Wilmington became the refining center of the country. Harbor expansion proceeded at a mind-boggling rate. Throughout the 1920s, the Los Angeles harbor was repeatedly expanded, mostly to handle the increased tonnage of oil shipped from the port; in fact, Los Angeles was the world's leading oil exporting region by 1923, a position it did not relinquish until the Depression decade.[25] The other major segment of the port—its lumber-handling facilities—also grew to serve the industry; in 1921 alone, the oil industry imported over 38 million linear feet of lumber, much of it old-growth redwood and some of it as large as 16-inch-square stock for derricks. Attracted by employment opportunities in these

Figure 5.2. Unidentified residential street on Signal Hill, probably early 1920s. Dwellings and wooden derricks were a common sight in Los Angeles's oil regions throughout the 1920s, as city councils were often reluctant to prevent oil drilling in local neighborhoods, especially in the early years of development. *Historical Society of Long Beach*

industries, working people and their families flooded into the burgeoning industrial areas of the southland.

The particular setting of any heavy industrial community structured its physical appearance in the Los Angeles area during the 1920s. Some communities were entirely dominated by such settings. The oil industry fostered many of these occupationally-specific communities. Oil towns, reported one authority, were frequently "distinguished by their squalor, where garbage and decaying vegetable matter, tin cans, old rags and scrap paper lie in heaps about temporary structures or are strewn over vacant lots. Flies swarm and the atmosphere reeks with offensive odors."[26] Splintered lumber, old tools, and rusted machinery lay abandoned near living quarters. Oil pipelines and steam pipes traversed the region. Water supplies and sewage systems were often inadequate.

In an area that was part industrial suburb and part residential community, workers' housing (and the provisions for such) varied throughout the region. Some families lived for years in rag rows: strings of tents and one-room shacks, often located near rail tracks or along strips of vacant land near oil districts.[27] One early resident of Huntington Beach remembered that, in the 1920s, this coastal oil town was filled with tents—in the tent city, in churchyards, in old campgrounds, and on the beach. Blocks upon blocks of shacks were built of cardboard, "structures that you could really just kick a hole through."[28] Other rag rows sprouted around oil districts in Long Beach, Wilmington, Carson, Norwalk, La Habra, and Inglewood. Elsewhere in the oil region, patterns of residence in company-provided housing on oil leases can best be described as scattered settlements comprised of loosely linked villages spread across a wide expanse of oil fields. Each village was the camp of one company.[29] The blue-collar towns of northern Orange County generally took this form. Despite the dispersed pattern of settlement, people derived their identity as residents of a particular oil community because, in the words of one early resident of Olinda, "we were mostly close together. All the people worked right there in the oil fields." Institutions also fostered an occupationally-specific sense of community. Olinda supported its own school district, run by the men who lived and worked in the oil fields, even into the 1950s, when the attendance at the local elementary school dwindled to just five pupils.[30] Even where living outside the purview of the company was an option, housing stock in the many small towns in the basin's oil districts was often not much better than that offered in the camps. Yet living in town provided workers with a sense of independence not easily attained by those people living on company property. In census samples of oil town populations, high percentages of household heads owned their dwellings outright, unencumbered by outstanding mortgages—indicating the likelihood that many of these buildings were self-built.[31] For workers, such a minimal investment in their dwellings could have real advantages: if employment in the oil fields declined, as it eventually did almost everywhere oil was found, workers would not have to leave behind an expensive house.

Both within and outside of the oil districts, workers' choice of housing was limited by many considerations. In choosing a residence, the work-home nexus was particularly important to oil workers, as public transportation to the oil fields and refineries was seldom adequate. In Los Angeles, working-class neighborhoods were often segregated by industry, as "each new industry—especially oil—creat[ed] a special community for the homes of each group of workmen."[32] Residents and nonresidents alike identified certain suburbs by the occupations of their residents. Bell, for example, was an autoworkers' town, while Huntington Park was most commonly associated with the steel industry.[33] Montebello had two industrial sites: a huge commercial brick kiln, whose workers lived in a neighborhood called The Brickyard, and an oil field. In the harbor area, slaughterhouses and fish canneries fouled local waters near the neighborhoods housing cannery workers and fishermen on Terminal Island and in the Barton Hill and Mexican Hollywood sections of San Pedro. Lumberyard workers tended to congregate in neighborhoods along Point Fermin, while longshoremen were scattered throughout San Pedro, described by one man as "an isolated little community with just one road leading into it" as late as 1930.[34] John Martinez grew up in company housing on the harbor site of the Long Beach Salt Works, along with the children of some twenty other families.[35] Such strong associations between industry and suburb had a clear basis in reality. In Wilmington, more residents were employed by the oil refineries than all other industries combined during the 1920s.[36] Some refineries there even maintained housing for some workers on site.[37] Another city populated mostly by oil and industrial workers and their families, Compton was described in the early 1930s as "a poor but respectable community. The homes are old and inexpensive. . . . It is not a town where men retire for life nor where tourists vacation."[38] In both small oil towns and larger working-class communities, residents could hear 24 hours a day oil field and industrial activity: the grind of rotary drills, the popping sounds of one- and two-cylinder pump engines, the screams of refinery whistles, the pounding of trip-hammers in boiler works, the roar of steel plants busily producing rotary drill pipe and well casings.[39]

Living in these towns afforded workers little sense of autonomy. El Segundo got its name for being the site of Standard Oil's second major California refinery. Residents there not only worked for Standard, but also shopped at the Standard Market, attended the Standard Elementary School, played baseball at the Standard Park, and were treated at the Standard Hospital when they became ill. In fact, according to one labor activist, it was only when one died that he found independence from the company's domination. Standard did not have its own cemetery.

The requirements of industry structured the lives of men, women, and children in the working-class communities of Los Angeles during the 1920s. In particular, the nature of oil work and the social relations of oil production deeply affected the lives of women and children. In material terms, the physical conditions of oil field communities, especially the lack of boundaries separating work and home, threw out of balance prevailing middle-class ideas about domesticity, women's proper roles, and the sanctity of the home. Despite the difficulties, some women willingly shouldered the challenges of oil field life. One woman recalled fondly that she "loved those fields, dirt and all," just as much as did her husband, who retired in 1961 after 45 years as an oil field worker.[40] Yet oil field life could be hard. For women, the daily toil of cleaning, cooking, and child care could be particularly tiresome.[41] Because men labored such long hours, children routinely helped with household chores, sometimes getting up before daybreak in order to finish their duties before leaving for school.[42] In blue-collar harbor communities, children commonly spent hours each day scavenging for driftwood that would be burned to heat their homes, or carried water from wells to their family water tanks in the years before indoor plumbing was commonplace.[43] Women living in rag rows as well as in some camps had to carry water in large bags, like wineskins, to their residences. Meals had to be prepared, including the substantial dinners men packed off to work.[44] Many women delivered meals to their husbands at work in the fields; wives of pumpers and firemen customarily tended the boilers as their menfolk ate. Women often could find groceries, clothing, and other supplies only at stores several miles from camp. Medical care was similarly distant.[45] In the harbor district, the county board of health encouraged local women to volunteer to work as unpaid visiting nurses in the homes of the ill and injured.[46] As well as usual child-care duties, oil field women were responsible for keeping their children out of danger—away from moving machinery, out of waste oil sumps where children might drown. Some women resourcefully taught their children to be self-reliant. When Leo Piantoni was still a toddler, his mother showed him how to avoid burning his bare feet by first spitting on pipelines to determine if they were hot or not.[47]

Cultural practices reinforced the importance of women to working-class families. Throughout the region's oil towns, newly married women were immediately welcomed into the community through the popular ritual of shivarees. The ritual was used both to celebrate a workmate's marriage and to initiate a young bride into the often rowdy industrial culture of oil work. The raucous parade normally began after nightfall at the house of the newlyweds, where dozens of friends would surprise the couple, and force them, sometimes physically, to the head of the parade. Amid the din of blaring automobile horns, noisy musical instruments, and the shouts and catcalls of fellow workers and their wives and sweethearts, the blushing groom and his equally blushing bride were driven around the town or oil camp in which they resided.[48]

There were individual variations to this ceremonial exercise: the crowd sometimes serenaded the newlyweds with old love songs; wedding gifts were often presented; the groom might be expected to make a speech before the participants were willing to disband.[49] In Brea, one young oil worker was handcuffed, placed in a sling, and raised to the crown block of a derrick; the crowd led his wife to him, but refused to free him for some time. Another young man tried to dissuade his workmates from giving him and his bride a shivaree by installing special locks on his lease house near Olinda immediately after his wedding in 1920. When the newlyweds returned from their week-long honeymoon, they found their house changed "completely around, the bedroom furniture arranged in the kitchen, the kitchen in one of the bedrooms where the stove was even hooked up." The shivaree occurred later that night, after the young couple had gone to bed. Nearly 60 years later, he recalled that marriage in those days "was kind of a scary proposition because you didn't know what was going to happen when everything [the shivaree] started."[50] Despite these variations, certain themes were common to oil field shivarees: a clamorous and sometimes bawdy introduction to oil workers' culture, an act which highlighted the importance of marriage and—by extension—family, a ritual staged by both men and women, a working-class rite seldom extended to those beyond the status of wage earner. Newspaper reports in other blue-collar towns suggest that shivarees were popular among many occupational groups in working-class Los Angeles throughout the 1920s.

Throughout one's life cycle, the experience of work shaped individual working-class identity as well as community structure. This was particularly true in oil towns. An oil worker's rough image sometimes clouded a man's various roles: worker, husband, parent. No matter how tough the other guy in the rig may be, advised one Signal Hill newspaper, "remember he may go home nights and crawl around on the floor while a yellow haired kid plays horse with him."[51] Popular institutions reinforced the strong linkages between family and work. Social organizations called Get Together Clubs proliferated throughout the southland's oil towns; club members specifically met to celebrate the births of babies to oil workers' families. Further, parents' expectations imparted working-class values to their children. "What your father did," said one longtime oil worker, "was still good enough for you. . . . [And] if you're going to wear overalls all your life, then it's good enough for your kids to wear overalls all their lives."[52]

Oil workers introduced their children at an early age to oil field work, on occasion bringing young children to work with them. One man's memory of his first night spent in the oil fields of Brea was so vivid that more than 60 years later he remembered the experience as if it had just happened. When only three or four years old, Leland Kinsler persuaded his father to take him to work. Charles Kinsler, Leland's father, let his son watch the drilling process for a while, then bedded down young Leland in the tin belthouse for the remainder of his night shift. Leland Kinsler remembered trying to sleep amid the tremendous racket made by the big, wide belt slapping around as the crew continued to drill, the noise reverberating inside the tin shack.[53] Other children, both boys and girls, also accompanied their fathers to the job site. Sometimes a child assisted a father with his duties in an emergency; other times a child stood at a father's side as he visited from well to well organizing for the union; many times a child followed a father into the fields in the absence of a second parent and when no other child-care provisions could be made. As in Leland Kinsler's case, most often children joined their fathers on the job just occasionally, when a man felt it time for a youngster to be introduced to oil field work life.[54] In addition, children routinely played in oil fields; by the early 1930s, many oil companies in the Los Angeles area had to hire private guards to keep children off oil equipment, especially the walking beams that served as the equivalent of mechanical horses to oil field children. There was a lot of camaraderie between oil field children, asserted another man, "because all of the people grew up in the same way."[55]

In other industrial settings, work identity structured many aspects of the social life of working-class communities, even for children. Among Wilmington's residents, all of the longshoremen's children "hung around together because they had that something in common: that our dads were down on the docks and everything."[56] In other communities, working-class children similarly segregated themselves by fathers' occupation; such social groupings by occupation sometimes transcended ethnic divisions, as children of Finnish, Anglo, and Mexican longshoremen met to play.[57] Regardless of the industry, young children frequently brought hot lunches to their fathers at the job site, sometimes traveling miles via the interurban railways to do so.[58] Fishermen commonly took their sons to sea with them during summer months, while during school vacations young teenagers, especially girls, were employed in the fish canneries where their mothers labored. Other children accompanied widowed parents or guardians to work, often on the night shift.[59] The strategy of using children's labor both to maximize family income and to lighten the nonpaid labors of working-class women was so prevalent in Los Angeles's blue-collar suburbs during the 1920s and 1930s that social workers frequently pointed out the consequences: truancy, social alienation, and juvenile delinquency. The members of some street gangs in the region's blue-collar towns even took their names from the work identities of their parents and local communities.[60]

A common working-class identity was forged in the realm of the community as well as the job site. Even at very young ages, working-class children were sensitive to the radicalizing influences of their parents' struggles on the job and in the community. One man who was raised in Signal Hill remembered that residents of his neighborhood—who were all working people, poor people—divided into two fractious camps when a strikebreaker and his family moved into the neighborhood. Tensions were so high that some residents moved out of the neighborhood rather than live next to a scab.[61] In other instances, playmates compared their fathers' work experiences, and in the process, some children realized the nature and depth of their own working-class identities. One man whose father was blacklisted for being a union organizer in the early 1930s remembered that he "began to be aware of what my father was up against" only after he and his friends compared notes about their fathers' experiences on the job, since all of the men were longshoremen.[62] Further, residents of both the harbor towns and other communities prided themselves on sucessfully maintaining their own forms of local government, sometimes against the desires of the large metropolis of Los Angeles. As late as the 1940s, harbor area unions sponsored programs in opposition to L.A.'s importation of bus-lines and government into the harbor communities.[63]

This look at the development of working-class Los Angeles suggests several new paths of inquiry. First, historians need to reexamine the familiar dichot-omy between the public world of the workplace and the private world of the home, and instead search for ways in which home and work were con-nected. The rigors of the workplace—be it steel plant shop floor, lumber dock at the harbor, oil drilling rig, or any number of other industrial set-tings—invaded the home, thus structuring the labors of men, women, and children. We should not forget that Los Angeles emerged as one of the country's leading industrial and manufacturing centers during the 1920s and 1930s; its population grew accordingly, especially in the region's south-ern suburban ring, a primarily working-class area.

Second, we should reevaluate the concept of suburb to be more inclu-sive, encompassing many sorts of communities in all stages of development. How do we define suburb, neighborhood, and community? While the re-cent work of historians and geographers is promising, we need to go much further.[64] Suburbs were not simply commuter residential districts, spatially separated from an older industrial core, whose defining characteristics were architectural uniformity and demographic homogeneity, as sociologist Ben-nett Berger suggested more than forty years ago.[65] I would argue for a more generic definition of a suburb as an entity, such as a town, neither urban nor rural in character, and often differentiated from the metropole by an inde-pendent political identity. In this definition, suburbs are towns that need be neither wholly industrial nor entirely residential in character. Neighbor-hoods and communities, on the other hand, are the human manifestations of the suburb's separate identity.

Third, we need to investigate in greater depth and detail the process and timing of Los Angeles's suburban development. As historians, we need to rid ourselves of the anti-urban ethos model of Los Angeles's suburbaniza-tion with as much haste and vigor as those suburbs did in the 1920s. At the same time, however, we need to recognize that the *antimetropolitan* perspec-tive of local residents was firmly rooted in their consciousness as industrial workers, as members of the working class, and as residents of towns that

Figure 5.3. Realtors in Torrance advertised working-class developments as "garden courts," but landscaping alone could not mask the industrial settings of these neighborhoods, as shown by the oil derricks in the background. *Long Beach Public Library*

celebrated their status as industrial centers separate from the city of Los Angeles. We need to acknowledge that the Roaring Twenties looked very different to the working class than it did to the hordes of corporate men, real estate promoters, Hollywood moguls, starstruck tourists, stock swindlers, and others who peopled Los Angeles during this decade.[66]

NOTES

1. Lorecia East, *The Boomers: The Autobiography of a Roughneck's Wife* (Baton Rouge: Legacy Publishing, 1976), 53–55.

2. Dyer Bennett, interviewed by Jean Howlett, October 20, 1981, Brea, Calif., for the Brea Community History Project, Oral History Program–California State University, Fullerton (hereafter, OHP-CSUF).

3. John Royal, interviewed by Daniel Beagle and David Wellman, September 16, 1982, San Pedro, Calif., for the International Longshoremen's and Warehousemen's Union–National Endowment for the Humanities Oral History Project, in the ILWU Archives, San Francisco (hereafter, ILWU-NEH OHP, in ILWUA).

4. Bill T. Ward, interviewed by Harvey Schwartz, November 3, 1981, San Francisco, ILWU-NEH OHP, in ILWUA.

5. Lomita *News-Letter*, August 31, 1923; *California Oil Worker* (Long Beach), December 2, 1922; Fred Jackson, editor of the Long Beach *Labor News*, typically referred to L.A. as "Louse Angeles" throughout his tenure as head of the paper, 1923–26.

6. The most important works to examine the suburbanization of Los Angeles are Robert Fogelson, *The Fragmented Metropolis: Los Angeles, 1850–1930* (1967; Berkeley and Los Angeles: University of California Press, 1993); Scott L. Bottles, *Los Angeles and the Automobile: The Making of the Modern City* (Berkeley and Los Angeles: University of California Press, 1987); Reyner Banham, *Los Angeles: The Architecture of Four Ecologies* (London: Penguin, 1971); Carey McWilliams, *Southern California Country: An Island on the Land* (New York: Duell, Sloan and Pierce, 1946); Kevin Starr, *Inventing the Dream: California through the Progressive Era* (New York: Oxford University Press, 1985) and *Material Dreams: Southern California through the 1920s* (New York: Oxford University Press, 1990); Stephan Thernstrom, "The Growth of Los Angeles in Historical Perspective," in Werner Z. Hirsch, ed., *Los Angeles: Viability and Prospects for a Metropolitan Leadership* (New York: Praeger, 1971); Mark S. Foster, "The Decentralization of Los Angeles in the 1920s" (Ph.D. dissertation, University of Southern California, 1971), and "The Model-T, the Hard Sell, and Los Angeles' Urban Growth: The Decentralization of Los Angeles during the 1920s," *Pacific Historical Review* 44 (November 1975): 459–84; Greg Hise, *Magnetic Los Angeles: Planning the Twentieth Century Metropolis* (Baltimore: Johns Hopkins University Press, 1997). See also Hise's essay in this volume.

Fred Viehe offers a different view of the process of suburbanization in "Black Gold Suburbs: The Influence of the Extractive Industry on the Suburbanization of Los Angeles, 1890–1930," *Journal of Urban History* 8 (1981): 3–26.

7. Viehe, "Black Gold Suburbs."

8. See Mike Davis, *City of Quartz: Excavating the Future in Los Angeles* (New York: Vintage, 1990).

9. Nancy Quam-Wickham, *The Power of Oil: Culture, Politics, and Development in the American West, 1900–1950* (forthcoming, University of California Press).

10. See Viehe, "Black Gold Suburbs," 13.

11. The importance of the oil industry to Los Angeles's economic development is well documented by Viehe, "Black Gold Suburbs"; James Clifford Finley, "The Economic Boom of the 'Twenties in Los Angeles" (Ph.D. dissertation, Claremont Graduate School, 1958), 341–78; Starr, *Material Dreams*, 85–89; John Ise, *The United States Oil Policy* (New Haven: Yale University Press, 1926), 91.

12. Fogelson notes the importance of single-family subdivisions in the decentralization of the Los Angeles region in *The Fragmented Metropolis*, 147, 151, 154, 164, 190–91.

13. Lomita *News-Letter*, January 20, February 3, and February 24, 1922.

14. Lomita *News-Letter*, March 31, June 2, July 14 and 28, 1922.

15. *California Oil World*, July 13, 1922.

16. Lomita *News-Letter*, March 31 and April 7, 1922; Torrance *Herald*, April 14 and September 1, 1922; Lomita *News-Letter*, July 7 and 28, 1922.

17. Lomita *News-Letter*, November 10, 1922.

18. Lomita *News-Letter,* September 22, 1922.

19. Lomita *News-Letter,* December 22, 1922.

20. Lomita *News-Letter,* January 19 and 23, 1923.

21. Lomita *News-Letter,* January 20, 1922.

22. Lomita *News-Letter,* August 24 and 31, 1923; January 19, 1923.

23. Lomita *News-Letter,* January 14, 1926.

24. Gardena *Reporter,* May 12, 1923.

25. San Pedro *Daily News,* September 6 and 26, 1923.

26. "Cleaning Up the Oil Camps," *Literary Digest,* October 22, 1921: 20.

27. Eileen McKay, "Growing Up in the Early Oil Fields," *The Pumper* 7:2 (September 1988): 6–7.

28. Delbert "Bud" Higgins, interviewed by Harry Henslick, May 19, 1968, Huntington Beach, Calif., for the Huntington Beach Community History Project, OHP-CSUF, p. 60 of transcript.

29. Ella Armstrong Post, interviewed by Jackie Malone, in Ken Beko et al., eds., *Pipelines to the Past: An Oral History of Olinda, California* (Fullerton: Oral History Program, California State University, 1978).

30. Jessie Isbell, interviewed by Patricia English, in Beko, *Pipelines to the Past.*

31. On mortgage practices and home owning in the United States, see M. J. Daunton, "Rows and Tenements: American Cities, 1880–1914," in Daunton, ed., *Housing the Workers, 1850–1914: A Comparative Perspective* (London: Leicester University Press, 1990), 249–86; Olivier Zunz, *The Changing Face of Inequality* (Chicago: University of Chicago Press, 1982), 170–76; Richard Harris correspondence with author, February 18, 1992.

32. Louise Colton Appell, "An Historical Folk-Survey of Southern California: A Narrative of the Peopling of the Southland" (M.A. thesis, University of Southern California, 1927), 99–100.

33. Bill T. Ward, interviewed by Harvey Schwartz, October 27, 1981, San Francisco, ILWU-NEH OHP, in ILWUA.

34. Bill T. Ward interview, November 3, 1981.

35. John Martinez, interviewed by Harvey Schwartz, May 29, 1984, Stanton, Calif., ILWU-NEH OHP, in ILWUA.

36. Pete Moore, interviewed by Harvey Schwartz, May 24, 1984, San Pedro, Calif., ILWU-NEH OHP, in ILWUA.

37. Walter E. Holstein, "A History of Wilmington" (M.A. thesis, University of Southern California, 1931), 67; Joseph Crabtree [pseudonym], interviewed by Harvey Schwartz, May 24, 1984, Carson, Calif., and John Royal interview; *Cal-Pet Rotary* 2:6 (November 1926): 16.

38. George Knox Roth, "The Compton Unemployed Co-operative Relief Association: A Sociological Study, 1932–1933" (M.A. thesis, University of Southern California, 1934), 10.

39. "Boom Town," *The Pumper* 9:1 (February 1990): 4–5; Joy Elliott, interviewed by Kaye Briegel, December 13, 1989, Signal Hill, Calif., for the Signal Hill Oral History Project, Special Collections, California State University, Long Beach; Thomas V. Talbert, interviewed by Barbara Milkovich, February 15, 1988, Huntington Beach, Calif., Oral History Resource Center, California State University, Long Beach.

40. Whittier *Daily News,* May 19, 1980.

41. The drudgery of doing laundry is a common complaint of both men and women who lived in the nation's oil fields and oil communities in the first decades of this century. See Delbert "Bud" Higgins interview, p. 63 of transcript; Richard R. "Jack" Gauldin, interviewed by Jackie Malone, and Merle Van Ness Hale, interviewed by Jackie Malone, both in Beko, *Pipelines to the Past;* Roger Olien and Diana Davids Olien, *Oil Booms: Social Change in Five Texas Towns* (Lincoln: University of Nebraska Press, 1982), 95–96; East, *The Boomers,* 27–28.

42. Myrtle Warner, interviewed by Annette Frye, April 13, 1972, Orange, Calif., for the Brea Community History Project, OHP-CSUF, p. 13 of transcript. After 1917, most oil field workers in California worked eight hours per day, although some companies did work 12 hours per day. Refinery workers generally worked 10–12 hours per day. However, the seven-day workweek did not disappear until late 1928. In the copper industry, the impact that men's long working hours had on children's lives is discussed in the Montana Writers' Program, Works Progress Administration, *Copper Camp* (New York: Hastings House, 1943), 137–61.

43. John Martinez interview; Frank and Mike Salcido, interviewed by Harvey Schwartz, March 27, 1984, Torrance, Calif., ILWU-NEH OHP, in ILWUA.

44. See Thelma Henderson, interviewed by Bruce Rockwell, in Beko, *Pipelines to the Past;* Bill T. Ward interview, October 27, 1981.

45. McKay, "Growing Up in the Early Oil Fields," 6.

46. John Martinez interview.

47. Leo Piantoni, interviewed by Bruce Rockwell, October 22, 1981 [Brea, Calif.?], for the Brea Community History Project, OHP-CSUF, pp. 1–2 of transcript.

48. Bryan Palmer discusses similar marriage rites among the working class more generally in "Discordant Music," *Labour/Le Travail* 3 (1978): 5–62.

49. Oil field shivarees are described in *The Aoco Record* (Associated Oil Company), 3:1 (January 1922): 18, and 3:9 (September 1922): 18; East, *The Boomers,* 9.

50. Richard R. "Jack" Gauldin interview.

51. Signal Hill *Producer,* March 9, 1928.

52. Dyer Bennett interview, pp. 67–68 of transcript.

53. Leland Kinsler, interviewed by Bruce Rockwell, in Beko, *Pipelines to the Past.*

54. Merle Van Ness Hale interview; Thelma Henderson interview; Leo Piantoni interview; Oscar Stricklin, interviewed by Barbara Milkovich; James E. Herley, interviewed by Ann B. Andriesse; E. D. Mitchell, interviewed by Kaye Briegel; all in Beko, *Pipelines to the Past.*

55. Voloney Siebenthal, interviewed by Ann Towner, in Beko, *Pipelines to the Past.*

56. Bill T. Ward interview, October 27, 1981.

57. Pete Moore interview; Tony Salcido, interviewed by Harvey Schwartz, April 25, 1985, Long Beach, Calif.; Henry Gaitan, interviewed by Daniel Beagle and David Wellman, May 14, 1983, San Pedro, Calif., both ILWU-NEH OHP, in ILWUA; Frank Sunstedt, interviewed by Harvey Schwartz, March 26, 1984, San Pedro, Calif., ILWU-NEH OHP, in ILWUA.

58. Bill T. Ward interview, October 27, 1981.

59. Frank Sunstedt interview.

60. Willis Winfield Clark, "A Study of 102 Truant Boys" (M.A. thesis, University of Southern California, 1918); T. R. Marshall, "The Recreation Problems of 735 Junior and Senior High School Pupils in Torrance, California" (M.A. thesis, University

of Southern California, 1942); Elsa Longmoor, "An Ecological Approach to the Study of Juvenile Delinquency in Long Beach, California" (M.A. thesis, University of Southern California, 1935); T. I. Quarton, "Social Background of Juvenile Predelinquents in the San Pedro District" (M.A. thesis, University of Southern California, 1937).

61. Pete Moore interview.

62. Bill T. Ward interview, October 27, 1981.

63. Bill T. Ward interview, November 3, 1981.

64. Geographer Richard Harris has resurrected the study of working-class suburbs; see, especially, "Working-Class Home Ownership in the American Metropolis," *Journal of Urban History* 17 (1990): 46–69, and "Self-Building in the Urban Housing Market," *Economic Geography* 67 (1991): 1–21. Sociologists have studied working-class suburbs, including a large number of M.A. students at the University of Southern California during the 1920s and 1930s; see also Bennett Berger, *Working-Class Suburb: A Study of Autoworkers in Suburbia* (Berkeley and Los Angeles: University of California Press, 1960), and William Kornblum, *Blue-Collar Community* (Chicago: University of Chicago Press, 1974). The strong associations between home, community, and workplace in Los Angeles in some ways parallel the links between neighborhoods and worksites in Chicago that Lizabeth Cohen has analyzed in *Making a New Deal* (New York: Cambridge University Press, 1990), 17–31.

65. Berger, *Working-Class Suburb*, 6–8.

66. See Jules Tygiel, preface to Upton Sinclair, *Oil!* (Berkeley and Los Angeles: University of California Press, 1997).

PART TWO

Metropolitan Identities

BERATED BY PUNDITS for being the exclusively white western capital of the Midwest, 1920s Los Angeles was in reality a tremendously diverse city. That diversity, of race, class, and ethnicity, is the subject of essays by Douglas Flamming, Douglas Monroy, and Clark Davis. Flamming examines the coherence of the city's African American community, as well as the simultaneous molding of a regionally specific African American cultural identity. Monroy's essay explores the Mexican and Mexican American world of 1920s Los Angeles, a world at once near and far from the Mexico many had only recently left. Lastly, Clark Davis examines Los Angeles identity from a different perspective; his essay investigates the formation of a new urban class with real Los Angeles roots: the white-collar worker.

CHAPTER SIX

The Star of Ethiopia and the NAACP

Pageantry, Politics, and the Los Angeles African American Community

Douglas Flamming

The Hollywood Bowl, 1925. On a beautiful June night, with stars shining faintly in Southern California's purple-blue sky, an audience of blacks and whites watched as spotlights came up on the grandeur of ancient Africa, c. 50,000 B.C. In five acts, history in motion swept across the stage. As centuries passed, beautiful Ethiopia began a slow, painful demise, which ended with Africa's tragic descent into the slave trade. To the accompaniment of orchestral music, all of it composed by African Americans, several hundred local black actors—volunteers all—danced, marched, and sang their way across the stage, presenting an epic theatrical version of black history, carrying the story from African splendor through the darkness of American slavery and finally to the rise of the "New Negro" in the 1920s.

Such was the opening night in Los Angeles for W. E. B. Du Bois's grand theatrical pageant, *The Star of Ethiopia*. Du Bois was the nation's most famous African American, as well as its foremost black intellectual and the editor of the *Crisis,* the official magazine of the National Association for the Advancement of Colored People (NAACP), the leading civil rights organization in the country. He had arrived from New York to oversee the pageant, which was directed by his longtime theatrical assistant, Charles Burroughs, also a New Yorker. *Star* got plenty of buildup in the local black newspapers— "Race papers" as the African American community called them—and it even received a nice plug from the *Los Angeles Times*. But the turnout for opening night—and for the second (and last) performance three days later—was poor. Most of the 10,000 seats in the Bowl were empty. Worse, the process of staging the pageant nearly tore apart the black community of Los Angeles.

Paradoxically, though, the fallout from the *Star of Ethiopia* fiasco proved curiously positive. The mess shook up the entrenched leadership of the local branch of the NAACP and cleared the way for a more united, decisive generation of leadership, which, by the end of the 1920s, had built a much stronger organization in Los Angeles. What's more, Du Bois, despite taking some serious flak in Los Angeles in 1925, was charmed by Southern California and its possibilities. The Los Angeles Branch began to play a stronger, more visible role in the national circles of the NAACP. This growing regional clout became clear when the NAACP decided to hold its national convention in Los Angeles in 1928, an event that marked an important stage in the evolution of the city's African American community.[1]

Staging *The Star of Ethiopia* in Los Angeles was the brainchild of the NAACP's "Junior Branch." Newly organized by black students from UCLA and USC, the Junior Branch had ambitious plans. The NAACP's national Junior Branch program was actually intended to promote the organization among teenagers, but by the mid 1920s Los Angeles's NAACP had not established a Junior Branch, which gave the city's college students an opening to apply for and receive a charter from the national office in early 1925. There was some generational gamesmanship at work here. These young men and women were fired with enthusiasm, and they viewed Los Angeles's established NAACP leaders as inactive relics who barred the way of younger, more aggressive activists.[2]

The leading lights of the college crowd were James McGregor, Naida Portia McCullough, and Fay Jackson. McGregor and Jackson served as president and vice president of the Junior Branch. A senior at USC, McGregor was a rising star in black Los Angeles. Active and popular in church and social circles, he was national vice president of Alpha Phi Alpha, a leading black fraternity. In January 1925, McGregor made a tour of the East, which included a stop in New York, where he dined with Du Bois at the New York City Club.[3] Another high-profile USC student, Naida Portia McCullough, took a similar tour, representing the Alpha Kappa Alpha sorority at its annual convention. McCullough, a talented musician, also met with Du Bois, and she spoke with him about the possibility of the Los Angeles's Junior Branch producing his popular theatrical pageant, *The Star of Ethiopia*.[4] Fay Jackson was already writing articles for the *California Eagle* and, later in the decade, would serve as editor of the local literary journal, *Flash*.

Leaders of the Los Angeles Junior Branch identified themselves as "New Negroes"—a term heard everywhere among the African American middle class of the 1920s. To be a New Negro was to be an educated, assertive proponent of black freedom and black progress. Usually, the term implied the younger set, the new cadre of university students who looked toward Du Bois and other intellectual-activists for inspiration, and the rising generation of black artists, such as Langston Hughes and Los Angeles's own Arna

Figure 6.1. The Junior Branch of the Los Angeles NAACP, c. 1924. *Shades of L.A. Archives/Los Angeles Public Library*

Bontemps, who were on the leading edge of the New Negro Renaissance. Of McGregor, the *California Eagle*, Los Angeles's leading black paper, wrote: he "embodies the ideals and intellectual aspirations of the New Negro, . . . he has implicit faith in the power of true education to surmount all obstacles and to solve the Negro's problems."[5] McCullough, the *Eagle* stated, was "a woman whose comprehensive culture and winning personality bespeaks eloquently of the entrance of the New Negro woman into a field of endeavor which is unquestionably for the good and ultimate liberation of the Race."[6]

By staging *Star of Ethiopia* as their initial project, by seeing pageantry as politics, the Junior Branch placed itself squarely within the New Negro Arts Movement. Also called the New Negro (or Harlem) Renaissance, this flowering of African American artistry electrified American culture in the mid to late 1920s, and the current was sharply felt in Los Angeles. There arose in urban America a white fascination with black literature, music, and art; at the same time, there was a new assertiveness on the part of black Americans to be recognized by whites as serious artists. For Du Bois, art *was* political. In his view, white racism rested on assumptions of black inferiority. Path-breaking art by black Americans would undermine that assumption and, thereby, white racism. By the end of the 1920s, most of the younger generation of New Negroes would dismiss this simple political formula; but in 1925, Du Bois's idea fired the imagination of the Junior Branch and set *Star* in motion. Los Angeles's middle-class leadership fully embraced the ideal. "To the white world," wrote one enthusiast, "the pageant will be a tremendous revelation. To the Black world its picture of our life will be a stirring inspiration. Its purpose is to educate each one of us—Black and White alike."[7]

Du Bois's *Star of Ethiopia* was a bit late coming west. He first staged the pageant in 1913, as part of New York's Emancipation Exposition, held to commemorate the fiftieth anniversary of the Emancipation Proclamation. Despite many difficulties in production, *Star* was a smash, playing to some 14,000 blacks and whites. Strong demand for its restaging led to two subsequent performances—in Washington, D.C., in 1915, where 6,000 attended; and in Philadelphia the following year, to celebrate the African Methodist Episcopal Church's hundredth anniversary. Du Bois himself selected the music for his pageant, almost all of it written by black composers. Charles Burroughs served as Du Bois's right hand in each production, directing the acting or music at Du Bois's wishes.[8]

Star demanded a cast of hundreds, and the novelty of the thing was that the host community—New York, Washington, Philadelphia, and finally Los Angeles—had to supply the actors, dancers, singers, musicians, everything. Everything, that is, except ultimate control over the pageant, which remained firmly in Du Bois's hands. Back East, he got his way. Always there were flare-ups over who would direct what, but Du Bois, who rather liked conflict, always came out on top. Always, that is, until he brought *The Star of Ethiopia* to Los Angeles.

In early February 1925, when the Junior Branch announced its plans to stage Du Bois's pageant, the news electrified Central Avenue, the heart of the black community: Du Bois himself might direct the pageant; it might be held at the Hollywood Bowl! The *Eagle* reported that the announcement "swept intelligent Los Angeles like wild fire." Indeed it did. Men and women, young and old, rich and not-so-rich—it seemed that all of black Los Angeles lined up to support the project. "The past week alone," noted the *Eagle,* "witnessed an army of capable and enthusiastic workers who, after aligning themselves together, are now out to ensure the successful enactment of the story of their suffering, but nevertheless triumphant race."[9] In late February, Fay Jackson issued "a call for talent," asking for 1,000 participants for the stage production. McCullough estimated the music would require a 50-piece orchestra and a 2,000-voice chorus. The community buzzed with excitement.[10]

The Junior Branch had taken black Los Angeles by storm. Suddenly, they were the leaders and everyone else was following. An editorial in the *Eagle* praised their "daring and enterprising" campaign to stage *Star.* Predicting that "this thing will mean more in a racial way to Los Angeles and its environs than any other single effort of its kind in the last generation," the *Eagle* dubbed the Junior Branch "a growing and powerful civic organization" and concluded: "Young people our eyes are on you."[11] Back in New York, Du Bois had his eye on them, too. When in March the NAACP Director of Branches, Robert W. Bagnall, took a trip to Los Angeles, Du Bois personally requested that he try to visit the Junior Branch—and, he added, "boost the Pageant."[12]

Throughout February and March, the pageant generated tremendous interest, and all seemed well. The Junior Branch held mass meetings. The young people from Pasadena got involved. Auditions drew lines of eager actors and dancers. Financial donations large and small rolled in. One woman who had no money to spare baked a few pies and then sold them so that she could contribute a little something. The principal of Jefferson High School offered use of the school's auditorium for auditions and rehearsals. The churches helped out, and the YWCA served as pageant headquarters.[13]

But as March gave way to April—with the pageant little more than two months away—the fabric of enthusiasm and cooperation began to unravel. When the news broke that Du Bois was indeed on his way to Los Angeles, the *Eagle* warned that "social jockeys" would "endeavor to ride on his back in an effort to advertise themselves under the pretext of generous entertainment and hospitality." The Junior Branch had done all the work, but the *Eagle* openly wondered whether those who had never supported the NAACP would now take over. In part, this speculation was merely the usual scramble for the spotlight whenever a big social or political event was in the works. Du Bois had seen it before, in every previous production of his pageant, and somehow things always worked out in the end. In Los Angeles, though, the conflict turned bitter and nearly undermined the pageant.[14]

Tensions grew between the Senior Branch and the Junior Branch. Not without some justification, perhaps, the older leaders who had founded and led the Los Angeles Branch thought the juniors were a little too brash. In an early April letter to the national NAACP office, longtime secretary of Los Angeles's Senior Branch, Mrs. Beatrice S. Thompson, voiced her annoyance with the juniors and their lofty plans. "Our most active field workers are assisting the Junior Branch to stage 'The Star of Ethiopia' this summer," she wrote. "In fact, the entire program of the Juniors seems to parallel in many ways the work of the older Branch, which fact does not strengthen the efficiency of either."[15]

By early April, reports of the pageant preparations had become a bewildering mix of booster rhetoric, conflicting claims, and vague accusations. The April 10 edition of the *Eagle* illustrates the point. On that day, the newspaper began a "Who's Who in the Production of the Pageant" column, offering as its first installment a glowing commendation of Naida McCullough.

The story emphasized that "it is especially gratifying to learn that she is to have complete personal supervision of the musical score of the pageant." At the same time, though, the *Eagle* reported that Du Bois had settled the issue of control, and it would be his. "Settling definitely and for all time the questions as to who shall have supervision of the pageant . . . announcement was made this week of the receipt of a letter from Dr. W. E. B. Du Bois stating that he and his casting director, [Charles] Henry Burroughs, will have complete charge and management of the production." Suggesting that everyone was happy with this news—that Du Bois himself (and not some unknown from New York) would stage the pageant in Los Angeles—the *Eagle* had misread the message. The real message was that the Junior Branch would not stage the pageant; they could sponsor it, but it was not theirs to take. The very story that heralded Du Bois's personal direction and unchallenged supervision of *Star* also noted, apparently without recognizing the imminent collision, that Mrs. Arthur Prince (a young newlywed in the Junior Branch) had already selected 100 dancers for the African dance numbers, choreographed the dances, and begun the rehearsals, and that McCullough was already arranging the musical numbers for the show.[16] And so things continued, with Du Bois claiming control from New York and the Junior Branch pressing forward in Los Angeles.

Burroughs came to town in the second week of May to take charge. He was armed with a letter from Du Bois, which emphasized that "Mr. Burroughs is a director of dramatic action and knows exactly what he is doing." Burroughs immediately called a casting meeting for May 18, at which time he would "select the principal characters and groups."[17]

If Burroughs's blunt takeover did not insult the Junior Branch, an *Eagle* editorial on May 22 surely did. Claiming knowledge from "very reliable sources," the editors charged that the Junior Branch was simply "a cover under which a few social 'High Brows' of Los Angeles are operating to stage DuBois' Pageant in an effort to gain prominence and have their names broadcast in glaring headlines as the social marvels of this community. What is it all about?" That quickly, the *Eagle* shifted from being a strong supporter of the Junior Branch to being its adversary. "We challenge the president, or any bona fide authority of that organization to deny our statement. We are out to turn the covers of this thing right now. . . . Who is staging DuBois' Pageant? The Junior Branch of the N.A.A.C.P. or a group of old time social 'war-horses' of Los Angeles?"[18]

Shortly thereafter the Junior Branch voted to boycott the pageant. If they could not finish what they had started, if they could not stage the thing on their own terms, they would not participate. As Du Bois later put it, "we ran afoul a strike of the young colored intellectuals."[19]

The issue was control, but the lines of conflict were many and varied. One was an age-old aspect of racial and ethnic minority culture in America.

To those barred from mainstream opportunities, moments in the spotlight were rare and highly prized; minority communities were often small and familiar, and there was not much room at the top; for that very reason, minority strivers clashed over who should lead whom and how. This had been a source of tensions in Du Bois's three previous productions, and it was now apparent in the *Eagle*'s editorial against social "war horses." Nothing unusual, really; stage a pageant, expect a spat.

But in 1925, in Los Angeles, there was more to the story. Time and place mattered. *Star*'s troubles in Los Angeles reflected cultural and political trends of the 1920s, and they reflected regional tensions between East and West. First, the decade of the 1920s saw the generation gap move front and center in American culture—for all racial and ethnic groups. The Junior Branch of Los Angeles, organized by smart, restless college students, viewed the regular branch as deadwood. The Junior Branch saw themselves as the *real* NAACP in town. That was the twenties. So, too, was the notion that pageantry counted as politics. The New Negro Renaissance was in the air, and at its center, at least initially, was the idea that black artistry was a force for civil rights. No doubt the growing weakness of African American voters within the Republican Party had something to do with this shift from ballots to *beaux-arts,* but the roots of the idea are of less importance here than the implications for the Junior Branch. For them, staging *The Star of Ethiopia* at the Hollywood Bowl was no mere showcase for their talent. For them, it was the New Negro ideal personified, a clear and visible claim that young black intellectuals were on the move, obstacles be damned.

Finally, there was region. Somehow, down deep, it mattered to the Junior Branch that arrogant easterners rode into town and stole their show. They were not about to take that. Their elders, despite having boosted "the Grand West" for a generation, still felt slightly like outsiders in black American life, still longed to have Du Bois come to town. Indeed, when Du Bois arrived in Los Angeles to direct *Star,* the NAACP regulars wined and dined him, slightly in awe. One observer noted, writing of a banquet at which 200 attended, that the presence of Du Bois "caused the Los Angeles Branch to appreciate that even tho far away from the Central Headquarters on the Atlantic, they are at the same time closely woven and in reality an integral part of the great organization." The same report concluded: "It was indeed a history making event and an inspiration for the sons and daughters of the West to enlist their full quota in the service of the N.A.A.C.P."[20] The last line missed the spirit of the age by a substantial margin. In the 1920s, the sons and daughters of the West were not in awe of Du Bois or any highbrow easterner. When McGregor and McCullough went on their eastern tours in 1924–25, they met and talked with Du Bois as a matter of course. For them it was no pilgrimage. They were a confident bunch. And proud. Their boycott spread beyond their membership; Burroughs simply could not get enough young people to play parts in the mass-drama scenes. On the eve of the pageant, he was still several hundred short. And the youth boycott hurt the orchestra even more. Few young people crossed the line. The "strike" held firm. Du Bois later said the production "nearly floundered" because the young people simply would not participate.[21]

The show went on. The *Eagle* flip-flopped again and promoted the pageant down the home stretch. Remarkably, Du Bois and the pageant even got a nice big write-up in the *Los Angeles Times* entertainment section the Sunday before performance week. Du Bois himself wrote most of the piece (the *Times* rightly felt it necessary to introduce him to its white readers), and he offered a clear overview of what the "New Negro Renaissance" was all about, as well as a dramatic preview of what the pageant would hold. It would be, he assured white readers, "a beautiful spectacle in brown and black skins."[22]

There were two performances at the Hollywood Bowl. The premier on Monday, June 15, drew a biracial audience of 1,651—an audience scarcely larger than the number of people in the show itself, and by far the lowest attendance for any of Du Bois's stagings of *Star*. The second performance at the Hollywood Bowl, on Wednesday, June 18, drew 1,763. Compared to the turnouts back east, it was a flop. Black Los Angeles was disgraced.

Du Bois tried to put a good spin on it. In a summary report to the local Race papers, he offered a positive assessment. First, he tersely detailed the costs and the attendance figures for the performances, and noted that only Burroughs (not himself) received salary and travel money. The bottom line financially was a debt of $749.70. "It would have been a fine thing to have made enough to pay all expenses," Du Bois wrote, "but this our pageant has never done," and he added that he had learned that no pageant ever presented at the Hollywood Bowl had ever made a profit: "So much for business." Turning from resignation to praise, he wrote, "As a spectacle the pageant was a success. If we had a larger number of participants it would have equaled Washington in spectacular effect and Philadelphia in Artistry." He thought that Miss Ada Gaines, who played the key role of "Ethiopia," was "the best we ever had." There was in all this an unusual weariness in Du Bois's prose ("the band was not so good as we could wish for, but Mr. John Spikes worked faithfully"), but he revived near the end of the piece and closed the report in fine style: "Above all let me thank Los Angeles for loyal co-operation, and dogged grit in putting over a beautiful thing. It was a fine and moving picture. Who will ever forget it? The golden jewel of light and movement and song beneath the stars, making the history of black folk visible. It was a fine adventure in souls."[23]

But if Du Bois went home to savor the adventure in souls, the black community of Los Angeles was saddled with the debt and, more important, it was left with the embarrassment of the moment and the internal conflicts that had torn the pageant apart. The Los Angeles attorney and legal adviser for the local NAACP, E. Burton Ceruti, offered a somewhat chagrined explanation to the NAACP national secretary, Walter White. "In spite of some embarrassing circumstances," Ceruti wrote, "the Pageant was 'put over.' Dr. Du Bois and Prof. Burroughs labored indefatigably, making it an artistic success, notwithstanding a small financial loss."[24] What mattered was not the small financial loss but those "embarrassing circumstances." The local community had begun with the notion that the pageant would throw black Los Angeles in the national spotlight. It did, but for reasons not intended.

In the usual list of commendations printed in the local black press, not a single member of the Junior Branch of the NAACP was mentioned, despite the lavish praise poured on them only weeks before. Once they went "on strike," McGregor, McCullough, Jackson, and the others simply disappeared from view. The *Eagle* and Du Bois both praised Dr. John A. Somerville and Dr. Vada Somerville, a husband and wife team of dentists who "headed" the pageant. If one read only the final reports, one might think that the college students had never had any part in it.[25] The Junior Branch disbanded in protest, which was a relief to both the Los Angeles Senior Branch and the national office. In the wake of the juniors' boycott, McGregor's fraternity, Alpha Phi Alpha, held a banquet in honor of Du Bois, and Du Bois, angry at McGregor, refused to attend. McGregor then wrote several articles attacking Du Bois, angering both the New York office and the Senior Branch in Los Angeles.[26]

The national office of the NAACP hoped that a "citizens' committee" in Los Angeles would assume the pageant debt, but the local NAACP wound up shouldering it. Actually, the debt was pretty small potatoes. There was plenty of money in black Los Angeles. Even if there had not been, the local NAACP had some very wealthy white supporters, including the millionaire progressive and reformer John Randolph Haynes, who was an NAACP member.[27] No, the problem with the debt was not paying it; rather, the problem was that the debt had become linked to weightier issues—status, blame, responsibility, pride. Instead of being quickly paid and forgotten, the debt basically sat there, simmering in the overheated emotions ignited by the pageant.

At the center of this storm, struggling to hold things together, was the recently elected president of the Los Angeles NAACP, Dr. H. Claude Hudson, and he was neither happy about inheriting the problem nor optimistic about overcoming it. But in truth, the local branch would have been hard pressed to find a better leader at such a difficult time. Like many in black Los Angeles, Hudson was a product of Louisiana and Texas. Born (in 1886) and reared in Louisiana, he later moved to Marshall, Texas, to attend Wiley College. He then traveled north to dental school at Howard University. Having graduated, he moved back to the South to practice dentistry, first in Shreveport and later in Houston. In Houston, he took on the dangerous

task of standing up for black civil rights, and he became president of the local NAACP, a decidedly risky office to hold in Dixie in the 1920s.[28]

Only one year after arriving in Los Angeles in 1923—where he set
up practice on Central Avenue—he reluctantly accepted the presidency of
the local NAACP chapter. Writing to the national NAACP field secretary,
William Pickens, in early 1925, Hudson confided his difficulties. "First," he
began, "these people elected me against my will to a dead thing and even
tho I have worked hard it does not appear that I shall be able to revive interest. The [local executive] board is made up largely of people who do not
take time to do anything, but get elected to the place." It did not help that,
as a newcomer, he really did not know whom he could depend on. And it
also seemed to him that the branch officers could never get together on
anything. Back in Houston, he wrote, the local NAACP board was so frightened of the white authorities that "they let me have my way and we were able
to go forward." But things were different in Los Angeles. "These are funny
people here. . . . The great outdoors call and they go in as many different
directions as there are automobiles to carry them."[29]

The fallout from the pageant absorbed most of Hudson's time, and the
national office, wanting him to get the debt paid and move on to other matters, quickly grew impatient. A frustrated Hudson finally spilled the ugly details to the national office. The debt was $1,000, not $700, and by mid-July
it was only half paid. Bad feelings abounded. The juniors "did all they could
to cause a failure." Beatrice Thompson and Eugene Walker, the secretary
and treasurer (respectively) of the Senior Branch, were in opposition to the
Junior-sponsored pageant from the beginning; they "were as contrary as
could be, and never helped any, but did all they could to retard the Pageant."[30] Before long, Thompson would resign, with a letter to the national
office that revealed a stiff upper lip, and a final barb for her detractors
about her city's "present splendid efficient N.A.A.C.P."[31]

By late 1925, then, the Los Angeles NAACP was in turmoil, and it was not
a good time for turmoil. The year had begun with such promise—a new
and vital Junior Branch, the possibilities of the pageant. Then things got
ugly within the community, and at the very time when the Ku Klux Klan was
gaining strength and visibility in Southern California. In the end, the KKK's
impact on black Los Angeles would be negligible, but no one could foresee
that in 1925. To make matters worse, residential segregation by race—the
barring of blacks from all-white residential areas through restrictive real
estate covenants—was growing in Los Angeles.[32] The rise of restrictive covenants and the KKK signaled the need for strong, united leadership in the
black community. The city's staging of *Star of Ethiopia* and its fallout suggested anything but that. One member of the local NAACP executive board,
Lulu Slaughter, felt obliged to tell Bagnall in a letter: "I suppose you know
Los Angeles is about the hardest town in the whole state to work."[33] It wore

Hudson out, as he confessed to Bagnall in late 1925: "I had run so completely down and was feeling the strain so I had to slow down and accept conditions as they developed."[34] Los Angeles membership in the NAACP, which had exceeded 1,200 in 1921, fell below 300 after the pageant.[35]

Remarkably, though, Hudson and the local branch of the NAACP made a strong comeback during the next two years. Important allies for Hudson in this resurgence were the Somervilles, a dynamic husband and wife who, in the early years of the century, became the first and second black persons to graduate from USC's dental school. Both were active in civic affairs and strong supporters of the NAACP. Equally important, they were close friends of W. E. B. Du Bois's. In fact, Du Bois later said that it was Vada who had convinced him to present *The Star of Ethiopia* in Los Angeles.[36]

In 1926, the Junior Branch was reorganized, this time under the direction of the Senior Branch and, more specifically, under that of Vada Somerville, who now served as "director" of what was now called the "Junior Division." McGregor's bunch was out, and an entirely new slate of junior officers took their place. This group was, in Vada Somerville's words, "a younger and more agreeable set." In an upbeat letter sent to the national office in the spring of 1926—almost exactly a year after the Junior Branch boycotted *Star*—she wrote that "we have never had as large a number of paid members before, and the future looks bright." Better still, a junior membership campaign had "been instrumental in bringing in a large number of senior memberships."[37]

Indeed, the Senior Branch grew stronger. Those who supported and worked faithfully for the pageant remained in office, including both Dr. Somervilles (John serving as one of the vice presidents of the branch, and Vada serving on the executive board). Those who had opposed the pageant left the organization. Only one of the initial juniors, Emma Lue Sayers, who had apparently not been a central figure in the pageant boycott, moved into the fold of the Senior Branch; she became secretary of the branch in late 1926. The branch also created a more expansive legal committee, consisting of five local attorneys, who were kept busy fighting off Jim Crow in residential housing and public swimming pools and seeking to curb police brutality—which meant the local NAACP was visibly active in local civil rights crusades, a fact that helped boost the organization's popularity and membership in Los Angeles.[38]

By the end of 1926, local NAACP membership had increased by the thousands, and the Los Angeles Branch had sent more than $3,500 to the national office to support the Legal Defense Fund. Leaders in New York acknowledged that the Los Angeles Branch had suddenly emerged as one of the largest and most active in the nation. As Robert Bagnall put it, Los Angeles "gave promise of very soon becoming our strongest branch."[39] By the time the national NAACP convention met in Indianapolis in the summer of

1927, officials in both New York and Los Angeles were thinking about Los Angeles as the site of the national convention in 1928.[40]

And so it came to be. Part of the draw was Los Angeles itself. Du Bois loved the place, the 1925 Junior Branch notwithstanding. And then there were the Somervilles. Like many famous leaders, Du Bois had few close friends. Known and admired, perhaps even feared, throughout black America, he was a rather overbearing individual who was not personally close to many people, not even his own wife and daughter. Somehow, though, he felt at home with the Somervilles in Los Angeles. Vada had helped persuade him to bring *Star of Ethiopia* to Los Angeles, and even the peculiar tensions surrounding that event failed to dampen the friendship. The Somervilles wanted Du Bois to bring the national conference to Los Angeles, and Du Bois was willing to entertain the idea, which took on greater possibility when the local branch began to advance after 1925.[41]

John Somerville went the extra mile. He committed himself and his own (borrowed) money to build a special hotel to host the 1928 convention. The need was there; no white hotel in the city was willing to play host to so many African American visitors, and no black-owned hotel was large enough to accommodate the crowds. But where to build? The heart of the black community, Central Avenue and 12th Street, was already crowded and built up, so Somerville bought land further south on Central Avenue, between 40th and 41st, where he built the elegant Hotel Somerville. It was a mostly white residential area, and a good 30 blocks from the traditional Central Avenue scene, and, as a result, some black leaders criticized him for building the hotel too far out. But the hotel was so fine, and the 1928 convention such a smashing success, that black businesses quickly located around the Hotel Somerville, and black residents to the area soon followed. So, as the 1920s came to an end, black Los Angeles had taken its historic leap southward along Central, and soon the neighborhoods between the "old" heart of black Los Angeles and the Hotel Somerville began to fill in with black homes and businesses.[42]

Whatever hint of disgrace remained from *The Star of Ethiopia* in 1925 was washed away by the stunning success of the NAACP's national conference in Los Angeles three years later. Du Bois, reporting on the 1928 meeting in the *Crisis,* fairly gushed about the quality of the local leadership, the beauty of Los Angeles, and, yes, all those automobiles—in which he toured Southern California with unabashed enthusiasm. "The boulevards of Los Angeles," Du Bois wrote, "grip me with nameless ecstasy. To sing with the sun of a golden morning and dip, soar and roll over Wilshire or out to Pasadena where one of the Seven Streets of the World blooms; or out Washington to the sigh of the sound of the sea—this is Glory and Triumph and Life."[43]

And it was "the West," as Du Bois also pointed out, noting, with a rare hint of a feeling of inferiority in his prose, that "we wise men of the East" were

Figure 6.2. In 1928, the Hotel Somerville on Central Avenue hosted the annual convention for the National Association for the Advancement of Colored People. It was the first time the NAACP had held its national convention in Los Angeles. Dr. John Somerville built his elegant hotel partly to attract the NAACP to Los Angeles; its location at 41st and Central set in motion the southward shift of the city's traditional black business district, which had originated closer to downtown. *Shades of L.A. Archives/Los Angeles Public Library*

small and lost amid the vigor and optimism of their western hosts. But the days of Los Angeles as "western" were almost over. In a real sense, the 1928 convention would be the last time black Los Angeles would serve as a western outpost of black America. The city was rapidly transcending its regional roots, and, in the ensuing decades, the irrepressible forces of Great Depression, New Deal, and World War II would further "nationalize" the city—and its African American community. Pageantry as politics would lose its potential, the regional differences among NAACP branches would gradually fade, and civil rights activism would find a new home within an increasingly liberal Democratic Party.

But in 1928, at the Hotel Somerville, flags flying, laughter ringing, horns honking joyfully in the sun-filled air, "the West"—as an ideal and as a place—still mattered to black Los Angeles. And surely the Somervilles and H. Claude Hudson felt exalted. Only three years after the embarrassment of

The Star of Ethiopia, Los Angeles had become, for the moment at least, the center of black America. To live in black Los Angeles in the 1920s was to confront the Klan, restrictive real estate covenants, police brutality, and Jim Crow swimming pools. But it was also to bask in the West Coast's ascent in national culture, to tune in to jazz on Central Avenue, to see the growth of prosperous black businesses, and to be part of a rising civil rights community. It was a town in which civil rights activists persistently bemoaned the lack of community spirit, but also a town that could, given the right circumstances, get things done. The city's individualistic culture incessantly clashed with its community-booster traditions. Lacking consistency, sometimes ugly, sometimes beautiful, and filled with fragile promise: that was Los Angeles in the 1920s. And in that sense, the city mirrored the decade itself.

NOTES

The author wishes to thank Bill Deverell and Tom Sitton for their support of this essay and for their editorial suggestions. The John Randolph Haynes and Dora Haynes Foundation provided financial support for my research. Randy Beohem of the Library of Congress, and financial support from the California Institute of Technology, made it possible for me to obtain a copy of the NAACP's Los Angeles Branch files. Special thanks to Eric Hill, who provided singularly outstanding research assistance for this project.

1. On black Los Angeles in the 1920s, see Lawrence B. De Graaff, "The City of Black Angels: Emergence of the Los Angeles Ghetto, 1890–1930," *Pacific Historical Review* 39 (1970): 323–52; Douglas Flamming, "A Westerner in Search of 'Negroness': Region and Race in the Writing of Arna Bontemps," in Valerie J. Matsumoto and Blake Allmendinger, eds., *Over the Edge: Remapping the American West* (Berkeley and Los Angeles: University of California Press, 1999); and Emory J. Tolbert, *The UNIA and Black Los Angeles* (Los Angeles: Center for Afro-American Studies, 1980).

2. The Junior Branch organized locally in December 1924 and was officially chartered by the national office of the NAACP on January 12, 1925.

3. *California Eagle* (hereinafter *Eagle*), 16, 30 Jan. 1925.

4. *Eagle,* 30 Jan., 10 Apr. 1925.

5. *Eagle,* 16 Jan. 1925.

6. *Eagle,* 10 Apr. 1925.

7. *Eagle,* 13 Feb. 1925.

8. Du Bois describes the first two productions in *Crisis,* Dec. 1915, pp. 91–93; and see David Levering Lewis, *W. E. B. Du Bois: Biography of a Race, 1868–1919* (New York: Henry Holt, 1993), pp. 459–60.

9. *Eagle,* 6, 13 (quote) Feb. 1925.

10. *Eagle,* 20 Feb. 1925.

11. *Eagle,* 13 Feb. 1925.

12. All of the NAACP correspondence cited in this essay may be found in Group I [1909–1939], Series G [Branch Files], Los Angeles Branch Files, Records of the National Association for the Advancement of Colored People, Library of Con-

gress, Washington, D.C. (hereinafter abbreviated as LABF, with the pertinent box and folder information added). James W. McGregor to W. E. B. Du Bois, 24 Mar. 1925 (which has Du Bois's handwritten note to Bagnall); LABF, Box 15, Folder: Jan.–July 1925.

13. See, for example, *Eagle,* 20 Feb.; 6, 13, 20, 27 Mar. 1925.

14. *Eagle,* 27 Mar. 1925.

15. Beatrice S. Thompson to Mr. Robt. W. Bagnall, 4 April 1925, LABF, Box 15, Folder: Jan.–July 1925.

16. *Eagle,* 10 Apr. 1925.

17. *Eagle,* 15 May 1925.

18. *Eagle,* 15, 22 May 1925.

19. *Chicago Defender,* 11 May 1946. In this article, because of either a typo or an inaccurate memory, Du Bois recalls the Hollywood Bowl pageant as being in 1924, rather than 1925.

20. *Eagle,* 29 May 1925.

21. *Eagle,* 22, 29 May 1925; quote in *Chicago Defender,* 11 May 1946.

22. *Los Angeles Times,* 14 June 1925, III:26–27.

23. *Eagle,* 26 June 1925.

24. E. Burton Ceruti to Mr. Walter White, 16 July 1925, LABF, Box 15, Folder: Jan.–July 1925.

25. *Eagle,* 19, 26 June 1925.

26. [Robert Bagnall] Director of Branches to Dr. H. C. Hudson, 15 July 1925; and H. C. Hudson to Mr. Robert W. Bagnal [*sic*], 18 July 1925, LABF, Box 15, Folder: Jan.–July 1925.

27. Haynes's membership noted in [Robert Bagnall] Director of Branches to Mrs. Beatrice S. Thompson, 6 Aug. 1925, LABF, Box 15, Folder: Jan.–July 1925.

28. *Who's Who in Colored Los Angeles—California* (Los Angeles: California Eagle, 1930), p. 91.

29. H. Claude Hudson to William Pickens, 16 Feb. 1925, LABF, Box 15, Folder: Jan.–July 1925.

30. Hudson to Bagnal [*sic*], 18 July 1925, LABF, Box 15, Folder: Jan.–July 1925.

31. Beatrice S. Thompson to Mr. Robert W. Bagnall, 30 Dec. 1925, LABF, Box 15, Folder: Aug.–Dec. 1925.

32. "This residential segregation seems to be getting worse. . . . It is becoming more acute here." H. C. Hudson to Mr. Robert W. Bagnall, 1 Oct. 1925, LABF, Box 15, Folder: Aug.–Dec. 1925. See also news clipping of an Associated Negro Press story, "Sells House to Negro; Sued," datelined Los Angeles, 23 Sept., in ibid.

33. Lulu Slaughter to Mr. Robert W. Bagnall, 25 Sept. 1925, LABF, Box 15, Folder: Aug.–Dec. 1925.

34. H. C. Hudson to Mr. Robert W. Bagnall, 1 Oct. 1925, LABF, Box 15, Folder: Aug.–Dec. 1925.

35. Statement of Memberships, Los Angeles Branch [no date, but c. 1 June 1926], LABF, Box 15, Folder: Jan.–June 1926.

36. *Chicago Defender,* 11 May 1946.

37. Vada Somerville to Mr. Bagnall, 29 May 1926, LABF, Box 15, Folder: Jan.–June 1926.

38. H. C. Hudson to Mr. Robert W. Bagnall, 17 Dec. 1926, LABF, Box 15, Folder: Jan.–June 1926.

39. Director of Branches [Bagnall] to Miss Emma Lue Sayers, 9 June 1927, LABF, Box 16, Folder: June–August, 1927.

40. H. C. Hudson to Mr. Robert W. Bagnall, 17 Dec. 1926; and [H. C.] Hudson to Dear Friend [William] Pickens [NAACP Field Secretary], 10 June 1927, LABF, Box 16, Folder: June–August 1927.

41. Field Secretary [William Pickens] to Dr. H. Claud [*sic*] Hudson, 6 July 1927, LABF, Box 16, Folder: June–August 1927.

42. John Somerville, *Man of Color* (Reprint Services Corporation, 1995), offers an account of how and why he built the Hotel Somerville. *Western Progress,* a photo-directory of black businesses in Los Angeles, c. 1930, indicates how quickly black businesses moved southward to the Hotel Somerville district; a photocopy of this book is located at the Henry E. Huntington Library, San Marino, Calif. The black residential movement on Central Avenue, occurring as it did during the height of restrictive covenants in Los Angeles, raises questions about residence and race that demand further research.

43. W. E. B. Du Bois, "The California Conference," *Crisis,* September 1928, pp. 311–12.

CHAPTER SEVEN

Making Mexico in Los Angeles

Douglas Monroy

The centrality of the decade of the 1920s for the Mexican history of Los Angeles cannot be disputed. The First Great Migration of Mexicans to the city their forebears founded in 1781 took place in the 1920s. This gigantic movement of people derived from the disruptive consequences of the cataclysmic Mexican Revolution (1911–20) and from the striking expansion of the economy of Southern California and the Southwest, which created so many low-wage jobs in the areas of service industries, transportation, and agribusiness. Thus the story of Mexicans in Los Angeles in the 1920s has usually been told as one of dislocation, the labor market and unionization, and adaptation to life in an American city.[1] Here, however, we will explore how Mexican immigrants placed themselves on the landscape of Los Angeles—how, in other words, they attempted to re-create the familiar via theater, sports, and religion.

To be sure, it was on a landscape nominally the domain of the United States upon which Mexicans situated themselves. But there are few things more important to remember than the fact that they understood themselves to be reestablishing Mexican communities in the new land. Their new places, whether *colonias, barrios,* or the old Pueblo de los Angeles around the city's central Plaza, were very much "*México de afuera,*" a popular phrase of the time which translates (approximately) as "outer Mexico," or "Mexico away." These were largely economic, sometimes political, emigrants who sought to sustain their families and find safety from violence and chaos. Blending into the American cultural, social, or political landscape was never the intent of the vast majority of them. Notions of white Protestant superiority kept that choice largely closed to them anyway. The objective was either to return to the homeland when conditions became more satisfactory or to reinstitute the familiar in the new place. The conservative Mexican

Figure 7.1. The old adobe houses from the Mexican period in Los Angeles became the new homes of 1920s Mexican immigrants. *Henry E. Huntington Library, San Marino, Calif.*

newspaper in Los Angeles, *El Heraldo de México,* noted in 1920 that those who migrated did so because of "the misery occasioned by the lack of work and the neediness of the laborers." But they "continue, in spite of that absorbing [American] civilization, feeling as Mexicans, with all of their defects and all of their virtues." The more liberal *La Opinión* similarly acknowledged in 1928 that even though *la gente* came north for better conditions than those "created by the revolution, we must always respond to the requirement of continuing to feel fully Mexican, in love, in intent, in deeds, [and] we have the clear right to express our opinions about our problems."[2] Significantly, "*nuestros problemas*" refers to Mexico.

Into a new Mexico they settled, one without many of the troubles of the old. Moreover, living in the new place seems to have enhanced their opinion of the old one.[3] "You see," stated a night school student in the 1920s, "our people love their country very much, and everyone hopes to go back to his own place some time." One who did become a citizen commented, "Most of the Mexican people do not want to be American citizens, though. I can see why they don't. They all think that they will go back to Mexico. You don't see many of them going, do you?" Community opinion pressured people away from naturalization: "Señor S.G." explained, "I have a store in the Mexican district. If I become a citizen of the United States the Mexicans wouldn't trade with me, because they wouldn't think that I was fair to them or loyal to my country. I read the papers and would like to vote, but I must not become a citizen. I have to have the Mexican trade to make a living." While the presumption of return played the largest role, these and other considerations maintained the formal allegiance of the residents of *México de afuera* to *la madre patria*. (One was, for example, relatively helpless in an American court if one was a citizen in legal trouble, but able to rely on the aid of the Mexican consul if not.) "Never will I become an American citizen. Never!" declared the glamorous movie star Dolores del Río, the most renowned resident of *México de afuera*.[4]

ENTERTAINMENTS AND SPECTACLES

With the family, where one heard the familiar language, smelled the familiar foods, and worshiped the familiar God, and also on certain Los Angeles streets, one knew that one lived in *México de afuera*. There was much to see walking south from the Plaza down Main Street. A solo worker, or a family with the patriarch or the grandmother watching carefully over their brood, or a small cluster of youths just escaped from the literal and figurative confines of the family, encountered signs in Spanish (some of the men and a few of the women could read them), and pictures indicating entertainments which they would find congenial. The railroad connections between the United States and Mexico enabled a variety of Mexican touring companies to come across the border, especially after the turn of the century. The years of the Revolution proved plainly inhospitable to theater in Mexico. Many artists and companies came north, especially to Los Angeles and San Antonio, to wait out the chaos; as we would expect, some stayed on. And there, on Main Street at the most prominent and enduring of the Mexican auditoriums in Los Angeles, Teatro Hidalgo (1911–34), Mexican companies found responsive audiences. Just over on Spring Street were the Teatro Zendejas (later Novel) (1919–24), and the first Teatro México. Farther down Main Street were the Teatro Principal (1921–29), the second México (1927–33), and the California (1927–34). These and several others provided a steady round of Mexican performances; more than a dozen others operated on a more irregular basis.[5]

These theaters represented different things to different people. The first Teatro México aspired to provide *la gente bien* with comforts, such as richly upholstered seats, and theater appropriate to their social status. Owners charged up to $1.50 for box seats and 60 cents for general admission for special events. But those of "the better sort" inconsistently supported the plays, operettas, and urbane touring companies, so genteel presentations had only sporadic runs; the first Teatro México apparently (the sources are confusing) came and went several times. (When it wasn't Teatro México it was the Walker Theater, also used by Mexicans for a variety of purposes, which had originally been the Lyceum.)

The demand for Mexican entertainments represented an opportunity to make some money. If the few *gente bien* could not support a house with high-priced seats, then *la gente trabajadora,* the working people, could compensate with their higher numbers of seats purchased. Most of *la gente* could be counted upon to frequent the less pretentious presentations which included *revistas* (variety reviews), *zarzuelas* (a format of musical plays or comedies originated in Spain), dramas of various themes and tempers, dance troupes, circus-type shows, comedy acts, burlesques, and, eventually, Spanish-language movies. In spite of their largely non-Mexican ownership, the theaters provided a wonderful variety of Mexican shows at assorted prices.[6]

A walker along Spring and Main Streets (the former angled into the latter at Ninth Street) typically saw the signs for such acts as the circus acrobats Trio Rivas; dramas including *La Dama de las Camelias,* by Alexander Dumas, and *La Mujer Adultera,* and historical dramas, *Maximiliano I, Emperador de México, La Guerra de México,* and the "extravaganza of *Don Juan Tenorio*"; or such dance presentations as "Amparito Guillot—la bailarina de los pies desnudos"; or maybe simply an *Orquesta Tipica.* On special occasions one could see promoted on the marquee "Virginia Fábregas, El Orgullo de la raza [pride of the people]," the famed Mexican actress whose company performed the latest European, and sometimes Mexican, plays. Often in the late 1920s and early 1930s one saw advertised Los Pirríns, whose *revistas* starred the picaresque comic Don Catarino.

Several theaters, especially the Hidalgo, showed the new motion pictures. At first, unlike in eastern cities, only Mexican men went to unrefined venues to see rough productions, often about the Mexican Revolution. By 1920 both movies from Mexico's thriving film industry and American ones with Spanish captions (both very much the fare in Mexico City and Guadalajara) flickered on the screens of the Mexican theaters catering to all of *la gente.* In February 1920 one could see at the Hidalgo Charlie Chaplin's *El Nuevo Portero* for ten cents, or the Mexican *Revelación* with "La celebrada artista Madame Nazinova." Several months later the marquee advertised, with faulty chronology, the ten-part "*Ramona,* an exquisite and vivid historical narrative of the times when California belonged to Mexico." The management showed consideration for, and reinforced, Mexican proprieties when it tendered such films as *Está Segura Su Hija?* which presented "*!La Verdad Ante Sus Ojos!*" Teatro California showed it for several weeks in 1927 for men only, and then later only for women, at 50, 40, and 25 cents per ticket.[7]

One could enter not only the salacious world of some Hollywood movies and their Mexican imitators, or that of escapist comedy, or the simplified world of some happy or oppressed or naive folk society. Mexican theater-goers could also choose portrayals of life in all of its complexities. Nicolás Kanellos's careful reconstruction of the Mexican theater scene in Los Angeles reveals its remarkable richness and depth. The popular *revistas,* offered at various prices and aimed at assorted appreciations of humor and parody, typically satirized such issues as the culture shock immigrants experienced upon arrival in the American metropolis, the resulting vitiation of Mexican culture, and, quite commonly, the Mexican Revolution. Los Pirríns' *revistas,* largely the creations of the ingenious Don Catarino, lampooned everything from Hollywood to Hell to the Depression to el niño Fidencio (a crackpot spirit boy in Mexico) to repatriation to "Whiskey, *morfina, y marihuana.*" Other writers, often under contract to one of the theaters, created *revistas* with similar themes, aimed at both working- and middle-class audiences.

Fleeing the turmoil of Mexico, several playwrights adopted Los Angeles as their semipermanent home. Eduardo Carrillo, Adalberto Elías González, and Gabriel Navarro made Los Angeles into a center of Mexican dramaturgy. These expatriates were fundamentally Mexican writers, but their themes often dealt with the predicaments of Mexicans in the North. (González's most successful play, an adaptation of *Ramona,* broke Los Angeles box office records in 1927, toured throughout the Southwest, and sometimes starred Virginia Fábregas.) [8] Mexican people of different classes and aspirations produced, staffed, and attended these theaters physically located in Los Angeles, but most certainly situated in *México de afuera.*

Yet other doorways afforded passage in and out of *México de afuera.* Emerging from one of the theaters, a walker on Main Street reentered the public and culturally assorted American city. On the way back to the Plaza, however, the doors of La Ciudad de México beckoned shoppers. According to its newspaper ads, this department store on North Main Street offered "*la colonia mexicana residente en Los Angeles*" everything from clothing to *chile* to milk to lunch boxes. A few doors away the Farmacia Hidalgo (with another store on Los Angeles Street) asserted that "we have the largest stock of medicines and Mexican herbal remedies." Many of the *colonias* around the county had such *farmacias,* which also functioned as typical drug stores tendering Mexican sodas, ice creams, and candies. A block further on North Main was the Repertorio Musical Mexicana which featured for 75 cents "Discos Victor" of the latest Mexican popular tunes. A loudspeaker proclaimed the availability of the familiar music to be played on the new machines and usually attracted an assembly of male listeners.[9] The area was not like the old Mexican village, because people came from all over, but it was fundamentally Mexico that Mexican people sought to build upon the cityscape of Los Angeles.

Figure 7.2. Hanging out at the Plaza, the historic center of Mexican Los Angeles. *Seaver Center for Western History Research, Natural History Museum of Los Angeles County*

THE PASSIONS OF *MÉXICO DE AFUERA*

We might say that cultural transplants blossomed differently in the new soil: *revistas* with Chicano themes; worship of the beautiful Virgin of Guadalupe; and other activities, such as baseball, expressing a universal male worldview, a *mestizaje* of sports. Indeed, Mexican men both consciously and intuitively sought validation in the new place through organized competitions. Perhaps, too, for similar reasons, they enjoyed strenuous recreation, especially boxing, and some at least found opportunities for making money through such passions.

In 1916 *El Heraldo de México* reported, "Several youthful companions, amateur enthusiasts of 'baseball,' have begun practicing this lovely sport in the lawn tennis patio of the club." This was the Club Anahuac, "where the principal families of our reputable society always meet." Club Anahuac likely combined recently arrived Mexican elites with the remnants of pre–Mexican War Californio society. (At a dance there, the attendees included "Señorita Couts," no doubt an offspring of the original marital alliance between the Californio Bandini family and the mildly Hispanicized Yankee entrepreneur Cave Couts.) [10] The appeal of the great game, though, could never be confined to such pretentious aristocratic circles.

By the late 1920s, teams sponsored by local Mexican businesses regularly competed with one another and with other ethnically identified teams, local Anglo clubs, and touring professionals from the United States and Mexico. The most renowned local Mexican teams of the era seem to have been El Paso Shoe Store, El Porvenir Grocery, and the Ortiz New Fords. El Porvenir Grocery, on First Street in Belvedere, had a ballpark next to it, El Gran Parque Mexicano, but El Paso Shoe Store had the best team. Itinerant workers could not have participated consistently of course, but, because of the high level of competition and the number of teams, doubtless a cross-structure of Mexican social classes took the field together. In 1929, Dr. A. C. Tellez, former catcher and captain of the University of California team, caught for El Paso Shoe Store.

Sports have greater meaning than the simple competition, and Mexican baseball in Los Angeles of the 1920s was no exception. It was one way the various people from south of the border forged an identity as Mexicans, a way for Mexicans to garner respect in the eyes of the *americanos,* and a public reinforcement of the traditional manly family values of forceful, dynamic activities. El Porvenir Grocery sponsored various baseball games and charged admission for "an afternoon of enthusiasm, healthy fun, and genuine emotions," quite openly "an afternoon simply Mexican." The crowds cheered for "their team," and their teams were often organized by ethnic group: when El Paso Shoe Store played the Nippons we can be sure that Mexicans rooted for their *"estrellas mexicanas,"* and that Japanese fans rooted for (as their uniforms were emblazoned) their "Nips." Mexicans in Los Angeles, at least the men, could feel a bit more upstanding when in the spring of 1929 El Paso Shoe Store defeated the Paramount Studios Sheiks and the Commercial Club Millionaires, and especially when, on Cinco de Mayo, they beat the Pacific Electric Trainmen in "an emotional game." Similarly when the championship team from Mexico, San Luis, played the Philadelphia Negro Giants in November 1929 (they split a two-game series), we can be quite certain about who was cheering for whom. The scene in the stands at such games was a remarkable one, as folk literally from all over the world played and watched baseball together in Los Angeles. Perhaps nothing is more emblematic of Los Angeles's emergence as an international city. And, it should be added, the sources do not mention altercations between the different peoples.[11]

Of course the appeal of the baseball games centered around the competition. Much was reflected in these contests: *"El evento beisbolístico más importante,"* exclaimed *La Opinión* about "the most important baseball event that has registered in the bosom of the Mexican colony in the past years, [which] will take place tomorrow afternoon in White Sox Stadium when the Mexicans of the mighty El Paso Shoe Store Club battle the orientals of the Los Angeles Nippons for the 'foreign championship of baseball' of the United States." I do not know how the Japanese press portrayed the series of games, and the *americano* press remained unsurprisingly silent about the matter, but what at least the Mexican press proclaimed as "the championship," the "Mexican stars" won by a score of 10 to 5 on May 12, 1929. Sports writers have always embellished the rhetoric about what constitutes a "world championship," but we can be sure that they expressed some truth when, after the Mexicans won the first game in April, *La Opinión* reported that the El Paso Shoe Store team "established themselves as the idols of the hundreds of *aficionados* [overwhelmingly male] of our *raza* who attended yesterday." [12]

Beyond the simple accounting of who won and who lost, much more complicated issues of allegiance were at stake as well, ones that have much to do with maleness and national identity. Appearances were important here: how *la raza* appeared to themselves and to others, how Mexicans imagined themselves in this curious new land of movie studio sheiks and Nippons. After one victory over the latter in April 1929, *La Opinión* noted, "The task these boys are undertaking on the sports field, which is the most appreciated among the American people, to elevate the good name of our *raza*, should not be overlooked." El Paso Shoe Store had demonstrated their suitability "to participate in the major leagues of Los Angeles," that is, the Triple A minor leagues which the Hollywood Stars and the Los Angeles Angels represented. (Perhaps some non-Mexican local promoters had suggested this possibility too.) [13] Simultaneously, then, baseball served to create cohesion and identity in "the Mexican colony," to provide recreation, and to display Mexicans' (at least the male ones) desire for the validation of the broader Los Angeles populace—for *mexicanos* to be acknowledged dwellers, Mexican ones, of the place.

Another Sunday activity provides a window into the female Mexican immigrant character in the decades of mass migration. Although men (in frocks) lorded over the ceremonies and males attended, the church embodied a feminine presence on the landscape. Catholicism arrived in Mexico in the 1520s and 1530s, but surely the great syncretic moment in the Christianizing effort came in 1531 when the Virgin Mary appeared to the Indian Juan Diego on the hill which had been home to the popular Tonantzin, the vanquished Aztec mother goddess of the earth, fertility, and corn. Indian-like in her features, this beautiful Virgin of Guadalupe came not only to attract many Indians to the True Faith, but to epitomize the *mestizaje* of Old and New World religions. She endures as a central figure of Mexican Catholicism and as the symbol of Mexican nationalism. On an institutional level, though, the American church in the Southwest, manned mostly by clergy of German and Irish descent (over 80 percent at the turn of the century), did not pay much attention to its Mexican believers until after World War II. Most of the sources note that no less than 90 percent of the Mexicans who came in the great migrations were nominally Catholic, but were and remained "mostly poorly instructed in the faith." A street paver named Bonifacio Ortega professed a common attitude in Los Angeles in 1926: "I am Catholic, but the truth is I hardly follow out my beliefs. I never go to the church nor do I pray. I have with me an amulet which my mother gave to me before dying. This amulet has the Virgin of Guadalupe on it and it is she who always protects me." A resident of the Pacoima *barrio* recalled how the place was reanimated with the spirit of the Virgen Morena, the Dark Virgin, every May. "To the practicing Catholics of our town, the month of May was *el mes de María,* dedicated to the Blessed Virgin Mary." It included "the nightly offering of flowers to Our Lady. This Mexican custom, brought by our parents to this country, was something I enjoyed."[14]

If religion and politics tend to cause disputes, then we can be sure that when the two are mixed, as they so often have been in Mexico, strife and contention will abound. Politically, such manifestations of religion reanimated the fights over the role of belief in people's lives, and the relationship of church and state. Most vocal in the 1920s were the "Liberales," the remnants of the anarchist Partido Liberal Mexicano who had lived communally, farmed fruit, and published an incendiary newspaper about the need for revolution in Los Angeles in the 1910s. One of their followers spoke in the Plaza in the era of World War I and said that "that old Roman Church opposite us is a nest of deceivers." A decade before, another had referred to "the clergy, this impenitent traitor, this servant of Rome, and irreconcilable enemy of free nations." And another pronounced that "Religion, whatever the denomination with which we are presented, is the most terrible enemy of woman." The *libre pensadores,* or free thinkers, also took to Plaza pulpits to chastize religion.[15]

Religious festivals, then, on the streets of *México de afuera* expressed not only religious feelings, but the highly charged politics of church and state in Mexico. In June 1928, an estimated 10,000 Mexicans took part in the church-sponsored *Fiesta de Corpus Cristi.* Believers marched from Nuestra Señora de Guadalupe church in Belvedere to La Soledad church. Participants included several consequential Mexican prelates "who live in California in exile." But the same year witnessed the first procession in honor of the Holy Mother. In what was a rather small undertaking at first, members of Hijas de María (the Daughters of Mary) paraded in adulation of the Virgin. The march soon found a sponsor in José David Orozco, a local travel agency owner and radio personality, who saw in the event an opportunity to further the prayer movement he had been organizing in support of the religiously persecuted in Mexico. In late 1929 he began forming chapters of the Asociación del Santo Nombre (the Holy Name Society), and by the next year had established about 40 chapters in Southern California. Urged on by his uncle, exiled Archbishop Francisco Orozco y Jiménez, Orozco mixed veneration of the Virgin with antigovernment politics when he persuaded Julio C. Guerrero, patron of Hijas de María, to cede sponsorship of the procession to Santo Nombre.[16]

For Orozco and Santo Nombre, these parades offered not only an occasion to express support for the church in Mexico but also the opportunity to promote what he called, in an interview with historian Francisco Balderrama, "Mexican consciousness." Aware that discrimination against Mexicans and the antipathy of the *americanos* to their culture would likely produce a sense of inferiority, Orozco understood Santo Nombre as a way to resuscitate *la raza*'s ethnic pride. Thus the shouts of "Viva Cristo Rey" (the slogan of the pro-church faction in Mexico); "the rosary beads slipping through rugged fingers, the hymn to Our Lady of Guadalupe on a thousand lips"; and an affirmation of Mexicanness in the streets of Los Angeles all merged in these remarkable processions.[17]

For the 1929 march *La Opinión* displayed her picture on the front page: She was "the Only and True Queen." "In Mexico," the article expounded, "one of the most powerful spiritual bonds is, undoubtedly, the veneration that all of the Mexicans—except the nonbelievers—feel for the Virgin of Guadalupe, Indian Virgin, of our *raza,* of our color."[18] Those who performed rituals around her figure, either prayers, votive candle offerings, pilgrimages, or processions, hoped that their actions would invoke her intervention in this dolorous world, either in their lives or in those of people they cared about or had an interest in. The immigrants transported these old rituals to the new land, but only those of the universal saints, like Mary. Many of the lesser spirits, peculiar to specific places in Mexico, were left behind. It was Mary, and her son, whom the Mexicans from diverse places had in common.

Then, too, on Sundays, while the men played with their bats and balls, a Mexican woman could see in this Virgen Morena a model of the most perfect love, the acme of all human relationships—the mutual adoration of mother and boy child. With her baby at her breast, Mary asserted the most profound presence of superiority over men and the state. Then Mary lost her precious son to the profane (male) world of temporal power, lust, and bloodletting—as did many other mothers.

Bert Colima was one of those mothers' sons of *México de afuera.* When "*el Mexicano de Whittier*" knocked down Bobby Corbett with a crashing right to the jaw, and then knocked him out with a blow to the solar plexus, the fans at Hollywood Boxing Stadium on June 20, 1924, "were on their chairs shouting their heads off." "The Whittier Flash" to the Anglo press, and "*el ídolo de Whittier*" to the Mexican press, Colima "was recognized as the best middleweight on the Coast" during the 1920s, according to one fight expert, "and his fights with such men as Oakland Jimmy Duffy were regarded as ring classics." *La Opinión* described how "in his ten years [in the ring] he has maintained Mexican supremacy in the 160 pound division, and has never lost his fame as the biggest ticket attraction for the aficionados [of boxing] of our *raza.*" Colima fought Anglos, blacks, and other Mexicans; sometimes he was "*noqueado,*" but mostly "*el noqueó*" his opponent. In those days the referees did not stop fights where one of the combatants had become defenseless.[19] They deferred to the shrilly expressed will of the crowd for a knockout: another mother's son left outstretched and bleeding on the canvas.

Nineteen twenty-four marked an important year for Los Angeles fight fans; three locals, Fidel LaBarba, Jack Fields, and Joe Salas, won medals at the Paris Olympic Games. LaBarba, the U.S. amateur flyweight champ, won a gold in that division, and Fields defeated Salas, national featherweight amateur champion, for the gold in the featherweight. Joe Salas from *México de afuera,* in other words, won a silver medal for the United States in the 1924 Olympics, and Fidel LaBarba, who, though an Italian, was no gringo Protestant, won a gold.[20]

While there may be a certain "purity" to the stark scene of two men going *mano a mano* in the ring, these were manufactured dramas. "To Dutch Meyers," noted a contemporary fight expert, "must be given credit for developing the biggest individual favorite during the days of the four round game in the southern part of the state. Meyers, an old friend and pal of Bert Colima, brought him along to the point where his every appearance meant a packed house."[21] Promoters arranged these fights for maximum appeal, of course. This meant that they exploited ethnicity, revenge, and the promise of brutality to increase the sale of tickets. *Aficionados* of the sport, almost inevitably deeply steeped in the history of famous bouts, have appreciated the remarkable skill levels which individual boxers have achieved, as well as the physical aesthetics of the ebb and flow of a bout. It has always been the blood and the knockout, though, which have provided the primary appeal of the big fights.

As in the eastern part of the country, boxers were often ethnically identified. "Joey Silver, Jew from San Francisco, won by technical knock out over the Mexican, Young González, from El Paso" was a typical entry in *La Opinión's* sport section. So was "*Colima noqueó al negro* Wolcott Langford." After "*Colima Noqueó Anoche* [last night] a Tiger Bob Robinson *en 1er. Round,*" the many Mexicans in attendance at Culver City Stadium enthusiastically applauded Colima, who on this occasion demonstrated much confidence and ability in his defense and in his delivery of blows, "*y un punch considerable.*" Colima "during the last ten years has maintained Mexican supremacy in the 160 pound division." Again, through identification with pan-Mexican figures such as Colima—*el mexicano de* Whittier who was briefly

middleweight champ of Mexico—village men from various parts of the republic could see themselves more and more as Mexicans.[22]

Such identifications, though, have their complexities. Through their ethnic emphasis, the matches separated people who may well have had, if not
some notions of brotherhood, at least some common interests and consciousness regarding their economic station in life. On one occasion when
Bert Colima was defeated it was because "Ace Hudkins *Peleó Ayer Muy Sucia-
mente* [fought very dirty]," as the headline blared: "*El Norteamericano destrozó
a Colima por medio de cabezazos* [head butts]." "It was," *La Opinión* concluded,
"one of the dirtiest fights we have ever seen in the rings of California." To
the extent that boxing has provided a paradigm for manhood, it has also
contributed to various groups' constructions of how other groups *are:* ma-
cho, crafty, slick, intelligent, strong-chinned, dirty fighters are adjectives
that come immediately to mind. While boxing arguably has offered a relatively safe outlet for such tribal loyalties, its different styles, often ethnically
associated, and the way promoters and the press have amplified them, have,
in the words of one boxing analyst, "reinforced the emotional perception,
if not the intellectual idea, that men are different physically and psycholog-
ically because they belong to different races." Any fight fan knows that "no
fighters in the world are more dedicated to the raw violence of the business
than Mexicans."[23]

Boxing gave youth a particular and Mexican notion of manhood to think
about, or, more likely, to imitate. "Two or three Mexicans have become famous boxers and gotten rich, like Colima, Fuente, and the like," noted a
Los Angeles playground director in 1926. "Nearly every Mexican boy has
the ambition to be a great boxer. This is the main thing that he thinks about
until he gets married and has to go to work digging ditches or working for
the railroad." It was acknowledged at the time that the sport manifested
"manliness and heroism." Frankie García provides one among many examples of the boxer as family man. A member of the Los Angeles Athletic
Club, García came to fame with a sensational knockout of Tamachula in the
International Amateur Championships held in San Francisco in 1917. This
flyweight turned pro and "is one of the cleanest boxers in the country and
one of the hardest right hand hitters, if not the hardest in his class. During
his time in the ring Frankie has saved enough money to provide a nice
home for his folks and family. He is the proud father of a fine little son, who
he claims some day will be the champion of the world in his class." Mexicans
rooted their family values in a variety of ways in the new land.[24]

Boxing has provided a path to success for young men, one that affirmed
in a public arena the masculine values of aggressiveness, forcefulness, and
immunity to pain. Almost every boxer has aspired to be a big winner, if
not a champion. What I have noted about Colima in regard to his physical

prowess and fortitude clearly marks him as an admirable man. After one of his several suspensions for fouls, Colima sought to open an athletic club "near the inhabitants of Pico" to instruct youth in boxing. Press clippings make clear that this great boxer (his ring violations notwithstanding) and others like him were men to be emulated in *México de afuera*. La Asociación Deportiva Hispano-Americana, for example, feted Colima as guest of honor at their *"Baile Deportiva"* held at the Masonic Temple in May 1927. (The middle-class *gente* danced to the Dixieland Mosby Bluesblowers, José Arias y los Monarcas del Jazz, and the Verdugo Imperials.) After European champion Paulino Uzcúdum won the Latin American championship in Mexico City in January 1928, this heavyweight received an *"entusiasta recepción"* at Teatro Hidalgo. Uzcúdum was actually a Basque from Spain, whom *La Opinión* adopted as a *"gran boxeador de la raza."* Bert Colima personally gave him the welcoming at this headline-grabbing event.[25] To be a contender, like Colima or Uzcúdum in their respective divisions, was for a working-class youth a way to be somebody.

EL FLAPPERISMO

In March 1928, *La Opinión* published an article with the headline: *"El Flapperismo Ha Hecho Iguales Las Mujeres."* They attributed the comment—that "Flapperdom Has Made All Women the Same"—with dateline in New York, to Helena Rubenstein. The editors clearly approved of Rubenstein's view that "With her short hair, with her painted cheeks and lips, with her skirts to her knees, they all seem the same. One no longer finds the true attraction and beauty with which women should be possessed." The comment typified complaints made generally about flappers. Then, too, the female figure evoked much attention: *La Opinión* often pictured *americana* models, emblematic of "the New Woman," in bathing suits. An article from June 1929 explained that such attire "would be the scandal of our grandmothers without any doubt. In these fast moving times we generally stifle the age-old and irreproachable sense of female modesty in favor of comfort and hygiene." (That is, the bare backs permitted "a healthy sun bath.")[26] These sentiments actually masked all manner of profound ambivalence about the flapper. Whether a culture based its ideal female on the model of la Virgen de Guadalupe or Queen Victoria, the notion that a woman could use physical allure to be an active participant, even initiator, in romantic occasions met with powerful repulsion, and attraction.

Of course, it was in the movies that these new images most enticingly manifested themselves. Several important stars developed in Mexico's thriving film industry made their way north to the international capital, Hollywood. Often their accents prohibited their making a transition to the talkies, but at least Ramon Novarro, Gilbert Roland, Lupe Velez, and Dolores del Río will forever be associated with Hollywood's early glory days. These were also ambiguous days. There was, on the one hand, ample demand and opportunity for Latino stars. But none of them could portray positive Mexican characters, because there were none in the scripts. Usually these actors were cast as generically exotic romantic figures.[27]

There is much more to be learned from the careers and legacies of Lupe Velez and Dolores del Río. *La Opinión* called del Río "our greatest screen star." In November 1928, a "Fiesta Mexicana . . . a royal event of homage and welcoming from the Mexican Colony" was held for her after her "triumphal return" from Europe. Los Angeles Mexicans had in her not only a compelling figure in the aristocratic del Río's own right, but a star whose beauty, fame, talent, and charisma equaled that of any other. And she provided an appealing model of womanhood, one that expressed a fuller range of feminine possibility than the usual well-known dichotomy. Of course, the movie star as archetype has been a problematic figure in the twentieth century; likely too many fans are "star-struck." A translation from an article of April 1929 in *La Opinión* allows one to imagine the Hollywood scene in *México de afuera*. The story discussed "the most sensational movie of the year: 'Evangelina,' based on the poem by Longfellow and directed by Edwin Carewe. Two Mexicans who have reached prominence on the screen have the principal parts in the production: she, the sublime (*excelsa*) Dolores del Río; he, Ernesto Guillén, best known in the cinema world by the pseudonym of Donald Reed." This could happen only in America, and only in Hollywood. On Mexican Independence Day in 1927, *La Opinión* included Dolores del Río among "five Mexicans who give prestige to *la raza*."[28]

While del Río embodied more the "grande dame" of the silver screen, red-haired Lupe Velez, "*la inquieta e inquietante* [the restless and disturbing], . . . embodies the genuine sort of sensual actress, vehemently without artifice or falseness." She was born into an elite family in San Luis Potosí, and took to acting when her father was wounded in the Revolution and her mother's stage career foundered in the turmoil. First known in the United States as the "The Wild Cat of Mexico," and later famous as the "Mexican Spitfire," she initially gained renown in the 1927 movie *The Gaucho,* in which she played the jealous lover of Douglas Fairbanks. Indeed, she provided quite a restless and disturbing figure for movie fans. The news about her romance with Gary Cooper—according to the paper in November 1929, "the only man with whom she had been in love in her whole life"—and of her illnesses, and speeding tickets (for "following her natural impulses") regularly made movie section headlines. She was, well, a "fast woman." Luella Parsons, whose syndicated column appeared regularly in translation on the paper's *Página Cinematográfico,* referred to her as a "Spanish beauty," an identity that Velez seemed at times to cultivate. *La Opinión* took umbrage not only at how "our Lupe Velez . . . had been mistakenly called 'Spanish,'" but as well at how the *"simpática artista mexicana"* herself seemed to connive in misleading fans about her identity.[29]

Such stars made popular appearances not only on the screen but at well-publicized events, especially at the openings of their films. Lupe Velez appeared in June 1928 at the downtown United Artists Theater "in person with her lively dances and songs at the first showing at popular prices of the Douglas Fairbanks film 'El Gaucho.'" Dolores del Río appeared from time to time at Teatro Hidalgo. Lupita Tovar, "the new Mexican star" from Fox Studios, introduced the El Paso Shoe Store baseball team at their Cinco de Mayo (1929) championship game against Pacific Electric. But many of these Mexican stars faded: "Lupe is one of the few of our stars who has been saved from the shipwreck occasioned by the talking picture." (Lupita Tovar starred in 1931 in the first talkie produced in Mexico, *Santa.*) Hollywood could accept the pretty faces of exotic Latinas but not their Spanish-accented voices.[30]

DEPRESSION

The 1920s was a neatly defined decade only within the Anglo-American paradigm. For Mexicans in Los Angeles, who overwhelmingly lived outside the mainstream of American culture and who usually worked under depressed conditions, neither the "return to normalcy" nor the stock market crash proved momentous. Certainly, the Depression harmed Mexican workers' wages and employment opportunities, and 1930 in particular witnessed reversals in Mexican attempts to build *México de afuera* in Los Angeles. Responding to what *La Opinión* and others called the threat of "disasters of *desmexicanización,*" or the undoing of traditional Mexican values and conduct, Mexican civic leaders had been attempting in the late 1920s both to create "Mexican schools" and to foster the making of Spanish-language films.

As they were described in May 1928, these afternoon and evening schools sought "to inspire in the students a powerful love for our country . . . they are taught . . . Spanish, national history, patriotic readings, stories of our heroes, [and] Mexican music," and "the responsibilities they have toward Mexico and the United States, while they live in this country."[31] But interest on the part of youth waned, and neither the Mexican government nor the local Mexican community could consistently support them financially, so that only three rural and isolated schools remained by late 1930 out of an original fifty. Similarly, both La Asociación Cultural America-Española, which sought to pressure Hollywood studios to produce better Spanish-speaking films, and the independent Hollywood Spanish Pictures Company, which sought actually to produce them, saw the Depression quickly ruin their efforts.[32]

Of course the sports and the faith would continue in the new land; no Depression could kill those passions. But the efforts to create Mexican institutions that attended to the young in the places where they spent the most time outside their families—schools and movies—fell to the lack of support of the Mexican middle class and the preference of Mexican youth for American spectacles. In the 1920s *México de afuera* could only be partially built on the landscape of Los Angeles.

NOTES

1. Ricardo Romo, *East Los Angeles: History of a Barrio* (Austin: University of Texas Press, 1983); George J. Sánchez, *Becoming Mexican American: Ethnicity, Culture, and Identity in Chicano Los Angeles, 1900–1945* (New York: Oxford University Press, 1993); Douglas Monroy, *Rebirth: Mexican Los Angeles from the Great Migration to the Great Depression* (Berkeley and Los Angeles: University of California Press, 1999).

2. *El Heraldo de México*, May 13, 1920; *La Opinión*, November 24, 1928.

3. Ernest Galarza, *Barrio Boy* (South Bend, Ind.: University of Notre Dame Press, 1971), 200; Manuel Gamio, *Mexican Immigration to the United States: A Study of Human Migration and Adjustment* (Chicago: University of Chicago Press, 1930), 236.

4. Blanche A. Sommerville, "Naturalization from the Mexican Viewpoint," *Community Exchange Bulletin* 6 (May 1928): 11; Helen W. Walker, "Mexican Immigrants and American Citizenship," *Sociology and Social Research* 13 (1929): 468, 471; Emory Bogardus, "The Mexican Immigrant and Segregation," *American Journal of Sociology* 36 (July 1930): 76–78; *La Opinión*, April 20, 1928.

5. Nicolás Kanellos, *A History of Hispanic Theater in the United States: Origins to 1940* (Austin: University of Texas Press, 1990), 17–21.

6. Kanellos, *A History of Hispanic Theater*, 19–39.

7. William Wilson McEuen, "A Survey of the Mexicans in Los Angeles" (M.A. thesis, University of Southern California, 1914), 74. These examples are taken randomly from ads in *El Heraldo de México*, January 7, November 15, 18, 22, & 30, 1919, January 7, 30, & 31, February 6, 20, & 24, and June 12, 1920; and from *La Opinión*, March 7 & 15, April 2, and May 9 & 21, 1927; Kanellos, *A History of Hispanic Theater*, 26, 66. *Ramona* took place in the first decades of the American period of California history.

8. Kanellos, *A History of Hispanic Theater*, 44–59, 65–69.

9. *La Opinión*, December 22, 1926, January 2 and March 14, 1927, June 3, 1928, and November 28, 1930; *El Heraldo de México*, August 23, 1921; Sánchez, *Becoming Mexican American*, 182.

10. *El Heraldo de Mexico*, April 22 & 29, 1916; on the Couts family see Douglas Monroy, *Thrown among Strangers: The Making of Mexican Culture in Frontier California* (Berkeley and Los Angeles: University of California Press, 1991), 160, 192–193.

11. *La Opinión,* March 31, April 1, 21, & 22, May 6, 12, & 30, and November 22, 1929, and December 21, 1930.

12. *La Opinión,* April 13, 14, 15, & 16, and May 13, 1929.

13. *La Opinión,* April 16, 20, & 21, 1929.

14. William E. North, "Catholic Education in Southern California" (Ph.D. dissertation, Catholic University of America, 1936), 188–190; Sánchez, *Becoming Mexican American,* 157, 163; Manuel Gamio, *The Mexican Immigrant: His Life-Story* (Chicago: University of Chicago Press, 1931), 28; Mary Helen Ponce, *Hoyt Street: An Autobiography* (Albuquerque: University of New Mexico Press, 1993), 162.

15. Vernon Monroe McCombs, "Stopping the Reds," *El Mexicano* 7 (January–March 1919): 1; "Manifesto a la Nación del Plan del Partido Liberal *Mexicano* de 1906," reprinted in Juan Gómez-Quiñones, *Sembradores, Ricardo Flores Magón y el Partido Liberal Mexicano: A Eulogy and Critique* (Los Angeles: Atzlán Publications, 1973), 96; *Regeneración,* November 6, 1910; Samuel M. Ortegon, "The Religious Status of the Mexican Population of Los Angeles" (M.A. thesis, University of Southern California, 1932), 22–23.

16. *La Opinión,* June 10, 1928; Francisco Balderrama, *In Defense of La Raza: The Los Angeles Mexican Consulate and the Mexican Community, 1929 to 1936* (Tucson: University of Arizona Press, 1982), 76–77; Sánchez, *Becoming Mexican American,* 167–168.

17. Mike Davis, *City of Quartz: Excavating the Future in Los Angeles* (London: Verso, 1990), 330–331; Balderrama, *In Defense of La Raza,* 77; Sánchez, *Becoming Mexican American,* 168–169.

18. *La Opinión,* December 12, 1929.

19. *Los Angeles Times,* June 21, 1924; DeWitt Van Court, *The Making of Champions in California* (Los Angeles: Premier Printing Co., 1926), 136; *La Opinión,* January 21, 1930; Joyce Carol Oates, "On Boxing," in Joyce Carol Oates and Daniel Halpern, eds., *Reading the Fights* (New York: Henry Holt, 1988), 298–299.

20. Jeffrey T. Sammons, *Beyond the Ring: The Role of Boxing in American Society* (Urbana: University of Illinois Press, 1988), 27–29, 59–64, 257; *Los Angeles Times,* July 15 & 21, 1924; Van Court, *The Making of Champions in California,* 117. Van Court notes that Fidel LaBarba was senior class president at Lincoln High School. After the Olympics he turned pro to buy a house for his parents. In 1925 he quickly fought his way to the American flyweight championship, and then became world champion in 1927, at which point he took a year off to go to Stanford University.

21. Van Court, *The Making of Champions in California,* 136.

22. *La Opinión,* January 15 and March 21, 1928, April 1, 1927, and January 21, 1930.

23. *La Opinión,* March 9, 1927; Gerald Early, "Three Notes toward a Cultural Definition of Prizefighting," in Oates and Halpern, eds., *Reading the Fights,* 28; Hugh McIlvanney, "Onward Virgin Soldier: Lupe Pintor v. Johnny Owen, Los Angeles, September 19, 1980," in ibid., 191.

24. Emory S. Bogardus, *The City Boy and His Problems: A Survey of Boy Life in Los Angeles* (Los Angeles: Rotary Club, 1926), 86; Van Court, *The Making of Champions in California,* 2, 138–139.

25. *La Opinión,* May 26, 1927, and February 6, 7, & 9, 1928.

26. *La Opinión,* March 18, 1928, May 23 & 26, and June 2, 1929.

27. George Hadley-Garcia, *Hispanic Hollywood: The Latins in Motion Pictures* (New York: Carroll, 1990), 27–29.

28. *La Opinión,* November 27 and December 9, 1928, April 15, 1929, and September 16, 1927.

29. *La Opinión* March 16, May 25, and July 13, 1928, May 26 and November 17, 1929, January 19, 1930, and March 3 and April 26, 1927.

30. *La Opinión,* June 2, 1928, May 26 and November 3, 1929, and March 21, 1930; Hadley-Garcia, *Hispanic Hollywood,* 52.

31. *La Opinión,* November 29, 1926, and May 5, 1928.

32. *La Opinión* February 7 & 11, January 26 & 30, March 2, 4, 5, & 23, and April 30, 1930. Hadley-Garcia, *Hispanic Hollywood,* 54.

CHAPTER EIGHT

The View from Spring Street
White-Collar Men in the City of Angels

Clark Davis

In 1928, throngs of Americans in cities throughout the nation streamed to local movie palaces to watch *The Crowd,* an MGM feature directed by King Vidor. The two-hour silent film presented a devastating vision of modern life. The story begins on July 4, 1900, with the birth of Johnny Sims in an idyllic small town. Upon seeing his new son, Johnny's father triumphantly announces, "There's a little man the world is going to hear from all right. . . . I'm going to give him every opportunity." Twenty-one years later, however, Johnny Sims is working as no. 137 in a New York City insurance company, toiling away in what can only be described as white-collar hell. His desk is in a vast room where hundreds of identically dressed young men sit in evenly spaced rows turning page after page of documents in perfect unison. Johnny's home life proves equally stifling as his wife and in-laws grow bitter over his inability to climb in the firm. When he finally gets a break and wins $100 in an advertising jingle contest, an automobile strikes and kills his youngest child during the celebration. Incapacitated by grief, Johnny quits, narrowly averting being fired. The film closes with Johnny and his wife escaping to the movies. He sits in the theater having a great time, but as the camera fades, viewers see him watching amid a crowd of thousands who appear and act exactly like him. Even in this brief moment of pleasure, he remains immersed in the crowd.

The Crowd offered Americans a bleak appraisal of urban life in the 1920s. Small-town kids were moving to cities, only to find themselves enveloped in urban jungles where opportunities for personal autonomy and individual achievement were at best rare. Grueling and distasteful white-collar positions in big corporations seemed the likely fate of even the most ambitious young men. Yet *The Crowd,* and a host of other films in a genre I call "corporate noir," were not the only vision of middle-class life presented to

179

Americans during the 1920s. While negative depictions of urban life usually centered on New York City or some fictionalized eastern metropolis, life on the other coast seemed to promise a very different experience. Boosters and developers touted western cities as lingering frontiers where good weather, cheap land, and swelling economies promised relief from midwestern monotony or eastern despair.[1]

No city promised to overcome the perils of modernity and to provide "the good life" more than Los Angeles. While urban scenes occasionally began to appear in Southern California promotional literature during the 1920s, the text and images almost never departed from the ideal of a Mediterranean oasis. Typical was a 1924 promotional pamphlet that characterized the region by its "mystery, romance, charm, splendor . . . The vastness of far-flung spaces . . . Trees in bloom throughout the year, flowers in bloom all the time, fragrant orange blossoms . . . snow-covered summits . . . the fullness, the richness, the magic out of doors inviting always. . . ."[2] "No crowd here!" the literature seemed to blare, certainly not in a city where skyscrapers themselves were illegal.[3]

The gap between the devastating critique of urban life seen in *The Crowd* and the vision of a Mediterranean oasis ever-present in Southern California promotional images was as ironic as it was expansive. *The Crowd* may have been set in New York, but it was conceived in Los Angeles, which itself had become a major city with all the challenges of modern urban life. For all the attention to difference paid by Los Angeles boosters, it, as much as New York City, emerged as the nation's prototypical corporate metropolis in the 1920s.[4] By that decade, Los Angeles was home to a number of the nation's largest corporations—firms such as Union Oil, Pacific Mutual Life Insurance, Southern California Edison, Security-First National Bank, and the Pacific Electric Railway—whose headquarters congregated in an area surrounding Spring Street, which locals dubbed the "Wall Street of the West." A crowd of salaried employees, the majority of whom were white men, became key to the growth and management of these and other companies throughout the region.[5] By the 1920s, thousands of Johnny Simses poured into downtown office buildings each morning. In fact, by 1930, more than 100,000 men, representing a fourth of the city's male workforce, held white-collar jobs.[6] For every film star or business tycoon in Los Angeles, there were thousands of white-collar employees working for modest pay.

Of all the images associated with Los Angeles in the 1920s, legions of white-collar employees working in crowded downtown offices rarely come to mind, but this reality underlay the city's much heralded prosperity. This essay explores the world of Los Angeles "company men" in the 1920s. They were part of the first national generation of Americans to grow up in a significantly white-collar economy, and, like their colleagues around the nation, they struggled to make sense of what it meant to be a corporate em-

Figure 8.1. Interior view of Pacific Electric administrative offices, 1923. *Henry E. Huntington Library, San Marino, Calif.*

ployee.[7] An office job had long been considered an appropriate starting point in a young man's career, but the rapid feminization of clerical work and the steadily bureaucratizing nature of corporate life increasingly threw into doubt the meaning of white-collar work. Despite these changes in the nature of office work, however, Los Angeles business leaders recruited their career employees from the ranks of young Anglo-American men, one of the most privileged groups in the region's social hierarchy. Hollywood's most devastating silent-era critique of urban life—young ambitious man moves to city, only to have his dreams dashed by the stifling control of big businesses in urban economies—poignantly documented the fears and angst of this first generation of white-collar men. Raised in a society which held economic autonomy and occupational independence as the very measures by which one became a man, the young men who filled the rosters of growing corporations found themselves entangled in complex hierarchies, subordinated to a rigid chain of command, and lacking any realistic opportunity to direct the enterprise. These men's ambivalence about long-term white-collar employment would challenge daily the efforts of executives to build stable and profitable corporations. As we enter the world of white-collar Los

Angeles during the 1920s, we thus find *The Crowd* to be a profoundly L.A. story.

THE WHITEST OF COLLARS

Few Los Angeles corporations ever struggled to find applicants for white-collar openings. As the small nineteenth-century town with a limited agricultural economy grew into a major corporate metropolis within the span of barely three decades, the labor pool swelled daily with the arrival of new residents looking for good jobs. While demographers point to specific population booms in 1906 and 1923, journalist Carey McWilliams aptly noted after World War II that "the growth of Southern California since 1870 should be regarded as one continuous boom punctuated at intervals by major explosions."[8] From 1920 to 1924, the city's population increased by more than 100,000 each year, and it would reach one million in 1930. Los Angeles County's population soared from 936,455 in 1920 to nearly 2.25 million in 1930, with an additional million in the greater metropolitan area.[9] This booming population provided a vast and steadily growing labor pool for business leaders in Los Angeles, where the number of working adult men rose from approximately 30,000 in 1900 to over half a million in 1930.[10]

Yet however impressive the region's growth, executives assessed with caution the adequacy of the labor pool for salaried men. Rather than seeing a massive population from which to recruit employees, they looked down from their offices onto a community that they divided into explicit categories of desirable and undesirable applicants. Leaders had a distinct vision of the kinds of men they wanted to hire for white-collar "career" positions, and in their considerations, experience, training, and skills were not the only important items. Officials began with fundamental conceptions about what kind of people would best suit corporate interests, and, more often than not, these reflected dominant constructions of gender, race, and ethnicity. When the Security-First National Bank of Los Angeles promoted J. A. H. Kerr in 1930, for instance, its leaders noted in a laudatory article that "Kerr looks like a banker." They meant this explicitly. The square-jawed, silver-haired, handsomely dressed Anglo-American personified their vision of the ideal employee.[11]

In Los Angeles, where corporate executives were a significantly monolithic group intent on replicating themselves among new hires, an infatuation with appearance and lineage dominated personnel practices. Avidly self-proclaimed Anglo-Saxon males, the city's business elite never questioned that only men would fill significant positions leading up the corporate ladder, and talked often and fervently about the importance of racial and ethnic divisions in the region's social and economic structure. Chamber of Commerce members and city officials spoke of Los Angeles as the most "American of cities," and home to true "red-blooded Americans." And in these discussions, they were specific about what a "real American" was. Los Angeles, they argued, represented the last bastion of "true Americans," whom they explicitly defined as persons of Anglo-Saxon descent. This was not an issue of vagueness, subtlety, or inference. Chamber members laced their annual banquet speeches and toasts with direct comments about Anglo-Saxon superiority. This phenomenon was well established by the 1890s, when J. S. Slauson, for instance, fondly described Southern California as a place of "the soft-voiced Spaniard, the shrugging, pantomiming Frenchman, the guttural German, the musical Italian, the progressive Japanese, the industrious Chinaman, and the sharp, decisive American."[12] The quote speaks volumes about how Slauson and his colleagues, who responded with frequent applause, defined "Americans." Not only were "Americans" not people of Asian, southern European, or "Spanish" descent (probably a euphemism for Mexican, considered by them pejorative); Los Angeles's Anglo elite also placed German or French Americans at the margins of American society. By the 1920s, when Congress enacted national immigration policies that codified these attitudes, a cult of "Anglo-Saxonness" had become an established feature of elite life in Los Angeles. In 1924, for instance, a Chamber of Commerce magazine author noted that "for centuries the Anglo-Saxon race has been marching Westward. It is now on the shores of the Pacific. . . . The apex of this movement is Los Angeles County."[13]

The cult of Anglo-Saxonness which flourished among Los Angeles elites directly affected the ability of the region's young men to find work. Paralleling civic and business leaders' efforts to market and celebrate the city as an Anglo-Saxon community, corporations privileged native-born white men in hirings and promotions. As much as possible, Los Angeles companies hired men of Nordic appearance who presented themselves in terms they would have described as "all American."[14] In practice, this meant normative Anglo physiognomy and a lack of distinctive regional accents or characteristics.[15] The composition of Southern California's population made it relatively easy for corporate leaders to engineer their white-collar ranks along these lines, and native-born white Americans dominated migration to the region. By 1890, roughly three out of every four Los Angelenos were native-born whites, a significantly higher percentage than in many other major American cities. And Los Angeles's population growth thereafter came predominantly from an influx of native-born persons from the midwestern and eastern United States.[16]

Out of this populace, businessmen staffed their firms with the very "whitest of collars." A sample of men from the 1910 and 1920 censuses in Los Angeles suggests that foreign-born persons and people of southern European, Asian, or Mexican descent were largely confined to jobs in agriculture, domestic service, and manual labor. All the other major occupational groups, including clerical/sales workers, craftsmen and foremen, managers/officials/proprietors, operatives and kindred workers, and professional/technical workers, had overwhelming majorities of native-born northern European men.[17] Among these categories, however, white-collar men were distinctive on several points. First, in both 1910 and 1920, native-born men comprised a higher proportion of white-collar men than any other occupational category. Eighty-six percent of the sample was native born in 1910; 80 percent was native born in 1920. Second, the vast majority of most white-collar men's parents were also native born. In both census years, more than two-thirds of white-collar men's parents were born in the United States, a figure matched only by professional and technical workers. Third, of those white-collar men whose parents were foreign born, between 35 and 40 percent claimed English as their parents' native tongue, a figure again matched only by professional and technical workers.[18]

Other sources confirm the Anglo lineage of Los Angeles's white-collar ranks. A cursory reading of company magazines finds that Anglo-American faces and names dominate their pages. Numbers from a sample of white draft registrants from the city in 1917, illuminating the city's young male workforce (men between the ages of 18 and 29) near the dawn of the 1920s, further makes this point. Of these men who worked in white-collar positions, 96 percent of corporate professionals, 94 percent of men in managerial positions, and 92 percent of the remaining general white-collar employees were native born, figures significantly higher than those for any other occupational group. Furthermore, of the 8 percent of general white-collar employees in this sample who were foreign born, nearly half were from Canada or the United Kingdom. The remainder hailed largely from Germany, Scandinavia, or Russia. This contrasts sharply with other occupational groupings. Slightly more than one-fourth of all blue-collar workers who were "white" were foreign born, as were approximately half of all independent proprietors. Both groups were more likely to come from Mexico, or southern or eastern Europe.[19]

In the early twentieth-century world of corporate Los Angeles, a white-collar job was thus a possibility if one could present a truly *white*-collar appearance. Yet the fact that the city's company men became a bastion of native-born Anglo-Americanism obscures the ambivalence with which these men often viewed these positions. Such jobs were not the fruits California dreams were made of, and the fact that these men moved so steadily into these positions tells us more about the opportunities they found in Los Angeles than the aspirations they took there.

MEN ON THE MAKE

In *The Crowd,* Johnny Sims arrives in New York City via its harbor. As his ship steams past Manhattan Island, he is stunned by the ominous and colossal wall of skyscrapers. Those arriving in Los Angeles in the 1920s would have experienced a very different visage. Most immigrants would have disembarked from a train at one of three downtown depots where odds were good they would find sunshine, pleasant temperatures, and possibly even palm trees. Except for the city's distinctive City Hall, completed in 1928, they would not see buildings over twelve stories. Meteorological and architectural differences aside, however, Los Angeles's urban character, like that of New York City, instilled both awe and trepidation in many of its new residents who, like Johnny Sims, arrived from small towns with big dreams.

The apparent ease with which local firms staffed their white-collar positions with native-born white men proved deceptive, for these men shared Johnny Sims's ambitions and did not believe they were signing on for dutiful lifelong service in a single firm. Privileged by their race and sex, and emboldened by their age, they were the bearers of the "rags to respectability and riches" ideal of American culture, and dreamed of grand futures, whatever that might mean.[20] Their ambitions were often very high, and Southern California's social and cultural milieu only fanned them further, for, once there, they found themselves part of a local elite. The prospect of white-collar jobs in complex hierarchies certainly did not drive men from the Midwest and the East to cross the great western deserts and continue on to the Pacific Coast. If the simple ability to secure a livelihood was the ultimate goal, most would have found it sooner along the way and settled there, as many indeed did. Rarely "pushed" to migrate by social, political, or economic despair, Southern Californians were instead largely a self-selected class of people willing to relocate far away in order to reap the region's many rewards. Their hopes were fueled by Los Angeles's celebrated and incessant booster campaigns. Southern California thus attracted settlers for whom a "better quality of life" meant many different things, and they journeyed there with high expectations, seeking to enact their own "American Dream."[21] Once in California, young white men in search of better things found their status only heightened by the region's significant populations of Mexicans, Japanese, and African Americans. Los Angeles's sizable numbers of peoples of color, who were particularly vulnerable to economic exploitation, strengthened the social and economic position of white immigrants who were already bringing to the city comparatively privileged backgrounds.[22]

But once settled in California, did young, white male immigrants realize their high expectations? According to historian Stuart Blumin, by the turn of the century the divide between "office jobs" and manual labor had become one of the key elements in Anglo-American conceptions of status and success.[23] On these terms, Los Angeles appeared a promising city to young men, one that offered a broad range of middle-class opportunities. Its economic development in the 1910s and 1920s rested on a swelling workforce in every economic sector, but its commercial and professional ranks saw the most growth. The proportion of nonmanual workers in Los Angeles surpassed the national average by a significant margin during this period. By 1930, more than 40 percent of all gainfully employed adult men in Los Angeles served in nonmanual positions, a figure significantly higher than the national average of 25 percent, and higher than those for most other major urban centers.[24]

Yet despite the seemingly middle-class nature of Los Angeles's economy, young white men found a much more limited range of opportunities. When they actually set out to find work, the wide diversity of jobs seemed to shrink. The large number of small businessmen, professionals, and managers in the city were rarely young men. We can gain some perspective on how the workplace looked to young men from the 1917 sample of draft records. Approximately 40 percent of the men in this sample worked in some kind of nonmanual position. Yet while citywide, half of all men in nonmanual work were independent professionals or small businessmen, such opportunities were more rare for this cohort. Only 10 percent of white men who registered for the draft worked as professionals or owned their own business. Stricter educational and licensing requirements were making many highly desirable professions, such as medicine and law, increasingly difficult to enter.[25] And despite the appeal of owning one's own business, this was a difficult route. Would-be entrepreneurs needed start-up capital, and even if one had the resources, competition was fierce and rates of business failure high.[26]

If one hoped to acquire a middle-class occupational status via nonmanual work, finding an office job in a local company seemed the best bet. One-quarter of all the men in the 1917 sample of Los Angeles's draft registrants (well over half of those in the sample's nonmanual sector overall) worked in white-collar posts. White-collar jobs, however, were not a "natural" career pathway for young men. Despite the rapidly increasing prominence of these positions, this type of work loomed as a new and confusing proposition. Office jobs in small businesses had long been seen as an obvious starting point for young men's careers, but as companies grew larger and their management bureaucratized, such entry-level posts seemed less and less attractive.[27] Young men who, accurately or not, felt they understood professional or small business life stared at the office buildings in downtown Los Angeles, pondering: Who did these companies hire? What kind of opportunities were available? And what would a corporate career mean?

Figure 8.2. Spring Street looking north from Sixth Street, 1929. *Henry E. Hunting-ton Library, San Marino, Calif.*

The image of white-collar work presented in *The Crowd* testifies to the kinds of concerns Americans had come to have about the suitability of such positions for ambitious young men. In focusing on the increasingly routine nature of office work and the growing size of corporate bureaucracies, *The Crowd* cast the spotlight on features of corporate life that were by the 1920s giving young men in Los Angeles great pause. When twenty-year-old Frank Graves moved to Los Angeles with his Vermont-born parents in the 1910s and accepted a position as a clerk in a downtown bank, for instance, he was following in the footsteps of many before him who had taken such entry-level white-collar jobs as stepping stones to promising futures. By the 1910s and 1920s, however, the size, systematization, and dominance of the big banks and other corporations which gripped Los Angeles's economy fore-shadowed a more ominous career trajectory for men like Graves.

Few confronted this transition as directly as Clarence Bowerman. Bower-man grew up in the suburb of Monrovia in the 1880s. After finishing high school, he did coursework at the University of Southern California and the Throop Polytechnic Institute in Pasadena (now Caltech). Business courses at the latter helped him, in 1900, to secure his first job, as stenographer and balancer of passbooks with the First National Bank of Monrovia. By 1906 he had become an assistant cashier, but he decided that he wanted to work out-doors; as a result he joined the ranks of a local contracting company. After seven years he left that job to start up a general merchandising business in the San Fernando Valley. His business put him in contact with the president of a small, local, institution, the Bank of Lankershim, which, in 1919, of-fered him the position of vice president and manager.

Bowerman entered the 1920s an icon of middle-class success. Raised in the nation's new glamour capital of Southern California, he had made con-siderable money in entrepreneurial ventures and, by his forties, helped di-rect a thriving local business. In 1928, however, the massive Security-First National Bank of Los Angeles acquired the Bank of Lankershim. Suddenly Bowerman found himself one of more than 150 branch managers in a 3,500-employee institution. Ironically, Security-First assigned this former entrepreneur and business leader, now well down the large corporation's chain of command, the task of helping to solve its turnover problem. Bank executives were intent on developing a dedicated staff of educated Anglo-American men, but they found these men difficult to retain. Many aspired to the kinds of careers Bowerman had had, and would not long remain white-collar employees in a large bureaucracy.[28]

As Los Angeles firms grew into major regional, national, and interna-tional corporations, the city's company men found themselves bound in of-ten rigid chains of command where they were subjected to paternalistic, if not authoritarian working environments. By the mid 1920s, for instance, the Pacific Mutual Life Insurance Company required its employees to keep elaborate productivity reports charting the number of clients interviewed per hour, the number of policies sold per hour, and thereby the hourly value of their time.[29] White-collar personnel were also vulnerable, like small businesspersons and farmers, to larger market and other forces, but had less control over the firm's ability to survive such difficulties. Many employ-ees found their jobs abruptly terminated when their firms suffered financial setbacks. When changes in the ownership of shipping routes forced the dis-solution of the Pacific Mail Steamship Company in 1925 and 1926, for in-stance, employees received sudden termination notices. Men such as Eu-gene C. Walsh, who had served the company as clerk for seven years and had been promoted twice, received a letter which said, "as stated today we very much regret the necessity of severing your connection with the com-pany. . . . during the long period that you have worked for the company your service has been most satisfactory." Nonetheless, "with utmost regret"

Walsh's boss fired him.[30] More-junior employees received less compassionate notices stating, "Owing to the discontinuance of shipping board operations it is necessary to reduce forces and therefore advise you that effective immediately you will be released."[31]

And if white-collar work conferred middle-class status while blue-collar work did not, money was less of a factor in this distinction. Lower-level white-collar men often received working-class wages. Security-First National Bank, for instance, one of the city's elite banks, paid entry-level male employees just over $70 a month in 1929, only marginally more than what local operatives made.[32] Nor was white-collar work necessarily more dependable. Most companies paid office personnel on a weekly or biweekly basis with no contract. Status and semantic distinctions formed much of the difference between the two groups. Even though their terms of payment were often similar, American companies paid "wages" to manual "workers," while white-collar "employees" received "salaries."[33]

For all these reasons, young white men in Los Angeles viewed white-collar employment with considerable uncertainty. In the best of cases, office jobs provided excellent platforms from which to pursue more grandiose ambitions. But in most circumstances, these aspirations dulled any potential luster of an entry-level position. One does not have to dig far into the lives of Southern Californians to find young white-collar men expressing resentment at their employment status. Ray Hindman's early career biography, for instance, includes a laundry list of grievances. He obtained his first job in San Francisco in 1924, when he was hired as a clerk at Woolworth's retail chain. The company soon transferred him to a Southern California store and promoted him to assistant manager, but Hindman then learned, to his disappointment, that at Woolworth's, everyone, "even janitors," was soon given that title. Hindman subsequently sought work in a local lumber company, but it turned out they wanted him primarily as a laborer, so he again quit and went to work for another retailer, the Kress Company. He became a receiving clerk at Kress and was given a better salary and more interesting tasks, but soon found a harsh side to his employment contract: no store employee but manager could own an automobile because the company had strict views about how their salary should be spent. Hindman recalls that employees were expected to "dress properly—suit, white shirt, and tie—and live in a proper kind of an apartment house . . . that would make the Kress Story look good." Company managers told Hindman they did not believe an employee could buy an automobile and still "live the way they thought you should live." Hindman quit yet again and in 1927 went to work for the National Cash Register Company as a salesman. He stayed with NCR less than two years, however, tired of being continually relocated. "What they were doing with me was making a yo-yo out of me. . . . Whenever a salesman would be pulled out of a territory or quit his job, I could be sent into the territory." He noted that once he was sent to Tacoma for a short stint because "a man's wife didn't like the rain."[34]

Transferred to distant offices, asked to perform tedious tasks, and finding his private life subject to company policies, Hindman joined the chorus of those who longed to own their own business, or at least have more control over their working environment. He never did own his own firm, but in 1928, he went to work for a small typewriter shop, essentially becoming a junior partner in an enterprise where he spent 33 years.[35]

We can best sense the ambivalence and transience of Los Angeles white-collar men in the 1920s by walking through their neighborhoods. At the dawn of the 1920s, white-collar employees lived in virtually every district in Los Angeles. The young white men who formed the heart of the white-collar labor force, however, were concentrated in an approximately 40-block area just west of downtown, stretching from approximately First and Tenth Streets to the north and south, and Spring Street and Figueroa Avenue to the east and west.[36] Known as Bunker Hill, this district once housed the city's elite. By the 1920s, however, lower-middle-class renters were taking over the stately homes and moving into new apartment buildings. At the heart of this district lay the intersection of South Grand Avenue and Second Street. Walking down Grand Avenue, one would pass a large apartment house called "The Minnewska." The building's 58 units housed primarily married couples ranging from those in their twenties to those in their sixties. Less than a dozen units were occupied by single renters. All the tenants were white, and 45 of the 58 families or individuals were native born. All but three of the foreign-born residents were from Canada, the United Kingdom, or Scandinavia. White-collar types comprised a minority of the Minnewska's residents. Most were workers or proprietors, with a smattering of professionals. Carl Taylor was one of the white-collar men in the building. A 35-year-old married Nebraskan with two children, he worked as a ticket clerk for a local railway firm.[37]

Next door to the Minnewska stood a house shared by seven young single women, working as either stenographers or nurses. Adjacent to them was an eight-unit apartment house where eight couples lived, half of whom had children. The residents included both blue- and white-collar workers. Among them was Scott Hazel, a bookkeeper who had come from Minnesota with his parents several years before, and his partner, Ida Pamplin, a 28-year-old manicurist. Large homes converted into boarding houses took up the remainder of the block with one to four families or lodgers residing in each. All the residents were "white," though people of Mexican descent appeared occasionally in this neighborhood. The ages of residents varied from the twenties through the sixties, and their occupations were relatively evenly divided between proprietors, workers, and white-collar employees.

Farther south on Grand Avenue, the neighborhood slowly changed from one encompassing a few apartment buildings with many homes, to an area dominated by large apartment complexes. The demographics of these blocks shifted slightly as well, with a younger population and fewer families. The 400 block of South Grand Avenue, for instance, included the 46-unit "Zelda" and the 85-unit "Granada." Both buildings were entirely white and included significant numbers of white-collar men. In the Zelda, for instance, resided John Seiner, a 32-year-old married billing clerk for a local supply company. And in the Granada lived single 21-year-old Samuel King from Missouri, who was working as a freight clerk for a local railroad. White-collar men shared these buildings with a roughly equal number of blue-collar workers. In the Granada, for instance, 22-year-old Ray Roberts, a salesman for a local drug company, lived next to 21-year-old George Roitsch, a laborer.

By the 700 block of South Grand Avenue, lodging houses filled largely by single white men predominated. The residents continued to be mostly native born (immigrants were primarily British or Canadian), and were divided among white-collar employees, proprietors, professionals, and workers. In one 68-unit complex, for instance, Frank Graves, the bank clerk we met earlier, lived across from William Read, a 23-year-old laborer from England.[38]

Los Angeles's young white-collar men were clearly living in a remarkably fluid neighborhood. Residents varied greatly in age, social class, and family status. The only measures of demographic homogeneity, in fact, were that residents were renters, and mostly white. There did exist, however, some ethnic diversity. A small number of Jews, Mexicans, and southern Europeans, all people of questionable descent in the eyes of Southern California's Anglo elite, lived in this neighborhood. And in its midst was an apartment complex housing 55 Japanese American lodgers and families.

In the minds of young white men, all these factors made their careers seem distinctly in transition. When they left their apartments to go to work each morning, they passed the doors of few neighbors whose lives they hoped to emulate. Those of their neighbors who were recent immigrants from southern or eastern Europe were probably not the "type of people" among whom they expected to live. And many people whom they greeted in the halls or on the stairwells were laborers, whose presence ensured that the prospect of a working-class status loomed constantly.

Perhaps most troubling, these men lived in immediate proximity to many white-collar women, and many older white men working in low-level white-collar positions. Such figures must have kindled considerable anxiety about the status and long-term implications of white-collar work. The increasing presence of women who held jobs with comparable titles, even if such women received less pay, had less authority, and worked in different physical locations within the corporate workplace, forced white-collar men to question their own social status. The added continual presence of older white-collar men in low-level positions aroused further anxieties. Thirty-four-year-old Fred Laughlin, for instance, likely hoped his position as clerk would provide a future that would take him and his wife out of a crowded lodging house shared by 14 people including a mechanic, a marble tiler, and a plasterer. One of his neighbors, however, a 47-year-old clerk named George Mitchell, must have given him some pause about his future opportunities for social mobility.

The transient nature of Los Angeles's young white men alerts us to the fact that while few companies in Los Angeles struggled to find employees, personnel problems commenced almost immediately upon hiring. Young men simply viewed their positions as stepping stones to better opportunities elsewhere. Motivating these young men to work with enthusiasm and commitment and keeping them in the firm's service over the long haul proved a continual challenge. Corporate leaders who hired and then neglected company personnel learned quickly that employee loyalty could not be taken for granted. Lacking the occupational cohesion often seen among skilled laborers and rarely in this period participating in collective bargaining or unions, white-collar workers did not often exert power in ways easily visible to historians. Yet corporate employees did "bargain" with leaders. They bargained in subtle ways by simply not offering their maximum efforts. From clerks to senior managers, their frequent contact with consumers and their role in the daily coordination of company activities made them important players in company operations. While not every employee had to fit the corporate ideal for a firm to prosper, a substantial number did. Leaders never forgot that, on any given day, individual workers could seriously help or hurt the firm, and continually demanded that employees act with greater loyalty.

White-collar employees also bargained with their feet. A 1919 volume on office management published for business executives noted that "during the last few years much attention has been directed to the loss involved in the frequent leaving of employees." Citing recent research, the author noted that "a high rate of turnover is not confined to factory employees."[39] Indeed, in most firms, employee turnover plagued company operations. While the severity of the problem depended on how many and which employees departed in any given period, it was always a concern. The desire of corporate leaders to staff their firms with native-born white men, primarily of Anglo-Saxon descent, doomed them to a continual struggle. In asking men who had ambitions of independence, wealth, and power to accept white-collar jobs, they assumed a difficult challenge. These "men on the make" were usually more than willing to change companies if better opportunities arose. Job-hopping, in fact, was a central element in their career histories. Fred Pearson, for instance, transferred from company to company. He became a senior statistician at the Atlantic and San Francisco Railroad Company in 1908, and stayed with the firm until 1918, receiving at least two promotions, but left in that year for a better position in the Bethlehem Shipbuilding Corporation. This new firm terminated Pearson in 1921, after which the Pacific Mail Steamship Company hired him. Though receiving a promotion six months later, Pearson resigned in 1922 to take a "more remunerative position" elsewhere. He sought upward mobility through white-collar work but in no way limited his opportunities to those found in a single company.[40]

Most large Los Angeles companies struggled to combat high rates of turnover among their young male employees throughout the 1920s. Among banks, the problem seemed particularly severe. In 1929, for instance, Security-First National Bank experienced an alarming turnover rate of 35 percent. Even in the following year, as the Depression set in, turnover declined only to 20 percent.[41] Nothing captures the world of Los Angeles's white-collar men in the 1920s better than these measures of occupational fluidity, for they testify to young men's efforts to search for better opportunities and more promising futures.[42]

CONCLUSION

Perhaps nowhere in the United States did the angst of white-collar men reverberate in business life more dramatically than in Los Angeles, where corporate concentration proceeded with greater speed than anywhere else in the country between 1890 and 1930. During this period, local executives needed a rapidly growing pool of employees to staff their corporations, and they placed enormously high expectations upon them.[43] To their good fortune, the city's soaring population translated into hundreds of thousands of people searching for work. Yet while there were always plenty of applicants for positions in the rapidly expanding white-collar ranks of local companies, Los Angeles business leaders were selective about whom they considered for such posts. Neither the cost of labor nor education and skills alone shaped hiring and promotion decisions. Rather, leaders added to these issues a desire for what one called the "pearl and white Anglo Saxon" male, a term that meant volumes in the worldview of Los Angeles business leaders.[44] In fishing for employees only in this pool, businesses faced a challenging labor market. They placed themselves in the position of making heavy demands on comparatively privileged young men who often had severe reservations about long-term corporate employment.

It is not surprising that Vidor's *The Crowd,* one of Hollywood's most celebrated films in the 1920s, centered on the fate of ambitious young white men in modern urban economies. Though the film was set in New York, one could have found thousands of Johnny Simses as in Los Angeles. Lewis Ives Pierce, for instance, moved to Southern California from Chelsea, Massachusetts, in 1918. His family had been in the United States for more than seven generations, and over that time had come to secure a comfortable existence, of which summers on Cape Cod were but one family tradition. Pierce first settled in Pasadena because of fond impressions from a lengthy family holiday there years before. Shortly after his arrival in Southern California, he accepted a job as statement clerk with the Pasadena branch of Security Trust & Savings. As a young, educated, Anglo-American male, Pierce was exactly the sort of public ambassador the bank wanted to interact with customers, and he did not disappoint. He became known for his effective service, his late evenings, and his active involvement in the bank's speakers' bureau where he spread news of its merits to the community. Pleased as his employers were with his performance, however, Pierce proved to be a problem. He not only met the high expectations of Security Trust & Savings leaders, but also matched the employee profile of many other local companies, a fact that did not go unnoticed by his superiors. Though he remained with the company for many years, it was a tenuous alliance. Only two months after his hiring, Pierce complained of boredom. Shortly thereafter, the bank transferred him to its head office downtown. This initial promotion began a pattern of continually improving pay, positions, and perquisites in an effort to retain the services of Pierce and other valued employees.[45]

Throughout the 1920s, business leaders in Los Angeles struggled to motivate and retain men such as Lewis Pierce. Late in the decade, many firms could report considerable success in having constructed elaborate corporate cultures that were the envy of major firms nationwide. The release of *The Crowd* in 1928, however, reminded executives in Los Angeles that turning men like Johnny Sims into loyal employees was a complicated and ongoing process. Viewing Los Angeles from Spring Street reveals a city where the rise of big business forced hundreds of young white men to negotiate new relationships between work and success. Miles from the famous Southern California beaches, mountains, and deserts, the view from Spring Street was far from tranquil. Los Angeles, the city of great weather, glamour, and individual ambitions, became a site where a new generation of Americans would construct the nation's modern corporate culture.

NOTES

1. On Southern California boosterism, see: Glenn S. Dumke, "Advertising Southern California before the Boom of 1887," *The Quarterly of the Historical Society of Southern California* 24 (March 1942): 15–16; Tom Zimmerman, "Paradise Promoted: Boosterism and the Los Angeles Chamber of Commerce," *California History* 64 (Winter 1985): 22–33; Clark Davis, "From Oasis to Metropolis: Southern California

and the Changing Context of American Leisure," *Pacific Historical Review* 61 (August 1992): 357–86.

2. *Southern California, All the Year, Winter 1924–25* (Los Angeles: All Year Club of Southern California, 1924).

3. Buildings higher than 150 feet were not allowed in Los Angeles until the 1950s because of concerns about earthquakes and what early residents referred to as "Chicagoization." Kevin Starr, *Material Dreams; Southern California through the 1920s* (New York: Oxford University Press, 1990), 78.

4. For an economic history of Los Angeles in the 1920s, see James Findley Clifford, "The Economic Boom of the 'Twenties in Los Angeles" (Ph.D. dissertation, Claremont Graduate School, 1958). On the general process of corporate formation, see Alfred D. Chandler Jr., *The Visible Hand: The Managerial Revolution in American Business* (Cambridge: Harvard University Press, 1977).

5. By the 1920s, roughly a third of all white-collar workers in the United States were women, but men and women occupied very different spheres within the corporate workplace. Women were segregated largely in lower-level positions with no opportunity for significant advancement. Most companies assumed these positions would be filled by young women who would work only until marriage. "Career employees," that is, employees who were expected to devote their lives to the company, and would be rewarded by steady promotions up the company ladder, were primarily men. Angel Kwolek-Folland explores these details in length in *Engendering Business: Men and Women in the Corporate Office, 1870–1930* (Baltimore: Johns Hopkins University Press, 1994). See also Olivier Zunz, *Making America Corporate, 1870–1920* (Chicago: University of Chicago Press, 1990), 147–48.

6. U.S. Department of Commerce, Bureau of the Census, *Fifteenth Census of the United States, 1930, Vol. IV, Occupations, by States* (Washington, D.C.: United States Government Printing Office, 1933), 173–83. The proportion of white-collar workers in the nation's civilian labor force had grown from approximately 6 percent in 1870 to approximately 30 percent in 1930, comprising over 14 million people. United States Department of Commerce, Bureau of the Census, *Historical Statistics of the United States from Colonial Times to 1970, Part 1* (Washington, D.C.: United States Government Printing Office, 1975), 139–40. Jurgen Kocka, *White-Collar Workers in America, 1890–1940: A Social-Political History in International Perspective* (London: Sage, 1980), 94–95.

7. Excellent studies of white-collar work in this period include Kocka, *White-Collar Workers in America;* Ileen A. DeVault, *Sons and Daughters of Labor: Class and Clerical Work in Turn-of-the-Century Pittsburgh* (Ithaca: Cornell University Press, 1990); Kwolek-Folland, *Engendering Business;* and Zunz, *Making America Corporate.*

8. Carey McWilliams, *Southern California; An Island on the Land* (1946; Salt Lake City: Peregrine Smith Books, 1990), 114, 135.

9. On this growth, see Robert Fogelson, *The Fragmented Metropolis: Los Angeles, 1850–1930* (1967; Berkeley and Los Angeles: University of California Press, 1993), chapter 4; Oscar Osburn Winther, "The Rise of Metropolitan Los Angeles, 1870–1900," *Huntington Library Quarterly* 10 (1947): 391–405; "Facts about Industrial Los Angeles: Nature's Workshop" (Los Angeles: Los Angeles Chamber of Commerce, 1922); Reyner Banham, *Los Angeles: The Architecture of Four Ecologies* (New York:

Harper and Row, 1971), 203; Glen Dumke, *The Boom of the Eighties in Southern California* (San Marino, Calif.: Huntington Library, 1944); McWilliams, *Southern California*, 113–25.

10. *Fifteenth Census of the United States, 1930, Volume IV*, 172.

11. "Introducing J. A. H. Kerr," *Security-First News Bulletin*, May 15, 1930: 6.

12. J. S. Slauson, *The Members' Annual* (Los Angeles: Los Angeles Chamber of Commerce, 1895), 32.

13. Clarence Matson, "The Los Angeles of Tomorrow," *Southern California Business* 3 (November 1924): 37.

14. National management texts of the period promoted such practices by urging employers to ask about hair texture, complexion, and lineage on application forms. Employers were also urged to give careful attention to the eyes and faces of applicants. See Joseph French Johnson et al, *Modern Business, Volume 19: Office Management* (New York: Alexander Hamilton Institute, 1919), 85–86.

15. This phenomenon, which blossomed in the racial discussions surrounding the Spanish-American War, lasted at least through the Great Depression. In his study of Okie migration to California during the Dust Bowl years, for instance, historian James Gregory notes that "those hoping to gain access to white-collar jobs and middle-class social circles realized that it was important to shed behaviors that identified them as Okies." James N. Gregory, *American Exodus: The Dust Bowl Migration and Okie Culture in California* (New York: Oxford University Press, 1989), 121–22.

16. Robert Fogelson offers a useful survey of demographic data pertaining to Los Angeles's population growth in *The Fragmented Metropolis*, chapter 4.

17. The 1910 and 1920 census samples used in this research comprise 588 and 651 gainfully employed men, respectively, and come from Steven Ruggles and Matthew Sobek, *Integrated Public Use Microdata Series: Version 1.0* (Minneapolis: Social History Research Laboratory, University of Minnesota, 1995), hereafter referred to as IPUM–95.

18. IPUM–95.

19. These numbers are based on a randomly selected population of 4,223 white men who registered for the draft in the city of Los Angeles in 1917. Draft registration records housed in federal archives in Atlanta, Ga.; hereafter referred to as 1917 sample.

20. See Richard Weiss, *The American Myth of Success: From Horatio Alger to Norman Vincent Peale* (Urbana: University of Illinois Press, 1969), 3–15; Daniel T. Rodgers, *The Work Ethic in Industrial America, 1850–1920* (Chicago: University of Chicago Press, 1974). On the construction of manhood and masculinity during this period, see E. Anthony Rotundo, *American Manhood: Transformations in Masculinity from the Revolution to the Modern Era* (New York: Basic Books, 1993).

21. Morrow Mayo, *Los Angeles* (New York: Alfred A. Knopf, 1932), 310.

22. As would become increasingly evident throughout the twentieth century, race and class interacted in complex ways in multiracial and multi-ethnic urban centers, often resulting in patterns of social, residential, and occupational segregation to the economic benefit of whites. See Lisbeth Haas, *Conquests and Historical Identities in California, 1769–1936* (Berkeley and Los Angeles: University of California Press, 1995); Tomas Almagar, *Racial Fault Lines: The Historical Origins of White*

Supremacy in California (Berkeley and Los Angeles: University of California Press, 1994). On the racial and ethnic demographics of Los Angeles's population, see Fogelson, *The Fragmented Metropolis,* chapter 4.

23. This is the argument made in Stuart Blumin's book *The Emergence of the Middle Class: Social Experience in the American City, 1760–1900* (New York: Cambridge University Press, 1989).

24. The percentages of nonmanual male workers in other major cities are as follows: New York City, 40; Chicago, 35; St. Louis, 36; San Francisco, 38. Bureau of the Census, *Historical Statistics of the United States from Colonial Times to 1970, Part 1,* 139–40. For metropolitan figures, see *Thirteenth Census, 1910, Volume IV,* 132–49, 166–79, 186–203, 205–21, 222–38; *Fourteenth Census, 1920, Volume IV,* 153–207; *Fifteenth Census, 1930, Volume IV,* 173–83, 208–9, 447–49, 884–90, 1130–32.

25. See Burton J. Bledstein, *The Culture of Professionalism: The Middle Class and the Development of Higher Education in America* (New York: W. W. Norton, 1976).

26. On the history and culture of small business in America, see Mansel G. Blackford, *A History of Small Business in America* (New York: Twayne, 1991), and Stuart Bruchey, *Small Business in American Life* (New York: Columbia University Press, 1980).

27. Cindy Sondik Aron, *Ladies and Gentleman of the Civil Service: Middle-Class Workers in Victorian America* (New York: Oxford University Press, 1987), 34–35. C. Wright Mills discusses the degrading nature of white-collar work in *White Collar; The American Middle Classes* (New York: Oxford University Press, 1956), 227. See also Harry Braverman, *Labor and Monopoly Capital: The Degradation of Work in the Twentieth Century* (New York: Monthly Review Press, 1974).

28. "Introducing C. C. Bowerman," *Security-First News Bulletin,* April 15, 1933: 4.

29. "How the Pacific Mutual Is Helping the Agent to Organize His Time," *Pacific Mutual News* 25 (September 1926): 328.

30. Eugene C. Walsh, personnel file, Pacific Mail Steamship Collection (PMSSC), Box 30, Huntington Library.

31. Daulton Mann, letter to Mr. Albert Walker, freight clerk, June, 1925, PMSSC, Box 30, Huntington Library.

32. "Personnel Plan and Policy Outlined," *Security-First News Bulletin,* January 1, 1931: 6.

33. Kocka, *White-Collar Workers in America,* 82–83.

34. "An interview with Raymond S. Hindman, September 14, 1988, by Craig Carter," San Diego Historical Society Oral History Program.

35. Ibid.

36. This information is based on the 1917 draft sample.

37. United States Department of Commerce, Bureau of the Census, microfilm copy 1920 census manuscripts from California, enumeration district 206, Reel #108, precinct 187.

38. Ibid., enumeration district 478, precinct 248.

39. Johnson, *Office Management,* 109–10.

40. Fred Pearson, personnel file, PMSSC, Box 30, Huntington Library.

41. "Personnel Plan and Policy Outlined," *Security-First News Bulletin,* January 1, 1931: 6.

42. Mobility studies in other parts of the country seem to confirm that most large firms encountered significant turnover, particularly in lower-level positions. Walter Licht, *Getting Work: Philadelphia, 1840–1950* (Cambridge: Harvard University Press, 1992), 229; Johnson, *Office Management*, 109–10; *Proceedings of the Northwestern University Conference on Business Education,* June 16 & 17, 1927 (Chicago: Northwestern University, 1927), 42, 63–68.

43. For a detailed discussion of these expectations, see Clark Davis, "You Are the Company: The Demands of Employment in the Emerging Corporate Culture, Los Angeles, 1900–1930," *Business History Review* 70 (Autumn 1996): 328–62.

44. This term would appear continuously in the words and writing of Los Angeles elites. For an early reference, see J. S. Slauson's introduction of Senator Stephen White, *Members' Annual,* 32.

45. "Introducing Lewis I. Pierce," *Security-First News Bulletin,* October 15, 1933: 4.

PART THREE

Faith in the Metropolis

LOS ANGELES in the 1920s became an urban haven for eccentric and mystical religious groups. Writers delighted in describing wide-eyed newcomers to the city transformed into slavish followers of proselytizers like Aimee Semple McPherson and Robert "Fighting Bob" Shuler. Yet as the following essays by Michael Engh and Philip Goff demonstrate, mainstream religious bodies were the dominant forces in the spiritual life of 1920s Angelenos. Outlandish and entertaining clergy received remarkable publicity, but traditional figures, like Charles E. Fuller, exercised greater influence on religious development in the City of Angels.

CHAPTER NINE

"Practically Every Religion Being Represented"

Michael E. Engh, S.J.

"Los Angeles is the most celebrated incubator of new creeds, codes of ethics, philosophies and near philosophies and schools of thought, occult, new and old," wrote journalist-turned-historian John Steven McGroarty in 1921, describing the city in which he lived. McGroarty observed that a multiplicity of religions thrived in Los Angeles during the prosperous years after World War I. He worried, however, that the city was acquiring a reputation as a "rendezvous of freak religions" which lured "people pale of thought." Like later civic boosters, McGroarty hastened to reassure readers that "sane religion" had a safe haven in the City of Angels. In the following year, one publicist of the Los Angeles Chamber of Commerce also reassured residents that "Los Angeles is a church going city, practically every religion being represented in 350 church edifices."[1]

This uneasy balancing of wariness and reassurance continued in subsequent decades, and the leading guide to Los Angeles returned to McGroarty's themes in 1941. Authors of the Works Progress Administration's handbook to the city scoffed at certain exotic faiths and then vigorously defended the city's spiritual health. After 1918, religion had burst into "full and spectacular bloom," and "religious fakers" such as "soothsayers, fortune tellers, and swamis" overran the city. Nonetheless, mainline churches and synagogues prospered and formed "a dignified background against which the fantastic stands out in garish high lights."[2] Religiously, something distinct from the rest of the nation was happening in the City of Angels in the first decades of this century.

Commentators since McGroarty have repeatedly wrestled with the challenge of how to interpret Los Angeles and to understand this city unlike others. During the 1920s in particular, the multiplicity of faiths and the variety of the forms of worship aggravated the apprehension of many outside observers and the skepticism of many residents. From the perspective of the twenty-first century, however, it is more obvious that Los Angeles was experiencing the spiritual consequences of its enormous growth in population. The vast numbers of newcomers to the city and the region hailed from a wide variety of countries and states in the Union. Ethnically, culturally, and religiously, they did not resemble those who resided in the city before 1920.

Dubbed "Iowa by the Sea" and "Double Dubuque," Los Angeles in 1900 was one of the three most homogeneous cities west of the Mississippi River.[3] Its 103,000 residents were primarily Euro-American transplants from the Midwest who brought with them a staunch mainline Protestantism. They vastly outnumbered the few surviving Native Americans, Irish and Mexican Catholics, African American Protestants, and the Chinese and Japanese who followed Confucianism, Taoism, and Buddhism. Seeking to redefine civic virtue, the more recently arrived Angelenos promoted a variety of causes and reforms which ranged from Sunday "blue laws" and the prohibition of alcoholic beverages to municipal reform and women's suffrage. They also vigorously boosted the region's attributes—particularly its climate—to attract further migration to the city.

By 1920, Los Angeles counted 576,673 residents, and in 1930 the census listed a population of 1,238,000. Unlike the "boom" of the 1880s, the post–World War I migration attracted significant numbers of people from outside the United States. Census enumerators were notoriously inaccurate in tallying the Spanish-speaking population, but the 1920 census reported 21,598 Mexicans within the city limits. By 1930, the total was 97,000 in the city and 100,000 elsewhere in the county.[4] Japanese, African American, and other arrivals in these decades further diversified the population so that Los Angeles exceeded every metropolis in the nation save one (Baltimore) in the percentage of its population that was nonwhite. Nowhere, Robert Fogelson notes, "on the Pacific coast, not even in cosmopolitan San Francisco, was there so diverse a mixture of racial groups, so visible a contrast . . . as in Los Angeles."[5]

Such significant growth in population and in racial and ethnic diversity manifested itself in the religious traditions that set down roots in the metropolis in the 1920s. Federal religious censuses in 1916, 1926, and 1936 document the remarkable expansion of congregations and facilities, as well as an impressive pluralism in beliefs.[6] Although these decennial enumerations do not include a tally of the city's total population in those years, they do provide important statistics revealing denomination growth. Not surprisingly, the diverse mixture of racial groups that Fogelson observed was revealed in a corresponding variety of faith traditions.

Denominational membership totaled 122,697 persons in 1916, swelled to 326,446 in 1926, and grew at a slower pace to reach 427,348 in 1936.[7]

Only in 1916 did census officials offer an estimate of the total city population for the same year that they tabulated religious membership. Out of an estimated 504,878 Angelenos in 1916, 122,697 professed a religious affiliation, approximately 24.3 percent. This is a decline from 1890, when the census reported that 36 percent of the city's residents claimed church or synagogue membership.[8] One can only speculate as to the causes of this reported decrease. Historian James Gregory noted that among later Dust Bowl immigrants in California, many remained religiously isolated because of the difficulty in finding a congregation whose worship resembled what they had left and where they would feel comfortable.[9]

Another aspect of change in Los Angeles religion was the impressive construction boom beginning after World War I. Church and synagogue officials reported religious facilities in the city worth $6.7 million in 1916, while the value had soared to $29.5 million ten years later. An architecture of success and prosperity emerged along Wilshire Boulevard in particular. During the 1920s most of the city's older congregations relocated westward from downtown Los Angeles to sites along the developing "Miracle Mile." As one commentator noted, "Wilshire boulevard is sometimes called the 'Five Million Dollar Church Street,' and, probably, has more new modern church buildings than any similar street in the world."[10]

Important congregations that left the city's historic core included First Baptist (completed in 1927), First Unitarian (1930), Immanuel Presbyterian (1927–29), First Congregational (1930–32), and the community's original synagogue, Congregation B'nai B'rith, which changed its name to Wilshire Boulevard Temple (1929). Additional houses of worship dedicated in that era were Wilshire Methodist (1924), Wilshire Boulevard Christian Church, (1922–23), St. James Episcopal (1918), and the nearby Wilshire Ward Chapel of the Latter-day Saints (1928). Elsewhere in the city, other impressive religious structures arose, such as St. Paul's Cathedral and St. John's (both Episcopal), Temple Sinai East (Jewish), Second Baptist, and St. Vincent's (Roman Catholic) at Adams and Figueroa.[11] None proved as famous, however, as Angelus Temple, the center of the ministry of the Canadian-born evangelist Aimee Semple McPherson.

After ten years as an itinerant preacher, McPherson drove her mother and two children three thousand miles to Los Angeles in 1918. Within five years she had built and paid for Angelus Temple, a $1.5 million "revival tabernacle" in the Echo Park district of the city, filling its 5,300 seats three times every Sunday. Staging "illustrated sermons" and "sacred operas," casts of hundreds dramatized scenes from Scripture and from "Sister Aimee's" imagination. The central attraction was McPherson herself, who often appeared in costume. On one occasion she rushed on-stage dressed as the quarterback for USC's football team, the Trojans. At another service she wore the uniform of a city police officer and rode a motorcycle onto the

Figure 9.1. Aimee Semple McPherson, founder of Angelus Temple and the Church of the Four Square Gospel, c. 1930. *David du Plessis Collection, Fuller Theological Seminary*

temple stage with light glaring and siren wailing. Holding up her hand, she shouted into the microphone, "Stop! You are speeding to ruin!"[12]

McPherson's L.I.F.E. Bible School joined other religiously affiliated schools and universities which expanded in the city during the prosperous decade of the 1920s. The Methodist University of Southern California erected eight major buildings in this decade, for example, while other institutions relocated to larger campuses. Reflecting the rising aspirations of Roman Catholics, Loyola College, the Marymount School, and Mount St. Mary's College all moved to the west side of the city and initiated major building campaigns in this era. Occidental College continued to thrive with the strong support of Presbyterians from across Southern California.[13] Other educational efforts included the multi-service Church of All Nations, pastored by G. Bromley Oxnam, which received Methodist support in an effort to assist impoverished inner-city children.[14]

Oxnam's labors on behalf of immigrants and their families represents

the best of local Protestant outreach to foreign-born people in need. His social services at Church of All Nations sprang from his desire to assist immigrants, Mexicans in particular, by improving the conditions in which they
lived and worked in Los Angeles. His investigative writings, such as *The Mexican in Los Angeles*, reveal a deep sympathy for Spanish-speaking newcomers
based upon his broad knowledge of the poverty and prejudice they faced in
the city.[15] Only three years prior to the appearance of Oxnam's study, for example, a Congregationalist minister, George Warren Hinman, expressed
different sentiments, shared by many in the city: "The objective missionary
work for immigrants, undertaken by American churches . . . has, naturally,
been directed toward those immigrants coming from non-Christian or Roman Catholic countries, immigrants whose previous religious history gave
little or no promise of making them good American citizens." Hinman
fretted about the estimated 110,000 Slavs, Russians, Croatians, Poles, He-
brews, Italians, Armenians, Greeks, "Orientals," and Mexicans found in Los
Angeles and the threat they supposedly posed to the city.[16]

Increasing numbers of African Americans migrating to Los Angeles also
elicited a nervous response from racially bigoted residents. Numbering only
15,579 in 1920, by 1930 black Angelenos increased to 38,894, and their
churches reflected this influx.[17] The federal religious census of 1926 listed
33 identifiable African American congregations with over 10,000 members;
a decade later, 17,296 congregants worshipped in 54 churches. These denominations included the Negro Baptist, the Church of God in Christ, the
African Methodist Episcopal, the African Methodist Episcopal Zion, and
the Colored Methodist Episcopal.[18] African Americans belonged to other
churches as well, such as the Pentecostal, Presbyterian, and Roman Catholic, but their numbers went unrecorded. Black newspaper publisher Charlotta A. Bass recalled that the most prestigious houses of prayer in that decade were the older established congregations, Second Baptist and First
African Methodist Episcopal Churches, where the elite of the black community gathered to worship.[19]

Throughout the 1920s, these historic congregations struggled to keep
pace with the spiritual needs of the increasing black population by expanding services, staffing, and facilities. The most notable example of such
growth was Second Baptist Church, one of the two oldest black congregations in the city. In 1921 the church selected a new pastor and chose a seminary graduate who was a married man, father of four, Army chaplain in
World War I, and a dynamic preacher. Reverend T. L. Griffith moved quickly
after his arrival in Los Angeles and initiated a campaign to relocate the
church to a site at 24th Street and Griffith Avenue, adjacent to the Central
Avenue business district in the heart of the burgeoning African American
community. In 1926, Griffith presided at the dedication of the completed
brick church, worth $175,000, and the choice of the preacher on that occa-

Figure 9.2. Members of the Faith League, First African Methodist Episcopal Church, at Eighth and Towne Streets in central Los Angeles, 1918. *Shades of L.A. Archives/Los Angeles Public Library*

sion suggests the rising national importance of Los Angeles black churches among African Americans.[20] Reverend Adam Clayton Powell Sr., pastor of the renowned Abyssinian Baptist Church of New York City and Griffith's seminary classmate, praised the new complex as the "most elaborate" structure on the West Coast for black Baptists.[21]

Elsewhere in Los Angeles, growing numbers of white, English-speaking Angelenos feared the newcomers and sought to protect their neighborhoods from suspected crime (much as some residents today seek private and gated communities). Common in the city by 1920, racial and religious restrictive covenants in real estate deeds were one means to limit people of color, Jews, Mexicans, and Italians in their ability to purchase homes in certain areas of the city. Until declared unconstitutional by the United States Supreme Court in 1948, these deed restrictions applied to homes in virtually all sections of Los Angeles and in surrounding communities such as Glendale, Beverly Hills, Azusa, Montebello, and Inglewood.[22]

Others in the city turned to "Americanization" efforts, particularly in the public schools, to integrate newcomers into local society and the predominant culture. George Sánchez notes a significant "religious undertone" in the Americanization materials developed by city officials for use in Mexican neighborhoods. Only members of Protestant denominations were allowed to prepare these primers and lesson plans, and for many leaders of this effort, successful Americanization meant conversion to Protestantism.[23] Coinciding with these efforts, another movement of a more sinister nature arose, the Ku Klux Klan, with local manifestations of its nationwide revival.

The original antagonism of some whites toward Mexican Americans expanded in the 1920s when the Klan directed its ire against Jews, Roman Catholics, and immigrants from southern and eastern Europe. Anaheim and Inglewood boasted the largest klaverns, with Reverend Leon Myers, pastor of the First Christian Church of Anaheim, serving as Exalted Cyclops from 1922 to 1925. Masked klansmen in Inglewood terrorized that community's only Mexican family in April 1922 for allegedly bootlegging liquor. In a night-time raid on that family's home which involved the exchange of gunfire, a mortally wounded klansman was revealed to be the town's constable.[24] As elsewhere in the nation, KKK activity in the Los Angeles area manifested the fears of many mainstream Protestants that local society was changing far too rapidly and threatening the stability of both their community and the nation.

Amid such antagonisms, immigrants and other new residents organized themselves to provide strength in numbers and to support one another in the often hostile metropolitan environment. One Roman Catholic who stands out for his efforts is José David Orozco, a Los Angeles radio announcer from the Mexican state of Jalisco whose uncle was the archbishop of Guadalajara. Orozco organized chapters of the Santo Nombre (the Holy Name Society) to encourage religious practice among Mexican men and to pray for Catholics suffering in Mexico. Between 1929 and 1930, he founded forty chapters of the society in the Los Angeles area and emerged as an important leader in local religious affairs.[25] Orozco also desired to stir Mexican pride by promoting an ethnic consciousness among immigrants and exiles in Los Angeles. He furthered public expression of Mexican piety by sponsoring a procession of 20,000 Catholics through the streets of East Los Angeles in December 1930. First organized in 1928 by a women's group, the Hijas de Maria (Daughters of Mary), the demonstration honored Mexico's national patron, the Virgin of Guadalupe. Orozco later publicized the December devotion by radio, so that by 1934 over 40,000 Catholics participated.[26] This success led Orozco to organize another annual procession on the feast of Corpus Christi every June, attended by thousands in the 1930s.[27]

Orozco's vigorous efforts reveal the striking ability of members of the exile community to organize and publicly articulate their faith. Mexican religious associations that appeared in the 1920s ranged from Orozco's Santo Nombre for men to the widely popular Asociación Guadalupana to promote devotion to the Virgin of Guadalupe. Mutual aid societies, such as branches of the Sociedád Mutualista de San José, were founded in many eastside parishes, as were pious associations including El Santisimo and El Apostolado de la Oración, and women's charitable groups like the Hijas de Maria and the Damas de Caridád.[28] Groups for young people included the Juventud Catolica Femenina Mexicana and the Asociación Catolica de los Jovenes Mexicanos.[29] When Mexican priests were unavailable, leaders from organizations such as these assumed responsibility for the continuance of devotional activities for weekly worship and for social activities on important occasions.[30]

Working alongside clergy and among immigrants, Mexican religious women also experienced a variety of reactions to conditions in the United States. Over two hundred Mexican nuns fled to Los Angeles in the 1920s and turned their attention to the widespread religious needs of their fellow immigrants. Outnumbering male religious but attracting little scholarly attention, these women fled northward during the antireligious violence in Mexico associated with the Cristero revolt in the state of Jalisco. Their challenges and adaptations in California shed additional light on the religious experience of Mexicans in Los Angeles. These women also assumed positions of leadership and manifested creativity in coping with their new environs. Members of one religious order, the Carmelite Sisters of the Sacred Heart, offer a clear example of how immigrant religious women responded to conditions in the City of Angels.

Mother Maria Luisa Josefa de la Peña, founder and first mother superior of the order, fled Guadalajara in 1927 with two companions, Sisters Teresa Navarro and Margarita Hernandez. They arrived penniless in Los Angeles, and only Hernandez spoke a little English. They soon made their way to Long Beach, where they located a fellow refugee, Mrs. Nicolosa Flores, who welcomed them to her boarding house as she had done for numerous other poor religious on the run. When additional sisters escaped Mexico, they established a small convent and set to work in the *colonia* in Holy Innocents parish, Long Beach. They taught catechism and prepared children for the sacraments, distributed food baskets and organized *Las Posadas* (a commemoration of the holy family's search for an inn in Bethehem) at Christmastide, and opened a series of facilities in Los Angeles County for Mexican women which eventually included a residence for girls at risk, a tubercular sanitarium for young women, parochial schools, and a women's retreat house. Even when it was safe to return to Mexico, many of the sisters remained in California, corresponding with their convents in Mexico, and maintaining a steady coming and going across the border not unlike their fellow emigrés throughout the Southwest.[31]

These and other Mexican nuns in the Los Angeles area focused their attention on the needs of other immigrant women and on work with young people. The gender-specific nature of their ministry was typical of what was expected of women within Mexican culture, as well as within the ethos of Roman Catholicism that they found in Southern California. As Bishop John Cantwell had written upon the arrival of the first Mexican nuns in 1923, their vocation as "spouses of Christ" is "to help others."[32] The labors of these women on the West Coast paralleled the experience of Irish religious women in the eastern United States in the nineteenth century.[33] Both offered their fellow female immigrants an alternative to marriage, as well a model of women living independently from men and ready to aid women faced with poverty, domestic violence, alcoholism, and illness. Along with thousands of family members and hundreds of priests, the nuns reveal aspects of the move to a new land in the adaptations they chose to make, the issues that confronted them, and the creative responses they formulated.[34]

Alongside Mexicans who settled in the Boyle Heights district of eastside Los Angeles were thousands of Jewish immigrants, who developed another vibrant ethnic and religious community.[35] They created numerous secular and religious associations, such as *folkschules,* labor unions, Yiddish dramatic, cultural, and political clubs, Zionist societies, social and recreational groups, and a plethora of religious institutions. The Orthodox congregation Talmud Torah, the "Breed Street *shul,"* erected the largest of the local synagogues in 1912 and continued services until the early 1990s.[36] Across the river in downtown Los Angeles, Sephardic Jews from Rhodes, Salonika, Aleppo, and Turkey gathered their first *minyan* before World War I and eventually formed Congregation Tifererth Israel. Rabbi Max Nussbaum led a more acculturated Reform congregation at Temple Israel, and Sinai Temple's rabbi, Jacob Kohn, was an outspoken defender of the worker's right to unionize.[37]

Further west across the city, Jews in the 1920s began developing the Fairfax district, which would be the destination of upwardly mobile immigrant Jews in following decades.[38] Nearby was the city's most prominent Jewish congregation, Wilshire Boulevard Temple, headed by Rabbi Edgar Fogel Magnin. Magnin emerged in the 1920s as an eloquent and gracious representative for Los Angeles Jewry. Often touted as the "Rabbi to the Stars," he included among his congregants numerous Hollywood movie moguls, and his extensive civic service continued until his death in 1984. His efforts served to blunt the edge of anti-Semitism in Los Angeles in the 1920s, when xenophobia and suspicion of non-Christian religion ran high.[39]

Other ethnic religious believers appeared in the city in the 1920s and often had difficulty gaining social acceptance. Asian immigrants introduced a wide variety of spiritual beliefs and practices to western cities like Los Angeles.[40] Buddhists, Confucians, Taoists, and Shintoists established local congregations, which inspired Christian proselytizers to initiate missionary outreach to these peoples. These ethnic groups struggled to define their own

Figure 9.3. Celebrants at a service held every six years to commemorate the elevation of the Hompa Hongwanji Buddhist Temple to "Betsuin" status, in the Little Tokyo district of Los Angeles, c. 1931. *Shades of L.A. Archives/Los Angeles Public Library*

identities, to resist prejudice, and to establish themselves economically in this new land.[41] Religion played a significant role in the process of Asian adaptation to American society. Buddhism provided the Japanese with the means to interpret their experiences as a racial minority in the United States and also a religious minority in a Christian country. Buddhist temples also assisted many Japanese to adapt to their surroundings and to develop the foundations of a Nisei culture prior to World War II.[42]

Interest in Asian religion blossomed nationwide in the 1960s, but its Los Angeles roots dated back to the lectures on Hinduism given in 1889 by Swami Vivekananda, disciple of the famed Ramakrishna. In 1912, Albert P. Warrington established the 15-acre Krotona colony in the Hollywood Hills as a branch of the Theosophical Society of America. Affiliated with the international Theosophical headquarters in Adyar, Madras, India, believers studied a synthesis of Asian and Occidental wisdom. One important outgrowth of the pageants staged at Krotona was the 1919 formation of the Theatre Arts Alliance, which eventually established the Hollywood Bowl. Because of rapid residential growth in Hollywood, Krotona's education work relocated in 1928 to Ojai, where thousands came to hear the widely heralded spokesman, Krishnamurti.[43]

The closure of Krotona occurred at the height of the popularity of Asian religion and philosophy in Los Angeles in the 1920s. In 1929, Swami Prabhavananda established the Vedanta Society of Southern California in Hollywood to offer lectures and spiritual guidance drawn from the Hindu and Ramakrishna-Vedanta traditions. One of the most noted of the swami's later disciples was the writer Christopher Isherwood, who edited *Vedanta for Modern Man*.[44] Another important group established locally in the late 1920s was the Self-Realization Fellowship, headquartered on Mount Washington. Born and educated in India, Swami Paramahansa Yogananda taught yoga and the philosophy underlying it, using the scriptures of various religions.[45]

Other Asian faith traditions appeared in Los Angeles with the arrival of immigrants in the first decades of the twentieth century. Followers of the B'ahai Faith, which originated in Persia, gathered in 1909 and elected their first Local Spiritual Assembly in 1924. Christian Koreans, mostly Presbyterians, also immigrated to Los Angeles in the 1920s and began forming congregations. Japanese immigrants introduced Zen Buddhism with its rich tradition of meditation through the establishment in 1922 of the Zenshuji Soto Mission. In 1931, Nyogen Senzaki began teaching Zen in Los Angeles from his home on Turner Street near the railroad yards. Aided by Mrs. Kin Tanahashi, Senzaki gathered a small circle of devoted followers, to whom he explained, "Zen is not a puzzle; it cannot be solved by wit. It is spiritual food for those who want to learn what life is and what our mission is." Senzaki, Tanahashi, and other disciples continued the practice of *zazen* (zen meditation) even while interned at the desolate Heart Mountain Relocation Camp in Wyoming during World War II.[46] Upon release, the monk returned to Los Angeles and continued instructing a growing circle of students until his death in 1958. Interest in Japanese Zen blossomed in California in the 1960s, and an acquaintance of Senzaki, Mazumi Roshi, founded the Zen Center of Los Angeles/Buddha Essence Temple, which flourishes today. Other branches of Japanese Buddhism include the "Pure Land" or Jodo Shinshu Buddhism, represented locally by the Higashi Hongwanji Temple (1921) and the Hompa Hongwanji Temple (1917); and Shingon Buddhism, with its Koyasan Temple (1940).[47]

Angelenos witnessing the spread of so many new spiritual traditions in their city reacted in a variety of ways. Not everyone was welcome, as noted earlier, and the pluralism even within Christianity was often bewildering. Residents discovered that the followers of Christ in Los Angeles now included Antiochene and Armenian Christians; Copts; Chaldeans; Melkite, Maronite, and Byzantine Catholics; the Russian pacifist sect, the Molokans; and the Greek, Serbian, and Russian Orthodox.[48] The religious demographics of Los Angeles staggered the imagination and led commentators and journalists to expressions of derision or alarm.

The importance of the proliferation of faiths in the decade of the 1920s, however, transcends its impact on local culture and society. The massive immigration into Los Angeles from across the nation and from Europe, Mexico, and Asia faced Angelenos with a society that was far more multicultural than anything yet encountered in the nation. Religious manifestations of this emerging polyglot metropolis provided yet another example of difference and diversity. Most residents did not yet possess the necessary attitudes and tolerance to accept or appreciate the variety emerging in local religion. Some ridiculed new forms of ancient faiths, such as Aimee Semple McPherson's Four Square Gospel or the Pentecostal churches, and manifested overt hostility and suspicion.[49] Others, however, acted in a manner more consistent with the American ideals of toleration. These people manifested interest, explored the spiritual riches appearing in the city, and formed personal friendships with believers different from themselves, and some joined these religious groups new to the city. The often tentative efforts to understand the religious differences in their midst marked Angelenos as pioneers of religious diversity in the United States in the twentieth century. These efforts would become formalized in the 1940s with the establishment of city and county Human Relations Commissions, ably assisted by the B'nai B'rith Anti-Defamation League in meeting challenges from intercultural conflicts.

These shifts in demographics and church affiliation in the city in the 1920s coincided with broader trends affecting American Christianity. Commentators have described this as the beginning of the post-Protestant era, when a greatly expanded religious pluralism weakened Protestant cultural hegemony in the United States. In this regard, church life in Los Angeles differed little from that in Chicago and New York. Issues of immigration restriction and prohibition, for example, possessed strong religious implications for urban centers nationwide. What distinguished the City of Angels was the relatively recent urbanization of the community, the particular patterns of migration to the city, the broader racial diversity, and a rapid appearance of distinct and novel religious groups. Such changes in a mere three decades confronted church leaders and their congregations with the need to find adequate structures, attitudes, and skills to grapple with the consequences of such profound shifts.[50]

What began in Los Angeles with struggling efforts in that decade after 1920 was an effort to articulate a new model beyond that of the melting pot to accommodate the religious pluralism more widespread in the city than anywhere else in the nation. Because existing paradigms proved insufficient to address the breadth of religious expression, Angelenos struggled through subsequent generations to fashion a working relationship among the faith

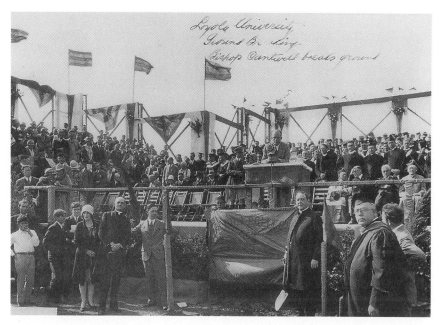

Figure 9.4. Groundbreaking for Loyola College (now Loyola Marymount University), May 28, 1928, in present-day Westchester. *Foreground, left to right:* Archbishop Edward J. Hanna of San Francisco; Harry Culver, donor of the site; Bishop John J. Cantwell of Los Angeles; Father Joseph Sullivan, president of Loyola College. *Department of Special Collections, Charles Von der Ahe Library, Loyola Marymount University*

communities. The repatriation of Mexicans during the Great Depression, the relocation of Japanese and Japanese Americans in World War II, the Zoot Suit Riots of 1943, and the urban unrest of 1965 and 1992 were all significant manifestations of fear and antipathy toward peoples viewed as "other." Religious leaders themselves would not form the all-encompassing interreligious Council of Southern California until 1970, to welcome leaders of all faiths into dialogue among equals.[51]

Not until the 1990s did the nation fully comprehend the challenges of multiculturalism which the city encountered seventy years earlier. Present efforts focusing on racial and ethnic concerns continue to include issues of religious diversity, particularly with the enormous growth of Islam and other faiths in recent years. Church leaders played significant roles in the efforts to grapple with the causes of the violence that exploded across the city in April 1992. One such endeavor, the Interfaith Coalition to Heal LA, sponsored community-building projects such as the 1993 Religious Leaders Summit, to facilitate discussion among pastors confronting the problems facing their congregations and the city. Though this is a definite sign of progress when compared to religious life in the 1920s, Angelenos still face enormous difficulties.

The challenge to religious believers in Los Angeles today is to avoid the close-mindedness of the twenties and to embrace a more cooperative and proactive approach to ethnic, racial, and religious diversity and issues of social justice. Seventy or eighty years ago, religion in the city did not override factors of social location and did not sufficiently challenge the widespread suspicion of newcomers to the region. Denominations whose institutional ties crisscrossed the city did not adequately utilize their considerable resources to minimize strife and prejudice. Church leaders frequently reflected the cultural biases of the age. Contemporary urban problems are of such urgency that members of churches, temples, and synagogues need to work together in effective coalitions to provide leadership, example, hope, and, on occasion, sufficient political pressure to improve civic life for all Angelenos.

In contrast with the 1920s, increasing numbers of religious leaders are aware that the city requires broad spiritual foundations if there is to be peaceful coexistence among its diverse peoples. Rather than support culturally homogenizing programs as did earlier pastors, present-day leaders must seek means to assist people in deepening respect for others while also promoting cohesive bonds of civic unity. As one recent USC study concluded, the best of such religious leaders help residents "to value, even to love, their multiethnicity."[52] These collaborative efforts are more likely to succeed today because of the breadth of mutual assistance and consultation which pastors of an earlier era could never fully imagine. Those who hold this vision are far more likely now to welcome the aid of people of all faith traditions, rather than to scorn or dismiss those spiritually different from themselves.

Like John Steven McGroarty in the 1920s, writers and commentators continue to watch Los Angeles with fascination, awe, and occasional dismay. Residents have not adequately resolved the challenges that emerged so abundantly in McGroarty's time, as violence, racial tension, and poverty remind us daily. The religious dimensions to urban growth, however, offer great hope for Angelenos. Despite occasional friction among religious believers, residents today manifest a far greater tolerance and acceptance of spiritual pluralism than did their predecessors in the twenties. This attitude is a necessary precondition for the ongoing work that civic unity entails. What remains to be seen is what these faiths will contribute to healing and unifying the city where they have long labored—and prayed—to find a congenial home.

NOTES

The author wishes to acknowledge the aid of research assistants Felipe Andalón and Denis Delja.

1. John Steven McGroarty, *Los Angeles: From the Mountains to the Sea* (Chicago: American Historical Society, 1921), 322; and Morris M. Rathbun, "Statistical Facts about Los Angeles," in *Los Angeles City Directory* (Los Angeles: Los Angeles City Directory Company, 1922), 8.

2. Writers' Program of the Works Progress Administration in Southern California, *Los Angeles: A Guide to the City and Its Environs* (New York: Hastings House, 1941; rev. ed., New York: Hastings House, 1951), 72, 73.

3. U.S. Bureau of the Census, *Twelfth Census of the United States. 1900. Population,* vol. I, Part I (Washington, D.C.: Government Printing Office, 1901), cxxii.

4. U.S. Bureau of the Census, *Fourteenth Census of the United States. 1920. Population,* vol. III, Part I (Washington, D.C.: Government Printing Office, 1922), 123; *Fifteenth Census of the United States. 1920. Population,* vol. III, Part I (Washington, D.C.: Government Printing Office, 1932), 252, 260.

5. Robert M. Fogelson, *The Fragmented Metropolis: Los Angeles, 1850–1930* (Cambridge: Harvard University Press, 1967; rpt. Berkeley and Los Angeles: University of California Press, 1993), 83.

6. U.S. Bureau of the Census, *Religious Bodies: 1916* (Washington, D.C., 1919); *Religious Bodies: 1926* (Washington, D.C., 1930); *Religious Bodies: 1936* (Washington, D.C., 1941).

7. U.S. Bureau of the Census, *Religious Bodies: 1916,* I, 330, 336, 431–33; *Religious Bodies: 1926,* I, 348–49, 457–59; *Religious Bodies: 1936,* I, 424–25, 568–70.

8. Lawrence H. Larsen, *The Urban West at the End of the Frontier* (Lawrence: Regents Press of Kansas, 1978), 29.

9. James N. Gregory, *American Exodus: The Dust Bowl Migration and Okie Culture in California* (New York: Oxford University Press, 1989), 203.

10. Nathaniel Wheaton, "Glance at the Churches of Los Angeles," *Saturday Night,* January 3, 1931, 11–12.

11. David Gebhard and Robert Winter, *Los Angeles: An Architectural Guide* (Salt Lake City: Gibbs Smith, 1994), 195, 200, 202–3, 205, 267; and WPA, *Los Angeles: A Guide to the City and Its Environs,* 186–87.

12. Shelton Bissell, "Vaudeville at Angelus Temple," *The Outlook,* May 23, 1928, 126–27, 158; and Aimee Semple McPherson, "Foursquare!" *Sunset* 58 (February 1927), 15, 80.

13. Laurence L. Hill, *Six Collegiate Decades: The Growth of Higher Education in Southern California* (Los Angeles: Security-First National Bank, 1929), 12–15, 18–28, 34–55; Mary Germaine McNeil, *History of Mount St. Mary's College* (New York: Vantage, 1985).

14. Robert Moats Miller, *Bishop G. Bromley Oxnam: Palladin of Liberal Protestantism* (Nashville: Abingdon Press, 1990), 73–79.

15. G. Bromley Oxnam, *The Mexican in Los Angeles: Los Angeles City Survey* (Los Angeles: Interchurch World Movement of North America, 1920).

16. George Warren Hinman, "Religious Work among Immigrants," in Joseph A.

Benton, ed., *Religious Progress on the Pacific Slope* (Boston: Pilgrim Press, 1917), 176, 182.

17. *Fourteenth Census. 1920. Population,* II, 47; and *Fifteenth Census. 1930. Population,* III, Part 1, 280; see also Lawrence B. DeGraaf, "The City of Black Angels: Emergence of the Los Angeles Ghetto, 1890–1930," *Pacific Historical Review* 39 (August 1970), 334–36, and Octavia B. Vivian, *The Story of the Negro in Los Angeles County* (Los Angeles: Federal Writers' Project, 1936; rpt. San Francisco: R and E Research Associates, 1970), 28–29.

18. *Religious Bodies: 1926,* I, 457–58; and *Religious Bodies: 1936,* I, 568–70.

19. Charlotta A. Bass, *Forty Years: Memoirs from the Pages of a Newspaper* (Los Angeles: C. A. Bass, 1960), 17.

20. Ada R. Barnes, "The History of Second Baptist Church," in *The History of Second Baptist Church, 1885–1931,* 45th Anniversary Edition (Los Angeles: The Mirror, 1930), 18–19; *Southwest Builder and Contractor,* February 22, 1924, 51; June 20, 1924, 52; October 31, 1924, 56; December 5, 1924, 51; December 19, 1924, 54; January 9, 1925, 61; February 6, 1925, 56; *California Eagle,* February 29, 1924, 1, and October 10, 1924, 1; and *Los Angeles Times,* January 3, 1926, II, 3.

21. Bass, *Forty Years,* 19.

22. DeGraaf, "The City of Black Angels," 336–38; Kevin Allen Leonard, "Years of Hope, Days of Fear: The Impact of World War II on Race Relations in Los Angeles" (Ph.D. dissertation, University of California, Davis, 1992), 284–90; Max Vorspan and Lloyd P. Gartner, *History of the Jews in Los Angeles* (San Marino, Calif.: Huntington Library, 1970), 205; Fogelson, *Fragmented Metropolis,* 145–46, 195; Ricardo Romo, *East Los Angeles: History of a Barrio* (Austin: University of Texas Press, 1983), 84; John Modell, *The Economics and Politics of Racial Accommodation: The Japanese in Los Angeles, 1900–1942* (Urbana: University of Illinois Press, 1977), 58; and Bass, *Forty Years,* 23–24.

23. George Sánchez, *Becoming Mexican American: Ethnicity, Culture, and Identity in Chicano Los Angeles, 1900–1945* (New York: Oxford University Press, 1993), 155.

24. Kenneth T. Jackson, *The Ku Klux Klan in the City, 1915–1930* (New York: Oxford University Press, 1967), 187–93; Christopher N. Cocoltchos, "The Invisible Empire and the Search for Orderly Community: The Ku Klux Klan in Anaheim, California," in Shawn Lay, ed., *Invisible Empire in the West* (Urbana: University of Illinois Press, 1992), 97–120; L. L. Bryson, *The Inglewood Raiders: The Story of the Celebrated Ku Klux Case at Los Angeles* (Los Angeles: L. L. Bryson, 1923), 5; and *"Citizen's Raid on Blind Pig Ends in Tragedy,"* Inglewood *Californian,* April 26, 1922, 1.

25. Francisco E. Balderrama, *In Defense of La Raza: The Los Angeles Mexican Consulate and the Mexican Community, 1929 to 1936* (Tucson: University of Arizona Press, 1982), 76–77.

26. *The Tidings* [Los Angeles], November 30 and December 14, 1934; Balderrama, *In Defense of La Raza,* 76–82; Sánchez, *Becoming Mexican American,* 168–69.

27. Rudolfo F. Acuña, *Community under Siege: A Chronicle of Chicanos East of the Los Angeles River, 1945–1975* (Los Angeles: Chicano Studies Research Center, University of California, Los Angeles, 1984), 407–9. Orozco also proposed to Bishop John Cantwell the establishment of a Spanish-language newspaper for Mexican Catholics,

though the bishop's response is not preserved. See Orozco to Cantwell, October 4, 1935 [Los Angeles]; Box 138, Archives of the Archdiocese of Los Angeles, Mission Hills, Calif., hereafter cited as AALA.

28. A valuable description of one such branch of the Mutualista de San José is found in James Hourihan, *History of St. Andrew's Parish* (Tappan, N.Y.: Custombook, Inc., 1986); for further explanation, see also Allan Figueroa Deck, *Second Wave: Hispanic Ministry and the Evangelization of Culture* (New York: Paulist Press, 1989), 66. For the Damas de Caridad, see the *Annual Report* of the Associated Catholic Charities, Diocese of Monterey and Los Angeles (1920), 21.

29. Cited in Archbishop Cantwell's report to the Holy See, "Relatio Prima Archdioecesis Angelorum in California, Sacra Congregationi Consistoriali" (1939), 21, AALA.

30. For a helpful discussion of Hispanic spirituality and values, see Rosa Maria Icaza, C.C.V.I., "Prayer, Worship, and Liturgy in a United States Hispanic Key," in Allan Figueroa Deck, S.J., ed., *Frontiers of Hispanic Theology in the United States* (Maryknoll, N.Y.: Orbis Books, 1992), 136–53.

31. See Helenita Colbert, *To Love Me in Truth: Mother Maria Luisa Josefa of the Blessed Sacrament, Servant of God* (Los Angeles: Carmelite Sisters of the Most Sacred Heart of Los Angeles, 1987), 25–53. To compare the experience of Mexican sisters with similar religious immigrants, see Suellen Hoy, "The Journey Out: The Recruitment and Emigration of Irish Religious Women to the United States, 1812–1914," *Journal of Women's History* 6 (Winter/Spring 1995), 64–98.

32. *The Tidings* [Los Angeles], July 23, 1926.

33. See Hasia Diner, *Erin's Daughters: Irish Immigrant Women in the Nineteenth Century* (Baltimore: Johns Hopkins University Press, 1983), 130–38.

34. As late as 1936 eleven convents still remained in the Archdiocese of Los Angeles where Mexican nuns engaged in a variety of ministries among the Spanish-speaking. See John J. Cantwell to Amleto Giovanni Cicognani, October 31, 1936, Los Angeles, AALA; and *Official Catholic Directory* (New York, 1936), 392–93.

35. Reva Clar, *The Jews of Los Angeles: Urban Pioneers* (Los Angeles: Southern California Jewish Historical Society, 1981), [7]; Neal Gabler, *An Empire of Their Own: How the Jews Invented Hollywood* (New York: Crown, 1988), 266–72, 276–77, 280–85, 306–9; Deborah Dash Moore, *To the Golden Cities: Pursuing the American Jewish Dream in Miami and Los Angeles* (New York: Free Press, 1994), 123–52. See also Mitchell Brian Gelfand, "Chutzpah in El Dorado: Social Mobility of Jews in Los Angeles" (Ph.D. dissertation, Carnegie-Mellon University, 1981), and Stephen Stern, *The Sephardic Jewish Community in Los Angeles* (New York: Arno, 1980).

36. See also the film about the Boyle Heights Jewish community, *Meet Me at Brooklyn and Soto* (Los Angeles, 1995), produced and directed by Ellie Kahn, written by Ellie Kahn and Stephen J. Sass, and sponsored by the Jewish Historical Society of Southern California.

37. Vorspan and Gartner, *History of the Jews of Los Angeles*, 116, 158–59, 161–62, 215; and Lewis M. Barth, ed., with Ruth Nussbaum, *Max Nussbaum: From Berlin to Hollywood: A Mid-Century Vision of Jewish Life* (Malibu, Calif: Joseph Simon/Pangloss Press, 1994).

38. Lynn Channah Kroznek, "Establishing the Boundaries: Fairfax to the Mid

1930s," *Legacy: Journal of the Jewish Historical Society of Southern California* 1 (Spring 1990), 7–13.

39. William M. Kramer and Reva Clar, "Rabbi Edgar F. Magnin and the Modernization of Los Angeles Jewry," *Western States Jewish History* 19 (April 1987), 233–51, and (July 1987), 346–62.

40. Michael Quinn, "Religion in the American West," in William Cronon, George Miles, and Jay Gitlin, eds., *Under an Open Sky: Rethinking America's Western Past* (New York: W. W. Norton, 1992), 145–66.

41. See, for example, Ronald Takaki, *Strangers from a Different Shore: A History of Asian Americans* (Boston: Little, Brown, 1989); Sucheng Chan, *Asian Americans: An Interpretive History* (Boston: Twayne, 1991); Gail M. Nomura, "Significant Lives: Asia and Asian Americans in the History of the American West," *Western Historical Quarterly* 25 (Spring 1994), 69–88; and Gary Okihiro, *Margins and Mainstreams: Asians in American History and Culture* (Seattle: University of Washington Press, 1994).

42. David Yoo, "Enlightened Identities: Buddhism and Japanese Americans of California, 1924–1941," *Western Historical Quarterly* 27 (Autumn 1996), 281–301; Yoo, "Growing Up Nisei: Second-Generation Japanese Americans of California, 1924–45" (Ph.D. dissertation, Yale University, 1994); and Brian Masaru Hayashi, *"For the Sake of Our Japanese Brethren": Assimilation, Nationalism, and Protestantism among the Japanese of Los Angeles, 1895–1942* (Stanford: Stanford University Press, 1995).

43. Swami Nikhilananda, *Vivekananda: A Biography* (New York: Ramakrishna-Vivekananda Center, 1953; rpt. New York: Self-Realization Fellowship, 1989), 153–54; Robert S. Ellwood Jr. and Donald E. Miller, "Eastern Religions and New Spiritual Movements," in Francis J. Weber, ed., *The Religious Heritage of Southern California* (Los Angeles: Interreligious Council of Southern California, 1976), 100–101; Carey McWilliams, *Southern California: An Island on the Land* (New York: Duell, Sloan, and Pearce, 1946; rpt. Salt Lake City: Peregrine Smith, 1973), 254–55; Mary Lutyens, *Krishnamurti: His Life and Death* (New York: St. Martin's Press, 1990). See also Joseph E. Ross, *Krotona of Old Hollywood* (Montecito, Calif.: El Montecito Oaks Press, n.d.), vol. I; and Pravrajika Vrajaprana, "What Do Hindus Do?—The Role of the Vedanta Societies in North America," *Cross Currents* 47 (Spring 1997), 69–85.

44. Christopher Isherwood, ed., *Vedanta for Modern Man* (New York: Viking, 1945); and Katherine Bucknell, ed., *Christopher Isherwood: Diaries*, Volume One: *1939–1960* (London: Metheun, 1996).

45. Paramahansa Yogananda, *Autobiography of a Yogi* (New York: The Philosophical Library, 1946; rpt. Los Angeles: Ramakrishnas-Vivekananda Center, 1993), 407, 408.

46. Nyogen Senzaki, "An Autobiographical Sketch," in Nyogen Senzaki and Ruth Strout McCandless, eds. and trans., *The Iron Flute* (Rutland, Vt.: Charles E. Tuttle Company, 1961), 161–62; Robert Aitken, *Original Dwelling Place: Zen Buddhist Essays* (Washington, D.C.: Counterpoint, 1996), 11–13; and Charles S. Prebisch, *American Buddhism* (North Scituate, Mass.: Duxbury Press, 1979), 9.

47. Ellwood and Miller, "Eastern Religions," 106–8, 114; see also Rick Fields, *How the Swans Came to the Lake: A Narrative History of Buddhism in America* (Boston: Shambhala, 1986).

48. See, for example, Stavros Nicholas Akrotirianakis, *Byzantium Comes to South-*

ern California: The Los Angeles Greek Community and the Building of Saint Sophia Cathedral (Minneapolis: Light and Life, 1994); Susan Wiley Hardwick, *Russian Refuge: Religion, Migration, and Settlement on the North American Rim* (Chicago: University of Chicago Press, 1993), 91–95, 174–76; Lillian Sokoloff, *The Russians in Los Angeles* (Los Angeles: Southern California Sociological Society, 1918), 2–4, 7–8; and Aram S. Yeretzian, *A History of Armenian Immigration to America with Special Reference to Los Angeles* (San Francisco: R and E Research Associates, 1974), 53–57.

49. McPherson's major clerical nemesis was Reverend Robert "Fighting Bob" Shuler, pastor of Trinity Southern Methodist Church, Los Angeles, who utilized his radio programs and magazine to attack "McPhersonism." See Mark S. Still, "'Fighting Bob' Shuler: Fundamentalist and Reformer" (Ph..D. dissertation, Claremont Graduate School, 1988).

50. See Gregory H. Singleton, *Religion in the City of the Angels: American Protestant Culture and Urbanization, Los Angeles, 1850–1930* (Ann Arbor: UMI Research Press, 1979), 180–81.

51. Alfred Wolf, "Introduction," in Weber, ed., *Religious Heritage of Southern California,* iv.

52. John B. Orr et al., *Politics of the Spirit: Religion and Multiethnicity in Los Angeles* (Los Angeles: University of Southern California, 1994), 9.

CHAPTER TEN

Fighting Like the Devil
in the City of Angels

The Rise of Fundamentalist Charles E. Fuller

Philip Goff

A change has occurred in American religious studies that has just begun to affect the writing of Los Angeles religious history. Over the past two decades scholars have moved away from a national model emphasizing a Puritan Protestant foundation that degenerated over the centuries into a secularized, "post-Protestant" civil religion, devoid of transcendent meaning. The challenge to this interpretation came from two sources. The first reflected a renewed interest in those groups that retained their spirituality outside the traditional power structures and focused on religious experiences of immigrants and the disfranchised. The more recent objection was formulated by injecting religion into the marketplace paradigm, whereby it is seen as a commodity that must be continually refashioned to meet the demand of consumers. Rather than understand religion's constant transformation as degeneration, one can analyze its steady interaction with the developing democratic economy—thus religion sells itself in the marketplace of ideas by continually adapting to that market. Religion itself changes in the very process of reforming society.[1]

Gregory Singleton's seminal study *Religion in the City of Angels* is a fine representative of scholarship before the transition. It traced the effects of Los Angeles's urbanization on the cooperative Protestant system that had formed before the turn of the century. The religious ethos that governed the city's power structure, popular myth, and accepted behavior resulted in a common boosterism that attracted economic growth in the early twentieth century, particularly the 1920s. That Protestant cooperation gave way to a corporate religiosity that by 1930 rendered the urbanized metropolis a compartmentalized society, leaving civic-mindedness to politics and the search for spiritual meaning to peripheral sects and cults.[2]

Michael Engh's *Frontier Faiths*, however, did not limit the collaboration to

Protestants. Although more limited in chronology, 1846–88, Engh's book expanded the religious contours of the city significantly by tracing the shared civic values of Protestants, Catholics, and Jews. His challenge to Singleton's work represents that first objection to traditional religious history: the need to enlarge the scope of religious studies to place more people on the playing field—or better, the praying field. Those peripheral "small sects and cults" that Singleton passed over can offer yet another powerful challenge to the traditional approach. Protestant Pentecostals provide a fascinating and helpful glimpse of the role of modernization in 1920s Los Angeles. Edith Blumhofer's study of Aimee Semple McPherson, for instance, furnishes an example of the strange ways the sacred and profane intersect in the marketplace, indicating just how far religion can be adapted to an area's culture in an attempt to convert people to a certain religious worldview.[3]

The more ordinary fundamentalists found in 1920s Los Angeles, the focus of this essay, can further extend our understanding of religion along both these lines—non-mainstream groups making room for themselves in the marketplace of culture. Encompassing tens of thousands who feared urbanization and modernism, local fundamentalists attempted to balance some semblance of Protestant cooperation with separatist beliefs. What resulted was a religious controversy that split fundamentalists not just in Los Angeles but across the country, as many turned their sights and later their backs on the epicenter of this debate, the Bible Institute of Los Angeles. In the midst of this struggle emerged a new national figure, native-born and native-trained Charles Fuller, who through this experience found the right mixture of conservative fundamentalist beliefs and Los Angeles–type religious cooperation to popularize the movement.

The story of these fundamentalists is important on at least three levels. First, it challenges the notion that religious life in 1920s Los Angeles fell into either secularized civil religion or cultic detachment. The truth is, there were many shades of Protestants in the region, many thousands of whom sustained their spirituality outside both boosterism and complete separatism. Second, it illustrates how national religious movements interact with, and attempt to overwhelm, local traditions and practices. The 1920s proved to be one of the most contentious decades in American Protestantism, and the battles between the national fundamentalist movement and regional cooperatives in Los Angeles constitute one of the most significant and understudied aspects of that period. Third, this story simultaneously transcends the 1920s and Los Angeles and also sheds light on the region's influence in shaping modern American religion, for the pitched battles deeply influenced the pioneer religious broadcaster who set the patterns most religious media follow today. Charles Fuller's response to the episode set the stage for modern religious broadcasting, which is built upon cooperation, rather than contentious competition, of faith groups. Further, Fuller's unique blend of separatist substance and nonconfrontational style eventually convinced millions of religious conservatives to remain engaged in social and political life, thus making him an important part of the story of American fundamentalism and its emergent influence in American politics.

FUNDAMENTALISTS AND THE BIBLE INSTITUTE OF LOS ANGELES

Strictly speaking, "fundamentalists" were conservative Protestants in the early twentieth century who reacted against the effects of modernism, particularly higher criticism of the Bible and acceptance of Darwinism. Highly intelligent leaders of the movement—some were leading scholars in universities—pooled their collective arguments regarding what they believed to be the essential elements of Christianity in twelve booklets produced from 1910 to 1915 called *The Fundamentals;* hence their appellation. The articles proved uneven and at times even contradictory, which is no surprise since they represented a group scattered among several religious traditions.[4]

George Marsden, regarded as the most knowledgeable historian of the topic, delineates four early-fundamentalist varieties according to their relation to American culture during the 1910s and 1920s. First, the Presbyterian intelligentsia at Princeton Seminary offered a worldview premised on the consecration of depraved society on a solid Reformed Protestant intellectual basis. Most of them held to a *postmillennial* (or even amillennial) view of society, that is, they believed that the world could be saved through right Christian thinking and action to establish the Kingdom of God. Meanwhile, those hoping to save "that old-time religion" epitomized by the Great Commoner William Jennings Bryan grew increasingly anti-intellectual and antimodern in reaction to developing theories of biblical higher criticism and Darwinism. Many, though not all, held the developing *premillennial* worldview that emphasized society's downward spiral, claiming that only Jesus' return could usher in the Kingdom. Third, the *dispensational premillennialists* pessimistically taught that society had become so saturated by sin that human effort was useless, that Jesus would imminently rapture believers to heaven and return to earth soon thereafter to begin the millennium. They understood history as broken into separate stages, or "dispensations," and believed they now stood near the brink of the final act. The last type of fundamentalist, and for our purposes the most important, wore each of the others' colors. They were a strange ideological mixture that proved to be a distinct assembly, satellites circling the urban Bible Institutes. Like the Princeton crowd, their nexus largely remained in places of higher learning—although education in the Bible Institutes was as practical as it was academic. Like the preservers of Christian America, they partook in the enduring nineteenth-century evangelical consensus. Like the dispensationalists, they were usually committed to the imminent return of Jesus.[5]

The Bible Institute of Los Angeles enjoyed a fundamentalist pedigree from the beginning. Union Oil Company millionaire Lyman Stewart, who later bankrolled *The Fundamentals,* hoped to establish a West Coast version of Chicago's famed Moody Bible Institute when he teamed with Thomas C. "Big Daddy" Horton in 1908 to create a training center for Christian men and women. Horton had left his position in Dallas's YMCA in 1905 to join the staff at the Immanuel Presbyterian Church in Los Angeles, to which Stewart belonged. In 1906 Horton founded the "International Fishermen's Club" to train Christians in the art of proselytization. The two men planned citywide revivals and conducted classes to ready workers to blanket the streets with evangelical witnesses. In 1911 they invited Reuben A. Torrey, noted conservative theologian, international lecturer, and former dean of Moody Bible Institute, to take the position as the first dean of the newly constituted Bible Institute of Los Angeles, the outgrowth of Horton's Bible classes.[6]

With Torrey as dean, Horton as superintendent, and Stewart as president and chief contributor, the Institute grew at an astounding rate and began to affect religious life throughout Southern California. The school's new building on the corner of Hope and Sixth Streets took up a city block and boasted a 4,565-seat auditorium for the Church of the Open Door, a non-denominational congregation under Torrey's pastorate. It also contained 683 dorm rooms with modern conveniences housed in twin 13-floor towers. The five boilers provided steam not only for the Institute but also (for a fee) for ten surrounding buildings housing hotels, restaurants, and stores. By 1923 the school's publishing operation ran nearly 42,000 copies each month of the leading western fundamentalist journal, *The King's Business,* edited by Horton, as well as books, hymnals, and contracted outside publishing projects. While mainline Protestant traditions trod water, Biola (as the Institute came to be known) rushed full ahead. The six social workers hired in 1923 by the Episcopal Diocese of Los Angeles could not hope to keep pace with Biola's students, who were required to report their Christian service each week to the dean of students. In 1917 alone they conducted 6,417 evangelistic meetings, taught 9,912 classes, distributed over 17,000 Bibles, Testaments, and Gospels, handed out more than 213,000 tracts, directly witnessed to nearly 50,000 people, and converted nearly 5,000. Is it any wonder that Los Angeles's six mainline Protestant denominations grew by only 64 percent during the 1920s, while those "small sects and cults" garnered a 381 percent increase?[7]

Biola advertised nationally for students, using all the advantages of a fundamentalist school in Southern California. The 1920 catalog's list of "Advantages and Privileges" placed its location second only to its esteemed

Figure 10.1. Biola student body in 1921, standing before the large Institute building. Charles Fuller is the large man with the bow tie standing in the center of the
second row; seated in front of him are (left to right) Reuben A. Torrey, T.C. Horton, and Lyman Stewart. *David du Plessis Collection, Fuller Theological Seminary*

faculty. "There is probably no more healthful climate in all the world," it
claimed. Students in Los Angeles suffered under fewer physical strains than
those elsewhere. "Many coming to Los Angeles in run-down physical condition, soon regain abounding health." Meanwhile residents also enjoyed
"marvelously fertile soil, its rich mines, its cheap fuel, and a citizenship of
rare quality." Besides, where else could one interact with so many cultures?
Since Los Angeles dominated the Pacific coast, it influenced Japan, China,
and Korea. "This is the critical hour, and those who believe in the Bible and
its matchless power to influence, not only individuals, but also society as a
whole, and the commercial life of nations as well as their religious life,
should seize the present opportunity at any cost." And speaking of cost,
there was no tuition, only the nominal price of registration.[8]

By the early 1920s, Biola had gained a reputation as an aggressive school
that brandished a conservative Protestantism not only on the streets of Los
Angeles, but throughout the surrounding community. Some local pastors
were repelled by the strict creedalism and increasingly separatist style of the
Institute. Other high-ranking ministers saw it as a bastion of traditional,
orthodox evangelical Protestantism. Fundamentalism proved extremely
popular in the American West, especially in Los Angeles. Whatever their
stripe—intellectuals, evangelical old guard, premillennial extremists—Los
Angeles fundamentalists found in Biola their common ground. Still, its
preeminent position was tenuous, since the "institutional fundamentalists"
Marsden described disagreed on numerous issues, though before 1925
those differences seemed less important than what they held in common.

But the Bible Institute of Los Angeles always had the potential to become a lightning rod in fundamentalist disputes since so many opinions were housed there.[9]

THE RISE OF CHARLES FULLER IN LOS ANGELES'S FUNDAMENTALIST COMMUNITY

Unlike the more colorful local evangelicals most scholars highlight, particularly the flashy Aimee Semple McPherson and the irrepressible Bob Shuler, Charles Fuller (1887–1968) was Los Angeles–born and never lived outside Southern California. As such, he kept a provincial character about his faith that most displaced eastern evangelicals lacked. Fuller knew well the cooperative spirit that Singleton described, having grown up locally in the Methodist Episcopal Church. His father was known for great faith, wealth, and generosity to favored conservative projects, particularly foreign missions. That Southern California experience served to create in Fuller a cooperative and diplomatic spirit, unlike the attitudes of many of his later Los Angeles colleagues.

Charles Fuller was born across the street from Central Park (now Pershing Square), less than two blocks from where the Institute was built a quarter century later. After Henry Fuller made a large profit from selling furniture, he moved his family to Redlands, where his orange groves became the envy of his neighbors. The fourth of four sons, Charles received little attention from his family and was nearly denied the opportunity to attend college since he had never shown any academic promise. Henry relented, however, and young Charles attended Pomona College, taking his degree in chemistry magna cum laude in 1910. After working for his father and marrying, he entered the citrus industry by buying a small grove. The freeze of 1913 quickly ended that, however, and he moved to Placentia, where he landed a job as packing house manager with the Pacific Mutual Orange Association.[10]

Nothing about Fuller's first thirty years gave any indication of his future. Although he grew up in a religious setting, he exhibited little interest in spiritual matters. He joined the Placentia Presbyterian Church in 1913 and was elected a Ruling Elder the following year—precisely the route one would expect of a young man hoping to move up in the community. In 1916 he underwent a significant change. Reading in the *Los Angeles Times* that a famous boxer-turned-preacher was to speak at the Institute's Church of the Open Door, he attended the evangelistic service alone. Deeply moved by Paul Rader's message, Fuller was converted to fundamental Christianity.

Feeling called to the ministry and suddenly flush with cash after leasing his new small grove for oil drilling, he enrolled at Biola in the fall of 1919. The curriculum had been refined to a two-year program leading to a dip-

Figure 10.2 Pamphlet
issued by Biola in 1926
advertising their newest
field evangelist, Charles E.
Fuller. *David du Plessis
Collection, Fuller Theological
Seminary*

loma. Each of the six terms required about twelve hours of class time per
week, the largest portion being devoted to "Bible Doctrines." Other courses
included homiletics, Bible analysis, public speaking, teacher training, and
music. Each week students turned in reports of study and practical work by
which the dean of students could ascertain their efforts at maintaining high
grades and Christian practice. They reported all meetings attended, classes
taught, Bibles and tracts distributed, numbers of people talked to about the
faith, people converted, visits to the hospital, and hours of Bible and music
study.[11]

Fuller's class notes reveal his complete submersion in Los Angeles's fundamentalist subculture. Torrey's popular book *What the Bible Teaches* dominated the Bible Doctrines course. Written in the form of an evangelical
catechism, it covered the major tenets of fundamentalism: the nature of

God; the divinity, virgin birth, death, and physical resurrection of Jesus; the role of the church in this present age; sin and punishment by torment in hell; the return of Christ and the resultant millennium; and Satan. Several courses steeped Fuller in biblical typology, training him to read Christ images back into the Old Testament. That skill later served him well, especially during the Cold War, when he read apocalyptic symbolism into current events.[12]

Perhaps most important, Fuller fell deeply under the sway of the popular dispensational interpretation of the Bible given in the notes of the *Scofield Reference Bible*. A layman who sought a unity behind the Bible from the perspective of premillennialism, Cyrus Scofield claimed that history is divided into seven dispensations, arranged under three large eras. The world was currently in the period when Gentiles receive the blessings of God's covenant, but soon the Jews would again become the people of God as the apocalypse neared. Those holding to earlier forms of premillennial thought charged that this "dispensational premillennialism" was hopelessly pessimistic, for it taught that Jesus' return was imminent and that Christian engagement with the outside world only served to taint the faith. But despite such arguments, dispensationalism attracted more and more fundamentalists who felt the significance of their culture slipping away. Unlike most mainline Protestant traditions, which optimistically taught that the world is redeemable and will slowly be turned to the gospel of peace (postmillennialism), these fundamentalists became increasingly pessimistic about the surrounding culture. The changing world seemed more and more sinful, rejecting the authority of the Bible and accepting scientific theories that ran contrary to the Genesis account of creation.[13]

Fuller's behavior upon graduation reflected his fundamentalist training. He became disenchanted with many aspects of his Presbyterian church, notably its belief that social work was the route to a better society, and began to teach a Sunday School class, under the church's auspices, in the Placentia Women's Club across the street. By 1924 the class outdrew the 11:00 service by a three-to-one margin, causing the church's new pastor to cut ties with it in hopes of drawing good Presbyterians back to the fold. Fuller and many in the class broke from the congregation to form an independent, interdenominational, premillennial church. Trained for Christian service but unordained, Fuller drove with a half-dozen like-minded separatists to Modesto to be ordained by the Baptist Bible Union, a fundamentalist wing of the Northern Baptist Convention.

Biola became an important fixture for such people as Fuller, pastoring an independent congregation, and for those mainline Protestant ministers unhappy with their denominations' acceptance of moderate positions in the fundamentalist-modernist debates. According to Marsden, those connected with the urban Bible Institutes, whether in Chicago, Minneapolis, New York, Philadelphia, or Los Angeles, became increasingly pessimistic and dispensational in the face of defeats for fundamentalism within denominations. Publicity surrounding the Scopes trial did little to alleviate fundamentalists' fears of further loss of power. As they began to discard "any clear view of the organized church above the local level, the Bible institutes played a major role in giving them some unity." In Los Angeles that harmony was furthered by *The King's Business* and the school's downtown radio station, KTBI, which broadcast shows featuring many local fundamentalist leaders, from both independent and fundamentalist-leaning mainline congregations.[14]

Clearly the social and cultural transformation of Los Angeles during the 1920s drove local fundamentalists' fears as much as any doctrinal debate did. An increased Catholic and non-mainstream Protestant presence threatened the long-standing cooperative system that still existed as an ideal, even if often unrealized, in the minds of many. Several of the mainstream Protestant denominations, once the heartbeat of nineteenth-century evangelicalism, now flirted with modernist theology. Ethnically and religiously, the city was changing. Fundamentalists reacted by founding parachurch and separatist organizations that they hoped would remain beyond the corrupting influences infiltrating society and the historic Protestant churches. The Southern California Premillennial Association, which emphasized the degradation of society and Christ's imminent return, was but one of a multitude of regional responses. Biola, as an established fundamentalist institution, took on greater significance, as it represented both a connection to evangelicalism's past and a more narrow biblical interpretation of society.

Fuller's Calvary Church quickly became one of Biola's dispensational outposts in Orange County. His messages mirrored the school's concern for the "signs of the times" that portended Christ's coming to rapture all true believers away to heaven. Scores of sermons turned the congregation's attention to world events that Fuller interpreted as fulfilled prophecy. For instance, in May 1926 he discussed "the Chinese situation." The *Placentia Courier* claimed, "This is an opportunity to hear first hand news. China, Japan, and Russia play an important part in closing events of today, and just prior to the Second Coming." A few years later Fuller joined with other dispensationalists who closely watched Italy's Benito Mussolini to see if he might be the fateful Antichrist who would bring great calamity to earth around the time of the rapture, shortly before the Second Coming. In a series of sermons entitled "Mussolini and the Vatican," Fuller compared Scripture and newspaper accounts in order to link the foretold ten kingdoms in the prophetic Book of Daniel to the world federation forming in Europe.

Shortly, Rome and Russia joined the sermon series, as the pastor pictured "a world-wide union of the Churches and how the stage will be set for the last conflict of the ages." The following week he added "Western Europe and the Sunrise Kingdoms of the East." Clearly, though, the connection was Mussolini, "The Wild Man of Europe," who would resurrect the Roman Empire which had tortured Christians in the early church. Russia's role as "The Bear Out of the North" would become increasingly important in Fuller's sermons during the Cold War, when Mussolini was gone from the world stage and America faced its greatest challenge from Moscow, but at this point Russia was simply one among a number of nations that would follow Antichrist against Israel.[15]

While dispensational fundamentalists shared many Americans' fears of fascism and communism as world powers, they proved distinct in their attitude toward Jews. If anything, they were pro-Semites. They believed Jews were the chosen people of God who were outside the divine plan only during this particular stage of history. Jews were soon to be restored to their former glory. The first sign would be their return to Palestine, which would usher in the final stage of time, during which Antichrist would try to destroy God's people, but to no avail. Fuller's understanding of Jews as "God's Timepiece" and his belief in their imminent reinstatement peppered his sermons and those of his guest speakers.[16]

Darwinism in public schools proved virtually the only local issue to appear in Fuller's sermons, which were usually dominated by world events. Several times he invited to his church Gerald Winrod, often called the "Kansas Cyclone" or the "Bryan of Kansas," founder of The Defenders of the Christian Faith, who was known for his anti-evolutionary rhetoric before the California state legislature. One sermon Fuller delivered was creatively entitled "Creation vs. Evolution, or Monko-Homo the High Brow, King of the Zoo." He advertised the message as one of great importance, for "Atheism is sweeping our country and the American Association for the Advancement of Atheism is promoting the teaching of Evolution in the schools to undermine the faith of our young people in the written Word of God." By controlling children's textbooks, the notice argued, the infidels hoped to abolish theism. Fuller included a poem entitled "The Creed of the Evolutionist," which clearly pointed to modernist higher education as the core problem.

> Once he was a pollywog, beginning to begin,
> Then he was a toad with its tail tucked in,
> Then he was a monkey up a bam-yan tree,
> Then he was a Doctor with a big D.D.
> A pollywog, a toad, a monkey and a man,
> Glory be to nature for the great big plan.

"In the course of his message," the *Placentia Courier* explained about the chemistry graduate, "Mr. Fuller will display some of the diagrams he had drawn while a college student. He will also have some books containing the teaching of Evolution which are now being used in the grammar schools."[17]

Charles Fuller proved himself a Biola man in more than his message and interests; he also became part of the cooperative network that surrounded the downtown school like a wheel's spokes extending throughout Southern California. He spoke against Pentecostalism, no doubt referring obliquely to the exploits of Aimee Semple McPherson, who remained an unmentionable topic in the school throughout the late 1920s. Fuller became a recurrent speaker at numerous local Bible conferences and throughout the West, particularly at the Native American's Sherman Institute in Riverside and the Southwest Bible and Missionary Conference at Flagstaff, Arizona. By 1926 he had developed into an official worker for the school's "Field Extension" department. It even sent him to the East Coast in hopes of drawing new students and financial support to the Institute, which operated on a tight budget after Stewart's death in 1923.[18]

While Fuller remained a second-tier speaker at fundamentalist conferences east of the Rocky Mountains, he established himself as a major power among conservatives in the Los Angeles area. In the summer of 1928 he joined T. C. Horton of Biola, Frederick Farr of Los Angeles's Calvary Baptist Church, and Stewart MacLennan of Hollywood's First Presbyterian Church as one of the speakers at a two-week-long "Fundamentals Bible Conference" at Camp Bethel near San Dimas. He also joined the faculty at the Los Angeles Baptist Theological Seminary to teach Bible doctrines several days each week. It proves no surprise then that Biola's "Society," the self-sustaining core of twenty-four school supporters who elected the board of directors, chose him as a member in February 1927 and immediately elevated him to fill a vacancy on the board.[19]

THE BOOK

Charles Fuller had no notion of the trouble that lay ahead. The school had undergone numerous changes since his graduation six years before, leaving problems in their wake. Lyman Stewart was dead. Amid controversies and internal power struggles, Dean Reuben Torrey had resigned to return to worldwide evangelistic work. Superintendent T. C. Horton had retired from the school, but remained very active in the Biola Society and in the Southern California Premillennial Association. Before they departed, however, the old guard had amassed a large debt and were operating at a deficit.[20]

It was impossible to replace Stewart, whose pocketbook seemed as deep as his faith. Charles Hurlburt and John Murdoch MacInnis filled Horton's

and Torrey's positions, respectively. Hurlburt was highly respected by conservative Protestants throughout the nation as co-founder of the African Interior Mission. MacInnis had worked with Torrey in Bible conferences previously, but was not known as a dynamic speaker, opting for a more reflective
faith that came by way of his studies in philosophy at Syracuse University,
where he took his Ph.D. Having joined the Biola faculty in 1922 as a Torrey
associate, and noted for his attacks against modernists among East Coast
Presbyterians, he carried the credentials to lead the Institute as dean. However, a struggle among Los Angeles fundamentalist types ensued, with the
nature of the Bible Institute as the battleground.[21]

MacInnis hoped to bring to the school a cooperative spirit, which once
characterized both Los Angeles and the larger Protestant scene under the
unifying ministry of Dwight L. Moody. He began a new era of "constructive
fundamentalism" to diminish many of the tensions between Biola and the
ruling committees of mainline churches. MacInnis saw himself as a conservative, but not as a fundamentalist as the term was beginning to be used,
having been co-opted by dispensationalists. In attempting to hew a middle
path between separatist and accommodationist territories, he left himself
with little room to maneuver. Ever vigilant against the slightest hint of het-
erodoxy, Horton had voiced misgivings about MacInnis since his nomina-
tion to the post in 1925. He feared that MacInnis's secular, philosophical
education had turned the new dean's thinking aside from such staple doctrines as the second coming of Christ and creationism, to say nothing of the
fundamentals themselves. Horton and others watched closely as the curriculum and new faculty began to reflect MacInnis's highly academic approach to religious education. One San Francisco alumnus and reader
of *The King's Business* complained to the new editorial staff, "Two years ago,
we had a graduate of B.I. in our home for four weeks,—a *firm defender of
Dr. MacInnis,* and yet so filled with Psychology that he finally admitted that
he didn't know what he believed any longer." Horton, meanwhile, collected
data that would prove MacInnis was not worthy to wear the mantle of those
who led the Institute in its early years.[22]

Failure to sustain the belief in Jesus' imminent return proved one of the
first and most often heard criticisms about the new leadership. This is hardly
surprising. Coming from a highly trained and well-regarded background in
Presbyterian theology (the first of Marsden's four fundamentalist types),
MacInnis was less likely to hold to the strict dispensational premillennialism
that Horton and others increasingly felt the mark of a true believer. The issue became a litmus test for the new administration, especially when it chose
not to air a radio Bible class supported by Horton and a number of Biola patrons. Based on the *Scofield Reference Bible*—which had taken on the aura of
an icon for dispensationalists—the course had been successfully taught by

two leading premillennialists, John Roach Straton in New York City and J. Frank Norris in Dallas. Meanwhile, in February 1926 the Biola Society, which Horton still dominated, voted to amend the school's creed given in the "Rules, Regulations and Discipline." Dominated by dispensationalists, the Society hoped to insert its beliefs into two places where Jesus' return is mentioned ambiguously and in a nondivisive manner. The board of directors, however, rejected the proposal, claiming that Biola's "Statement of Doctrine could never be changed" since God's truth is immutable. Therefore, while the Society, which acted as an advisory board for the school, turned increasingly conservative and pessimistic in its response to the changing culture in Los Angeles and in America at large, Biola's leadership refused to go along and even interacted more readily with churches the Society viewed as too modernist.[23]

Horton's actions during this period reveal an issue that, if not as deep as the doctrinal struggle, had equally important implications for the school's reputation and future: the Institute's finances. In an attempt to save Stewart's bequest, the board had used much of its capital to bolster flagging Western Enterprise Engine Company stock that it owned. In addition, as support for Western Enterprise Engine one struggling client deeded to the school a virtually defunct farm in Arizona. Pima Farms thus joined Western Enterprise as a financial burden around the neck of the Bible Institute. Time and again, the school borrowed money just to make ends meet, accruing more than $900,000 of debt by 1928. Rumors about Biola's financial situation worried many of its local supporters, including Horton, who saw the radio Bible class as an opportunity to produce income. Indeed, he understood the school's doctrinal and fiscal "drift" as the result of the new administration. "I suppose the Institute has made at least $50,000 from selling the Scofield Bible in the last fourteen years," he wrote to the president of the board, Joseph Irvine. If the radio Bible class enlisted only ten thousand listeners, then the income from class entrance fees, Bible sales, subscriptions to *The King's Business,* sales of other books, and making friends with potential contributors—all these would help the school financially as well as keep it on the ideological track laid by Lyman Stewart.[24]

The increasingly apparent cracks completely fissured in 1927 when Biola Press published MacInnis's book *Peter, the Fisherman Philosopher: A Study in Higher Fundamentalism.* This work attempted to weave together the best of modern philosophy and science into the essentials of evangelical Christian faith. "The Higher Fundamentalism is that insight of a living experience which is the light of life," claimed an advertisement for the book. "An adequate philosophy or interpretation of life is the explanation that satisfactorily solves the problem which life itself presents and makes possible the truest and highest kind of living." The difficulty, of course, was that many fundamentalists had already decided upon life's answers. But particularly because the book was based in part on lectures he had given at both Moody Bible Institute and Biola, MacInnis was unprepared for the intense reactions from both local and national fundamentalists.[25]

Horton, who had just suffered a manuscript rejection from Biola Press, led a faction of the Society criticizing the work as modernist. He even began considering legal action to require Biola to return all financial gifts to fundamentalists to pressure the board further. Flyers canvassed Los Angeles County advertising a review by local fundamentalist Leon Mayer entitled, "Is the Bible Institute Sold to Modernism?" which interested parties could order for one dollar from Mayer's Eagle Rock address. Not known for holding back his feelings, Mayer admitted there was much to recommend in this book, "but arsenic and ground glass are best administered in choicest bon bons." Soon national leaders joined in. William B. Riley, founder and president of both the influential World Christian Fundamentals Association (which Biola hosted for its 1922 world conference) and Northwestern Bible School in Minneapolis, squared off against the book in his publication *The Christian Fundamentalist.* "The book is utterly lacking in clarity of thought, felicity of expression, and gives little evidence indeed of careful research," wrote Riley. "It is unscholarly, anti-scriptural, and the moment all the fuss made about it dies down, its sales will cease." The problem, of course, was that Riley and his ilk were the ones making all the fuss. James Gray, dean of Moody Bible Institute in Chicago and editor of *Moody Monthly,* also published a negative review, which chastised the book for its "blending of non-Christian and non-biblical philosophizing with inspired revelation."[26]

It was, however, Charles Trumbull, a leading Philadelphia fundamentalist and editor of *The Sunday School Times,* the most popular national fundamentalist journal, with a weekly circulation nearing 100,000, that caused MacInnis and the Institute the most trouble. "One of the gravest dangers of this generation confronting the Church of Christ in America has arisen at the Bible Institute of Los Angeles, California," Trumbull began. "In this volume of more than two hundred pages the Dean of the Institute publishes mature convictions that are contrary to the Scriptures and the evangelistic Christian faith." Recognized modernists are quoted in the book, a sure sign that the lines of demarcation had fallen. "The expression 'The Higher Fundamentalism' is a significant one. The author obviously believes that Fundamentalism is not high enough." MacInnis's error, it appears, lay in his attempt to show that orthodox Protestantism was based on a deeper truth that is also reflected in true science and philosophy. Trumbull and others could never admit such a breach in the high wall separating their faith from the corrupted rationalism and "atheistic science" that resulted from modernism. He hoped the dean would prayerfully reconsider his stated position and "disavow his book and the teachings it embodies." The obligation Trumbull put on MacInnis was heavy, and he left no doubt that he intended no negotiation.[27]

Feeling the pressure from fundamentalist leaders outside Los Angeles, MacInnis and Keith Brooks, managing editor of *The King's Business,* answered Trumbull's charge. Brooks pointed out, "The devil has no greater dupes and none serve him so well as those who roar against Modernism and come short of the type of life which many Modernists live. . . . 'Higher Fundamentalism' will never be a popular thing, but it ought not to be a thing objected to by those who stand in the places of orthodox leadership." MacInnis also pointed to Satan's role in sowing discord. Harkening back to the serpent's actions in Eden, he claimed the devil now "has started lies about the Bible Institute of Los Angeles." He avowed that the fundamental beliefs (scriptural inerrancy, the divinity of Jesus, the atonement, the resurrection, and the second coming) were behind his book; the misunderstandings arose from its style, as it was cast "into philosophical molds in order to meet certain difficulties young people are meeting in schools, colleges, and universities."[28]

Locally, with the steady rise of a pessimistic dispensationalism in Southern California, Biola became the battleground for the different types of fundamentalists. Smarting over their treatment in the press, some became increasingly defensive and militant, and a dispensational pessimism made greater sense to them. Having separated from mainline denominations, they rallied around the Institute and felt threatened by conservatives who did not fall into step with their worldview. These feelings could spill over in strange ways, like their mistrust of the famed G. Campbell Morgan—who joined the faculty precisely because of MacInnis's intellectual reputation— simply because he smoked. Presbyterian fundamentalists, who leaned toward the first type of fundamentalist Marsden described, had their own doctrinal battles raging in Princeton Seminary, and thus could offer MacInnis little help. In all, as more dispensational separatists found their home in the Institute, MacInnis looked increasingly out of place. Still the school's board, only some of whom were dispensationalists, stood by him in a spirit of Christian unity.[29]

The board that defended the dean included several area notables. Alexander MacKeigan, of Mines & MacKeigan appraisers, had been involved in Los Angeles real estate and promotion since 1893. William Hazlett, twice a trustee of the Los Angeles Bar Association, served as a superior court judge for Los Angeles. Nathan Newby, one of fifteen freeholders elected in 1923 to draft the Charter of Los Angeles, was also a prestigious lawyer in the area and director of Seaboard National Bank and Aero Corporation of California. He later led Southern California's prohibition drive, no surprise since he attended Robert Shuler's church. Lula Stewart, Lyman's widow, remained a wealthy participant in the life of Christian women in the region and even directed the Bible Women, a club at Biola. Charles Fuller himself had moved into the arena of landed gentry, owning acreage in Redlands and around Orange County, growing and packing oranges, and leasing land to oil companies.[30]

In hopes of stilling the tempest, the board of directors appealed to the local network of cooperative fundamentalist leaders, asking a committee of Los Angeles area ministers to review MacInnis's book. The committee of nine included stellar local fundamentalists: Bob Shuler of Trinity Methodist, Fred Hagin of Figueroa Christian Church, Walter E. Edmonds of Glendale Presbyterian, Stewart MacLennan of First Presbyterian in Hollywood, Frederick Farr of Los Angeles's Calvary Baptist, Gustav Briegleb of St. Paul's Presbyterian in Los Angeles, Louis Bauman of Long Beach First Brethren, William McCulloch of the Los Angeles First United Presbyterian, and Lincoln Ferris of the Methodist Episcopal Church. They unanimously agreed that MacInnis was a true believer in the fundamentals and that the book's problem arose from its language and style, which were philosophical rather than doctrinal or theological. Only one, Louis Bauman, went so far as to put the onus on MacInnis to be clearer in the future since many who "hear his lectures and read his books are children in the faith."[31]

Generally the faculty stood behind its leader, as evidenced by a handwritten proclamation signed by twenty faculty members. G. Campbell Morgan, the school's most famous faculty member, wrote MacInnis, "I resolutely declare that you have put nothing in this book which can lay you under one moment's suspicion of holding any other position than that of the Bible in all matters of faith and practice. I am not inclined to go further. I am perfectly well aware that the devil has great ingenuity in taking sayings out of their context; and am shrewdly suspicious that any charge leveled against you on account of this book is the vicious offspring of that ingenuity."[32]

But the pressure did not stop. Clearly the attempt to use the local network had failed, and Horton continued to lob grenades at the dean. The board stood by MacInnis and warned Horton as one of the school's founders "to give to the loyal men who are carrying it forward the confidence and sympathy which is their due." By this point, however, Horton had enlisted the Southern California Premillennial Association to enter the fray. This was not a difficult task, as the usually irenic MacInnis had lost patience with the rumors spread by dispensationalists and lashed out at the popular member of that association who made the initial charge against him before the board. MacInnis derided Marion Reynolds, who had since lost his job at Biola, for his "absolute disloyalty and unchristian conduct" in a letter to the association's members. One wrote back to MacInnis, stating, "Few men on the coast have the hearts of the common man as Mr. Reynolds has. . . . His friends are looking at this charge as a very unethical procedure." He felt MacInnis's explosion would cost the Institute many of its local friends.[33]

Meanwhile the national campaign continued. In mid-May Charles Trumbull extended his criticisms to the board and, by implication, the faculty. Obviously, local and national criticism could deeply affect the school's ability to survive. Knowing this, MacInnis and Brooks ran a full-page ad in *The King's Business* with the names of each faculty member at Biola, stating that Trumbull's attack was "an assault on the *moral integrity* of every member of the faculty. . . . The attack upon our Institution has resolved itself into a one-sided battle of mud throwing. If men must throw mud, they should remember they cannot keep their own hands clean."[34]

While Trumbull might have held Biola's future in dirty hands, he held it nonetheless. Despite personal conversations between MacInnis and Trumbull throughout the summer, neither would budge—which posed a greater danger to Biola than to Trumbull's popular position. After trading public comments through the summer, Trumbull wielded his influence. He withheld Biola from his list of "Bible Schools That Are True to the Faith" in August just as students were preparing to begin the new session. The following month he sounded conciliatory in his tone toward MacInnis personally, but unmoved in his opinion of the book and the new and dangerous "constructive instead of controversial policy" vis-à-vis mainline denominations of *The King's Business,* of which MacInnis was editor in chief. Trumbull asserted that he was among many Christians who believed "that the errors in teaching that have crept in there are so serious, so unscriptural, that they threaten its testimony and its very life." Targeting the board, he maintained that contact with Biola over the summer had deepened his belief and hope that "God will guide and enable those who have the sacred stewardship for this great Christian institution to see its dangers and to safeguard the school and its magazine from every harmful policy and unscriptural teaching." Since MacInnis could not see the light, perhaps the board would feel the heat.[35]

Throughout the summer the board had stood by MacInnis, but they began to feel the pressure exerted from above and below. In June 45 graduates signed a letter stating their concerns about the dean and the school. Lula Stewart, now dean of women's ministries as well as an active board member, insisted that all guest speakers must sign the school's statement of faith, a move that MacInnis arrested by pointing out that all lecturers were chosen by the school's leaders, who themselves had signed the pledge. But it was clear that he was losing Mrs. Stewart's support. Meanwhile, income dropped precipitously as donations plummeted and Western Enterprise Engine Company and Pima Farms spiraled into bankruptcy. Soon the board set up a special committee to investigate the financial state of the school while they sold off assets to keep its doors open.[36]

These problems began to wear down the resolve of some board members. They faced a difficult question: Who would offer the school benefaction? Dispensational fundamentalists had grown wary of the school's dean; mainline supporters feared the militant stance of many local Biola partisans. Therefore, neither constituency came through with the requisite cash. Of course, in its early days, Lyman Stewart had picked up the bill, but even before his death Biola had incurred $500,000 of debt because of business difficulties and the school's expansion. Now it faced nearly a million dollars in loans, and some dispensationalists, particularly W. A. Hollis, purposefully spread rumors about Biola's administration in order to inspire patrons to liquidate their annuities. The board threatened lawsuits against these agitators. John MacInnis and several board members felt it was time Lula Stewart liquidated the $500,000 trust fund her husband left to preserve Biola in case of a financial emergency. But Lula Stewart only allowed the school to borrow against it, while she used the interest from this money to run the Bible Women club she headed.[37]

Exactly what happened next is unclear from extant evidence. The minutes of the board of directors meeting of 13 November 1928 state abruptly, "Dr. MacInnis tendered his resignation as Dean of the Bible Institute. On motion of Mr. Newby, seconded by Mrs. Stewart, it was accepted." Apparently the finance committee of the board decided to reactivate MacInnis's resignation, which he had courteously offered and the board had immediately rejected the previous February. Now, by a five-to-four vote, the resignation was accepted. What is clear, however, is that nearly half the board— Joseph Irvine (president), J. M. Rust, Alexander MacKeigan, and Judge William Hazlett—resigned, for two reasons. "It appears that as an attempt to allay unfounded criticism of the Dean and the Board of Directors, made by persons not connected with the Institute," wrote the four resigning members, "the majority of the Board of Directors, over our protest, have accepted his resignation, at the same time expressing the same confidence and approval of the Dean." Meanwhile, Mrs. Stewart, employing the trust fund for her pet ministry, refused to use it for its intended purposes. These debts now hung "as a millstone around the neck of the Institute and in a measure has depleted and will continue to deplete the funds donated by the friends of the Institute for its religious work." Fearing they might eventually be held responsible for these mounting debts, these four jumped ship.[38]

Within a week the remaining board members tried to work out a settlement with John MacInnis that paid him for six more months "so long as Dr. MacInnis shall maintain toward the Institute an attitude of Christian fellowship, and not manifest a spirit of antagonism that will retard the growth and development of the work of the Institute." But that was not to be. Hunkered down and taking hits from the right and the left, the board soon learned that playing to their dispensational friends would not silence their critics, who now included MacInnis himself. Following the capable leadership of Nathan Newby, the experienced and highly regarded lawyer who apparently led the coup, and sticking close to Lula Stewart, who still held the financial trump card, the remaining board members attempted to placate both the mainline churches and dispensationalists. Charles Fuller was absent from each meeting, speaking at Winrod's Defenders' Annual National Bible Conference in McPherson, Kansas. Although his role in planning the takeover is unknown, he returned to a firestorm, and quickly became the center of it.[39]

BETWEEN THE DEVIL AND DEEP BLUE SEA

The Bible Institute of Los Angeles nearly broke apart in the wake of John MacInnis's "resignation." Many faculty members quit, the Presbytery of Los Angeles met to exonerate MacInnis of error and denounce the separatist character of the school, MacInnis made serious charges about the board's bookkeeping, and there remained the problem of pleasing Horton's local contingent and the national fundamentalist leaders. The board pushed Fuller—the only member with something resembling a national reputation—into this quagmire by electing him second vice president and to committees in charge of settling down the remaining faculty and students, selecting the next dean, seeing that classes continued, and representing the school at the annual Founders Week Conference upcoming in February 1929 at Chicago's Moody Bible Institute.[40]

The board attempted to put out the many fires that threatened to engulf the school. Regarding local matters, they prepared a statement about the MacInnis controversy (2,500 copies) to be distributed among the ministers of the Los Angeles Presbytery and selected others. They pulled the book from the famed Biola Bookroom shelves, and adopted a concise resolution to be made public: "RESOLVED, That, having already withdrawn from sale and circulation the book, 'Peter, the Fisherman Philosopher,' the Board of Directors of the Bible Institute of Los Angeles hereby declares that this book does not represent the thinking and teaching of the Bible Institute of Los Angeles today."[41]

The board reconsidered their statement at the insistence of then-president Newby, perhaps because MacInnis threatened a lawsuit against the school, the board having intimated that the former dean's failure to sustain evangelistic programs had been behind his loss of job. The new statement, issued one month after the first, stood above the fray, claiming that "many sincere Fundamentalists throughout the world have maintained that the book was modernistic in its teachings, and doctrinally unsound from the fundamentalist point of view," while many others "of equal sincerity . . . have asserted their belief in the doctrinal soundness of the book." Since the controversy had injured the great cause of the school, MacInnis's resignation had been accepted, and the book was no longer being sold by anyone connected to the Institute. The statement kept away from admitting wrong while making it clear the school no longer had any link to the national controversy. The board then voted that Charles Fuller and Lula Stewart take copies of the new statement to Chicago for the Founders Conference for presentation to all interested parties. The following month T. C. Horton expressed his approval of the statement and moved in the annual Society meeting that the statement be published in the April issue of *The King's Business*. There was reason to hope the storm was subsiding.[42]

Fuller had already scheduled an evangelistic crusade with Gerald Winrod in Indianapolis during the Chicago conference, but planned to take the short jaunt to Chicago to represent Biola and carry the statement to James Gray, dean of the Moody Bible Institute, and Charles Trumbull. Stewart sent word to Fuller from Chicago that Gray found the statement's moderate tone unacceptable and that Fuller would not be allowed on the conference platform to represent Los Angeles. Fuller regarded this as an attempt by national fundamentalist outsiders to run local affairs. He telegraphed Stewart, "To prepare a statement that would suit Dr. Gray will force an issue in our Board. Under the present final statement we are all agreed and I for one cannot see why this statement should not [*sic*] and is not satisfactory. I believe with all my heart that Dr. Gray while professing helpfulness is at the same time wanting to dominate over and have his hands in the affairs of the Bible Institute of Los Angeles. I believe this is the game they are playing." He doubted the Chicago fundamentalist kingpin's motives. "I am coming to believe that Dr. Gray does not want the Bible Institute of Los Angeles to be a competitor of the Moody Bible Institute and at the same time I am sure that he wants to dominate the situation and be king of the situation, if possible."[43]

Here Fuller showed his native California stripes. He understood that Biola had always been supported by a conservative cooperative that did not seek approval outside its region. "If we prepare a statement that would suit Dr. Gray, we would alienate hundreds of loyal conscientious friends of the Pacific coast and if we would gain Dr. Gray's and Dr. Trumbull's friendship, I am afraid it would only be temporary and some other excuse would come up that might break further relations," he warned Stewart. Cognizant that the pastoral committee which had exonerated MacInnis the previous year would be placed in a tenuous position among national fundamentalists, he reminded her, "We must face the fact that eight of our loyal friends on the Pacific coast would be alienated with a statement which would suit Dr. Gray."

Besides, he had been elected to carry the board's statement, not to nego-tiate a new one with those national leaders who caused such local prob-lems. He refused to be placed on the defensive. After all, "Dr. McInnis [*sic*] is gone, the book is not on sale, and if Dr. Gray and Dr. Trumbull are not big enough to come in and help them [*sic*] I believe we had better go ahead ourselves." He understood the traditional Los Angeles–based coalition and proved unwilling to sacrifice it yet.[44]

Stewart replied quickly, greatly distressed that Fuller now refused to leave his meetings and join her in Chicago. She disagreed with his assessment of Gray and asserted that Biola should not be allowed on the platform so long as the issue of the book remained unsettled. Newby had forced the board to write the unfortunate declaration, which left ambiguity about the board's thoughts on the matter. Stewart understood that it was ambiguity that in-jured MacInnis in the first place. She felt certain that Newby, like MacInnis, lacked "a real Bible Institute vision" and that a new president should be elected. "Please, Mr. Fuller, don't go back on me now," she implored. "I came east for the express purpose of trying to establish friendly relations with Moody and I feel that this conference on Friday is a vital matter. . . . I feel the very existence of our Institute depends on lining up with our Fun-damentalist brethren. . . . This is a real S.O.S. call."[45]

Lula Stewart returned to Los Angeles touting two helpful conferences with Trumbull and Gray and relayed that "all these friends are earnestly desirous that a statement may be issued by the Board of Directors which will satisfactorily clarify the Board's attitude toward the book." Meanwhile the board received a letter from Horton rescinding his endorsement of the statement he once wanted published in *The King's Business*. Obviously, he had learned of the national fundamentalist leaders' rejection of the statement and tailored his opinion to meet theirs. The same pressure that squeezed MacInnis out of his job and Newby out of his presidency contin-ued to grip the new board, including its new president, Charles Fuller.[46]

Charles Fuller found himself over a barrel, an uncomfortable position for a man who had watched MacInnis ride one over the falls only weeks be-fore. Certainly Fuller, a graduate of Horton's Biola, trained in the *Scofield Reference Bible*, agreed ideologically with the dispensationalists. After all, he had led a separatist movement in Placentia when he started his own church. He had ridden to Modesto for ordination with Marion Reynolds, the Biola worker who initially blew the whistle on MacInnis's book. He was a member of the Southern California Premillennial Association. But Fuller was also old enough to remember the cooperative spirit that once existed among churches in Los Angeles. Since he was the most outspoken dispensational-ist on Biola's board, it must have been his memory of cooperation that had kept him defending MacInnis's "constructive fundamentalism" throughout

Figure 10.3. Cadle Tabernacle in Indianapolis, February 1926, after an evangelistic meeting. During this revival Fuller refused Mrs. Stewart's pleas to join her in Chicago to placate eastern fundamentalists. Back row (right to left): Charles Fuller, Gerald Winrod, and Paul Rader. *David du Plessis Collection, Fuller Theological Seminary*

the entire controversy. In fact, MacInnis had even spoken in Fuller's church. Still, Fuller announced that the book and its plates had been destroyed.[47]

Several faculty members and T. T. Shields, the famous Canadian fundamentalist preacher, helped to iron out yet a third statement which everyone hoped would be acceptable to the powerful faction that ran the Society and to the national fundamentalist leaders. This one clearly stated that the school erred in commending the book, that the author had resigned and "has now absolutely no connection with the Institute," and that not only was the book taken out of circulation but "all remaining copies, together with the type-forms, have been destroyed." Reiterating the school's strong doctrinal stand, the board also now required that all teachers must "pledge themselves without reservation" to it. Approved unanimously, the statement was to bear the signature only of the board's new president and best-known figure, Charles Fuller.[48]

Just as political revolutions eventually devour their own, so religious coups tend to throw off those unwilling to move in lockstep with others. Nathan Newby, the member who led the takeover, found himself in that unenviable position two days later when yet another addition was suggested for the statement. Newby refused to go along with it, and was dismissed from the board, which felt "that the acute conditions prevailing at the Institute at the present time make it necessary that the Board proceed unanimously with their policy." No doubt, Fuller was correct in his assessment to Stewart the previous month: locals were losing control of the school in pursuit of national approval.[49]

MacInnis struck back. He questioned the school's financial housekeeping and the purpose of independent Bible Institutions, claiming denominations should train their own ministers in approved seminaries. Rumors swirled through Los Angeles and the national fundamentalist subculture that Milton Stewart, Lyman's surviving brother, continued to support MacInnis financially as he planned a counterattack to take over the school and transform it into a Presbyterian seminary. This, of course, was not to be. Certainly, though, one hears the pathos in MacInnis's writing when he responded to Fuller's published statement. Questioning why the board vigorously defended him and the book only to turn its back later, he asked, "Why degrade religion by the use of pious phrases when everybody knows perfectly well that the change has come because Dr. Charles G. Trumbull . . . and others have demanded it as the price of recognition?" He pointedly assessed their actions, and found them behaving like Judas, who betrayed the truth for a price. "In other words, tell the people frankly that you have sold your convictions and Christian freedom for the favor of an extreme group whose favor is hardly worth thirty pieces of silver."[50]

Over the following months Fuller traveled throughout the country, continuing his speaking tours on behalf of Biola, in search of a dean and president of the school—something it had lacked since Stewart's death. They settled on Elbert McCreery of Pittsburgh, former faculty member at Moody, for dean, and William White, Moody's West Coast representative, as president. The reorganization of Biola had begun—a plan that laid the groundwork for a Moody-style national establishment that lacked local character.[51]

LOS ANGELES AND TWENTIETH-CENTURY FUNDAMENTALISM

What can be learned from this strange controversy that rocked Los Angeles fundamentalists and held captive for two years the attention of others around the nation? Its implications affect our understanding of religion in 1920s Los Angeles, American fundamentalism, and the importance of Los Angeles in twentieth-century American religion.

First, we must revise our notion that during the 1920s Protestants in Los Angeles either became secularized or sought spiritual fulfillment in small sects and cults. Such an understanding fails to recognize the complexity of the situation. Many conservative pastors of mainline churches, whose denominational leadership tended toward liberal religion and social services, became part of a cooperative substructure that found its core at the Bible Institute of Los Angeles. Some of Biola's leaders pastored Los Angeles's principal denominationally affiliated congregations. Likewise those sectlike separatists, who were supposedly so heavenly-minded, did not remain aloof from the area's urbanization and its modernizing effects on the city. Indeed, Protestant fundamentalists like Fuller, who separated from denominations, were obsessed with modernism, which must be understood as the more abstract result of urbanization. At the same time they used every available modern means—magazines and radio, especially—to voice their response to the transforming metropolis. There was far more give and take between Protestant types and the changing city than a dichotomous model of Protestants indicates.

On a wider level, Los Angeles's case provides an example of how a national religious worldview and transdenominational movement can overwhelm a local religious structure. When John Murdoch MacInnis attempted to build a constructive relationship with mainline Protestants, he encountered resistance from a vocal contingent of the school's supporters and national leaders of the movement to whom those locals now paid homage. While it is impossible to know, an interesting question is whether MacInnis could have been ousted and the Biola board so buffeted without insurgents from both above and below. Certainly the sum effect of both contributed to the school's difficulties. Equally clear, though, was that Horton took his cues from the national leaders, having accepted the board's second statement only to reject it once Gray and Trumbull announced their misgivings.

All of which indicates that the Bible Institute of Los Angeles, while similar to other urban Bible Institutes as a place where different types of fundamentalists gathered, held together in a precarious unity that reflected the variety of beliefs found in the Los Angeles area. Each breed of fundamentalist was creedal-conscious. Generally speaking, once publicity surrounding the Scopes trial made a contingent of them particularly militant, they began to turn on each other. Locally, that strain was intensified by the changes in the once overwhelmingly white Protestant city. Biola became the lightning rod of fundamentalist debates, as old-fashioned conservative evangelicals like MacInnis tried to keep a large tent in the tradition of Dwight L. Moody, while dispensationalists saw any negotiation with moderates as a signal of failure to uphold the faith. Ultimately, Biola could go in only one direction—and one side would be sacrificed for the other to survive.

A firm belief in a dispensational premillennialism that emphasized the imminent return of Jesus held together the alliance of Los Angeles insurgent fundamentalists and their national leaders. Clearly they became increasingly pessimistic as the 1920s saw the city transformed in ways that further frightened religious leaders, who felt their cultural significance slipping away. Darwin had made his way into public schools, and the Bible was often spoken of as a historical artifact, if at all. Interpreted a certain way, all the "signs of the times" were, in both the world and local news, indicating that Jesus would soon rapture true believers and return shortly thereafter to judge the world and bring the millennium. Anything that detracted from world evangelism or tainted the purity of the church—particularly a Bible Institute book that smacked of modernism—must be jettisoned as the church entered its final stage of preparation.[52]

Less ideologically, the Biola controversy reveals the mechanics of an institution attempting to place itself successfully in the religious market of Los Angeles. When MacInnis changed the school's focus in 1925 toward cooperation with mainline groups, he clearly wanted to expand the base of support. Joseph Irvine, then president of the board, chastened Horton for trying to make this shift into an ideological issue. If Biola were opened to others, they would in return open their doors to Biola "as feeders for the Institute both as to students and to funds." But he missed Horton's point, which was actually akin to his own interest: Horton thought the Scofield Bible Radio Class would expand the school's base and bring in more supporters. MacInnis defended his rejection of the class by pointing out that it would only further divide those who already supported the school. Why identify oneself with a school of thought to which "less than one-fourth of the evangelical membership" adheres? That logic eventually cost MacInnis his job and Biola half its board. MacInnis recognized this when he accused Fuller and the board of acting like Judas, selling their souls for the silver of an extremist group. One can almost read the debates in the board minutes,

then, as a struggle within a corporation for control of the advertising project. In the very act of appealing to people in order to bring them in, religious institutions are changed by the market.[53]

Finally, it is in Charles Fuller's role that the complexity of the fundamentalist movement in Los Angeles Protestantism finds its greatest expression. Scholars are usually drawn to the enigmatic Aimee Semple McPherson
or the bombastic Bob Shuler, but Fuller's Los Angeles background and
eventual worldwide influence disclose a powerful provincial religious movement. Having grown up in the cooperative atmosphere articulated by Gregory Singleton, he converted to a sectarian faith and trained in its foremost
social institution in Los Angeles. His early career shows every sign that he
was both a dispensational fundamentalist and an Angeleno. Clearly he
played a part—although an ambiguous one—in ousting MacInnis, but his
subsequent actions reveal a man attempting to retain the local character of
his city's long-standing religious atmosphere. He was no mere separatist. His
independent church was not just nondenominational, it was interdenominational, a fact he advertised weekly. As a member of Biola's board, he attempted to steer a middle course between the separatists and the more
cooperative spirit of Los Angeles's churches. His efforts, though, were defeated, and he oversaw the school's reorganization along a foreign line.
Soon thereafter, he turned to radio—having been exposed to it through
the school's KTBI and through preaching over the air on eastern speaking
engagements—to unite fundamentalists across the nation under a more
cooperative, less controversial banner.

Charles Fuller went on to popularize a more moderate form of fundamentalism predicated on his early Los Angeles experience. The local religious culture he knew as a young adult remained in his mind a model even
for extreme conservatives like himself who believed in the imminent return
of Jesus. Despite doctrinal differences, he underscored shared interpretations of world events that united fundamentalists throughout the nation.
"We are allied with no denomination," he told his listeners in 1937. "We are
fundamental, premillennial and our desire is to bring up no controversial
questions, but only to preach and teach the Word of God. . . ." By 1944,
he enjoyed an estimated weekly audience of over twenty million listeners. His popularity was based on a conservative message, both theological
and political, coupled with a more irenic evangelical image that reflected a
cooperative spirit. The most popular radio preacher in history, for a quarter century he commanded worldwide audiences in the tens of millions
who learned his premillennial interpretation of world events—all made
possible by the Los Angeles–style fundamentalist who never left Southern
California.[54]

As Charles Fuller recedes from the limelight, those he mentored have
continued to follow his script closely. Billy Graham tapped Southern Cali-

fornia talent to produce several influential films, including the award-winning anti-Nazi story of Corrie Ten Boom, *The Hiding Place*. More than a decade ago Bill Bright, charter student of Fuller Theological Seminary and founder of Campus Crusade for Christ (begun at UCLA and headquartered in Los Angeles until 1993), hired filmmakers who had worked on the musical hit *Grease* and the L.A. crime film *Chinatown* to create a film about the life of Jesus. Not released in American theaters, the motion picture was made available to missionaries around the world. Thus far it has been dubbed into over 520 languages, with 200 more on the way, and viewed by over 2 billion people. While *Variety* follows the numbers-crunching on Hollywood productions, *Jesus* has quietly become one of the most-watched films in history. Meanwhile, other Los Angeles–based worldwide ministries walk in Charles Fuller's steps in taking advantage of mass media opportunities available in Southern California, utilizing satellite technology and cable television. Trinity Broadcasting Network (based in Santa Ana) has grown in its thirty years to worldwide coverage and weekly audiences estimated at 50 million viewers. Glossing over doctrinal, political, and social differences, the network has consolidated many traditions into a "pan-evangelicalism" that enables smaller groups like the Christian Coalition to tap into that unity and challenge public opinion by politically energizing believers. Likewise, Robert Schuller of the Crystal Cathedral (Garden Grove), who grew up listening to the *Old Fashioned Revival Hour* and credits it with inspiring the best aspects of his own program, now draws more American viewers than any other television preacher. Known for incorporating pop psychology into his biblical sermons, he teaches tolerance and cooperation among faiths, expanded hallmarks of Fuller's religious culture.

The recent advent of religious music videos shown on cable television most clearly exhibits the give-and-take relationship between religion and culture in the twentieth century that Fuller helped to generate. Until the mid 1970s religious music remained a small part of the industry, usually categorized simply as "gospel." But in the past three decades many "Christian artists" have challenged the traditional dichotomy of "secular" and "sacred" music. These cross-over talents sell tens of millions of albums each year, and now are awarded Grammies right alongside those singing pop, rap, and rock music. Presently cable television carries a 24-hour religious counterpart to MTV, replete with Christian music videos and musical talk shows. Here fashion, artistry, and musical style clearly imitate nonreligious forms in an attempt to increase the audience—all in hopes of converting viewers.

Other faith groups have used their proximity to Los Angeles to set aside the doctrinal debates that often divide their religious communities in order to buy television time. By underscoring shared principles and practices, groups as varied as the Baptist Men's Association and American Muslims have unified their constituencies across the country. They often employed "entertainment," that is, common ritual practices their groups shared and enjoyed hearing or watching together, in this process, thereby more easily sidestepping controversial dogma—exactly as Fuller did. This shows no signs of slowing down. Los Angeles is today the most ethnically and religiously diverse city in the world, and its media role has not abated. As future ethnic religions arrive here and grow accustomed to American religious pluralism, they will doubtless find the "entertainment over doctrine" road an easy one to follow. Pan-Hindu (rather than sectarian) and pan-Islamic (rather than separate national programs) as well as East Asian television religious broadcasts already serve both to consolidate diasporic communities and to create better public relations with the larger American public. By placing themselves in the living rooms of traditional Americans, these groups make themselves less exotic to occasional viewers.

All of which underscores the importance of Charles Fuller's experiences in 1920s Los Angeles. The Biola training he received turned his sights and hopes to the return of Jesus and gave him the desire to convert others to Protestant fundamentalism. His obsession with world events came through over his national radio program by the late 1930s and made sense to religious conservatives as America moved into a new position as world leader. His style purposefully did not turn off evangelicals of any ilk, and his message kept separatists engaged with the world around them if for no other reason than to decipher the imminent return of Jesus. His immensely popular show laid the national framework for fundamentalists to reenter the public fray by giving them an interpretation of world events that could explain both the problems in public schools and Russia's evil role in the future. Certainly today's political conservatives look back on the last four decades and consider the presidential might that came out of Southern California, but its religious roots were laid long before by a different Angeleno.

NOTES

I wish to thank the John Randolph Haynes and Dora Haynes Foundation, which funded this study. I also wish to thank Kate McGinn of the Charles Fuller Collection at the David du Plessis Archive, Fuller Theological Seminary, Pasadena, Calif., and Sue Whitehead of the Biola University Archive, La Mirada, Calif., for their valuable aid, and Daniel P. Fuller for his helpful comments.

1. For a good discussion of the shift away from the Protestant mainstream, see Thomas A. Tweed, "Introduction: Narrating U. S. Religious History," in *Retelling U. S. Religious History*, ed. Thomas A. Tweed (Berkeley and Los Angeles: University of California Press, 1997). The marketplace model is best exemplified in R. Laurence Moore, *Selling God: Religion in the American Marketplace* (New York: Oxford University Press, 1995); and Leigh Eric Schmidt, *Consumer Rites: The Buying and Selling of American Holidays* (Princeton: Princeton University Press, 1996). See the review of this

new approach in Philip Goff, "Spiritual Enrichment and the Bull Market: Balancing the Books of American Religious History," *Religious Studies Review* 22, no. 2 (April 1996): 106–112.

2. Gregory H. Singleton, *Religion in the City of Angels: American Protestant Culture and Urbanization, Los Angeles, 1850–1930* (Ann Arbor, Mich.: UMI Research Press, 1979).

3. Michael E. Engh, S.J., *Frontier Faiths: Church, Temple, and Synagogue, 1846–1888* (Albuquerque: University of New Mexico Press, 1992). Edith Blumhofer, *Aimee Semple McPherson: Everybody's Sister* (Grand Rapids, Mich.: William B. Eerdmans, 1993). Singleton paid attention to Southern California fundamentalists in a different study; see "Fundamentalism and Urbanization: A Quantitative Critique of Impressionistic Interpretations," in *The New Urban History: Quantitative Explorations by American Historians,* ed. Leo F. Schnore (Princeton: Princeton University Press, 1975).

4. My understanding of modernism and fundamentalist reactions is based largely on Bruce B. Lawrence, *Defenders of God: The Fundamentalist Revolt against the Modern Age* (San Francisco: Harper & Row, 1989), chapter 1.

5. George M. Marsden, *Fundamentalism and American Culture: The Shaping of Twentieth-Century Evangelicalism, 1870–1925* (New York: Oxford University Press, 1980). Marsden's book has been supplemented but never supplanted by the myriad of fine works on twentieth-century fundamentalism and evangelicalism.

6. Robert Williams and Marilyn Miller, *Chartered for His Glory: Biola University, 1908–1983* (La Mirada, Calif.: Associated Students of Biola University, 1983). For an excellent overview of the Bible Institute movement in America, see Virginia L. Brereton, *Training God's Army: The American Bible School, 1880–1940* (Bloomington: Indiana University Press, 1990).

7. Williams and Miller, *Chartered for His Glory,* 33, 35; "Dr. MacInnis Reply to Crit. of TCH in letter," 21 May 1926, and quoted in Joseph Irvine to T. C. Horton, 28 May 1928, Biola University Archive (hereafter, BA); Singleton, *Religion in the City of Angels,* 156, 159, based upon Diocese of Los Angeles, *Annual Report* (Los Angeles, 1924), 213–217.

8. *1920 Catalog of the Bible Institute of Los Angeles,* 10–11, 17.

9. For studies of fundamentalism's popularity in Southern Californa during this period, see Singleton, "Fundamentalism and Urbanization"; William D. Edmondson, "Fundamentalist Sects of Los Angeles, 1900–1930" (Ph.D. dissertation, Claremont Graduate School, 1970); and James G. Lewis, "An Historical Survey of Radical Sectarianism in Los Angeles" (M.A. thesis, Occidental College, 1950).

10. For a good biography of Charles Fuller, see Daniel P. Fuller, *Give the Winds a Mighty Voice: The Story of Charles Fuller* (Waco, Texas: Word Books, 1971). For a brief period after graduation Charles Fuller worked on his father's gold-dredging operation along the American River in Northern California.

11. "Weekly Report of Study and Practical Work," David du Plessis Archive, Fuller Theological Seminary (hereafter DDA).

12. Charles Fuller's Classnotes, DDA. Reuben A. Torrey, *What the Bible Teaches* (New York: Fleming Revell, 1898).

13. Fuller first learned of premillennialism in William Blackstone, *Jesus Is Coming* (Chicago: F. H. Revell, 1898). Fuller read Blackstone's book soon after his con-

version in 1916. It continued to affect his thought and behavior throughout his life. Cyrus Scofield, *Scofield Reference Bible* (New York: Oxford University Press, 1909). For a good history of premillennialism, see Timothy Weber, *Living in the Shadow of the Second Coming: American Premillennialism, 1875–1982* (Chicago: University of Chicago Press, 1979); and Paul Boyer, *When Time Shall Be No More* (Cambridge: The Belknap Press of Harvard University Press, 1992).

14. Marsden, *Fundamentalism and American Culture*, 128.

15. *Placentia Courier*, 31 May 1926; 5 April 1929; 19 April 1929; 28 April 1929; 11 October 1929; 25 October 1929.

16. *Placentia Courier*, 18 September 1924; 5 January 1928; 13 September 1929; 20 September 1929; 27 September 1929; 28 March 1930.

17. Sermon book, n.d., internal evidence 1925–29, DDA. *Placentia Courier*, 30 June 1927; 15 December 1927; 5 January 1928; 27 October 1927. The strange sermon title doubtless came from a popular fundamentalist pamphlet of the period attacking evolution.

18. Brochure entitled "Charles Fuller, Evangelist," DDA. Bible Institute of Los Angeles Board of Directors minutes, 24 February 1927 (hereafter referred to as Board minutes).

19. *Placentia Courier*, 21 June 1928. Bible Institute of Los Angeles Society minutes, 24 February 1927 (hereafter referred to as Society minutes).

20. The Reverend Gustav A. Briegleb claimed, "Jealousy was rife at the Bible Institute at the time of R. A. Torrey. Dr. Torrey left the Bible Institute with a broken heart. No two men can ride the same horse without one man riding behind, however good he may be. And so between Mr. Horton and Mr. Torrey there did develop an element of jealousy which resulted in Mr. Horton also resigning." See "Prelude Speech" by Rev. Gustav A. Briegleb, delivered Sunday evening, 2 December 1928, at St. Paul's Presbyterian Church, BA. Gustav Briegleb, "The Trouble at the Institute, Some Facts for Fair Minds: 'A Whited Sepulchre,'" delivered at St. Paul's Presbyterian Church, 9 December 1928, BA.

21. In an unpublished paper, Diana Butler traces the early days of John Murdoch MacInnis's tenure as Biola's dean and his welcome reception among mainline Protestants. See "The Lost Puritan City: Los Angeles' Fundamentalist-Modernist Controversy, 1925–1928," written for the Young Scholars in American Religion meeting, Indianapolis, Ind., June 1996. For a good overall history of the MacInnis years in relation to national fundamentalism, see Daniel W. Draney, "John Murdoch MacInnis and the Crisis of Authority in American Protestant Fundamentalism, 1925–1929" (Ph.D. dissertation, Fuller Theological Seminary, 1996).

22. *Los Angeles Times*, 7 April 1925, II, 1. MacInnis Statement, Typed Document (1925), John Murdoch MacInnis Papers, Presbyterian Historical Society, Philadelphia, quoted in Draney, "John Murdoch MacInnis," 176. Oscar Zimmerman to Keith Brooks, 7 November 1927, BA. J. Paul Hatch to T. C. Horton, 5 May 1925, BA; J. E. McKee to T. C. Horton, 15 March 1925, BA.

23. Society minutes, 25 February 1926; Board minutes, 5 November 1926. A number of faculty and students were unhappy with MacInnis's views on eschatology. He apparently rejected dispensationalism, which many began to understand as fundamental to the faith rather than simply an interpretation of the earth's final days.

24. Thomas C. Horton to Joseph Irvine, 21 May 1926, BA.

25. John Murdoch MacInnis, *Peter, the Fisherman Philosopher: A Study in Higher Fundamentalism* (Los Angeles: Bible Institute of Los Angeles, 1927; rpt. New York: Harper Bros., 1930). *The King's Business* (November 1927): 750.

26. T. C. Horton to J. M. Irvine, 4 November 1925, BA. Leon B. Mayer, "Is the Bible Institute Sold to Modernism?" BA. William B. Riley, "Breaking the Bible School Defense" (April 1928); "Biola Boiling: Dean MacInnis and Modernism Again" (May 1928); "The MacInnis Controversy" (quoted) (June 1928), all in *The Christian Fundamentalist. Moody Monthly*, March 1928, 346.

27. Charles Trumbull, "Simon Peter—Philosopher or Apostle?" *The Sunday School Times* (5 May 1928): 277–278, 282.

28. Keith Brooks, "Higher Fundamentalism—What Is It?" *The King's Business* (May 1928): 270–271. John MacInnis, "Peddling the Devil's Lies," *The King's Business* (May 1928): 276.

29. E. J. Hazelton to Marion Reynolds, 4 February 1928, BA.

30. "Alexander MacKeigan," "William Hazlett," "Nathan Newby," "Charles Fuller," *Who's Who in California* (1928–29); W. W. Robinson, *Lawyers in Los Angeles: A History of the Los Angeles Bar Association and the Bar of Los Angeles County* (Los Angeles: The Ward Ritchie Press, 1959), 316, 321.

31. Board minutes, 2 March 1928.

32. Handwritten proclamation signed by twenty faculty members and four student body officers, BA. G. Campbell Morgan to John MacInnis, 12 January 1928, BA.

33. Board minutes, 6 January 1928. The board also rejected Horton's request for a special meeting of the Society for 21 February since a special meeting had just been held on 3 February and the annual meeting was scheduled for 23 February; see Board minutes, 14 February 1928. John M. MacInnis to "Dear Brother" (members of Premillennial Association), 25 January 1928, BA. Charles A. Nethery[?] to John MacInnis, 2 February 1928, BA.

34. Charles Trumbull, "The Los Angeles Crisis Continues," *The Sunday School Times* (19 May 1928): 310. "Write Your Own Headline," *The King's Business* (June 1928).

35. Trumbull, "Bible Schools That Are True to the Faith," *The Sunday School Times* (11 August 1928): 469; "The Bible Institute of Los Angeles," *The Sunday School Times* (29 September 1929): 558.

36. Board minutes, 1 June 1928; 6 July 1928. Draney refers to a letter from Ida MacInnis to her family saying that Lula Stewart had turned against John MacInnis: Ida MacInnis to family, 28 October 1928, Draney, "John Murdoch MacInnis," 266.

37. Briegleb, "The Trouble at the Institute, Some Facts for Fair Minds." Draney, "John Murdoch MacInnis," 267ff. *Los Angeles Times*, 29 December 1929. The school had borrowed $350,000 against the fund.

38. Board minutes, 13 November 1928; 16 November 1928; 19 November 1928. "We the undersigned" to Nathan Newby and the Board of Directors of the Bible Institute, 19 November 1928, BA.

39. Board minutes, 23 November 1928. *Placentia Courier*, 16 and 23 November 1928.

40. Board minutes, 7 December 1928. Minutes of the Presbytery of Los Angeles,

1929; "Pro Re Nata Meeting, First Presbyterian Church, Los Angeles," in Butler, "Lost Puritan City," 27–28. For Fuller's expanded role, see Board minutes, 20 December 1928; 23 November 1928; 12 December 1928; 21 January 1929.

41. Board minutes, 20 December 1928; 21 January 1929.

42. *Los Angeles Times,* 29 December 1928. Board minutes, 28 January 1929. Lula Stewart voted against reconsideration of the first statement. Society minutes, 28 February 1929.

43. Charles Fuller to Lula Stewart, 5 February 1929, DDA.

44. Fuller to Stewart, 5 February 1929, DDA.

45. Lula Stewart to Charles Fuller, n.d.; internal evidence suggests 6 February 1929, DDA. She also questioned Fuller's insistence that Gerald Winrod—who stood behind MacInnis throughout the affair—should come on board as dean, as she had "heard things that make me fear he may not be all that you think him to be." Under the influence of the Chicago crowd, Stewart no doubt heard rumors—later proved true—about Winrod's anti-Semitic sentiments. These became more pronounced in the 1930s, when he often teamed up with Gerald L. K. Smith and others to argue the merits of Nazi Germany. Twice Winrod was indicted for sedition against the United States.

46. Board minutes, 7 March 1929.

47. *Los Angeles Times,* 28 March 1929.

48. Board minutes, 18 March 1929.

49. Board minutes, 20 March 1929. Apparently Newby's dismissal was part of the moment's drama, but nothing more. He appears back on the board within weeks, without mention of the incident in the Board or Society minutes.

50. L. W. Munhall, "The Bible Institute of Los Angeles," *The Methodist* (19 March 1931). "Dr. MacInnis Replies," *Faith and Fellowship* (2 April 1929).

51. Board minutes, 29 May 1929. During that meeting they also sent a letter of appreciation to James Gray at Moody "for his help and counsel in matters concerning the Institute during the past several months."

52. *The King's Business* (April 1929): 188; and monthly thereafter.

53. Joseph Irvine to T. C. Horton, 28 May 1926, BA. "Dr. MacInnis Reply to Crit. of TCH in letter," 21 May 1926, BA.

54. "Heart to Heart Talk," 17 April 1937. For an analysis of the rise to prominence of Fuller's radio program, see Philip Goff, "We Have Heard the Joyful Sound: Charles E. Fuller's Radio Program and the Rise of Modern Evangelicalism," *Religious Studies Review: A Journal of Interpretation* 9, no. 1 (January 1999): 67–95.

PART FOUR

Metropolitics

POLITICS IN 1920S Los Angeles encompassed a complicated web of groups and individuals who played various roles in making public policy. From City Hall to corporate boardrooms, workplaces, and pulpits, an array of elected officials, civic leaders, business moguls, and representatives of economic or social organizations competed for influence with varying degrees of success. The following essays explore elements of this busy 1920s milieu. Steven J. Ross and Laurie Pintar focus on the conflicts between capital and labor unions in the film industry as case studies of the struggle for economic gain and the political power to retain it. Tom Sitton looks at elites and their rivals in the contest to influence municipal policy making, while William Deverell concentrates on a forgotten but once important figure in the power plays of 1920s Los Angeles politics.

CHAPTER ELEVEN

How Hollywood Became Hollywood

Money, Politics, and Movies

Steven J. Ross

Settling into their seats eagerly anticipating an evening of entertainment, millions of moviegoers soon found themselves shaken by the powerful scenes on the screen. *What Is to Be Done?* (1914), produced by socialist activist Joseph L. Weiss, showed national guardsmen massacring 24 striking miners and their families. *A Martyr to His Cause* (1911), made by the American Federation of Labor, showed manufacturers conspiring with local authorities to kidnap union leaders who fought to protect the rights of workers. Presenting a very different political perspective, *Steve Hill's Awakening* (1914), produced by the New York Central Railroad, revealed how thousands of railroad passengers were killed or injured in accidents caused by drunken railway workers, while *The Crime of Carelessness* (1912), produced by the National Association of Manufacturers, revealed how a sweatshop fire similar to the one that killed 146 employees of the Triangle Shirtwaist Company was caused by a careless cigarette-smoking employee and not, as unions charged, by manufacturers.

These are not the kind of films or producers we usually associate with Hollywood. Today when we think of "Hollywood," we think of multimillion-dollar productions made by wealthy studios that feature famous movie stars, dazzling special effects, and plots that generally avoid political controversy. But the movie industry was not always this way. In 1910, Hollywood, California, was a sleepy town of fewer than 4,000 residents and no movie studios. A decade later, the name "Hollywood" was synonymous with filmmaking, and Los Angeles reigned as the center of the movie industry: the United States produced 90 percent of the world's films and Southern California accounted for at least 80 percent of American production.[1]

Movies were far more self-consciously political and varied in their ideologies before Hollywood, California, became "Hollywood" than at any subsequent time in the industry's history. The minimal demands of technological expertise and the relatively modest costs of making films ($400 to $1,000 a reel in many instances) allowed large numbers of diverse groups and individuals to participate in this fledgling industry. Quickly grasping the medium's potential "for political, social, religious propaganda, for muckraking . . . [and] for revolutionary ideas," capitalists, unions, radicals, reformers, women's groups, religious organizations, and government agencies produced their own films or cooperated with established film companies in making films that presented their cause to a mass public.[2]

The rapid growth of American filmmaking in the 1920s signaled the rise of a new type of film industry and the birth of "Hollywood" as a metaphor to describe it. Filmmaking was less an art form than a multimillion-dollar industry with close ties to Wall Street and other major financial and industrial institutions. The eight studios that came to dominate the industry were run according to business principles that affected the economic organization of the industry and the politics of its films. By establishing itself as the center of the movie industry, Los Angeles and its studios exerted a tremendous influence over the political consciousness of the nation's citizens. Throughout the 1920s, figures on the political left and right agreed that movies played a vital role in shaping the ways in which millions of people looked at their world; there were an estimated 90 million admissions a week by 1927, a figure nearly equal to the entire population. "There has never been any means of scattering so many ideas and suggestions in so short a time before so many individuals," a *New York Times* reporter wrote in 1925. "The motion picture is the school, the diversion, perhaps even the church of the future." By reaching so many millions of people, concurred radical filmmaker William Kruse, movies had become an important weapon in the "struggle for the minds of the masses."[3]

Today, it is quite common for conservatives to bash Hollywood as the center of liberalism. Yet, in truth, the creation of Hollywood and its attendant studio system—located in the nation's most anti-union city—prompted a marked conservative shift in the ways in which American filmmakers dealt with problems of class conflict and class identity. Throughout the silent era, working-class filmmakers struggled to produce a regular array of films that dealt with class relations from a leftist perspective. Their efforts to affect the ideological direction of American film failed, however, as studios and government censors succeeded in forcing worker filmmakers off the screen. Consequently, Hollywood movies came to shape, not just reflect, the ways in which subsequent generations would think about what it meant to be working class or middle class. Indeed, for many Americans, Hollywood's political pronouncements today prove far more influential than those of the nation's politicians. As Republican Senator Arlen Specter recently noted: "Quite candidly, when Hollywood speaks, the world listens. Sometimes when Washington speaks, the world snoozes."[4]

This essay focuses on answering two important questions: How did Hollywood become "Hollywood" and what did that mean for the politics of American film? It also explores two related issues: the "myth" that producers respond primarily to audience tastes in deciding what films to make, and the extent to which events happening off the screen—in Los Angeles and around the nation—have affected the political images seen on the screen.

THE RISE OF HOLLYWOOD

The creation of "Hollywood" was a gradual process. In the years before the outbreak of World War I transformed the world's film industry, Southern California was only one of many production sites, and a minor one at that. The American movie industry began as a decentralized, small-scale business with hundreds of producers, distributors, and exhibitors. The astounding popularity of early moving pictures sparked a rapid expansion of movie theaters—from a few hundred in 1905 to 14,000 by 1914—and an accompanying demand for more films. Although early film production was dominated by the ten companies that comprised the Motion Picture Patents Company, a monopolistic group known as the "Trust," the constant shortage of movies and difficulties of enforcing patent laws created opportunities for dozens of independent companies. As ambitious entrepreneurs and farsighted political groups rushed to satisfy the public's taste for new products, film companies gradually spread outward from their initial centers in New York (home to American Mutuoscope and Biograph Edison, Kalem, and Vitagraph), Philadelphia (Lubin), and Chicago (Essanay and Selig) to cities such as Rochester, Boston, Jacksonville, Cincinnati, New Orleans, San Antonio, and Los Angeles.[5]

Southern California entered the movie age in 1906, when the New York–based Biograph company became the first to shoot in the Los Angeles area. Other eastern and midwestern film companies, whose operations were frequently curtailed by dark and inclement winter weather, soon realized that they could increase production by moving to a place where year-round sunlight and favorable weather conditions made it possible to shoot outdoors at least 300 days a year. The region's spectacular natural scenery—ocean, beaches, desert, forests, mountains—also allowed companies to make a wide variety of pictures. Several other factors drew filmmakers west: plentiful and inexpensive land to expand studio operations; relatively weak labor unions; and, for early independents, a site far from the reach of the Trust monopolists. By May 1911, at least ten motion picture companies had set up operations within greater Los Angeles—an area that included Santa Monica, Edendale, Glendale, Pasadena, Long Beach, and Hollywood.[6]

It took a number of years for Hollywood to establish its place in the movie world. As late as 1914, observed director William de Mille, "the name Hollywood meant nothing whatever to the people of this country; even the picture fans hadn't heard of it."[7] Located some twelve miles east of the Pacific Ocean, Hollywood was founded in 1886, became a city in 1903 (with an adult population of 166 residents), and was annexed by Los Angeles in 1910. Hollywood's first movie studio was founded in 1911, when transplanted New Jersey producer David Horsley moved his Nestor Film Company to Sunset Boulevard and Gower Street. Far from finding a welcome, the self-proclaimed socialist producer discovered that Hollywood residents considered filmmakers "a threat to the peace and good name of its citizens." On the other hand, some filmmakers found the local workforce too easygoing for their tastes. "This is semitropical country," complained movie star Francis X. Bushman, "and the people we were using weren't accustomed to working hard in this weather. As soon as we were out of sight they'd all loaf, start playing billiards or something."[8]

As companies replaced makeshift facilities with permanent studios, Los Angeles emerged as the rising center of film production. Yet it was not until after World War I that "Hollywood" became a generic term for a particular place and a particular way of doing business. When war broke out in 1914, the United States produced slightly more than half the world's movies. The subsequent decline of filmmaking abroad and the decline of the movie Trust at home provided ambitious American entrepreneurs like Adolph Zukor, Carl Laemmle, Jesse Lasky, and William Fox with an opportunity to monopolize the world market. But to do so they had to change the way they did business. More films were needed to replace European products; more efficient production facilities were needed to make them; more money was needed to finance them; and more theaters were needed to show them. To that end, studio executives abandoned the haphazard methods of the past in favor of more efficient modern business practices.[9]

Thomas Ince, a brilliant young producer, is generally credited with bringing film production into the modern era. While working in Los Angeles between 1913 and 1915, Ince adopted a "central producer system" that shifted control from the individual director units making films to a single producer who now oversaw several productions simultaneously. The studios, a *Variety* reporter observed in 1914, now preferred directors "who strive to make features commercially profitable" over "those who are victims of the 'artistic ideal' carried out to impossible degree, and with costs entirely disregarded." Directors who failed to follow instructions, or who came in over budget, soon found themselves looking for another job.[10]

Ince's emphasis on solid business practices set the trend for the future.

Figure 11.1. The first Hollywood studios were rather modest affairs. But outdoor sets and plenty of sunshine allowed producers to shoot year-round. *Title Insurance and Trust Collection, Department of Special Collections, University of Southern California Library*

Companies like Triangle–Fine Arts and Metro restructured their business operations and hired efficiency engineers to help meet increased production demands. The precision of this system evoked images of assembly-line factory production among many observers. "With the cogs of the big Ince machine oiled to the smallest gear," remarked one writer in 1913, "and the entire plant running as smoothly as an automobile in the hands of a salesman, the picture travels from the beginning to end without delays. To my mind this is the modern miracle."[11]

The increased emphasis on scientific management did not sit well with all industry personnel. Rudolph Valentino, the heartthrob of millions, was an outspoken critic of studios that "employed efficiency experts to keep down production costs." He told one reporter how, during the filming of *The Four Horsemen of the Apocalypse* (1921), an efficiency expert who knew "nothing of the artistic values" suggested "that the whole episode of the four

horsemen be eliminated . . . because he said it did not mean anything."
Director King Vidor, who referred to these new business practices as the
"sausage-factory method of making films," charged that studio-hired efficiency experts "knew more about assembly-line methods than what constituted first-class entertainment."[12]

Changes in production were accompanied by the establishment of Hollywood and its environs as the industry's main production site. The search for
cheaper and more efficient ways of making films on a year-around basis led
eastern and midwestern companies to restrict or shut down their operations
and head west. Filmmaking operations soon spread out into the San Fernando Valley, East Hollywood, and the recently created Culver City. In addition to the previously mentioned factors, moving to Los Angeles also provided the most ambitious filmmakers with a rare opportunity to exchange
the cramped spaces of their eastern operations for what one film scholar
dubbed "new palaces of production." Universal, Triangle, Ince, Lasky, Vitagraph, Metro, Hodkinson, and Fox all erected sprawling studio facilities so
imposing that tourists might well have mistaken them for factories.[13]

New York City remained the financial center of the movie industry
throughout the teens and twenties, but Los Angeles emerged as its production capital. In 1915, Los Angeles studios employed over 15,000 people and
produced between 60 and 75 percent of all American films. Four years later, the region's seventy-plus production companies turned out over 80 percent of the world's movies. Samuel Goldwyn explained the area's appeal by
noting: "Los Angeles is more efficient for us, more cheap. In Manhattan
the movie waits on the community and not the community on the movie."
Producers who were tired of battling powerful eastern unions were also
drawn to Los Angeles because of its reputation as the "model open shop
city of the world." Los Angeles's "rank and file of trade unionists," labor
organizer J. B. Dale complained in 1915, "are in a trance, or I might say a
comatose condition." The pro-business orientation of the courts and city
council helped local employers undercut the strength of organized labor.
The movie industry, in turn, helped spark the growth of the city's population and economy: from a modest 319,000 inhabitants in 1910 to 1.3 million in 1930.[14]

It was during the conservative, pro-business Republican climate of the
1920s that Hollywood emerged as a powerful corporate entity. "Nowhere in
the country," observes historian Clark Davis, "did the process of corporate
formation occur with greater scope, speed, or cultural impact during this
period than in Los Angeles." The geographically scattered small and medium producers, distributors, and exhibitors of the early years were gradually supplanted by an increasingly oligarchic, vertically integrated industry
centered in Los Angeles and dominated by a handful of studios that controlled production, distribution, and exhibition. The eight major studios

Figure 11.2. Larger lots and more elaborate sets paved the way for the cross-class fantasy films of the 1920s. *Title Insurance and Trust Collection, Department of Special Collections, University of Southern California Library*

of the 1920s—Paramount, Fox, Metro-Goldwyn-Mayer, Universal, Warner Brothers, Columbia, United Artists, and RKO—were closer in their business practices to General Motors, U.S. Steel, Du Pont, and other large corporations than they were to the movie companies of a decade earlier. Like other successful corporations, they realized they could greatly increase their profits by expanding into other parts of the business. Distributors moved into production, producers into exhibition, and exhibitors into production and distribution. Paramount, Fox, MGM, RKO, Universal, and Warner Brothers struggled to become integrated operations that could produce and distribute their own films, and then exhibit them in their own theater chains.[15]

To obtain the capital needed to realize their ambitious dreams of expansion, studio heads turned to the nation's financial and industrial leaders. Wall Street began seriously flirting with the movie industry in 1914–15 when a number of prominent investment banking firms arranged to sell stock for the World and Triangle Film Corporations. The failure of these companies to repay their debts quickly soured Wall Street on the movie industry. However, the expansion of the industry's share of the world market in the wake of war, coupled with its new emphasis on efficiency and improved management, brought investors back for a second look. And once they looked, they liked what they saw. Wall Street "financial interests," the socialist *New York Call* reported in 1919, "have made a survey of the whole industry and have concluded that it is a safe business for their money if they can control the box-office." The nation's 15,000 movie theaters took in an estimated $800 million that year; add to that the receipts from foreign sales and distribution, and potential profits were staggering.[16]

The movie industry entered the world of seriously big business in 1919 when several powerful investment banking houses arranged stock offerings of $10 million and $9.5 million ($75.5 million and $71.7 million in 1990 dollars), respectively, for Paramount and Loew's Inc. Links between Wall Street and Hollywood grew closer over the next several years as Pathe, Fox, Metro-Goldwyn-Mayer, and Universal all had their stock listed on the New York Stock Exchange. The nation's leading banks and corporations were quick to invest in the rapidly expanding movie industry. Fox got money from Prudential Life Insurance and New Jersey bankers; the Goldwyn Company from the du Ponts, Chase Bank, and Central Union Trust; and Triangle from the American Tobacco Company. By 1925, Wall Street handled shares for eleven movie corporations, and total capital invested in the industry skyrocketed from $78.2 million in 1921 to $850 million in 1930. Stock and bond issues for major studios rose from $21.9 million in 1925 to $47.8 million in 1929.[17]

The new corporate orientation of Hollywood precipitated dramatic changes in the composition of movie audiences and the nature of the moviegoing experience. Workers and immigrants were the industry's main patrons during the prewar years. However, studios and major exhibitors used their newfound wealth to expand their audience base and increase their profits by creating an experience of fantasy designed to attract millions of prosperous "middle-class" viewers, while also retaining the loyal working-class patrons. They did this by building exotic picture palaces and producing lavish pictures that were designed to turn moviegoing into a universal experience that both transcended and reshaped traditional class boundaries.[18]

The 1920s marked a period of unprecedented theater construction as studios battled for control of exhibition and its lucrative profits. The prime focus of new building was not the modest neighborhood theater but the opulent movie palace. "Plush and gilt movie palaces had mushroomed over the land," movie mogul Jesse Lasky recounted, "and became practically temples of worship, where the masses attended services faithfully at least once a week." Loew's laid out over $3 million ($22.3 million in 1990 dollars) for its Kansas City (Mo.) Midland Theatre, Paramount $3 million for its Times Square namesake, and the Stanley chain $2.5 million for the Baltimore Stanley. Although quite costly, palaces proved extraordinarily popular and became the industry's most profitable theaters. Paramount's general manager Sidney Kent estimated that 75 percent of the company's exhibition revenues in the mid 1920s came from only 1,250 deluxe houses. By 1926, "some 500 houses of the 'million dollar' type" were operating in 79 cities with populations over 100,000, and an equal number of a slightly "less expensive and luxurious grade . . . in the next group of cities, say down to 50,000."[19]

Lavish palaces demanded equally lavish movies. Studios began producing extravagant films replete with movie stars, spectacular costumes, exotic sets, and fabulous locations that set Hollywood films off from those of the rest of the world. Making these films, however, demanded unprecedented amounts of capital. The "orgy of extravagance that obsessed the studios from 1922 until 1927," recounted industry insider Benjamin Hampton, led many to spend millions of dollars for star-studded spectacles like *The Ten Commandments* or *The Thief of Bagdad*.[20]

The combination of spectacular films and luxurious theaters succeeded in expanding the industry's audience and turning moviegoing into a regular habit for virtually all Americans. "Nothing has done more to enlarge the motion picture theater audience during the present decade," the Wall Street investment house of Halsey, Stuart, and Company reported in 1927, "than the new type of [deluxe] theater construction. . . . The American public has spoken a decided preference for luxury in its houses of entertainment." Marveling at the rapid transformation of the industry, studio chief Jesse Lasky observed how in "the space of ten years motion pictures had grown from a suspect enterprise . . . to a major influence in shaping the fashions, the manners, and the taste of middle-class America, an influence felt throughout the world."[21]

In addition to shaping fashions, manners, and tastes, filmmakers and their films also shaped political sensibilities. Commenting on the subtle and sometimes almost unconscious ways in which this "molding" process occurred, radical film critic Paul Rotha claimed in 1931: "Whether it is aware of the propaganda or not, the general public is influenced by every film which it sees. Under the thin veil of entertainment, the hard fact is apparent that film is the most influential medium yet discovered for persuading an audience to believe this or to do that." Americans attended movies in unprecedented numbers throughout the 1920s. But what exactly did they see when they watched a Hollywood production? How and why did the rise of Hollywood change the politics of American cinema?[22]

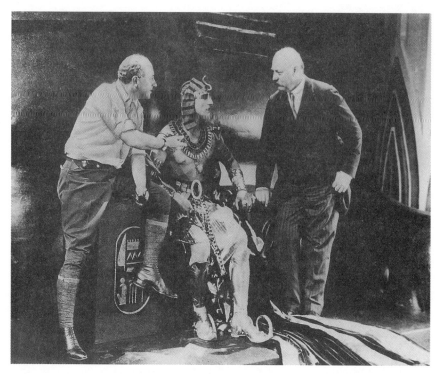

Figure 11.3. Cecil B. DeMille (left) was the master of the cross-class fantasy. He is shown here on the set of *The Ten Commandments* (1923) introducing Secretary of War John W. Weeks to Charles de Roche, the "French Valentino." *Title Insurance and Trust Collection, Department of Special Collections, University of Southern California Library*

THE MOVE TO THE RIGHT

The history of the movie industry is filled with countless myths and half-truths. One of the greatest of these is the idea that audiences determine the kinds of films that will be made. Although reporters often spoke of the power of audiences and the "inherently democratic" character of the movie industry, the Federal Trade Commission thought otherwise. The FTC considered the emerging studio system so antidemocratic that in 1921 it charged Paramount and five other organizations—which in 1919 released 82 percent of the nation's films—with conspiring to "control, dominate and monopolize the motion picture industry." In 1928, it charged the ten distributors who handled 98 percent of all films in the United States with violating antitrust laws; a year later, it charged Paramount, Metro-Goldwyn-

Mayer, Fox, and Warner Brothers with the same offense for producing 90 percent of the feature films made in the United States.[23]

By dominating the bulk of the nation's first-run movies and movie theaters, Hollywood studios exerted a powerful control over the political direction of American film and the collective political consciousness of the nation. In deciding what films to make, industry leaders of the 1920s based their choices, whenever possible, on predictable business considerations rather than on vague and unpredictable ideas about audience tastes. Although the full story of changing cinematic politics is too complex to analyze here, some broad trends can be identified. If we look at the ways in which filmmakers dealt with issues of class conflict and working-class life, we find that, far from signaling a new era of liberalism, the rise of Hollywood and its monopolistic studio system pushed representations of class and class conflict in increasingly conservative directions. This rightward drift in cinematic ideology was the result of several factors that interacted to reshape the political sympathies and ideological content of American film.

The ideological diversity of pre-Hollywood cinema can be attributed to the diversity of producers and the class composition of audiences. Since immigrants and workers comprised the bulk of regular patrons, it is not surprising that many pictures of the era focused on various aspects of working-class life. While most of these movies were rather innocuous romances, comedies, or melodramas, a small but significant number of films explored the most contentious class battles of the era. Encouraged by the low cost of production and easy access to the screen, class-conscious filmmakers inside and outside the movie industry (the latter including organizations such as the National Association of Manufacturers, the American Bankers' Association, the Socialist Party, and the American Federation of Labor) turned labor-capital struggles that had been confined to the often hidden realm of nineteenth-century factories into important parts of public culture in the twentieth century. Advancing ideological agendas that ranged from the far left to the far right, these politically engaged producers made movies that examined strikes, lockouts, labor violence, union organizing, and efforts by socialists and anarchists to overthrow the capitalist system. Indeed, class-conscious productions grew so prominent by 1910 that movie reviewers spoke about the emergence of a new genre of "labor-capital" films.[24]

Class identities were very much in flux during the first three decades of the new century, for it was still unclear whether the millions of new white-collar and service sector workers were working class or middle class. Labor-capital films helped translate abstract ideas about class, class conflict, and class identity into something people could see and understand. They showed people what strikes, labor leaders, labor unions, socialists, and businessmen looked like. In so doing, movies both reflected and shaped visual stereotypes of workers, capitalists, and radicals. Whether white-collar and service sector employees saw their interests as lying with employers or unions might well be determined by the images they saw on the screen.[25]

In telling their stories of class conflict, early filmmakers adopted one of five ideological perspectives. Liberal labor-capital films condemned the exploitation of workers and called for cooperation between labor and capital. Conservative films presented worker, union, or radical activities in the worst possible light and rarely explained the causes of strikes or employee discontent. Radical films offered positive depictions of socialists, radicals, and their struggles, and equally scathing critiques of capitalists and capitalism. Populist films preached a gut-level hatred of monopolists and showed how they undermined the welfare of ordinary citizens. Anti-authoritarian films, though not directly challenging capitalism, mocked the authority of those who gave workers the hardest time: foremen, police, judges, and employers.

Between 1905, when the nickelodeon first appeared, and April 1917, when American entry into World War I altered the politics of film and the film industry, producers released at least 274 films that explicitly dealt with labor-capital conflicts. Of the 244 films whose political perspectives could be determined, 112 (46 percent) were liberal, 82 (34 percent) conservative, 22 (9 percent) anti-authoritarian, 17 (7 percent) populist, and 11 (4 percent) radical. Given the fact that the industry was producing several thousand films a year during this period, 274 films may seem rather insignificant. Yet, it was by watching these films that many Americans drew their information about contemporary class struggles and perhaps formed their opinions about the meaning of those struggles and solutions to them.[26]

The political sympathies of labor-capital films dramatically changed in the 1920s as the emerging Hollywood studio system pushed the politics of American cinema in a more conservative direction. Between 1920 and 1929, 66 percent of the 96 films whose politics I could determine (excluding those made by labor film companies) were conservative, 21 percent liberal, 10 percent anti-authoritarian, and 3 percent populist. Not a single radical film was made by a studio. Four factors proved especially crucial in leading studios to reorient the ideological sympathies of their films: the desire to expand their audience base, the rising costs of production, the pressures exerted on studios by censors and investors, and the growing anti-union tensions in the studios and the nation.[27]

Filmmakers always walk a delicate line between responding to perceived audience desires and trying to create audience desires for films that pose few financial risks. Throughout the 1920s, studios moved to increase their profits by attracting greater numbers of prosperous "middle-class" patrons. In addition to constructing lavish movie palaces, they did this by shifting the class focus of their films from labor-capital movies that stressed conflict between the classes to cross-class fantasy films that emphasized love and harmony between the classes. The goal of producers and exhibitors was not to integrate the classes in any lasting way but to increase movie attendance and revenues by drawing them into the same theaters.

Cross-class fantasies were not confined to the screen but were part of a conservative national discourse that shifted public attention away from the problems of the workplace and toward the promises of consumption—a discourse articulated by business leaders, advertisers, and politicians that suggested old ideas of class no longer mattered, for participation in the new consumer society of the 1920s made previous class distinctions irrelevant. All who could afford a vaguely defined "middle-class" style of consumption could now consider themselves middle class. Democratized consumption, Calvin Coolidge boasted in 1919, was rapidly obliterating old class divisions: "We are reaching and maintaining the position where the property class and the employed class are not separate but equal."[28]

Operating in one of the most conservative, pro-business areas in the country, Hollywood studios helped spread and accelerate these new class visions. In the decade after World War I, studios and their investors believed they could lure new patrons and increase attendance by making movies about sex, jazz, wealth, consumption, and class harmony—movies "devoted almost exclusively to pleasing and mirroring the life of the more leisured and well-to-do citizenry." Features with alluring titles such as *Gigolo, Fashion Madness, Charge It,* and *Children of the Ritz* seemed far more appropriate to luxurious movie palaces than old-style stories of class exploitation. To attract prosperous audiences, explains historian Lizabeth Cohen, chains like Balaban and Katz moved "to expunge the working-class, neighborhood character from the movie-going experience." Films with strong working-class or socialist messages simply did not fit the movie palaces' new emphasis on cross-class fantasy.[29]

Fears of government censorship and the financial risks it posed also contributed to the industry's declining interest in labor-capital films. As strikes and labor violence swept the nation in the late 1910s and 1920s, local and state movie censors tried to halt the exhibition of any film or newsreel that offered sympathetic depictions of working-class life and struggles. Censors in Maryland, Pennsylvania, New York, West Virginia, Ohio, Kansas, South Carolina, Washington, and dozens of other states and cities banned or demanded extensive cuts in films "calculated to stir up . . . antagonistic relations between labor and capital." In addition to censoring first-run features like Famous Players–Lasky's *The Whistle* (1921), authorities also forced Pathe, Hearst, Gaumont, and Fox to remove scenes in newsreels showing ongoing strikes and labor agitation. Consequently, viewers rarely got to see positive images of labor activism on the screen. As one labor newspaper complained in August 1921: "The labor problem, you know, has become taboo in the motion picture because as soon as it is used it is bound to become radical and what with the censors and the American Legion, radical pictures will never do."[30]

Industry leaders could have chosen to fight censors, but doing so would have risked delaying or canceling a film's release in dozens of cities and states. By 1926, censorship boards were operating in 100 cities and nearly a dozen states, and each maintained a different set of standards. Trying to get liberal, let alone radical, labor-capital films past these boards would have been a time-consuming and costly task. When, in August 1921, Kansas censors banned *The Contrast,* a film made by the socialist Labor Film Service that portrayed radical miners defeating coal barons, the LFS went to court and won the right to show their movie. However, it took two years to do so and cost the company a great deal in legal fees and lost exhibition revenues. As studios expanded into production, distribution, and exhibition, the content of any one film was less important than securing its widespread distribution. First-run films were booked into theaters months in advance, and any changes ordered by censors could prevent a film from reaching its intended venues on time, thereby reducing profits for all three wings of a company's business.[31]

The heightened bottom-line mentality of industry executives also contributed to the rightward shift in the class content of Hollywood films. "New men from Wall Street, educated in finance," observed Lewis Jacobs, "became the overseers of the motion picture business." By the early 1920s, Wall Street firms and major industrial corporations—many of whom had strong anti-union policies—were represented in the boardrooms of virtually every major film company and used their power to bring in people to supervise production. Cecil DeMille sarcastically told how studio financial heads in New York, who placed more stress on "speedy productions" than artistic productions, sent experts from Kuhn, Loeb, and Company to Hollywood to bring greater "efficiency and economy into our wild and wonderful operations."[32]

With production costs skyrocketing and "Wall Street watchdogs" constantly offering what Jesse Lasky and others felt was "much unappreciated advice," industry leaders grew more conservative in deciding what films to make. While the cost of an *average* five-reel major studio production rose from $12,000–$20,000 in 1918 to $300,000 in 1924, expenses for special extravaganzas ran considerably higher: $2.5 million for *The King of Kings* (1927) and $4.5 million for *Ben Hur* (1926). As expenditures for first-run features rose, studio executives hesitated approving anything that might endanger a company's profits or their own personal success. And this meant not making any film whose subject matter or politics seemed too risky. After all, studios were in the money-making business, not the consciousness-raising business. The studio of this era, notes one writer, was "not only a place of business, but a theory of business economics, a belief in so much capital down yielding so much in receipt."[33]

Given the financial risks posed by censorship and their desire to build a new cross-class audience, studios decided to reduce the output of labor-capital films. Between 1910 and 1919, producers (excluding labor film companies) turned out 345 labor-capital films, an average of 35 per year; between 1920 and 1929 the number fell to 107, an average of 11 a year. Moreover, the labor-capital films studios turned out were unlikely to offend censors: 66 percent of the films released in the 1920s and 79 percent of those made after the publication of the industry's new production code in 1924 were conservative.[34]

Films about class relations did not disappear, but were presented in the form of less controversial cross-class fantasies. An examination of subject headings in one prominent film catalog reveals that between 1921 and 1929, "society films" (a subset of cross-class fantasies) outnumbered labor-capital films 308 to 67. Abandoning the contentious political edge that characterized labor-capital productions, cross-class fantasies such as *Saturday Night* (1921), *Poor Men's Wives* (1923), and *Orchids and Ermine* (1927) focused on love and harmony between the classes and suggested that class conflict and class organizations (such as labor unions) were things of the past. Taken collectively, cross-class fantasies stressed individualism rather than collective action, and told viewers that mobility and happiness would be found in the democratized world of consumption rather than in the deadening world of production. Since studios controlled most of what was made and shown, these were the visions of class relations to which moviegoers now grew accustomed. In so doing, these movies helped popularize and legitimize the class hierarchies and conservative Republican politics of the era.[35]

What viewers saw on the screen was also shaped by events off the screen. The increased emphasis on prosperity and the marked shift toward anti-union politics in 1920s films mirrored developments within greater Los Angeles and the movie industry itself. The rapid expansion of the movie, construction, and oil refining industries during the postwar decade sparked a regional economic renaissance. Surpassing San Francisco as the state's largest city by 1920, Los Angeles saw its industrial workforce grow by 127 percent during the 1920s and its residents' income far exceed the state average. By 1930, Los Angeles was the nation's fifth leading industrial city, and the movie industry reigned as the leading local producer and employer. As the value of the annual product coming out of its studios soared from approximately $79 million in 1921 to $850 million in 1930, so too did industry profits. Paramount/Famous Players–Lasky reported profits of $8.1 million for 1927, a 44 percent increase over the previous year. The proliferation of lavish Beverly Hills estates owned by studio moguls and movie stars testified to the riches enjoyed by those at the top.[36]

The studios' new prosperity did not extend to its workers. Believing they were entitled to a greater share of the industry's postwar wealth, a wide range of studio employees organized unions and launched strikes for higher wages and better working conditions. Although Los Angeles had long held the reputation of being the most anti-union city in the nation, the absence of studio labor conflict during the prewar era allowed producers to indulge the political sentiments of writers, directors, and working-class audiences by turning out liberal labor-capital films. However, the repeated outbreak of bitter strikes and organizing campaigns between 1917 and 1922 led studio heads to join the citywide Open Shop campaign. As labor militancy on studio lots increased, so too did the number of anti-union films coming out of Hollywood. Only after 1922, when the leading studios succeeded in crushing the insurgent studio labor movement did the industry back away from making labor-capital films.[37]

Audiences may have wanted to see more labor-capital films, but industry leaders were reluctant to make them. During the pre-Hollywood era, a diverse array of producers had provided audiences with a diverse array of ideological visions. However, the expansion of an oligarchic studio system and the subsequent decline of small production companies changed all that. "As a result," notes historian Lary May, "from 60 firms making over 2,000 movies in 1912, the 'Big Eight' made 90 percent of the 800 feature films made yearly in the twenties."[38]

By securing near monopolistic control over production, distribution, and exhibition, Hollywood studios were able to set the political agenda of American film and marginalize independent companies with markedly different political points of view. Although labor film companies such as New York's Labor Film Services and Seattle's Federation Film Corporation managed to make and exhibit radical labor-capital films in the early 1920s, they were soon driven out of business as the task of funding and exhibiting each successive production grew increasingly difficult. "All capitalists whom I have tried to interest in financing the [screen] play," explained aspiring labor producer Carl Clancy, "refuse to invest in it because they say it so strongly boosts the closed shop, and the cause of organized labor." Hollywood's power to dominate cinematic politics also lay in its ability to control what people did not see. Studio ownership of theaters, explained a *New York Times* reporter, deprived the public "of the power to influence exhibitors in the choice of films." Exhibitors outside the chains who were sympathetic to the cause of labor filmmakers also found themselves unable to satisfy potential audience demands for more class-conscious films because "block booking" practices required them to fill their entire annual program with a particular studio's releases or receive no films at all.[39]

The triumph of the studio system meant that Hollywood would play a central role in influencing the ways in which Americans thought, or failed to think, about class relations for the rest of the century. Hollywood studios have continually preferred to ignore questions of class conflict in favor of cross-class fantasies—like *Pretty Woman* (1990)—that promote visions of love and individual mobility as solutions to all problems. When studios do produce labor-capital films, they keep serving up the same conservative images that dominated screens of the 1920s—images of naive men and women mindlessly following corrupt union leaders, of radical agitators stirring up trouble among previously content workers, and of strikes that have no apparent cause. The few liberal films that reach the screen, like *Norma Rae* (1979) and *Reds* (1981), are greatly outnumbered by conservative productions such as *F.I.S.T.* (1978), *Blue Collar* (1978), and *Hoffa* (1992). Yet, the good wages, generous benefit packages, and high standards of consumption enjoyed by many Americans are not the products of employer benevolence, as conservative films suggest. They are the results of millions of employees embracing rather than fleeing from unions and collective action. By repeatedly disparaging unionism, radicalism, and collective struggles for justice, Hollywood has distorted the crucial role that organized working people played in the making of what we today conceive of as our "middle-class" nation.[40]

NOTES

1. Craig W. Campbell, *Reel America and World War I* (Jefferson, N.C.: McFarland, 1985), 124; Richard Koszarski, *An Evening's Entertainment: The Age of the Silent Feature Picture, 1915–1928* (New York: Charles Scribner's Sons, 1990), 104.

2. "Definition of Censorship Prepared by the National Board of Review of Motion Pictures. 1913," Subject Papers, Box 166, Papers of the National Board of Review of Motion Pictures, Special Collections, New York Public Library (hereafter Records NBRMP). Discussions of movies produced by various business, labor, radical, reform, religious, and government organizations can be found in Kay Sloan, *The Loud Silents: Origins of the Social Problem Film* (Urbana: University of Illinois Press, 1988); Kevin Brownlow, *Behind the Mask of Innocence* (New York: Alfred A. Knopf, 1990); Steven J. Ross, "Cinema and Class Conflict: Labor, Capital, the State and American Silent Film," in Robert Sklar and Charles Musser, eds., *Resisting Images: Essays on Cinema and History* (Philadelphia: Temple University Press, 1990), 68–107; Steven J. Ross, "The Unknown Hollywood," *History Today*, 40 (April 1990), 40–46.

3. *New York Times*, December 13, 1925; Chicago *Daily Worker*, October 6, 1924. For attendance figures, which vary greatly from source to source, see Halsey, Stuart, and Co., "The Motion Picture Industry as a Basis for Bond Financing, May 27, 1927," in Tino Balio, ed., *The American Film Industry* (Madison: University of Wisconsin Press, 1976), 183; U.S. Department of Commerce, *Historical Statistics of the United States. Colonial Times to 1970*, 2 vols. (Washington, D.C.: U.S. Government Printing Office, 1975), I: 400.

4. *Los Angeles Times,* May 30, 1997.

5. For overviews of the early history of production, distribution, and exhibition, see Benjamin B. Hampton, *A History of the Movies* (New York: Covici-Friede, 1931); Lewis Jacobs, *The Rise of American Film: A Critical History* (New York: Teachers College Press, 1968); Robert Sklar, *Movie-Made America: A Cultural History of American Movies* (New York: Random House, 1975); Lary May, *Screening Out the Past: The Birth of Mass Culture and the Motion Picture Industry* (New York: Oxford University Press, 1980); Charles Musser, *The Emergence of American Cinema: The American Screen to 1907* (New York: Charles Scribner's Sons, 1990); Eileen Bowser, *The Transformation of American Cinema, 1907–1915* (New York: Charles Scribner's Sons, 1990); Douglas Gomery, *Shared Pleasures: A History of Movie Presentation in the United States* (Madison: University of Wisconsin Press, 1992); and Balio, *American Film Industry.*

6. In 1911, the U.S. Weather Bureau suggested there were 320 days in the Los Angeles area that provided good photographic weather. For the move west and the advantages of California, see "Hollywood," in Frank N. Magill, ed., *Magill's Survey of Cinema,* 3 vols. (Englewood Cliffs, N.J.: Salem Press, 1982), 1: 74–78; Charles G. Clarke, *Early Film Making in Los Angeles* (Los Angeles: Dawson's Book Shop, 1976), 29; Kevin Brownlow, *The Parade's Gone By* (Berkeley and Los Angeles: University of California Press, 1968), 30–34; Musser, *Emergence of Cinema,* 455; Bowser, *Transformation of Cinema,* 149–65; and Hampton, *History of the Movies,* 77–82, 111–16.

7. William de Mille, *Hollywood Saga* (New York: E. P. Dutton, 1939), 82.

8. Ibid.; Bushman quoted in Brownlow, *Parade's Gone By,* 34. For other descriptions of early Hollywood, see Carey McWilliams, *Southern California: An Island on the Land* (New York: Duell, Sloan, and Pearce, 1946), 331–33. Despite his pioneer status, Horsley was not admitted to the Los Angeles Chamber of Commerce until April 1915. "Board of Directors Minutes," April 7, 1915, 106, Box 26, Records of the Los Angeles Chamber of Commerce, Regional History Center, University of Southern California. For a profile of Horsley, his politics, and later efforts on behalf of working-class filmmakers, see Steven J. Ross, *Working-Class Hollywood: Silent Film and the Shaping of Class in America* (Princeton: Princeton University Press, 1998).

9. Production figure for 1914 is taken from Jacobs, *Rise of American Film,* 159. American efforts to capture the European film market are described in Thomas H. Guback, *The International Film Industry* (Bloomington: Indiana University Press, 1969).

10. *Variety,* December 25, 1914. The origins of the central producer system and the evolution of new production techniques are most thoroughly explored in David Bordwell, Janet Staiger, and Kristin Thompson, *The Classical Hollywood Cinema: Film Style and the Mode of Production to 1960* (New York: Columbia University Press, 1985); and Koszarski, *Evening's Entertainment,* 108–10.

11. *New York Dramatic Mirror,* December 24, 1913, quoted in Bordwell, Staiger, and Thompson, *Classical Hollywood Cinema,* 136.

12. *Los Angeles Citizen,* March 30, 1923; King Vidor, *A Tree Is a Tree* (Hollywood: Samuel French, 1981), 70.

13. Jacobs, *Rise of American Film,* 161.

14. Goldwyn quoted in May, *Screening Out the Past,* 181; *Los Angeles Citizen,* February 2, 1912; *Proceedings of the Sixteenth Annual Convention. California State Federation of*

Labor (San Francisco, 1915), 63. Population figures are taken from Frederic Cople Jaher, *The Urban Establishment: Upper Strata in Boston, New York, Charleston, Chicago, and Los Angeles* (Urbana: University of Illinois Press, 1982), 654. By 1922, 84 percent of all American films were made in Hollywood, 12 percent in New York, and 4 percent in all other areas. Production statistics are taken from *Report of the Pennsylvania State Board of Censors, June 1, 1915 to December 1, 1915* (Harrisburg: William Stanley Ray, 1916), 4; *New York Times,* November 11, 1920; Bordwell, Staiger, and Thompson, *Classical Hollywood Cinema,* 123; Koszarski, *Evening's Entertainment,* 102–6.

15. Clark Davis, *Company Men: White-Collar Life and Corporate Cultures in Los Angeles, 1892–1941* (Baltimore: Johns Hopkins University Press, 2000), 3. For recent works that examine the rise of the studio system and the transformation of the movie industry, see Douglas Gomery, *The Hollywood Studio System* (New York: St. Martin's Press, 1986); Neal Gabler, *An Empire of Their Own: How the Jews Invented Hollywood* (New York: Crown, 1988); Thomas Schatz, *The Genius of the System: Hollywood Filmmaking in the Studio Era* (New York: Pantheon, 1988); Ethan Mordden, *The Hollywood Studios: House Style in the Golden Age of the Movies* (New York: Simon and Schuster, 1988); and the sources mentioned in note 5.

16. *New York Call,* October 17, 1919. Industry financing during this period is discussed in A. H. Giannini, "Financing the Production and Distribution of Motion Pictures," *The Annals of the American Academy of Political and Social Science,* 128 (November 1926), 46–49; Mae D. Huettig, *Economic Control of the Motion Picture Industry: A Study in Industrial Organization* (Philadelphia: University of Pennsylvania Press, 1944); Janet Wasko, *Movies and Money: Financing the American Film Industry* (Norwood, N.J.: Ablex, 1982), 1–45; and Koszarski, *Evening's Entertainment,* 63–94.

17. Dollar equivalences taken from John J. McCusker, *How Much Is That in Real Money? A Historical Price Index for Use as a Deflator of Money Values in the Economy of the United States* (Worcester, Mass.: American Antiquarian Society, 1992), 330, 332. Investment figures are from Wasko, *Movies and Money,* 31. For Wall Street's involvement in the movie industry, see *New York Times,* July 24, 1921; Chicago *Daily Worker,* December 22, 1924; *Film Year Book 1925,* n.p.; and sources in previous note.

18. There is a major debate over the composition of audiences in the prewar years. As I have argued elsewhere, part of the confusion over the class composition of movie audiences can be attributed to the confusion over the meaning and composition of "middle class" in the first three decades of the twentieth century. My own analysis suggests that immigrants and working-class people were the industry's main patrons before 1917. It was not until the 1920s that "middle-class" Americans—professionals, small business owners, corporate executives, and the amorphous ranks of white-collar workers whose class affiliations were still uncertain—began going to the movies in large numbers and on a regular basis. See Ross, *Working-Class Hollywood,* 19–20, 175–77, 182–94. For a summary of recent debates, see Ben Singer, "Manhattan Nickelodeons: New Data on Audiences and Exhibitors," *Cinema Journal,* 34 (Spring 1995), 5–35, and responses in ibid. 35 (Spring 1996), 72–128.

19. Jesse L. Lasky with Don Weldon, *I Blow My Own Horn* (London: Victor Gollancz, 1957), 173; Sidney R. Kent, "Distributing the Product," in Joseph P. Kennedy, ed., *The Story of the Films* (Chicago and New York: A. W. Shaw Company, 1927; rpt.

1971), 218; William A. Johnson, "The Structure of the Motion Picture Industry," *Annals of the American Academy of Political and Social Science,* 128 (November 1926), 27. Theater expansion and construction costs are described in *New York Times,* November 14, 1926; William Seabury, *The Public and the Motion Picture Industry* (New York: Macmillan, 1926), 277; Ben M. Hall, *Best Remaining Seats: The Golden Age of the Movie Palace* (New York: Da Capo Press, 1988); and Koszarski, *Evening's Entertainment,* 9–25.

20. Hampton, *History of the Movies,* 338.

21. Halsey, Stuart, and Co., "Motion Picture Industry," in Balio, *American Film Industry,* 184; Lasky, *I Blow My Own Horn,* 173.

22. Paul Rotha, *Celluloid: The Film To-Day* (London: Longmans, Green, 1931), 46.

23. *New York Times,* December 13, 1925; FTC, quoted in Hampton, *History of the Movies,* 276. For an examination of FTC charges in the 1920s, see *New York Times,* April 28 and June 21, 1928; Howard T. Lewis, *The Motion Picture Industry* (New York: D. Van Nostrand, 1933), 142–80, 265–66, 276–80, 371; and Hampton, *History of the Movies,* 317, 364–68.

24. Socialist newspapers often referred to the labor-capital film as a "proletarian playlet." *New York Call,* January 14, 1912. For more thorough analysis of the class content of early silent films, see Ross, *Working-Class Hollywood.*

25. For overviews of changing class identities, see Stuart M. Blumin, *The Emergence of the Middle Class: Social Experience in the American City, 1760–1900* (New York: Cambridge University Press, 1989); Daniel Horowitz, *The Morality of Spending: Attitudes toward the Consumer Society in America, 1875–1940* (Baltimore: Johns Hopkins University Press, 1985); Ileen DeVault, *Sons and Daughters of Labor: Class and Clerical Work in Turn-of-the-Century Pittsburgh* (Ithaca: Cornell University Press, 1991); C. Wright Mills, *White Collar: The American Middle Classes* (New York: Oxford University Press, 1951); Jurgen Kocka, *White Collar Workers in America 1890–1940: An Historical Perspective,* trans. Maura Kealey (Beverly Hills: Sage, 1980); and Ross, *Working-Class Hollywood.*

26. The figure 274 greatly underestimates the total number of labor-capital films. As I suggest elsewhere, a thorough investigation of every film made during this era is likely to yield several thousand labor-capital productions (at least 1,053 between 1911 and 1915 alone). For a more in-depth discussion of these films and the methodology used to compile these figures, see Ross, *Working-Class Hollywood,* 56–85, 297–98 note 3.

27. For a more extensive discussion of the methodology used in compiling these figures, see ibid., 116, 197–98, 312 note 4, 335 note 58.

28. Coolidge quoted in William Leuchtenburg, *The Perils of Prosperity, 1914–32* (Chicago: University of Chicago Press, 1958), 202–3. The rise of a consumer society and advertisers' efforts to link consumption and democracy are discussed in Horowitz, *The Morality of Spending;* Stuart Ewen, *Captains of Consciousness: Advertising and the Social Roots of the Consumer Culture* (New York: McGraw Hill, 1976); Roland Marchand, *Advertising American Culture: Making Way for Modernity, 1920–1940* (Berkeley and Los Angeles: University of California Press, 1985); Martha L. Olney, *Buy Now, Pay Later: Advertising, Credit, and Consumer Durables in the 1920s* (Chapel Hill: University of North Carolina Press, 1991); Jackson Lears, *Fables of Abundance: A Cul-*

tural History of Advertising in America (New York: Basic Books, 1994); and May, *Screening Out the Past.*

29. Jacobs, *Rise of American Film,* 271; Lizabeth Cohen, *Making a New Deal: Industrial Workers in Chicago, 1919–1939* (New York: Cambridge University Press, 1990), 125. For overviews of American films of the 1920s, see Sumiko Higashi, *Cecil B. DeMille and American Culture: The Silent Era* (Berkeley and Los Angeles: University of California Press, 1994), 142–203; May, *Screening Out the Past,* 200–236; and Jacobs, *Rise of American Film,* 395–415.

30. Morris L. Ernst and Pare Lorentz, *Censored: The Private Life of the Movie* (New York: Jonathan Cape and Harrison Smith, 1930), 42; *New York Call,* August 22, 1921. For censor actions against *The Whistle,* see *New York Call,* August 5, 1921; for newsreel censorship, see "In re: Censorship of News Weeklies by State Board of Censorship of Pennsylvania," c. March 1921, and W. D. McGuire to Samuel Gompers, July 12, 1922, in Subject Correspondence (AFL), Box 15; General Solicitation Letter by W. D. McGuire, March 16, 1921, and Charles Stelze to Dr. Herbert Gates, March 17, 1921, in Subjects Correspondence (Stelze), Box 43, all in Records NBRMP; State of New York, *Annual Report of the Moving Picture Commission for the Year 1922* (Albany: J. B. Lyon Co., 1923), 9; Chicago *Daily Worker,* April 1, 1924, March 18, 1925.

31. The plight of *The Contrast* is described in *Variety,* February 24, 1922, and September 20, 1923; W. D. McGuire to American Federation of Labor, September 24, 1921, Subject Correspondence (AFL), Box 15, Records NBRMP. The spread of censorship boards in the postwar era is discussed in Ford H. MacGregor, "Official Censorship Legislation," *Annals,* 128 (November 1926), 163–74, and Brownlow, *Behind the Mask,* 7–12.

32. Jacobs, *Rise of American Film,* 288; Cecil B. DeMille, *The Autobiography of Cecil B. DeMille,* ed. Donald Hayne (Englewood Cliffs, N.J.: Prentice-Hall, 1959), 211, 226; also see Lasky, *I Blow My Own Horn,* 144–46, 168, and Jacobs, *Rise of American Film,* 295–98.

33. Lasky, *I Blow My Own Horn,* 144; Mordden, *Hollywood Studios,* 5. Production costs are taken from Hampton, *History of the Movies,* 205, 308–21, 342; *New York Times,* December 13, 1925.

34. For the 96 films 1920–29 whose politics I could determine (excluding labor film companies), see above at note 27. Of the eight additional films made by labor film companies, six were radical and two liberal. For an analysis of the Motion Picture Producers and Distributors Association code and its efforts to forestall the negative and costly effects of censorship and public reaction to a spate of Hollywood scandals during the early 1920s, see Will H. Hays, "Supervision from Within," in Kennedy, *Story of the Films,* 46–50; William Marston Seabury, *Public and the Motion Picture Industry* (New York: Macmillan, 1926), 143–59; Garth Jowett, *Film the Democratic Art: A Social History of American Film* (Boston: Little, Brown, 1976), 154–84; Lasky, *I Blow My Own Horn,* 153–58; DeMille, *Autobiography,* 237–42; and Hampton, *History of Movies,* 281–303.

35. I computed the figures for society films by looking at the genre classification for all 6,606 films listed in volume one of the *American Film Institute Catalog . . . 1921–1930.* The figure of 308 includes "society dramas," "society melodramas," society comedies," and "society comedy-dramas." If we add in the dramas, melodramas, and

comedies dealing with cross-class love not included under "society" films, the total number of cross-class fantasies was undoubtedly over 400 films, or roughly 7 percent of the features made between 1921 and 1929. Since the AFI greatly underestimates the number of labor-capital films, I use my own numbers. Kenneth W. Munden, ed., *The American Film Institute Catalog of Motion Pictures Produced in the United States. Feature Films 1921–1930*, 2 vols. (New York: R. R. Bowker, 1971). For a more extensive analysis of the shifting class focus of American films of the 1920s, see Ross, *Working-Class Hollywood*, 194–239.

36. Population and economic statistics are compiled from *Twenty-Second Biennial Report of the Bureau of Labor Statistics of the State of California 1925–1926* (Sacramento: California State Printing Office, 1926), 131; U.S. Department of Commerce, *Biennial Census: 1935. Motion Pictures* (Washington, D.C., 1936), 3; *Milwaukee Leader,* March 31, 1928; Clark Davis, "'You Are the Company': The Demands of Employment in the Emerging Corporate Culture, Los Angeles, 1900–1930," *Business History Review*, 70 (Autumn 1996), 333; and Jaher, *Urban Establishment*, 654–60. For Los Angeles as an industrial center, see McWilliams, *Southern California;* and *Los Angeles Times, The Forty-Year War for a Free City: A History of the Open Shop in Los Angeles* (Los Angeles: *Los Angeles Times,* 1929).

37. For an overview of labor-capital relations in the Los Angeles movie industry during the 1920s, see Louis B. Perry and Richard Perry, *A History of the Los Angeles Labor Movement, 1911–1941* (Berkeley and Los Angeles: University of California Press, 1963); Michael Charles Nielsen, "Motion Picture Craft Workers and Craft Unions in Hollywood: The Studio Era, 1912–1948" (Ph.D. dissertation, University of Illinois, 1985); and Ross, *Working-Class Hollywood*. See also the essay by Laurie Pintar in this volume.

38. May, *Screening Out the Past,* 177.

39. Carl Stearns Clancy to Frank Morrison, July 29, 1919, reel 29, American Federation of Labor Convention 1919, American Federation of Labor Records: The Samuel Gompers Era (microfilm collection, Microfilming Corporation of America, 1979); *New York Times,* July 10, 1927. Block booking practices are discussed in Jacobs, *Rise of American Film,* 289–92, and sources cited in note 23. The rise and fall of the labor film movement is described in Ross, *Working-Class Hollywood*.

40. For a more detailed analysis of the labor-capital films from the 1930s to the present and the legacy left by the studios of the 1920s, see Ross, *Working-Class Hollywood,* 240–57.

CHAPTER TWELVE

My America or Yours?

Americanization and the Battle for the Youth of Los Angeles

William Deverell

The BAF thinks me dangerous.
THE REVEREND G. BROMLEY OXNAM, DIARY ENTRY, LOS ANGELES, 1920

It may be that the Better America Federation is working for God and humanity in its
opposition to extreme radicalism, but it is not working very hard along other lines in
which God and humanity might take interest.
DR. JOHN RANDOLPH HAYNES TO JUDGE BENJAMIN BLEDSOE, 1921

A school board election is generally not the most contentious political affair. But the election of 1923 in Los Angeles was different.[1] The fight over
board representation convinced powerful individuals and groups in Southern California to take off the gloves and wage a bitter public battle. It was a
contest—and collision—that had been coming for years. Investigation of
the debates and players in the board bout can tell us a great deal about regional political alignments, right and left, as well as those post–World War
cultural tensions which seem to characterize the "nervous 1920s." By taking
the school board fight apart, we can learn about the precursors of current
ideological factions in American political debate, and we might recognize
troubling continuity between the 1920s and today, particularly in the contested arenas of curriculum design, textbook adoption, and even what constitutes "Americanism."

In many respects, the 1923 Los Angeles school board fight resembled
a boxing match between two proxies: one representing "the left" and one
representing "the right." The labels are a bit crude, but they do at least hint
at the fundamental ideological divisions on either side of a deep divide.
From the left corner, an individual entered the ring against an organization
bound and determined to knock him down, if not out. This single warrior
was a Methodist minister in his early thirties named Garfield Bromley Oxnam. The principal organization that battled Oxnam from the right was the
Better America Federation (BAF) of Los Angeles.

Both Oxnam and the BAF have today faded from view. But their obscurity should not encourage dismissal of their importance, as symbols and performers, in helping to define fundamental contests in American public life before the Second World War. Of the two, perhaps Oxnam is the more remote. Born in 1891 in Los Angeles, Garfield Bromley Oxnam (named for the assassinated President James A. Garfield) came of age with the growing metropolis. His father, Thomas Oxnam, was a mining engineer, a strict, religious, and conservative man. As a teenager, Bromley Oxnam adopted the worldview of his father, whom he adored. Speaking before a church gathering, he opened with "Socialism is the biggest idiocy ever presented to the public." He ended on an establishment political note: "Vote for the strong old Republican Party . . . the party that stands for strongly organized companies, for advancement, and for the superiority of the United States over the entire world."[2]

But as he approached his twenties, something changed the way Bromley Oxnam looked at the world. He began to gravitate toward the ministry. He also felt pulled to progressive social causes. Part of this increasing commitment sprang from his observation of such Los Angeles adherents of the Social Gospel as the Reverend Dana Bartlett, an unsung activist who ran the Bethlehem Institute, one of the city's first and most important settlement houses. Oxnam also watched, and later tried to emulate, many of the first generation of municipal reformers active in the political arenas of the Progressive-era city.

His biggest influences, though, seem to have come from the classroom. At the University of Southern California, then a small Methodist school, Oxnam studied with a handful of prominent Progressive academics. Sociologist Emory Bogardus, whom Oxnam met not long after Bogardus arrived from the University of Chicago, was the most important. Oxnam occupied a regular seat in the courses Bogardus taught, and he took all three of Bogardus's classes during the latter's first summer term at USC. Bogardus impressed the young Oxnam greatly, and the student made an equally profound impression on the sociologist. Many years later, Bogardus introduced Oxnam as a man with "greater social vision" than anyone else in public life that he had ever known, a "scholar and author, seer and prophet, a friend to man."[3] He recalled that Oxnam "stood out in class. He always sat in the front row, always took copious notes and always asked many questions. He asked 'why' when others often asked 'what.' He often asked what could be done about a problem. Correct theory was important to him, but he always had the practical approach too."[4]

Oxnam also studied with historians Rockwell Hunt and James Main Dixon ("he knew almost everything about everything," Oxnam later recalled).[5] All three professors urged their students to study social problems and poverty on the ground, to get out of the classroom and into the neighborhoods of Los Angeles. Oxnam took to this task with characteristic enthusiasm; he signed on as an unpaid inspector for the Los Angeles Housing Commission and investigated the working-class districts at the edge of the Los Angeles River near downtown.

Bromley Oxnam also idolized the most famous American of his time. In President Theodore Roosevelt, he found a model of activity and energy. A campus athlete and "joiner" who took part in virtually every extracurricular pursuit available to him, Oxnam looked every bit the part of a West Coast version of the hyperactive president (with an added dose of "muscular Christianity" to his constitution).

By his early twenties, Oxnam had made a mark in social reform circles in Los Angeles. He had also formulated goals. "Someday," he wrote in 1913, "I am going to help lead the church against the slums and smash them forever. If our people would talk less and study and do more, the task would be easy."[6] Not one to rest much, Bromley Oxnam filled whatever quiet hours he had with study. His notes and personal papers are crammed full of sociological research from his own and his classmates' work. He typed notebook copies, word for word, of USC thesis projects that he had deemed important enough to study and keep in his expanding library.

From USC, Oxnam went east to Boston University's School of Theology, where he was ordained in 1916. Within a year, following a brief sojourn as head of a church in California's Central Valley, he returned to Los Angeles. There he presided over the Church of All Nations, a Methodist parish in the poorest section of downtown, amid those railroad yards, industries, small homes, and tenements that he had earlier wandered as a volunteer housing inspector. The All Nations parish existed in a diverse cross-section of ethnic Los Angeles. Its 213 city blocks, bounded by Third Street, Washington, Main, and Alameda, were sooty and run down. The district gave the lie to what realtors and Chamber of Commerce boosters always said about early twentieth-century Los Angeles, that it was a city without slums. "This," Oxnam succinctly recalled years later, "was the East Side."[7] "This part of the city is the least [desirable]," one of Oxnam's social work colleagues wrote, "because there are many factories, packing houses, warehouses, gas works, and railroad buildings. More foul air, less shade, more dusty and unpaved streets, and poorer houses are found here than in any other part of the city."[8]

All told, according to surveys Oxnam made, the All Nations parish took in upward of 60,000 people and over forty nationalities. Oxnam believed that reform in the district would require the concerted efforts of theology, sociology, and activist political organization. "This is an industrial section," he noted in a prophetic 1918 letter to another of his mentors, Sherwood Eddy of the Salvation Army. "The Labor Movement centers [here]. Our parish will be the center of the battle that is bound to come in the days of industrial and social reconstruction."[9] There was surely work to be done, more than enough to keep even a man of Bromley Oxnam's prodigious energies occupied. He went right at it, and he got noticed, by friend and foe alike. As Oxnam came of age, so too did the organization that would attack him.

The Better America Federation no longer exists. But in the 1920s, it was a powerful, if shrill, voice of reaction in Los Angeles, in California, and to some degree, across the United States.[10] The BAF grew out of an organization called the Commercial Federation of Los Angeles, which had taken an active role in promoting home front patriotism and industrial capitalism during the First World War, selling war bonds, drumming up support for war industries, and the like. As one member of the group remembered, the Commercial Federation had been "organized for the purpose of stimulating, protecting and advancing the interests of big business."[11] With the end of World War I, the Commercial Federation mutated, after testing out a few other names, into the more militant Better America Federation.[12] At a downtown meeting of the parent organization, businessman Harry Haldeman stood before his fellow Commercial Federation members and said that a new organization, the Better America Federation, was to be started. Haldeman, a pipe manufacturer described by one opponent as "a man of tremendous energy, a Prussian in thought and methods," would be BAF president. As Los Angeles reformer John Randolph Haynes recalled, Haldeman said that the newer organization would "kill—socially, politically and economically—anyone who disagreed with [it]."[13]

The BAF was incorporated in May 1920, with a constitution, bylaws, and a supposed war chest of $1 million, its letterhead listing a virtual who's who of local elites. As stated in its constitution, the organization aimed to "reawaken in America a realization of the responsibilities of citizenship" and to "induce a more general and intelligent acceptance of those responsibilities."[14] From such generalities, the BAF got down to business, keeping the (excessive) patriotic fervor generated by American involvement in World War I at high levels in Los Angeles.

The BAF sought to emphasize what it called the "Golden Rule" in relations between labor and capital and to defend private property. It was open to any person or any American corporation pledging allegiance to the U.S. Constitution. Dues were set up as voluntary contributions. The BAF's headquarters was, and would remain, in Los Angeles. The organization would be run by district representatives drawn from county-level aggregates of members. For instance, District One included the counties south of Los Angeles plus Santa Barbara; District Two was Los Angeles County (or the "Los Angeles County Unit"). The board of directors would meet quarterly; the entire Federation would meet once a year in the late fall. The BAF would staff and maintain a "Bureau of Analysis and Information" in Sacramento to keep a record of the voting behavior of state legislators.

The organization opposed "any other theories of government other than the United States Constitution," and it aimed to "oppose the development of class consciousness and the class domination of government, business or society." As Haynes put it, the BAF was "in fact opposed to everything progressive."[15] It suggested, in a pamphlet called "Beyond the Veil" that the initiative, referendum, and recall were communist-inspired legislative tools, and its functionaries worked hard to roll back these Progressive-era innovations. Hardly less insidious than the initiative process, the BAF intimated, were labor unions: the organization essentially picked up the open shop cudgel from where *Los Angeles Times* owner and publisher Harrison Gray Otis dropped it at his death in 1917. Haynes, probably the best-known and most important Progressive figure in Los Angeles, found the BAF and its "patrioteer" members ominous. As he wrote to California's governor, the "audacity of this attempt to put government in California and in America back a hundred years is almost unbelievable and incomprehensible."[16]

The BAF also worked to root out radical thought—and radical thinkers—from schools and school boards. Foreshadowing the school board controversies of 1923 in Los Angeles, the BAF *Weekly Letter* of March 1921 had stated that "a school board in America is no place for a socialist or a radical . . . and yet they do creep in."[17] Haldeman had charted a course of action at the very first meeting, Haynes recalled, when he proudly declared that the BAF "had students in a number of universities throughout the country who would take short-hand notes of any utterances or remarks made by fellow students, instructors, or professors at their colleges." The notes would then be forwarded to BAF headquarters, where an appropriate plan of action would be formulated. The offending student or faculty member might be "counseled" by BAF functionaries or sympathizers, or perhaps an employment blacklist would prove more effective.[18] In 1920s publications sent throughout the United States—"Making Socialists out of College Students" and "America Is Calling"—BAF managing director and publicist Woodworth Clum intimated that left-wing academics sought to poison the minds of the American young. Clum, son of famed frontier Indian agent John Clum, got right to the point: "It is the *subtle, highly intellectual, pink* variety that is boring into the very heart of America."[19]

A representative statement of BAF policies can be found in the organization's newsletter, the *Better America Federation Bulletin* ("a survey of Americanism") issued out of Los Angeles twice a month. The BAF opposed industrial reconstruction, what it called "unionistic radicalism"; historian Edwin Layton has written that "opposition to organized labor" was at the top of the list of BAF activities.[20] The group also staked out ground regarding compulsory education. Children should be required to stay in school only until age fourteen (not sixteen). Too much education could actually become "a handicap rather than an advantage." The organization lobbied for six-day workweeks, fought minimum wage laws, and opposed reform of workplace hours. The BAF opposed the abolition of night work for women and minors, arguing that such labor was "of ultimate benefit to the race." Equal pay for equal work was anathema to the BAF, as it argued that because women would always want to start families, they deserved less pay than men. The BAF even went on record blasting the Los Angeles YWCA for its vague endorsement of collective bargaining rights.[21]

The Better America Federation was, as much as anything, an Americanization vehicle. Americanization terrain during the interwar period was not limited to Progressives and social or political reformers active in settlement houses and night school work, out to "Americanize" the immigrants in cities, congregations, and schools. Americanization was not simply an agreed-upon list of do's and don'ts compiled by Progressives of the Jane Addams or (in Los Angeles) the Emory Bogardus stripe. On the contrary, Americanization was a battle, and pit bull organizations like the BAF played and played for keeps. "Americanization is a word that has been used so generally," the organization's *Weekly Letter* argued in 1920, "that it is almost threadbare."[22] Such a tug of war put schoolchildren at the center of the struggle *to* Americanize and, by argumentative extension, *for* America. The stakes were high, even somehow epidemiological. "You no doubt realize," the BAF preached to its membership,

> that the schoolchildren of to-day are the men and women of to-morrow, and perhaps you do not know that the radicals are making a strenuous effort to poison the minds of our school teachers in various ways, as they realize if they can succeed in this field the poison will be passed on to the pupils with whom the teachers come in contact, and it is vitally essential that a strong argument for constitutional Americanism and the doctrine of American ideals be placed in the hands of every school teacher in the state.[23]

Toward that end, the BAF sponsored soapbox speakers (at ten specifically chosen street corners in working-class districts), distributed pamphlets and leaflets, and even embarked on a concerted, and briefly successful, effort to get the *Nation* and the *New Republic* pulled from school libraries in favor of BAF literature.[24]

The Reverend G. Bromley Oxnam was an Americanization vehicle himself. He looked out across the sooty landscape of his All Nations district and saw urban poverty, hopelessness, disease. "It is evident that most of us have been asleep as to the menacing situation in our midst," he wrote. "Vital questions relating to the Americanization and moral salvation of large groups of our city population demand our immediate and serious attention."[25] The collision course seems, at least with the hindsight of historical vantage, nearly preordained. Bromley Oxnam spoke out about Americanization's "vital questions," and the BAF responded with speakers "to combat the Radical soap-boxer."[26] These two forces would meet in battle.

Bromley Oxnam posed a threat to organized power in Los Angeles because he saw Americanization as a reform tool, a way to approach labor problems in an aggressively open shop town. Even eighty years later, his tireless energy shines through his notes and diary entries, his speech drafts, and copies of his correspondence. He believed in reform, and he believed that Los Angeles would someday become the center of the world. He believed in doing sociological research in Los Angeles neighborhoods, something that doubtless threatened the commercial authorities in the city given Oxnam's pro-labor leanings. Oxnam's Church of All Nations was an intriguing mixture of religious doctrine, social work, community outreach, labor activism, and applied sociological research. "We must have accurate knowledge," the always ambitious young cleric wrote, "of population, industry, wages, housing, morbidity, and mortality rates, religious make-up, poverty, educational facilities, cooperating agencies in [the] city, forces tearing down social life—saloons, pool halls, disorderly hotels, clandestine prostitution, etc."[27]

This was not good news to the BAF, which had known of Oxnam even as the organization morphed from the Commercial Federation in the teens. Oxnam had, in fact, been under surveillance by the Commercial Federation as early as 1919.[28] Within a year, he noted in his diary that "the BAF thinks me dangerous." Oxnam, who had once worked as a stenographer for the Pacific Electric trolley system, and had signed an anti-union contract, was by now a labor champion at All Nations, publicly supporting walkouts and strikes. As he remembered years later, "I had the closest relationship with the labor movement, was intimately acquainted with the president and secretary of the Central Labor Council, with other officers, spoke often, and participated . . . in the settlement of industrial disputes."[29] As well, Oxnam quickly became known in Los Angeles, indeed throughout the Pacific coast, as a vibrant and forceful lecturer. He gave many talks, often to crowds of thousands, and deserves to be called one of the city's most important twentieth-century preachers. His biographer notes that in 1922, Oxnam spoke over five hundred times. Two years later, his combined annual audience had grown to 120,000 people.[30]

G. Bromley Oxnam was young, vibrant, and energetic. He spoke fast, apparently remarkably fast, he was on the left, and he could fill an auditorium and spellbind an audience. He did not like the BAF, and he made that clear as often as possible.[31] The feeling was mutual. "I soon learned," he wrote in his autobiography, "that there were men 'uptown' who were opposed to a young minister dabbling in matters that were none of his business."[32]

The opening round in the school board fight came in the spring of 1923. The city's schoolteachers had not been given a raise in years, and many of them wanted a larger say in curricular matters and school governance. A delegation approached Oxnam regarding a vacancy on the seven-member board. Oxnam's public pronouncements about education and his reputation as a progressive thinker and speaker probably made him an obvious choice. Would he run for the vacancy? He agreed to do so, a decision he later regretted as foolish.

Just as soon as he stepped into the race, alongside a dozen other candidates, the mud started flying, with the *Los Angeles Times* staking out anti-Oxnam territory immediately. At one late April speech at the Labor Temple in downtown, Oxnam wondered aloud why the *Times* had become so interested in discrediting him. Was it over disagreements about education or school governance? No, the combative young preacher answered, it was because he had come out in favor of labor. Los Angeles, the open shop headquarters of the West, if not the nation, could scarcely tolerate such a position from someone so closely associated with the industrial districts and industrial workforce. Oxnam essentially predicted the direction that the school board fight would take over the next few months (indeed several years). There would be, he said, a battle over "Americanism." He urged his listeners (among whom were right-wing spies, he claimed) to remember the Americanism of the Los Angeles Progressives, of crusading lawyer Francis Heney (who had helped prosecute political crooks in San Francisco), and of his hero Theodore Roosevelt. The *Times* claimed to be "American," but where had it stood in the fights for eight-hour legislation, for the initiative, referendum, and recall? The Reverend Oxnam promised more than a simple school board victory. "We are going to build a new society," he thundered.[33]

The *Los Angeles Times* hated such pronouncements, hated such public speeches, and hated such speakers. Oxnam earned a spot on its enemies list as the newspaper embarked on a series that examined the school board campaign. On one side, the *Times* claimed, stood the forces of decency and good, teachers who knew their place and would abide by the traditional hierarchies. These teachers were ably supported by the "Citizens [*sic*] School Committee," a group supposed to number upward of 1,000 members. On the other side stood the forces of radicalism, out to "sovietize" Los Angeles schools. Because Oxnam had been approached by teachers to run for the board vacancy, order had been sacrificed on an altar of radicalism. "And now enter Rev. G. Bromley Oxnam," the *Times* sneered, a pastor who "holds services in the Union Labor Temple."[34]

By the end of April, the young minister felt compelled to write to Harry Chandler, editor of the *Times,* and request that the paper refrain from personal attacks. He was no Wobbly, no Syndicalist. Would he be such a popular speaker in Los Angeles if he were the radical the *Times* said he was? He did support the reorganization of the school board. He did believe that the board ought to be run along, in fact, corporate lines, for the sake of both efficiency and oversight. He did want teacher input in curricular issues. But this by no means made him a proponent of "teacher control." "Hasn't the time come in American life when as citizens we can face issues as sportsmen, play the game like men, state our ideas accurately to the people and let them decide?"[35]

The *Times* apparently disagreed. Within days, Oxnam again wrote to Chandler to complain about coverage regarding the cleric's positions and his words. He was not at a certain IWW meeting as claimed, "and you know it." But damage had been done: various school and church organizations wrote to Oxnam retracting speaking invitations. Oxnam even had to write to the president of the University of Southern California to assure him that he had not called for the repudiation of Liberty Bonds as the newspaper had charged. "Oh that reaction could think," Oxnam confided to his diary. "They know no history, honor or law save their own selfish desires, and all the while are laying the foundation for trouble."[36]

The foundation *had* been laid. Also, the stakes had been raised. Oxnam was not simply a political opportunist or a political naif. He was, the *Times* claimed, part of a group of "outsiders" trying to "get control of the public school system of Los Angeles" by starting a "teachers soviet." The charge was essentially treason. The Citizens School Committee stood ready to fight against any movement "subvertive of American citizenship."[37] Acting on the heels of such stories, the conservative Sons of the Revolution (sort of a parlor subset of the BAF, with stricter blueblood membership criteria) sent Oxnam and the other candidates a series of six questions regarding their qualifications for the school board.[38] Bromley Oxnam should have sent it back unanswered or at least contemplated his answers a bit more carefully. But perhaps he thought that answers to school curriculum questions could not themselves become ammunition in a polarized battle? If so, he was terribly naïve. The Sons, after all, called themselves "the leading militant patriotic society of America."[39]

Oxnam answered the questionnaire right away, that same day. Yes, he did believe in representative government, he wrote. Then there was the seemingly innocuous curriculum question: Did he believe that American history ought to be written (or taught) "from the viewpoint of America ahead of all other countries, yet not unfair to other countries . . . ?" Oxnam probably did not even sense a trap. He simply wrote that history should not be written "from the viewpoint of any nation. History should be written from the fact. All history must be accurately written, honestly written, and in accord with all the facts."[40]

The trap had been sprung. Oxnam's "Rooseveltian utterances," as one supporter termed them, could be (and were) used against him more than ever, as his answers revealed a supposed lack of patriotism. Allies tried to rally to Oxnam's aid. A flyer, "To Teachers of Los Angeles," attempted to build solidarity with Oxnam's point of view:

> Considering that the chief function of the public schools is to protect and per- petuate the principles on which the American government was founded, it should be an established policy that both sides of all questions, political, in- dustrial, economic, shall be looked into in a thoroughgoing manner, and any effort to subvert the truth or to conceal or distort facts or figures in the inter- ests of any one group and at the expense of the great mass of the people should be not countenanced in our public schools.[41]

But the damage had been done.

Oxnam campaigned beneath the motto "Education for world service," a slogan far too international-sounding to suit his opponents. His platform was simple: he stood for the "enrichment of every child"; he stood for "de- mocracy"; and he stressed "goodwill" and "service" as goals. If elected, he promised to reorganize the school board on the pattern of the regular busi- ness practices of other boards, including the hiring of experts to examine particular issues and problems. He promised to utilize the teachers of Los Angeles as curriculum experts (a plan that particularly infuriated the *Los Angeles Times*). And he promised to end what he called "sectional control" of the board by certain influential members of the community.

The *Times* went after Oxnam virtually every day. He fought back, giving talks with titles like "The Truth about the Board of Education Campaign" and pushing for a new slogan for all of California, "The Elimination of *Times* Domination." He argued that the *Times* and the "forces of reaction," as he called them, were blaspheming the word "American" in their hyper- patriotic language and rhetoric. Oxnam's supporters, gathered together as the "People's Legislative Committee of Los Angeles," got up a pamphlet in answer to the BAF's attacks, "The People vs. The So-called 'Better America Federation' And Its Political Agency, So-called 'Association for Betterment of Public Service.'" In it, the BAF's checkered public record was succinctly reviewed: the organization's publications had been pulled from California classrooms, it had attacked the direct primary, the initiative, the referen- dum, and the recall.

The contest grew even hotter in the early summer. BAF surveillance of Oxnam increased. Even the FBI, which had concluded that he was a "local radical who is among the most influential of this section," had started a file on the young Methodist preacher.[42] BAF minions audited and copied Oxnam's public addresses. When Oxnam gave a lecture at the Central Labor Council on the topic of British labor, a BAF reporter attended and apparently sent a doctored copy of the speech to officials at the University of Southern California in an effort to discredit him.[43]

On June 3, Oxnam delivered a lecture before parishioners and others gathered on the playground of the Church of All Nations at Sixth and Gladys. The playground choice itself was interesting: playgrounds had become a focus of political battles in Los Angeles (as elsewhere in the nation) between advocates of reform, who believed that urban playgrounds could provide uplift for the children of immigrants and the poor, and their conservative opponents, many of whom balked at the notion. The talk, entitled "The Rise of the Reactionary Mind," offered Oxnam the chance to retaliate. "We face," he said, "an hour of reaction." Progressivism, which had made such important strides in Los Angeles, was in danger of dying out altogether, simply because reactionary forces had gathered strength and steam through the early 1920s. There were four categories of social outlook, Oxnam told those gathered on the blacktop, arrayed in a line stretching from reactionary to conservative to progressive to revolutionary. The conservative and the progressive were critically important stances, he insisted, lest the extremes at either end of the spectrum come to dominate discourse and policy. But Los Angeles reactionaries threatened to upset the balance and, in doing so, just might bring back the days of corporate domination that the Progressives had supposedly smashed.

As the election approached, Oxnam's opponents accelerated their assertions of his dangerous radicalism. This was particularly true of the *Times.* Throughout the spring, the paper had seen fit to refer to Oxnam simply as "Bromley Oxnam, radical." But as the election drew nigh, he became a "radical and associate of radicals." The school board ticket supported by the teachers became "the Oxnam slate." Before long, Oxnam had become the "continual storm-center of turmoil and agitation." By June, the *Times* insisted in headlines "Board of Education Issues Clean-Cut Between Radicals and Those Who Stand for Americanism."

This last jab went to the heart of one of the campaign's most critical features. What or who stood for "Americanism" and who did not? And what did it mean, exactly? It is clear that the *Times* and the Better America Federation utilized their own definitions of "Americanism" to battle Oxnam and others they deemed dangerous. One method of doing this was to use the United States Constitution (which the BAF equated with revealed truth, like the Bible and the decimal system) as a weapon, insinuating or in many cases declaring outright that opponents either did not believe or did not support constitutional tenets. Historian Layton correctly notes that BAF propaganda "was characterized by extreme, intolerant nationalism. [The BAF] attacked the men and measures which it opposed by associating them with treason and subversion."[44]

This was a brilliant move in many respects. It stole the thunder of those, like the infant American Civil Liberties Union, who sought to defend rights of speech and assembly by reference to the Constitution. The BAF and the *Times,* in effect, took the document from Oxnam's hands by insisting that the school board fight was a proxy for much grander constitutional battles.[45] The *Times* and the BAF made continual reference to constitutional issues and constitutional principles in their attacks on Oxnam and the teachers' ticket. In addition, the BAF and its "Southern California Citizens Committee" inaugurated a series of oratorical contests for college students around constitutional themes. These were heavily publicized in the *Times,* and the winning student's speech ("The Constitution, a Citadel of Freedom") was given great play in the paper and BAF literature. The *Times* also championed a new California law that mandated the teaching of the Constitution in California schools (public and private), especially the "ideals and principles of citizenship and government."

Oxnam, as ever, fought back, declaring to cheers at one meeting that "I stand for nothing that *The Times* stands for." But it was abundantly clear that he had been outmaneuvered. He tried to reason with the "uptown" forces. In one letter to the *Times* (which may not have been sent), Oxnam struck a rhetorical pose anticipatory of Joseph Welch's "have you no decency?" question put to Senator Joseph McCarthy thirty years later. "Isn't there anything of the old American spirit of fair-play left in the press?" Oxnam asked, adding that "I often wonder, though, what the conscience of men who attack a man falsely must speak during the quiet watches of the night."[46]

As the so-called storm center of the debate, Oxnam attracted vociferous opposition from powerful elites beyond the BAF and local newspapers. A particular thorn in his side was the Reverend Robert Shuler. Pastor of one of the largest Methodist congregations in the city, Shuler was the single most powerful and important cleric in Protestant Los Angeles, with the possible exception of Aimee Semple McPherson. When Shuler decided to break with Oxnam, the *Times* crowed that he "Scores Oxnam From Pulpit."

"Fighting Bob" Shuler, who had arrived in Los Angeles only in 1920, had already established himself as a moral crusader of note. His church, Trinity Southern Methodist, downtown at Twelfth and Flower, was within sight of Oxnam's All Nations district. But the two parishes, and the two religious leaders, were nearly as different as could be. Shuler, who had been honing his brand of conservative Americanism for several years, had earned BAF praise. For instance, following a sermon entitled "One Hundred Percent Americanism," the BAF congratulated "Fighting Bob" and reprinted parts of his address. "There has been," offered Shuler, "enough anarchy, Bolshevism, bitter contempt flung in the face of the flag and treason to the country vomited out in Pershing square and on Los Angeles [S]treet to float a submarine. . . . I like the idea of America being a melting pot, but I think we should have some process by which we could take care of the slag that can never be made American."[47]

Oxnam's answers to the curriculum questionnaire apparently horrified Shuler. "With a heart hurt to the depths," he wrote, "I cannot support you in your campaign anymore." Shuler wrote that he thought well of Oxnam, despite the fact that he had "never been able to think with you." But the young Methodist minister's responses to the Sons of the Revolution were, Shuler declared, "dreadfully wrong." "Never in my life have I faced a necessity that grieved me more than this," he continued, and ended the letter by making his break with Oxnam.[48] Not one to keep such pains private, Shuler sent a copy of the letter to the *Times*, which quickly printed it.

The break with Shuler was important, but Oxnam's most aggressive individual opponent in the school board battle was a man named LeRoy Smith, an assistant state service officer with the American Legion and affiliated with the Veterans' Bureau as well. By the late 1920s, Smith would be an official member (and officer) of the Better America Federation; it is difficult to imagine that he did not belong to it in the early 1920s, but he denied any such connection.

Smith doggedly shadowed Oxnam during the early twenties. He seems to have kept fairly regular "Oxnam watching" hours, which would not have been hard to do. Smith lived in nearby Echo Park, and Oxnam was fairly famous in the early 1920s as a robust champion of the city's poor and immigrant classes. The newspapers knew him, and Smith would not have had to work hard to establish surveillance. No doubt he saw what he expected to see: Oxnam active in progressive causes and spending time with known progressive activists. This tendency to pass time with "fellow travelers" particularly rankled Smith. Of real concern to him was Oxnam's friendship with, and political ties to, Upton Sinclair.

In the midst of the school board campaign, Oxnam agreed to speak at an important rally with Sinclair. The May meeting was called to protest recent actions by the Los Angeles Police Department in preventing rights of speech and assembly. Sinclair, a friend of Oxnam's for several years, had recently been arrested, along with dozens of others, near the waterfront in San Pedro, where they had gathered to speak about the rights of labor in the midst of a giant longshoremen's strike. The strike had been cruelly smashed by the police department. Oxnam had been appalled by the level of force utilized by the LAPD in arresting Sinclair (who had just begun to read aloud from the Constitution when he was carted off to jail). Oxnam apparently thought twice about appearing at the rally: "I know the Times will lie about it and I am tossing even the remote chance of being elected to the Board into the sea, but free speech is the surest guarantee of peace."[49] Oxnam went. Sharing the podium with him that evening were various civil libertarians and radicals, including John Packard, Prince Hopkins, Upton Sinclair, and Hugh Hardeman. LeRoy Smith sat in the audience taking notes (along with, he later claimed, as many as a dozen plainclothes policemen). Oxnam opened the meeting with a benediction. According to those shadowing the young minister, the audience at first did not recognize who he was. One man shouted, "Cut out that prayer," while another asked his neighbor, "Who the hell is that Bird?" Someone else answered, "That's Oxnam, the Wobbly Preacher." "Is he with us?" one wondered. "Is he? You ought to hear this blankety blank blank preacher sometime." Another man put in his two cents: "That's the dope—that's great, once we get a few of these Holy Joes coming our way, we'll be able to put the skids under the whole damned works, president, constitution, government and all."[50]

Smith had what he wanted: a reference that put Oxnam and the Industrial Workers of the World in the same sentence. Even better, Smith caught Oxnam uttering the word "America" at the meeting: "We SENSE, in this meeting, the true spirit of America." He gleefully noted that men sang IWW songs to the tune of "America the Beautiful." LeRoy Smith wasted little time in going after Oxnam with Methodist leaders in Los Angeles. He argued that Oxnam's "sense" at the meeting meant, in reality, that either Oxnam could not sense the "true spirit" of America at all, or that he ought not be representing the Methodist Church at such a meeting. In response, Oxnam made a simple, admirably succinct notation in his diary: "The reactionary mind is a simple mind."[51]

The *Times* continued to pummel Oxnam, even as he tried to fight back by claiming that he stood against the corruption of previous school boards.[52] Shuler's break and public opposition was accompanied by that of Reverend Gustav Briegleb of Westlake Presbyterian Church, who suggested that Oxnam wished to inject "politics" into the educational system of the city. This move, Briegleb asserted, would "present a serious menace to our free institutions."[53] Briegleb's intervention in the fight opened him up to attack by fervent Oxnam supporters. One wealthy Pasadenan and supporter of radical causes, Kate Crane-Gartz, jumped right into the fray and went after Briegleb following his repudiation of Oxnam. In what may have only served

Figure 12.1. Bromley Oxnam shortly after the conclusion of the Los Angeles school board fight. *Hearst Collection, Department of Special Collections, University of Southern California Library*

to cement Briegleb's opposition, Crane-Gartz wrote that men such as he "preach love (?) on Sunday, and hate on Monday. . . . we radicals are not afraid to admit that we are radicals."[54] She also flayed Shuler, suggesting that "your Christianity does not go deeper than just to skim a very thin surface. . . . you . . . think that your tiny voice will be listened to, in the face of the great issues at stake all over the world. Your children could be in no better hands than Mr. Oxnam's." Crane-Gartz reserved special venom for the *Los Angeles Times*. The paper's decision-makers were, she wrote, "beneath contempt." "The *Times* never even looked in the dictionary to learn the meaning of the word Radical and as for 'Red' that nightmare of a word to the unthinking Babbitts . . . stands for the red blood of humanity of all the world."[55]

With the election only days away, the BAF and *Times* officially joined forces. In a June 1 story headlined "Oxnam Is Flayed by War Hero," Oxnam's opponents played their trump card: Col. LeRoy F. Smith. The paper printed Smith's letter to the Reverend Byron Wilson of the Methodist Episcopal Church regarding Oxnam's prayer at the opening of the Sinclair rally. The *Times* added that Smith was a veteran of the First World War and that both his grandfathers and his father had been Methodist ministers.

On election day, Oxnam lost by a wide margin, coming in dead last in the field of thirteen. But as far as LeRoy Smith was concerned, repudiation at the polls did not end the Oxnam threat. In a later letter to Reverend Wilson, he continued to wage war. The letter laid out an entire series of objections to Oxnam, chief among them that the young minister was but a poor representative of "the ancient spirit of Methodism with its white history of high patriotism." Making an argument that appears nearly word for word in BAF writings of the period, Smith went on: "The insidious apostles of Russian Sovietism are 'boring in' to our schools, our labor unions, our fraternities, our homes, and our churches, by every possible means. They have abandoned to a large degree their early crude methods of sabotage and rapine, and are using the more dangerous methods of the skilled propagandist."[56]

Oxnam again tried to fight back. He wrote Smith, objecting to his charges and his tactics and naming him as a Better America Federation functionary. Smith returned fire, denying any BAF connection, and giving no ground: "you are giving aid and comfort to as rascally a lot of radicals as ever cursed the church. . . . the Methodist Church is on the grill with you."[57]

Smith kept on, dogging Oxnam "like Javert on the trail of Jean Valjean."[58] He complained to high Methodist officials that Reverend Wilson had not answered his charges or his letter. He gathered, thanks to the Los Angeles Police Department, literature on the American Civil Liberties Union, which he considered the "pet" of American Communist Party leader William Z. Foster. He claimed that Oxnam was "sullying the name of the church," that Oxnam had naively allied himself with "forces in the world" which would "erase the church from society" and "pull God out of Heaven." Sounding much like his anti-Communist counterparts of the 1950s, Smith insisted that the church "purge our forces of all the representatives of the enemy who may have gotten into our uniform."[59]

Methodist officials, Bishop Adna Leonard in San Francisco chief among them, responded that Smith ought either to make formal charges against Oxnam or to desist. Not one to back down, Smith responded with formal charges. These charges, accompanied by a questionnaire drawn up by Smith for Oxnam to answer, minced few words. By his positions and his words, Bromley Oxnam was "utterly unfit to represent the Methodist Episcopal Church as one of her ministers." He had allied with and spoken in defense of groups hostile to the Constitution and the United States government. For instance, Oxnam had spoken back in the spring of 1921 at a meeting to publicize the plight of political prisoners in the United States. He had, along with other well-known radicals, opposed the California Criminal Syndicalism Act. Smith also revisited the school board fight, pointing out that Oxnam had appeared on the same platform as Upton Sinclair, that he had in fact prayed for the well-being of Sinclair.[60]

There was more. The conduct of Oxnam's All Nations Church, and especially its Sunday school, rendered the young minister unfit, even dangerous; the church was a "hot-bed of radicals." A "trusted lieutenant" of Oxnam's was Mrs. Martha Kaschub, a Sunday school teacher, who had entertained Wobblies and Communists; as bad, "Kashub" (as Smith incorrectly spelled it) was "strong for [Eugene] Debs, right or wrong." Smith charged that she had been teaching socialism to ten-year-olds: a recent Sunday school class had devoted one hour to socialism, one hour to dancing, and twenty minutes to singing such songs as "The Worker's Flag Is the Red Flag."

Other Oxnamites also threatened the minds of the young people of Los Angeles. The Church of All Nations had a Boy Scout troop that was, Smith charged, led by a young Russian Socialist. The library had Socialist and Communist books, many of which had been donated by the "radical" Shelley Club. The librarian at All Nations had ties to the Socialist Lyceum that went back as far as "the days of Job Harriman," the well-known Socialist mayoral candidate in 1911. Indeed, members of the ACLU (which Smith and others were quick to point out was a "union"), women belonging to the progressive Severance Club, Socialists, Communists, and Shelley Club people "mingle together almost daily" at the Church of All Nations. "The institution is conducted under the name and cloak of 'Liberalism.'" Resurrecting the tactic of the questionnaire, Smith approached current and former members of the All Nations Church staff. Question one left little doubt as to the purposes of the inquiry: "Do you know G. Bromley Oxnam?" The questions, all 43 of them, went on from there, asking about Oxnam's ties to the IWW, his preachings ("are they of a gospel nature . . . that would bring people to a saving knowledge of God?"), and wondering about the content of the All Nations Church library. "Do you know anything about Mr. Oxnam going to San Pedro to help in the I.W.W. strike?" asked one ambiguous question. "In your public worship did you ever hear Mr. Oxnam repeat the Apostle's Creed or ask his congregation to do so?" asked another.

The questionnaire that went to Oxnam asked about his sympathies for the IWW and against the Criminal Syndicalism Law, and his thoughts on American government. "In substance, did you not say in the presence of witnesses that the present form of government would have to be overthrown before the new social order could be established and the right adjustment brought about between Capital and Labor?" Had Oxnam agreed to speak at the IWW meeting in San Pedro, and was it true "in consequence that thousands of handbills were distributed over Los Angeles and San Pedro, announcing you in big letters as one of the principal speakers?" "Did you not sit on the platform of the Walker Auditorium with Upton Sinclair and others who were sanctioning and sympathizing with the I.W.W. movement, and did you not take an active part in this meeting, leading in prayer and by clapping of hands in every way show your sympathy and approval of the attitude the I.W.W. had taken toward their employers?" A few questions bordered on the ridiculous: "Are you or have you been associated with an organization known as the Woman's Shelley Club?" A few questions were doctrinal and overtly religious: "What is your usual attendance at prayer meetings?" "Have you ever stated to anyone that there was no such thing as conversion or the enjoyment of a real Christian experience?" "Do you believe in all the doctrines of the Methodist Church involved in the Apostles Creed?"

A portion of the Oxnam questionnaire concerned the school board fight. Had Oxnam organized teachers to help him win the election? Had he put All Nations Church staffers to work on his behalf? There is no doubt that the questionnaire was every bit as sinister as it was silly. For instance, Oxnam was asked what "proportion of the children attending the different welfare classes connected with your work, are Jews?" "What proportion are Catholic?" "What proportion of those Jewish children attend your Sunday school?"

Oxnam probably did not send this questionnaire back: it lies unanswered in his papers at the Library of Congress. But Smith kept at it. An open letter in 1928 (mailed from the Better America Federation offices and listing Smith's affiliation as the BAF) resurrected, again, the IWW charges, saying that Oxnam was associated with "as scurrilous thugs as ever scuttled a ship." Oxnam kept a radical library. Another local minister had told Smith that Oxnam was "one of the most dangerous radicals in the United States of America."[61]

In a letter to Oxnam, Smith dared the minister to prefer countercharges against him. Oxnam responded by doing so. The young preacher, who by now had left Los Angeles to become president of DePauw University, had his former colleagues deposed (some several times over the next few years) to answer the scandalous charges. Librarian Alberta Martin (or Martyn) Millar pointed out that she had never met Job Harriman: she would have been a child at the time of Harriman's Los Angeles career. Nor had she ever taught at the Socialist Lyceum. Boy Scout leader Wes Klusmann, neither Russian nor Socialist, admitted that the All Nations Church had a Boy Scout troop, even a Pioneers group (but not the Young Pioneers of Soviet infamy). His sworn statement stated further "that during the time he was at the Church of All Nations the Boy Scout program was carried out according to the policies prescribed by the National Council of the Boy Scouts of America."[62] He said that he had been born and raised in Los Angeles, that both his parents were American citizens, and that he had never lived outside of California. Martha Kaschub Morse swore that she had indeed been a member of the Church of All Nations in 1922 and 1923, but she was not a regular Sunday school teacher during that time. When she did take over classes occasionally, she did not teach what the charges had suggested; she instead had taught the life of Jesus and had drawn a map of Jerusalem for the children to study. She had not taught socialism to the students; she was unfamiliar with the tenets of socialism. She had not taught the students to sing "The Workers Flag Is the Red Flag." She did not know that song. She did not know the book she had been charged with teaching. She further swore that she did not "teach dancing for the period of one hour or any other time. That affiant has never taught dancing nor does she dance herself, nor know how."[63]

From the president's office at DePauw, Oxnam went after the BAF as best he could. In August 1929, he contacted Los Angeles traction magnate and BAF leader Eli P. Clark at his downtown office. Oxnam wrote that he understood Clark to be important in the Better America Federation, which he was. LeRoy Smith had been attacking Oxnam for years, to the point of sending unsolicited and libelous materials to the board of trustees of the university. All this dated from the school board fight of six years before. Would Clark be able to meet with Oxnam? Could Clark call off the reactionary dog?[64]

Clark agreed to meet with Oxnam. The meeting, which Smith apparently attended as well, took place sometime that month. An "understanding" was reached, and Oxnam was invited to publish something about the charges in the BAF's newsletter.[65] But Smith did not let up. Oxnam wrote again to Clark in early 1930, pointing out that his former colleagues had refuted the charges of socialism and communism. Oxnam typed his prayer from the Sinclair meeting. He told Clark that he was not a radical, and he distanced himself from the IWW. He insisted that the meeting had its origins as a protest against the LAPD's strike-breaking. He included a statement for Smith to sign ("I have done him an injustice," it said in part).[66]

Again it seems all to have been for naught. Smith mimeographed Oxnam's statement and sent it out in a special (and seemingly very limited) edition of the BAF publication; Oxnam seems never to have seen it. And Smith chastised Oxnam for his statement, which he found "very incomplete and evasive." The Better America Federation Radio Hour revisited the Oxnam case in the late 1920s on radio station KFI. By March 1930, the BAF was crowing that "Oxnam Plays True to Form," that he would not provide them with the materials that they had requested.[67]

The final attack came in the early summer of 1930. Smith drew up two BAF position papers of sorts, something called "G. Bromley Oxnam: An Analysis of his Attitude toward Americanism," and another called "G. Bromley Oxnam: An Analysis in Three Parts." In them, Smith outlined the reasons for his original charges against Oxnam. "I had become convinced that Dr. Oxnam was guilty of a program of thought, feeling, and action which was contrary to the principles of the Methodist Church in America in relation to this Republic, and contrary to the principles of loyal American citizenship—not merely as I appraise those principles, but also as my Government, by consistent and repeated legislation and judicial procedure has ever appraised them."[68]

Smith wrote that Oxnam had protested his original charges, "making the veiled implication that I did not know what I was talking about." The long, rambling documents, with subtitles like "I Meet Oxnam," bring up yet again many of the charges which swirled around Oxnam and the All Nations Church staff in the early 1920s. Smith pointed out that it was "illuminating" that Boy Scout leader Wes Klusmann printed Boy Scout materials "on the Socialist printing press of Los Angeles." Oxnam again resorted to pleas to Eli Clark. Where was the printed statement that the BAF had supposedly agreed that Oxnam could make? Why couldn't the interested parties put this controversy behind them?

Apparently they could not. As late as the 1940s, the activities of Oxnam's All Nations Church in Los Angeles were the focus of attacks by superpatriots. For instance anti-Communist crusader Elizabeth Dilling, of the "Patriotic Research Bureau" in Chicago, issued a mimeographed flyer titled "Red Churchmen" in 1946. The passages on Oxnam revisited events of the 1920s in repetitive detail. Dilling paid homage to LeRoy Smith ("teacher of the largest Bible class of Los Angeles from 1923 on") beneath the subhead "Socialism, Dancing, Red Flag for Oxnam's Sunday School."

Today the Church of All Nations, what is left of it, sits abandoned, falling apart in downtown Los Angeles. Only 80 years ago, it was at the center of a progressive vision for reform in the city. But the brickbats of reaction began to fly when Bromley Oxnam tried for political office, and he soon departed, red-baited out of the city because organizations like the Better America Federation hated him, hated his vision, and hated how Oxnam defined "America" and "Americanism." *Plus ça change, plus c'est la même chose.*

NOTES

The author thanks Tom Sitton and Mike Engh for their help.

1. A good background discussion of the 1923 school board fight can be found in Judith Raftery, *Land of Fair Promise: Politics and Reform in Los Angeles Schools, 1885–1942* (Stanford: Stanford University Press, 1992), esp. pp. 102–106.

2. Quoted in Robert Moats Miller, *Bishop G. Bromley Oxnam: Paladin of Liberal Protestantism* (Nashville: Abingdon Press, 1990), p. 33.

3. On the relationship between Oxnam and Bogardus, see Bromley Oxnam Papers, Library of Congress (hereafter Oxnam Papers), esp. box 106. Bogardus's introduction of Oxnam occurred at a dinner of the Sociology Honor Society, March 11, 1927.

4. Quoted in Miller, *Bishop G. Bromley Oxnam,* p. 39.

5. From a commencement address, "The Meaning of Culture," before the Pratt Institute, June 5, 1959, Oxnam Papers, box 31.

6. Oxnam diary, February 17, 1913, Oxnam Papers.

7. "East" as in east of Main (as opposed to the Los Angeles River, which would increasingly demarcate poor—and ethnic—Los Angeles from other parts of the expanding metropolis). See Bromley Oxnam, *I Protest* (New York: Harper, 1954), p. 175.

8. See Alice Bessie Culp, "A Case Study of the Living Conditions of Thirty-Five Mexican Families of Los Angeles with Special Reference to Mexican Children" (M.A. thesis, University of Southern California, 1921), p. 26. Culp's study, and many others of the period, have been reprinted by R and E Research Associates of San Francisco, a valuable move.

9. See Bromley Oxnam to Sherwood Eddy, November 2, 1918, Oxnam Papers.

10. The only scholarly article written about the BAF is Edwin Layton's essay of the early 1960s: "The Better America Federation: A Case Study of Superpatriotism," *Pacific Historical Review* 30 (May 1961): 137–147. Jules Tygiel's excellent study of the Julian Petroleum scandal discusses some of the difficulties BAF "superpatriots" found themselves in by the late 1920s. See Tygiel, *The Great Los Angeles Swindle* (New York: Oxford University Press, 1994); see also Tom Sitton's contribution to this volume.

11. John Randolph Haynes to R. B. Baumgardt, July 16, 1928, John Randolph Haynes Papers, University of California, Los Angeles (hereafter Haynes Papers). My thanks to Tom Sitton for the making me aware of the BAF-related correspondence in the Haynes Papers.

12. As historian Albert Clodius writes, "the names varied to serve the occasion, but the purposes, leadership, and membership were essentially the same. In all these organizations a dislike of reform and an intent to destroy as much as possible of the accomplishments of the Progressive Movement were linking with and partially sublimated in a patriotism which, however sincere, seemed fanatically extreme to some Progressives." See Albert H. Clodius, "The Quest for Good Government in Los Angeles, 1890–1920" (Ph.D. dissertation, Claremont Graduate School, 1953), p. 542.

13. Haynes to Baumgardt, July 16, 1928, Haynes Papers. See also undated letter from Haynes to Governor Hiram Johnson, reprinted in *San Francisco Call,* August 18, 1920, Haynes Papers. Haldeman, the patriarch of an important conservative family of Southern California (his grandson would become Richard Nixon's chief of staff), would later find himself in very hot water regarding his role in the Julian Petroleum scandal. See Tygiel, *The Great Los Angeles Swindle.*

14. *Constitution and By-Laws; Better America Federation of California;* from Oxnam Papers.

15. Haynes to Baumgardt, July 16, 1928, Haynes Papers. In his January 15, 1921, letter to Bledsoe (ibid.; quoted in part as one of my epigraphs), Haynes listed some of the BAF's positions as he understood them. "They are opposed to the abolishing of night work for women and children. They are opposed to the establishment of the minimum wage. They are opposed to equal work and wages based on occupation and not on sex. Of course they are opposed to any form of collective bargaining.

They are opposed to government employment agencies. They are opposed to a women's industrial service department in the Department of Labor." Judge Benjamin Franklin Bledsoe was a high officer with the California chapter of the Sons of the Revolution, a superpatriot organization that had many members in common with the BAF.

16. See Haynes to Johnson, August 18, 1920, Haynes Papers. See also Haynes to Baumgardt, July 16, 1928, Haynes Papers.

17. Better America Federation, *Weekly Letter,* March 9, 1921. In its earlier incarnation as the Commercial Federation, the BAF had already been poking into classroom and pedagogical affairs, if tentatively. For instance, in March 1920, Special Agent W. S. Grassie of the Soldiers and Sailors' Employment Bureau, a postwar effort of the U.S. Department of Labor, urged that Federation to become a university watchdog. "There exists a big field for propaganda in the several State Universities," he wrote. "The University of Calif. has several men on their faculty who are teaching and lecturing in a way that creates wrong ideas." W. S. Grassie to Commercial Federation of California, March 27, 1920, Margaret Kerr Collection, Hoover Institution Archives, Stanford University.

18. See Haynes to Baumgardt, July 16, 1928, Haynes Papers.

19. Woodworth Clum, "Making Socialists out of College Students: A Story of Professors and Other Collegians Who Hobnob with Radicals" (Los Angeles: Better America Federation, n.d., c. 1925).

20. See Layton, "The Better America Federation," p. 140.

21. See Layton, "The Better America Federation," esp. pp. 143–145. Informative, too, is "A Brief Outline of Arguments" a pamphlet setting forth BAF positions on industrial and educational reforms (Los Angeles, c. 1920).

22. *Weekly Letter,* July 6, 1920.

23. *Weekly Letter,* May 18, 1920.

24. This magazine-pulling stunt was only partially successful; BAF pamphlets were themselves disallowed in state classrooms because of their aggressive propaganda.

25. Bromley Oxnam to Rev. Charles Locke, May 16, 1918, Oxnam Papers.

26. See Harry Haldeman to "Member Better America Federation of California," January 6, 1921; copy in the Haynes Papers.

27. Oxnam notes, c. 1918; Oxnam Papers. Regarding Oxnam's stripe of Americanization reform, I have found helpful insights in the California Commission of Immigration and Housing's *Report on an Experiment Made in Los Angeles in the Summer of 1917 for the Americanization of Foreign-born Women* (Sacramento: Commission of Immigration and Housing, 1917).

28. A 1919 letter from his bishop warned Oxnam about his being under surveillance by H. H. Haldeman and George I. Cochran of the Pacific Mutual Life Insurance Company. See Bishop A. W. Leonard to Bromley Oxnam, November 24, 1919, Oxnam Papers.

29. Miller, *Bishop G. Bromley Oxnam,* p. 82; see also Oxnam, *I Protest,* p. 175.

30. Miller, *Bishop G. Bromley Oxnam,* p. 81.

31. Federal agent A. A. Hopkins, who trailed Oxnam for J. Edgar Hoover, reported on Oxnam's anti-BAF activities in the spring of 1922. Oxnam, along with

Haynes, had delivered a "vitriolic attack again the B.A.F." and "called the leaders . . . a bunch of labor haters who were serving the corporations to the detriment of the common people." Hopkins wrote that Oxnam advocated political representation drawn on class lines—"that he was advocating the Soviet System of Government, most of his hearers did not realize." A. A. Hopkins to "Mr. Hoover," May 12, 1922, U.S. Department of Justice, Federal Bureau of Investigation, File #62-101302; from copy in author's files.

32. Oxnam, *I Protest,* p. 170.

33. See the transcript of this April 29, 1923, speech in Oxnam Papers.

34. *Los Angeles Times,* April 20, 1923. The five-part series ran April 17–20 and 22.

35. See Bromley Oxnam to Editor, *Los Angeles Times,* April 24, 1923, Oxnam Papers.

36. See Oxnam diary, May 19, 1923, in Oxnam Papers.

37. *Los Angeles Times,* April 18, 20, and 22, 1923.

38. "Sons of the Revolution in the State of California" to Bromley Oxnam, April 24, 1923, Oxnam Papers. The Sons of the Revolution pushed for immigration restrictions, adoption of laws mandating the teaching of the Constitution in California schools, and the banning of textbooks that supposedly cast doubt on the heroic aspects of the American Revolution and its leaders. The California chapter also later claimed to have played the key role in the school board defeat of Oxnam. See, for instance, *Roster of the Society, Sons of the Revolution in the State of California and Constitution of the United States* (Los Angeles[?], 1924), esp. p. 5: "Last year we were the determining factor in defeating the un-American and radical elements who sought election to the Board of Education of Los Angeles." The questionnaire likely came from Sons of the Revolution President Pierson Banning, a well-known local superpatriot and author of the wartime book *Hun Hunting at Home.* The ideological (if not organizational) connections between the BAF and the Sons can be divined from the 1923 BAF pamphlet *The Colonial Character: A Bit of Inspirational Fact Historic Reminiscence Interesting Conjecture* [sic]. The little pamphlet championed, in equal parts, New England's gifts to America: conservatism, the Constitution, and Calvin Coolidge.

39. See *Roster of the Society.*

40. See Oxnam's responses in Oxnam Papers.

41. In Oxnam Papers.

42. Federal agent A. A. Hopkins to "Mr. Hoover," November 13, 1923; U.S. Department of Justice, Federal Bureau of Investigation, File # 62–101302. Oxnam's FBI surveillance file, in the phrasing of Oxnam biographer Robert Moats Miller, eventually ran to "over four hundred chuckleheaded pages." Miller, *Bishop G. Bromley Oxnam,* p. 87. Through the Freedom of Information Act, I have acquired the whole file (less a few pages still too sensitive to open!).

43. USC had apparently sent its own representative to the event, who produced an accurate version of Oxnam's remarks. Oxnam related this story in a letter to Upton Sinclair. See Oxnam to Upton Sinclair, August 31, 1923, Sinclair Papers, Lilly Library, Indiana University. My thanks to Douglas Flamming for pointing out the Oxnam material in the Sinclair Papers.

44. Layton, "The Better America Federation," p. 141.

45. The BAF had recognized the power of Constitution-defending for several

years, as both a political and a business tool. Back in the spring of 1921, Haldeman had even engaged in a discussion with Bishop John J. Cantwell of Los Angeles about vigorous defense of the Constitution. Replying to Haldeman's assertion that extremism in the defense of the Constitution was no vice, Cantwell wrote that "a wrong interpretation has been placed on many of the fundamental principles in the Constitution. For instance, the phrase in the Constitution 'to promote the general welfare' had for its purpose to set forth an ideal of social justice to be striven after. It was a safeguard of human rights rather than a guarantee of property and profits." Cantwell further cautioned Haldeman—and by extension the BAF—that any political program aimed at schoolchildren demanded subtlety. "I think if our beloved country is to be insured against attack from too advanced liberals, the surest means is to inoculate in the minds of our citizens, and especially in the minds of our children of a school age, the enduring ideals of altruism and justice." It is interesting to note the recurrence of epidemiological metaphors for Americanization's programs, promises, and pitfalls. See Bishop John J. Cantwell to Harry Haldeman, May 21, 1921, Archival Center, Mission San Fernando, Los Angeles.

46. Bromley Oxnam to Harry Chandler, June 1, 1923, Oxnam Papers.

47. *Weekly Bulletin,* August 9, 1921.

48. Robert Shuler to Bromley Oxnam, June 1, 1923, Oxnam Papers.

49. Oxnam quoted in Miller, *Bishop G. Bromley Oxnam,* p. 84.

50. See [LeRoy Smith], "Charges Against Rev. G. Bromley Oxnam," c. September 1923, Oxnam Papers.

51. See Oxnam's notes on the Sinclair rally in Oxnam papers; Oxnam diary entry, May 19, 1923, Oxnam Papers.

52. See Oxnam to editor of the *Los Angeles Examiner,* June 2, 1923, in which he writes "I believe the better citizenship of Los Angeles will insist that the schools be run for the children, not for the purpose of allowing selfish interests to get building contracts"; Oxnam Papers.

53. At least one supporter of Oxnam thought Briegleb was himself in the pay of the BAF. See A. G. Matteson to Oxnam, May 30, 1923, Oxnam Papers.

54. Kate Crane-Gartz to G. Briegleb, May 30, 1923, Oxnam Papers.

55. Kate Crane-Gartz to Robert Shuler, May 30, 1923, and Crane-Gartz to Briegleb, May 30, 1923, Oxnam Papers.

56. LeRoy Smith to Byron Wilson, June 11, 1923; copy in Oxnam Papers.

57. LeRoy Smith to Bromley Oxnam, June 12, 1923, Oxnam Papers.

58. Miller, *Bishop G. Bromley Oxnam,* p. 86.

59. Smith to Bishop Adna Leonard, July 24, 1923, Oxnam Papers.

60. As noted above, Oxnam and Sinclair were well acquainted. Several years earlier, Oxnam had asked Sinclair to speak before the All Nations parish. Sinclair, who had sworn off speaking engagements, wrote that a "clergyman who is standing for social justice in Los Angeles is certainly in a position to demand support. So I will open your forum." Sinclair letter quoted in Miller, *Bishop G. Bromley Oxnam,* p. 84. See also [LeRoy Smith], "Charges Against Rev. G. Bromley Oxnam," c. September 1923, Oxnam Papers.

61. LeRoy Smith to "Dear ———," August 10, 1928, Oxnam Papers.

62. See LeRoy Smith's "G. Bromley Oxnam: An Analysis in Three Parts," unpublished typescript, Oxnam Papers.

63. Martha Kaschub, deposition, August 20, 1929, Oxnam Papers.

64. Bromley Oxnam to Eli P. Clark, August 13, 1929, Oxnam Papers.

65. Eli P. Clark to Bromley Oxnam, August 15, 1929, Oxnam Papers. As Smith later remembered the meeting, Oxnam began by saying, "Colonel Smith, I understand that you have expressed the possibility that I may have changed my attitude: I want to tell you that I have not changed my attitude one particle," whereupon Smith "expressed my sorrow." Smith, "G. Bromley Oxnam: An Analysis in Three Parts," Oxnam Papers.

66. Bromley Oxnam to Eli P. Clark, March 13, 1930, Oxnam Papers; see also Bromley Oxnam to LeRoy Smith, March 13, 1930, Oxnam Papers.

67. BAF *Bulletin,* March 7, 1930, Oxnam Papers.

68. Smith, "G. Bromley Oxnam: An Analysis in Three Parts," Oxnam Papers.

CHAPTER THIRTEEN

Did the Ruling Class Rule at City Hall in 1920s Los Angeles?

Tom Sitton

Many historians and other observers of Southern California's history ascribe to a belief that early twentieth-century Los Angeles was controlled politically, as well as socially and economically, by an informal oligarchy of wealthy business leaders and professionals. Composed of some of the heads of the city's major corporations, financial institutions, and business associations, partners in the most prestigious law firms, and a few wealthy social leaders, this power structure is commonly held to have promoted a regional program encompassing industrial, commercial, and residential development in its own class interest. At the same time it restricted opportunity for working-class residents and people of color and suppressed all political dissent. Working through the Chamber of Commerce, the Merchants and Manufacturers Association, and various community organizations and quasi-governmental commissions, meeting informally in the California and Jonathan Clubs, trumpeting its expansionist credo in the columns of the *Los Angeles Times* and other publications, and calling the shots at City Hall and the county supervisors' offices, the cabal is believed to have dominated local economic development, the social scene, and the political process into the 1950s. This "militarized power structure," as Mike Davis labeled it, "controlled the city for about three generations after 1889."[1]

While it cannot be denied that this particular slice of the upper economic and social strata exerted tremendous influence in politics and regional development, its hegemony was consistently challenged. This is especially true in the realm of city politics, where competing elites, interest groups, and coalitions vied with the entrepreneurial elite for control of elective offices in order to influence formal municipal policy making. During the 1920s, a decade in which the oligarchy is assumed to have been in complete control, there were many instances when it demonstrated that it was far from being all-powerful. It was defeated in two of four mayoral contests in that decade, and its candidate in the two "victories" soon turned against it; it did not succeed in a major attempt at limiting municipal ownership of public hydroelectrical power or in composing a more favorable city charter; some of its leaders were embarrassed (even indicted) in the decade's most notorious business scandal; and indeed it splintered on many occasions as its leadership differed on specific issues such as transportation systems, regional open space conservation, and the ideology and usefulness of municipally owned utilities. Defeated many times during the 1920s by cross-class alliances of competing interest groups, the entrepreneurial elite—which represented only a portion of the region's upper class—proved that it was not as dominant in municipal politics as its contemporary opponents and some later observers have claimed.[2]

The urban political milieu within which this competition played out was a product of structural changes that occurred earlier in the century. A progressive coalition embracing a variety of reform objectives successfully removed many of the props believed to be necessary for the support of organizations such as the typical city political machine that coordinated municipal politics in many American cities at the time. The establishment of a civil service system in 1903 limited the number of appointed full-time jobs available to precinct workers, which effectively eliminated patronage as a reward for political service. Municipal ownership of the city's waterworks, harbor, and later the hydroelectrical system reduced some of the possibilities of graft involved with granting franchises to private concerns and overseeing utility operations. The ban on political parties in municipal elections approved in early 1909 was especially detrimental, since the local party apparatus was frequently the framework and its workers the personnel of the big city machine or other urban political organizations. This measure abolished city political conventions, which had nominated party candidates, and created an open primary in which candidates ran without party designations. A candidate receiving more than 50 percent of the total primary vote for that office was declared elected and did not have to compete in the general election a month later.[3]

The population matrix of Los Angeles complemented these structural changes. Angelenos were primarily white, and a large proportion were middle-class migrants from the northern, southern, and midwestern states. In 1920, more than three-quarters of the city's residents were native-born Caucasians, as compared to eastern cities with large numbers of foreign born who became clients of the typical city machine. Los Angeles's rapidly growing population was also very mobile within the city limits, making it difficult for a ward heeler to organize and control his district for a long period of time. With the exception of certain working-class residential precincts and the downtown core, the dynamics of the city's population were not as conducive to machine-style organization as many other American urban centers of comparable or larger size.[4]

The emerging reform coalition in Los Angeles flowed in the mainstream of the urban progressive movement of this period. This organized combination of insurgents had a wide variety of agendas ranging from elimination of corruption in municipal government to a program of social justice objectives in cooperation with the city's political left. The majority of the local leaders of this movement were registered Republicans, although Democrats also participated. A number of them were active at the statewide level in electing California Governor Hiram Johnson, creating a short-lived state Progressive Party, and supporting progressive Republican officials in battles with more conservative Republicans through the 1920s. A few of them also helped to establish and support the national Progressive Party in 1912.[5]

The structural reforms advanced by nonpartisan progressives were instrumental in their accession to power in 1910, forcing out a combination of the Old Guard Republican establishment, the Southern Pacific Railroad, and Democratic ward politicians that had dominated city politics. Reform Mayor George Alexander and his advisers remained in office until 1913, when personality conflicts and a second threat from a labor-Socialist fusion forced them into another alliance with the Old Guard. When the Socialist was defeated in the municipal primary many conservatives deserted the alliance, and an independent candidate opposed to both the progressives and the city's social and economic elite won the mayoralty. For the next few years a power vacuum existed as progressives, the Old Guard, labor leaders, and others competed in an unstructured political milieu. Voters became increasingly apathetic during the period, as vice conditions and sex scandals were fashioned as the major campaign issues. The reformed structure of post-1913 Los Angeles hindered the creation of party-based organizations but did not produce the type of idealistic and elitist politics that the reformers had in mind. Instead, the progressive legacy witnessed the interplay of shifting alliances of diverse and often conflicting interests organized by transitory political strategists who relied on corporate and personal wealth, religious congregations and other interest groups, the underworld, and some combinations of all these elements to finance campaigns, organize administrations, and implement policies over the next few decades.[6]

The 1920s opened to this disorganization in urban politics and illustrates the challenges that the elite business leadership faced in establishing and maintaining control of the burgeoning metropolis. In the spring of 1921, the city electors would choose a new mayor. Although in the Los Angeles "weak-mayor" system the mayor's powers were limited, this officer was still the administrative and figurative head of city government, and the mayor's cooperation was necessary for any group interested in shaping and executing public policy. The incumbent, Meredith P. "Pinky" Snyder, was a Democrat who had served as mayor just before and after the turn of the century. He had been elected again in 1919 with the support of organized labor, progressives with a social reform agenda such as Dr. John R. Haynes, and the local Hearst press. During his administration, Snyder staunchly supported municipal ownership of utilities and a program that sought to balance the competing interests of the city's social classes.[7]

As in the earlier Snyder administration, the conservative business establishment opposed the mayor and was active in planning to replace him. In early 1921, a committee of clergymen approached Superior Court Judge Gavin Craig, a former progressive but by then a favorite of *Los Angeles Times* publisher Harry Chandler, to recommend a candidate to oppose Snyder. Craig suggested George E. Cryer, a former associate of progressive leader Edwin T. Earl, and Earl's candidate in 1913 for city attorney. By 1921, Cryer, too, had shed his progressivism and was finally induced to enter the mayoral race by Harry Chandler. The publisher promised the enthusiastic backing of the *Times* (which had consistently articulated the philosophy of the region's most boosterish and arch-conservative entrepreneurs for decades), the city's business community, and Judge Craig's considerable personal following. By early March, Cryer had begun his campaign, managed by an up-and-coming strategist who would become one of Chandler's chief personal rivals in city politics.[8]

Kent Kane Parrot, a native of Kennebunkport, Maine, moved to Los Angeles in 1907 to study law and play football at the University of Southern California. He was admitted to the California bar in 1909, and within a year he became a partner in a law firm that included the dean of the college of law at USC and several of his classmates. He soon entered the Los Angeles political world as a member of the reform wing led by newspaper publisher E. T. Earl. Although he called himself a progressive, Parrot was always more of a socialite than a social reformer.[9]

After the disintegration of Earl's faction following his death in 1918, Parrot gravitated to the political circle of Judge Craig, one of his USC law professors, whom he described as his "tutor, mentor, and guide." With financial success and the wealth of his recent bride, Parrot was able to leave his partnership in 1920 to devote more time to politics.[10]

His opportunity came the following year when he was chosen to manage Cryer's campaign. Parrot's achievement was the construction of one of the oddest political coalitions in the city's history. This alliance included, among others: leaders of the Central Labor Council, along with the anti-labor *Times* and the Better America Federation, a reactionary group of superpatriots committed to "Americanism" and suppressing labor and political dissent; a representative of the city's illicit liquor industry and the local chairman of

Figure 13.1. Kent Kane Parrot in May 1921, just after his successful management of the first Cryer mayoral campaign. *Seaver Center for Western History Research, Natural History Museum of Los Angeles County*

the Anti-Saloon League; several leading Protestant ministers and elements of the underworld and figures involved in past political and vice scandals; and Municipal League civic reformers and the chief lobbyist of the paving trust. Organized labor, a strong backer of Mayor Snyder in 1919, deserted the "Yellow Kid" because of his role in mediating a strike in favor of a street-car company and his alleged attempt to destroy the city firefighters' union. The *Times* and private utility companies attacked Snyder's record on municipal ownership and were sure that Cryer would promote unlimited business development. In keeping the support of clergymen and reformers, Parrot was aided by the *Times* which, just before the election, printed daily stories about Snyder's failure to suppress vice. Parrot proved an indefatigable political animal. In the last days of the campaign he even took over Cryer's forum in a newspaper space shared by Snyder in the neutral *Los Angeles Record*.[11]

The impressive array of interests Parrot organized to support Cryer left Mayor Snyder with few major backers. Dr. John R. Haynes, Marshall Stimson, and a few other influential progressives backed the incumbent because of his stand in favor of municipal ownership. William Randolph Hearst's *Ex-*

Figure 13.2. Mayor George E. Cryer at the time of his first election in 1921. *Seaver Center for Western History Research, Natural History Museum of Los Angeles County*

aminer and *Herald* were the only two metropolitan papers to endorse the mayor, as the others supported Cryer or remained neutral. Parrot made sure that vice was the central issue, and though Snyder was victorious in the May primary, Cryer narrowly defeated him in the June general election.[12]

The victory of the city's business elite—won with the help of some of its enemies—did not last very long. Within months Kent Parrot antagonized some of his allies in attempting to extend his personal influence in the city administration. At the same time, he began altering the composition of the alliance that had elected Mayor Cryer and molded it into a coalition of forces which effectively opposed the entrepreneurial elite's leadership for most of the remainder of the decade.

During Cryer's first term, Parrot quickly established himself as the administration's power broker. Although he failed to coerce the city council into approving his own appointment to the board of public service commissioners, this loss did not stop him from trying to dictate the operation of city agencies. Within six months of the 1921 election, he involved himself in Harbor Department affairs, describing himself as a "spokesman" for Mayor Cryer at a meeting in which he was accused of trying to dictate an appointment. Harbor commissioners complained that he meddled in department affairs and tried to have himself named as the board attorney. Parrot's interference in police matters was also evident, particularly in his relationship with Captain R. Lee Heath. Deposed Chief of Police Louis Oaks testified that Parrot funded Heath's efforts to organize police and fire department personnel backing for Cryer's 1923 reelection, set up a protection racket with tour bus drivers, and interfered in personnel matters to the point of personally arranging the transfer of police officers.[13]

Fortunately for Parrot, publicizing his role in these affairs began *after* the 1923 municipal election. To that time no major scandals had been uncovered, and Cryer was a popular mayor of a prosperous city. In the meantime, John R. Haynes and his coterie of municipal ownership activists and the Hearst papers had convinced Parrot and Cryer to embrace expansion of the city's hydroelectrical system and the statewide progressive program. These 1921 Cryer opponents now pledged to support him in 1923. Despite this shift on the public power issue, the *Times* and most important business leaders also backed Cryer again, since he and Parrot accommodated them by continuing to allow the Los Angeles Police Department and its "Red Squad" to be used in the interests of major businesses to keep industrial peace by suppressing union organizing, strikes, and radicalism. No doubt influenced by the start of a potentially violent IWW strike at the harbor, the *Times*'s editors reasoned that this was no time to desert the incumbent, even though Cryer's leading opponent, Bert Farmer, made the maintenance of the business leadership's anti-union "open shop" policy the foundation of his campaign. With the exception of a few conservative businessmen who deserted Cryer for Farmer, most of Cryer's 1921 coalition remained with him, and the mayor won a landslide victory in the primary.[14]

The *Times*'s deteriorating relationship with Parrot and Cryer, as evidenced by its lukewarm editorial support and failure to criticize Farmer, marked a shift in the alignment of the city's political interests. Prior to the election, Parrot worked well with the city's business elite, particularly *Times* publisher Harry Chandler, as both had campaigned for Cryer in 1921 and together served on various Republican Party campaign committees. By 1922, however, Parrot had also become an ally of Dr. Haynes and other prominent California progressives who continued to oppose Chandler and the Old Guard by working for expansion of state and local control of water and power resources and other measures. A major figure in this group was U.S. Senator Hiram Johnson, the old insurgent who had carried on a bitter personal rivalry with fellow Republican Chandler and his father-in-law and predecessor at the *Times,* Harrison Gray Otis. Although Parrot was able to keep both groups in his fragile alliance in 1923, he would eventually have to choose one or the other if he was to remain effective.[15]

For the sake of expediency and opportunity, Parrot chose the progressives, a portion of the city's elite often in political competition with the business leaders. As his relationship with Chandler was already deteriorating, Parrot prodded Cryer to embrace further expansion of the city's hydroelectrical system. At the same time he threw the support of his organization behind Senator Johnson, a move that prompted the enmity of Chandler and other conservative Republicans and the backing of the Hearst press (which consistently supported Johnson). With this shift in direction Parrot also acquired additional influence in police department affairs, since his price for supporting Johnson was the withdrawal of Hearst's endorsement of the city crime commission, a private group formed by Chandler and his associates who sought to dictate policing policies.[16]

The split with Chandler abruptly altered the positive image of Parrot and Cryer portrayed in the *Times*. Within months of the 1923 election, the newspaper sensationalized the controversies involving the harbor and the firing of the LAPD chief, and in 1924 began an all-out attack against the Cryer administration in a series of seventeen articles. The stories enumerated scandals in the administration and mismanagement of city departments, marking the final split between Parrot and the self-proclaimed organ of the city's business and industrial establishment.[17]

While the *Times* and other opponents referred to him by the pejorative term "boss," Kent Parrot most certainly was not the head of a typical city machine. He presided over an organization that actually included only a few members and had limited finances, more a committee of leaders representing diverse but related constituencies than a hierarchical machine with a permanent workforce. As leader of this apparatus, Parrot held a certain amount of control as long as he could balance the interests of the groups and individuals in his coalition and win elections. And in 1924, this organization was clearly the major organized opponent of the city's business leadership.

Parrot's allies formed one segment of this organization, an unofficial directorate of equals who worked with him. The composition of the group changed, but usually included representatives of the same interests. Dr. John R. Haynes, a board of public service commissioner and spokesman for public water and power forces and state and local progressives, was one of several liberals in the city's upper class who found it expedient to work with Parrot. Central Labor Council officers John Horn and J. W. Buzzell served on city commissions and organized union support, and Buzzell kept city employees in line and contributing to Parrot's campaign coffers. James Anderson and William "Pop" Sanders supplied votes in the African American Central Avenue district in return for patronage and political favors. Charley Crawford was Parrot's chief liaison with the underworld, consisting primarily of the city's reigning vice lords and their lieutenants. The Reverend Gustav Briegleb and, for a short time, the Reverend Robert Shuler, Protestant ministers with an interest in politics, proselytized their large congregations for Parrot. And occasional political figures such as Judge Gavin Craig (who had become estranged from Harry Chandler), and later "Queen Helen" Werner, who dispensed favors based on her contacts in local government, had personal followings that might be needed at a critical moment. These political activists represented singular interests often in competition with those of the business elite, although some became involved for purely personal reasons. Many could offer the support of their constituents as campaign workers, while Parrot's personal following, consisting of a few city department heads and commissioners, acted as a more stable force working within municipal government between elections.[18]

At its height in the mid 1920s, the Parrot organization operated at the municipal, county, and state levels with varying degrees of influence. It was most successful in city politics, where it opposed the business oligarchy with mixed results. In 1923 Parrot supported Haynes's efforts to block the creation of a retrograde city charter shorn of progressive amendments added in the last two decades. A Chamber of Commerce–led coalition of conservative civic and business groups pledged to a new charter nominated a complete ticket for the fifteen-seat Board of Freeholders, and a majority of the candidates won. The Parrot organization campaigned for the election of Haynes and labor leader John Horn along with a few progressive moderates and clubwomen. In the Freeholders' proceedings, Haynes fought to retain progressive measures such as direct legislation, to gain more administrative power for the mayor, and to protect public utilities by retaining the appointive commissions overseeing the proprietary departments. He also tried to replace the at-large city council election process with a proportional representation system, but lost in one of many compromises. The final product was not a radical change from the existing charter and, according to *National Municipal Review* editor C. A. Dykstra, did not incorporate any modern theories of city governance. But it did preserve most of the older progressive reforms. In the election that ratified this document, the voters also approved a separate call for districtwide council representation (proposed by organized labor), which limited the influence of the elite in electing a preponderance of sympathetic representatives from the more affluent areas in a citywide contest. With this latter change in the city's political process, the conservative elite lost whatever advantage it had gained in the composition of the new document.[19]

Parrot's organization was much more successful in the 1925 municipal primary election, when he responded to increasing criticism of his apparatus and some desertion from its ranks with a smashing victory for Mayor

Cryer and Parrot-approved council members over those of Harry Chandler and his elite cohorts. This offensive followed the conservative establishment's formation in early 1925 of a "Non-Partisan Association," which nominated federal Judge Benjamin Bledsoe as its candidate for mayor and set out to defeat Parrot and Cryer in the spring election. Supported by the *Times,* ex-Parrot ally Reverend Robert Shuler, and private utility companies, Judge Bledsoe became a rallying point for groups and individuals who opposed Kent Parrot.[20]

Parrot countered by making the city's expansion of electrical facilities the chief issue for Cryer's reelection campaign. This controversy revolved around the city's support of the proposed Swing-Johnson bill, which would give control of hydroelectrical power produced from a federally built dam in Boulder Canyon on the Colorado River to local government units without competition from private power companies. The bill also provided for construction of the All-American Canal, which would supply irrigation water to the Imperial Valley, thereby depreciating thousands of acres of land owned by Harry Chandler and his business partners just across the border in northern Mexico. In championing passage of the Swing-Johnson bill, Parrot and Cryer endeared themselves to the old progressives who advocated expansion of state and municipal power, the leaders of organized labor who were always battling Chandler and his open shop corporate allies, the Hearst press advancing the career of Senator Johnson (the bill's co-sponsor), and most of the other major newspapers, which favored Swing-Johnson and overlooked the shortcomings of politicians if they endorsed the measure.[21]

In the primary campaign Bledsoe and the *Times* tried to establish vice conditions as the major issue, just as Parrot had done in 1921. But Parrot made sure that Swing-Johnson remained center stage, as Cryer ignored the attacks on his administration and spoke almost exclusively on the importance of municipal power expansion. Even though Bledsoe eventually endorsed the Swing-Johnson bill, he made little headway with public power advocates, who castigated him as a puppet of Chandler and private power companies who would replace members of the Board of Public Service Commissioners with enemies of municipal ownership. Parrot then made Chandler himself a major campaign issue when he flooded the city with posters blaring "Harry Calls Him Ben," a reference to Chandler's control of Bledsoe.[22]

Parrot's pro-municipal ownership, anti-Chandler strategy worked well as Cryer easily won reelection in the primary. Eight of Parrot's choices for the city council were elected in the primary and general elections, compared to only two endorsed by the *Times.* The same eight had also been backed by organized labor, which the *Times* consistently opposed. The Republican

County Central Committee, which selected and endorsed Judge Bledsoe, a lifelong Democrat, to oppose the Republican mayor, caused further embarrassment. Although this was a nonpartisan election and the committee's chairman had warned that it should not be involved, some of the leaders tried to use the Republican organization to defeat a Republican incumbent and elect a Democrat, forcing the Old Guard Republican *Times* to endorse a member of the opposition party—and then lose. For the entrepreneurial oligarchy, and for Harry Chandler personally, the 1925 election was a disaster.[23]

Over the next year Parrot tried to extend his influence at the further expense of the Chandler group. He consolidated his power in the city by ordering the replacement of commissioners who did not go along with his program. At the same time he placated the oligarchy by allowing the appointment of Police Chief James E. Davis, a loyal Parrot follower whose hard-line stance on crime prevention and labor activism made him a favorite of Chandler and his Better America Federation friends. In late 1926, Parrot tried to branch out into county and state politics. He had little success at the county level, as he could count on the support of only one of the five supervisors and the district attorney. In the state election, however, Parrot played a critical role in lining up Southern California votes for the eventual governor, progressive Clement C. Young, who defeated the reactionary hero of the Old Guard establishment in the Republican primary.[24]

After this victory Parrot's political fortunes diminished. Northern California politicians ran the Young administration, leaving Parrot with little access to important state patronage. His county district attorney, Asa Keyes, was convicted in 1928 of accepting bribes from principals in the Julian Petroleum scandal, a stock-watering scheme of massive proportion that resulted in the indictment of BAF leader Harry Haldeman and other members of the business elite. In municipal circles, the success of Parrot's organization in 1925 bred an arrogance on the part of his associates, many of whom became involved in scandals that served to verify charges of corruption. Two Parrot city council members were removed after convictions of bribery; two of his city commissioners were forced to resign for conflict of interest; the LAPD was exposed as doing Parrot's dirty work in trying to frame an opposition city council member in a sex scandal; and other Cryer commissioners were accused of extortion and lesser misdeeds.[25]

The earliest of these scandals played a role in the 1927 municipal election as Parrot sought to increase his influence in the city council. The 1925 city charter had left the council with considerable administrative, as well as legislative, power, and a hostile majority could thwart a mayor's agenda. While the council in the 1920s was made up mostly of small businessmen— especially real estate agents—it included representatives of other interests as well, and became a battleground for the *Times* and allied forces favoring protection of private enterprise and opponents pursuing the progressives' public ownership initiatives. For a major organ of the business leadership, the *Times* had a poor record in electing mayors in the early twentieth century—only five victories in fourteen contests between 1900 and 1929, and these "victories" included the first two wins of George Cryer and that of a progressive reformer opposed by a Socialist. The newspaper's editors had a much better record of influencing the election of council members, however, and hoped to use that assembly to block the Parrot-Cryer administration agenda.[26]

In 1927 Parrot again attempted to reduce the municipal campaign to the single issue of support for the Swing-Johnson bill, while the *Times* brought up the scandals and the public ownership activism of Cryer's administration. The *Times* pulled no punches, smearing Parrot as a Socialist who promised "a sort of Bolshevik Utopia of municipal ownership of everything." But opponents of both Parrot and Chandler campaigned vigorously and won a number of seats on the council, which eroded the influence of both leaders. The Chandler forces were successful, however, in defeating two charter measures submitted by the public power advocates for which Parrot campaigned.[27]

With passage of the Swing-Johnson bill in 1928, that issue was dead, and newspapers like the *Record,* which had previously withheld criticism of the administration, began to publicize its shortcomings again. At the same time Parrot faced discontent within his organization as Mayor Cryer and others finally deserted him by early 1929. When the municipal election approached that year, Parrot's apparatus was in shambles, and shortly thereafter he moved out of the spotlight and into the shadows of city politics.[28]

Parrot's downfall did not result in a corresponding upswing in the fortunes of the Chandler forces as it came about partially because of the rise of another flamboyant political strategist who also opposed the entrepreneurial elite and fought it successfully. The Reverend Robert "Fighting Bob" Shuler, who arrived from Texas in 1920 to become pastor of Trinity Methodist Church, was a reactionary preacher who railed against Catholics, Jews, African Americans, the teaching of evolution, and criticism of the Ku Klux Klan. He had been a supporter of Parrot and Cryer until the 1925 election, when he chose to campaign for Judge Bledsoe, even though he hated Bledsoe's patron, Harry Chandler. After the election Shuler became more involved in city politics as a critic of the Cryer administration, and with his magazine and a radio station he attracted a large personal following beyond his religious congregation which included the clergy, moral reformers, and politicians not in Parrot's favor. Shuler spoke out against Parrot's city council choices in 1927 and spearheaded an attempt to recall Mayor Cryer late that year. In early 1929, Shuler selected John C. Porter, foreman of the crusading 1928 grand jury which investigated corruption in government, as the reform candidate for mayor and set out to defeat Parrot once and for all.[29]

The 1929 mayoralty election campaign opened with the Parrot apparatus in full retreat. Its leader was in New York, and a tired Mayor Cryer, who was advised by many to retire, did so. Without their strategist, Parrot's splintered forces had trouble settling on a candidate. The usually liberal *Record* eventually endorsed Porter, a decision its editors would regret when Porter opposed further expansion of municipal ownership. John R. Haynes and most of the public power advocates and Central Labor Council leaders belatedly campaigned for City Council President William G. Bonelli, a critic of both Chandler's group and the Cryer administration. Before the primary, Parrot himself gave his blessing to Perry H. Greer, an automobile dealer also backed by Hearst's *Examiner*. Greer placed a poor fourth in the primary, behind the inexperienced John R. Quinn, the very poor choice of the Chandler crowd. In the general election campaign, Parrot and his former associates united behind Bonelli, while the *Times* remained neutral. With the Swing-Johnson bill no longer at stake, vice conditions and morality in government again emerged as the major issues, along with accusations that both candidates had been members of the Ku Klux Klan. Shuler and the reformers took advantage of the recent scandals and a low voter turnout to elect Porter; both the Parrot alliance and the Chandler group were defeated by the religious right in this contest.[30]

The Porter administration proved to be an intolerant and inept group, favoring WASPish appointments and suffering many embarrassing moments and scandals of its own. The mayor angered all the old progressives when he began to block expansion of municipal power facilities, which was cheered by the *Times*. He further alienated organized labor and the left by allowing the LAPD to continue to be used in the service of major businesses in breaking strikes, harassing liberal and radical groups, and curtailing civil liberties in the guise of preventing crime. The Porter-Shuler program did not try to curry the approval of Chandler, but did grant the business establishment enough favors to garner the endorsement of the *Times* for Porter's reelection bid in 1933. In that contest Porter was defeated by Frank L. Shaw and the municipal ownership advocates, and the oligarchy lost again.[31]

In the 1930s, the Los Angeles entrepreneurial elite faced new political challenges and responded with the weapons at its command. But as in the 1920s, it found stiff competition from other interest groups and often was defeated. As in other cities such as Dallas and San Francisco in this era, the business leadership was powerful, but not in complete control of municipal politics. If it was successful in promoting its own policy of unrestrained industrial and residential expansion to benefit itself, it was limited—or in some cases blocked—in electing sympathetic officeholders and dictating policy decisions by the success of competing coalitions. In 1920s Los Angeles, the business elite was an important force in urban politics, but only one of several; and on many occasions it was not the winner. Although it exerted tremendous influence in regional development and negotiated concessions from municipal officers and political chieftains, the entrepreneurial ruling elite did not always rule at City Hall.[32]

NOTES

1. The informal Los Angeles power elite has seen many manifestations, from Mike Davis's late nineteenth-century and early twentieth-century power structure to a post-1950 "Committee of 25." References to this disparate oligarchy during the 1920s in different forms and with different emphases can be found in sources including: Louis Adamic, *Laughing in the Jungle: The Autobiography of an Immigrant in America* (New York: Harpers and Bros., 1932), 217–218; Carey McWilliams, *Southern California Country: An Island on the Land* (New York: Duell, Sloan and Pearce, 1946), 289–294; Robert Gottlieb and Irene Wolt, *Thinking Big: The Story of the Los Angeles Times, Its Publishers and Their Influence on Southern California* (New York: G.P. Putnam's Sons, 1977), esp. 189–201; Frederic Cople Jaher, *The Urban Establishment: Upper Strata in Boston, New York, Charleston, Chicago, and Los Angeles* (Urbana: University of Illinois Press, 1982), 654–685; Mike Davis, *City of Quartz: Excavating the Future in Los Angeles* (New York: Verso, 1990), 101–121; and various newspaper editorial essays over the years such as Joel Kotkin, "The Powers That Will Be," *Los Angeles Times*, December 14, 1997.

On the Committee of 25, see Al Martinez, "Committee of 25—L.A.'s Super Government," *Times*, December 3, 1972; Gottlieb and Wolt, *Thinking Big*, 457–458; Peter Wiley and Robert Gottlieb, *Empires in the Sun: The Rise of the New American West* (New York: G.P. Putnam's Sons, 1982), 104–107; and Davis, *City of Quartz*, 126–127.

2. Besides the examples of the limits of the entrepreneurial elite's effectiveness noted in this essay, see also: Vincent Ostrom, *Water and Politics: A Study of Water Policies and Administration in the Development of Los Angeles* (Los Angeles: Haynes Foundation, 1953), 59–61, 84–85, and Jaher, *Urban Establishment*, 662–663 (on disagreements between the Chamber of Commerce and the more militant Merchants and Manufacturers Association); Greg Hise and William Deverell, *Eden by Design: The 1930 Olmsted-Bartholomew Plan for the Los Angeles Region* (Berkeley and Los Angeles: University of California Press, 2000), introduction (on fundamental disagreements within the Chamber of Commerce); and the essays by Deverell and Becky Nicolaides in this volume.

On the larger question of the transition of Los Angeles from an entrepreneurial state to a statist regime in the 1906–32 era, see Steven P. Erie, "How the Urban West Was Won: The Local State and Economic Growth in Los Angeles, 1880–1932," *Urban Affairs Quarterly*, 27 (June 1992): 519–554, and his *Global Los Angeles: Growth and Crisis of a Developmental City-State* (Stanford: Stanford University Press, forthcoming).

3. *Times*, February 11, 1909; Martin J. Schiesl, "Politicians in Disguise: The Changing Roles of Public Administrators in Los Angeles, 1900–1920," in Michael H. Ebner and Eugene Tobin, eds., *The Age of Urban Reform: New Perspectives on the Pro-*

gressive Era (Port Washington, N.Y.: Kennikat Press, 1977), 102–116; Robert M. Fogelson, *The Fragmented Metropolis: Los Angeles, 1850–1930* (Cambridge: Harvard University Press, 1967), 229–236.

4. U.S. Department of Commerce, Bureau of the Census, *Historical Statistics of the United States, 1938* (Washington, D.C.: Government Printing Office, 1939), 22–23; Fogelson, *Fragmented Metropolis,* 114–147.

5. On the progressive movement in California and Los Angeles, see: George Mowry, *The California Progressives* (Berkeley and Los Angeles: University of California Press, 1951); Spencer C. Olin, Jr., *California's Prodigal Sons: Hiram Johnson and the Progressives, 1911–1917* (Berkeley and Los Angeles: University of California Press, 1968); and Tom Sitton, *John Randolph Haynes: California Progressive* (Stanford: Stanford University Press, 1992), 19–228.

6. Martin J. Schiesl, "Progressive Reform in Los Angeles under Mayor Alexander, 1909–1913," *California Historical Quarterly,* 54 (Spring 1975): 37–56; Fogelson, *Fragmented Metropolis,* 218–219.

7. Sitton, *John Randolph Haynes,* 166–167.

8. *Los Angeles Herald and Express,* undated clipping (1937) in Scrapbook 3, Eugene Biscailuz Papers and Scrapbooks, Special Collections, University of California, Los Angeles (UCLA); Marshall Stimson et al., "Why We Went to the Municipal Conference of 1913," *California Outlook,* April 5, 1913, 5; *Times,* August 30, 1920, March 27, June 18, 1921; John T. Morgan, "Mayor George E. Cryer of Los Angeles," *National Municipal Review,* 17 (January 1928): 27–32.

9. *Times,* October 31, 1931; J. C. Bates, ed., *History of the Bench and Bar of California* (San Francisco: Bench and Bar Publishing Co., 1912), 306, 425, 457–458; *Annual Announcement of the College of Law, University of Southern California, 1909–1910* (Los Angeles: University of Southern California, May 1919), 5–7, 22–24.

10. *Times,* August 23, 1914, July 16, 1916, January 10, 1926; *Los Angeles Record,* March 3, 1924; Ralph A. Arnold to Calvin Coolidge, April 7, 1926, box 228, Ralph Arnold Papers, Henry E. Huntington Library, San Marino, Calif.

11. *Record,* June 4, 5, 1921, March 3, 1924; *Los Angeles Citizen,* April 8, 22, May 6, 1921; *Times,* October 30, 1919, June 3, 1921. On the BAF, see Edwin Layton, "The Better America Federation: A Case Study in Superpatriotism," *Pacific Historical Review,* 30 (May 1961): 137–147, and the essay in this collection by William Deverell.

12. *Los Angeles Express,* May 2, 1921; *Los Angeles Examiner,* May 5–June 7, 1921; *Herald,* June 1–5, 1921; *Times,* June 3, 9, 1921; *Record,* June 3, 5, 1921.

13. *Times,* December 7, 1921, January 18, 1922, July 29, August 1–3, 16, 1923, May 13, 1933.

14. *Examiner,* April 30, 1923; *Times,* April 25–May 1, 1923; newspaper clippings in Scrapbook 17A, Edward A. Dickson Papers, Special Collections, UCLA; Fogelson, *Fragmented Metropolis,* 220; Louis B. Perry and Richard S. Perry, *A History of the Los Angeles Labor Movement, 1911–1941* (Berkeley and Los Angeles: University of California Press, 1963), 182–189.

15. "Moore for Senator Club" letters, August 21, 1923, boxes 221 and 232, Arnold Papers; Kent Parrot to John R. Haynes, August 25, 1922, Haynes to Rudolph Spreckels, February 8, 1923, and Haynes to Gov. William D. Stephens, January 23, 1922, box 59, John Randolph Haynes Papers, Special Collections, UCLA. For the ri-

valry between Hiram Johnson and Harrison Gray Otis and Harry Chandler, see Mowry, *The California Progressives,* 125–127, and almost any issue of the *Times* before a major election from 1910 to 1934.

16. *Record,* March 3, 1924; *Municipal League Bulletin,* March 15, 1924; Haynes to Parrot, April 28, 1923, box 59, Haynes Papers; Joseph Gerald Woods, "The Progressives and the Police: Urban Reform and the Professionalization of the Los Angeles Police" (Ph.D. dissertation, University of California, Los Angeles, 1973), 138–139, 228.

17. *Times,* July 29, August 1, 16, 18, 1923, July 13–29, 1924.

18. *Record,* March 3, 1924; *Times,* November 11, 1925, April 6, 1930, May 28. 1931; Parrot telegram to Hiram Johnson, March 8, 1927, box 65, and Frank P. Doherty to Johnson, June 4, 1931, box 34, Part 3, Hiram W. Johnson Papers, Bancroft Library, University of California, Berkeley; Edmund Wilson, "The City of Our Lady the Queen of the Angels," *New Republic,* December 9, 1931, 89–93; Woods, "Progressives and the Police," 110; Ostrom, *Water and Politics,* 78–80; Augustus F. Hawkins, Oral History Interview, conducted 1988 by Carlos Vasquez, UCLA Oral History Program, for the California State Archives State Government Oral History Program, 30–31; Richard N. Baisden, "Labor Unions in Los Angeles Politics" (Ph.D. dissertation, University of Chicago, 1958), 62–63.

19. Minutes of the Board of Directors, June 7, 1923, box 148, Los Angeles Chamber of Commerce Collection, Regional History Center, Department of Special Collections, University of Southern California; C. A. Dykstra, "The Pending Los Angeles Charter," *National Municipal Review,* 13 (March 1924): 148; Fogelson, *Fragmented Metropolis,* 222; Sitton, *John Randolph Haynes,* 173–174; Raphael J. Sonenshein, *Politics in Black and White: Race and Power in Los Angeles* (Princeton: Princeton University Press, 1993), 27.

20. *Municipal League Bulletin,* March 1925; *Times,* April 12, 1925; *Record,* April 13, 1925.

21. *Record,* April 30, 1925; Fogelson, *Fragmented Metropolis,* 220; Woods, "Progressives and the Police," 226–228; C. Wellington Koiner, "The Company Point of View Regarding Boulder Dam," and Hiram W. Johnson, "The Boulder Canyon Project," *Annals of the American Academy of Political and Social Science,* 135 (January 1928): 141–142, 150–156. On the wider dimensions of the Boulder Canyon project, see Norris Hundley, *The Great Thirst: Californians and Water, 1770s–1990s* (Berkeley and Los Angeles: University of California Press, 1992), 202–232, and Hundley, *Water and the West: The Colorado River Compact and the Politics of Water in the American West* (Berkeley and Los Angeles: University of California Press, 1975).

22. Haynes to Parrot, March 10, 1925, box 59, Haynes Papers; *Municipal League Bulletin,* April 1925; *Times,* March 30, April 15, 1925.

23. Ralph Arnold to George B. Bush, February 26, 1925, Arnold to William Butler, May 14, 1923, box 225, and Arnold to Herbert Hoover, April 30, 1926, box 226, Arnold Papers.

24. *Times,* January 10, May 23, 29, September 2, 1926; Frank Doherty to Hiram Johnson, January 21, 1927, box 34, Part 3, Johnson Papers; Woods, "Progressives and the Police," 256; Gottlieb and Wolt, *Thinking Big,* 199.

25. *Times,* October 23, 1925, July 30, November 2, 1926, February 6, April 27,

October 2, 1927, February 20, March 6, May 31, August 31, September 19, October 9, 1928; *Record,* May 8, 1928; Woods, "Progressives and the Police," 255. On the Julian Petroleum scandal, see Jules Tygiel, *The Great Los Angeles Swindle: Oil, Stocks, and Scandal during the Roaring Twenties* (New York: Oxford University Press, 1994).

26. Biography files of city personnel, Los Angeles Central Library; *Los Angeles City Directory,* various editions, 1920s and 1930s. Of the 41 city council members elected during the 1920s, at least ten were real estate brokers or agents, and several others were involved in building construction and real estate finance.

Regarding the *Times* and the city council in the 1930s, political scientist Francis M. Carney observed nearly 40 years ago that there was no clear evidence or a survey of voting records to indicate that *Times*-endorsed council members voted consistently as a bloc in favor of the paper's position on important issues. See Francis M. Carney, "The Decentralized Politics of Los Angeles," *Annals of the American Academy of Political and Social Science,* 353 (May 1964): 114.

27. *Times,* July 18, August 3, 20, 1926, January 16, April 16, 21–May 5, 1927; Ostrom, *Water and Politics,* 66–67.

28. *Times,* April 29, July 12, 1928, January 27, February 20, 1929; Woods, "Progressives and the Police," 256.

29. *Times,* April 26, August 31, 1927; *Bob Shuler's Magazine,* April 1930, 32–35; Duncan Aikman, "Savanarola in Los Angeles," *American Mercury,* December 1930, 426–429; William D. Edmundson, "Fundamentalist Sects of Los Angeles, 1900–1930" (Ph.D. dissertation, Claremont Graduate School, 1969), 389–424. For the Cryer recall attempt, see *Times,* January 3, 1928, and Frederick L. Bird and Frances Ryan, *The Recall of Public Officers* (New York: Macmillan, 1930), 241–246.

30. *Record,* April 23, 1929; *Municipal League Bulletin,* June 1, 1929; *Times,* March 1, 4, April 19, May 5, June 3, 1929; *Examiner,* May 6, June 4, 1929.

31. Sitton, *John Randolph Haynes,* 219–226.

32. William Issel and Robert W. Cherny, *San Francisco, 1865–1932: Politics, Power, and Urban Development* (Berkeley and Los Angeles: University of California Press, 1986), esp. 165–212; Patricia Evridge Hill, *Dallas: The Making of a Modern City* (Austin: University of Texas Press, 1996). For Denver at the same time, see Lyle W. Dorsett, *The Queen City: A History of Denver* (Boulder, Colo.: Pruett, 1977), 187–231.

CHAPTER FOURTEEN

Behind the Scenes

Bronco Billy and the Realities of
Work in Open Shop Hollywood

Laurie Pintar

In the early 1900s, G. M. Anderson, a young vaudeville actor in the East who could not so much as ride a horse, managed to bluff his way into a major role in Edwin S. Porter's *The Great Train Robbery*. But when the young actor fell off his trusty mount during filming in New Jersey, he promptly lost the part and was reduced to playing an extra in the classic movie. Despite such an inauspicious beginning, Anderson, who had previously changed his name from Max Aaronson, soon found a way to bridge the gap between on-screen depictions and behind-the-scenes realities. Within a few years, the easterner had transformed himself into "Bronco Billy" Anderson, a movie producer who, with the help of a stunt double, starred in his own western films. After a brief stint with the Selig Polyscope Company in Chicago, Bronco Billy helped establish the Essanay Motion Picture Company and in 1908 led a small troupe of employees westward to make movies. Searching for dramatic western landscapes as well as a suitable site to establish a permanent studio, Bronco Billy traveled through Colorado, Texas, and Mexico before finally settling in California in 1910.[1]

While Anderson was not the first motion picture pioneer to reach California, both his personal metamorphosis and his adventurous journey symbolize the industry's shift from East to West during the early twentieth century. Within just a few years of Bronco Billy's westward trek, California, and more specifically, Los Angeles, was home to scores of fledgling motion picture companies, hundreds of directors and players, and over a thousand motion picture workers. This geographic move from East to West was accompanied by an ideological shift: as moviemakers flocked to Hollywood—officially part of Los Angeles in 1910—the motion picture industry became increasingly associated with the myths of western opportunity and freedom which had pervaded the national consciousness since the mid 1800s. In a mutually reinforcing pattern, such myths were extolled in the early films produced in the West and shown in the rapidly proliferating movie houses of the East. Thus, it was not uncommon during the period for urban audiences to relieve the tedium of industrial work by watching a film such as *Bronco Billy's Sentence,* which featured Bronco Billy as the classic "good-bad man," roaming the open spaces of the West as a bandit before being converted to the side of law and order by the redeeming qualities of the region.[2]

Yet while a few individuals such as Bronco Billy were able to free themselves of eastern limitations, the vast majority of those working behind the scenes in Hollywood found that the vision of opportunity and freedom associated with both the West and the motion picture industry was more illusion than fact. In reality, by the time pioneer directors arrived in Los Angeles, the city was already entrenched in the hierarchical relationships of the East and sharply divided along class lines. More specifically, Los Angeles business owners were intent on maintaining power in labor-management relations by thwarting unionization among the city's growing industrial workforce. And as the motion picture industry developed in Los Angeles during the 1910s, producers replicated the general tenor of industrial relations in the city by refusing to recognize the right of studio workers to organize.[3]

Antagonistic labor relations in the city of Los Angeles and the motion picture industry did not wane with time. Instead, by the late 1910s and early 1920s, when the motion picture industry was firmly rooted in Los Angeles, the city had become a citadel of the "open shop," a euphemism for a policy whereby business owners built strong coalitions which were designed to deny employees the right to unionize. Such a hostile climate meant that when studio workers attempted to organize and demand higher wages, Hollywood became the site of a series of labor-capital conflicts which culminated with the 1921 studio strike. Making a mockery of the mythic images of western opportunity and freedom promulgated by the likes of Bronco Billy, producers did everything in their power to combat unions during these conflicts. For workers in Hollywood studios, behind-the-scenes realities were significantly impacted not only by hostile management policies but also by their own inability to coalesce as a unified workforce. Thus, while motion picture producers were able to unite as a class, studio workers were deeply divided by craft, rival union affiliations, and gender, all of which undercut the effectiveness of their labor activism. These divisions among workers proved doubly unfortunate. For the outcome of these labor conflicts was far reaching, not only sealing the fate of motion picture workers during the decade of the twenties, but also setting a hostile tone for labor-management relations which would continue to reverberate in Hollywood through the post–World War II era.

On April 23, 1896, patrons filed into Koster & Bial's Music Hall in New York City to witness the first commercial screening of motion pictures in the country. Treated to a series of short films, the audience watched women dancing, waves crashing, and men boxing while listening to the accompaniment of the Music Hall band. The debut was reportedly a huge success, eliciting both critical acclaim and commercial clamor, and over the next several years the seemingly insatiable demand for films fueled the dynamic growth of the nascent motion picture industry. By the second decade of the industry's development, movie producers, who had previously established studios in cities such as New York and Chicago, began to search for alternative sites that would increase productive capacity and provide fresh locales for their films. While some producers gravitated toward Florida, many began to view Southern California, with its attractive climate, diverse geography, and abundant land, as a viable wintertime production site.[4]

The pioneer directors—noteworthy and otherwise—who traveled west during the winter months to make movies generally worked in makeshift studios. For example, the Selig Company's Francis Boggs's ingenuity in adapting a Chinese laundry in 1909 was matched in that same year by the New York Motion Picture Corporation's Fred Balshofer, who made western films using what one reporter described as "only a horse corral and a stage."[5] Similarly, D. W. Griffith, working at the time for New York's Biograph Studio, arrived in Los Angeles during the winter of 1910 and promptly rented an empty loft, which he converted into a dressing and storage room. Adjacent to the loft was a vacant lot that Griffith used for outdoor shooting. "Our stage, erected in the center of the lot," Griffith's wife, actress Linda Arvidson, later recalled, "was merely a wooden floor raised a few feet off the ground."[6]

Despite the industry's humble beginnings in Los Angeles, the region's natural resources ensured that winter forays soon gave way to year-round production, as eastern companies reaped the profits of a steady supply of films made in the West. In 1915, George Blaisdell, a reporter for *The Moving Picture World*, enthusiastically described what the region had to offer the industry in terms of locations. In the process, Blaisdell made Southern California sound like a veritable Garden of Eden: "There are mountains, even with snow; there are desert plains and valleys, some in flower, some sterile; there are city streets and high buildings; there are palaces set in gardens of semi-tropical luxuriance and marvelous beauty; there are trees, from the pine and the cedar to the eucalyptus and the palm; and there is the ocean." "Los Angeles," Blaisdell concluded, "will hold its strong grip on the industry . . . just so long as its varied backgrounds continue to charm the eye of the picturegoer."[7]

Not surprisingly, the trend toward year-round production led to a rapid improvement in the makeshift facilities used by directors in the city. Just two years after Francis Boggs's arrival in Los Angeles, the Selig "mission studio" was built. The facility, which was modeled after the San Gabriel and Santa Barbara missions, included a stage, projection room, cutting room, garage, wardrobe department, carpenter shop, prop room, negative developing plant, executive offices, and directors' offices.[8] Even more impressive than the Selig studio was Carl Laemmle's Universal City, which opened in 1915. In addition to numerous stages and workshops, the studio, which was situated on 250 acres in the Hollywood Hills, also included a zoo, fire station, police station, and city hall.[9]

The gold rush had finally hit Southern California, and between 1915 and 1920, studios continued to expand at a phenomenal rate. For example, the Goldwyn facility, which was established in 1915, had already undergone $100,000 worth of expansion projects by 1920. Not to be outdone, the Metro Studio, also built in 1915, was planning a $250,000 expansion project in 1920 which was to include five new studio buildings. Reporter Rene R. Riviere's description of the rapid growth of the Brunton Studios, which now included a 500-acre location ranch in the Hollywood Hills, could be applied to numerous other studios in 1920: "The expansion of the plant during the past year," Riviere enthused, "has been nothing short of marvelous."[10] Such rapid growth of the motion picture industry meant that by 1920, 53 studios operated in Los Angeles with a product value of over $31 million. By the end of the decade, the value of motion picture production in the city would more than quadruple, to $129 million.[11]

The rapid expansion of the motion picture industry in Los Angeles reflected not only the advantageous natural resources of the region but also the financial benefits that the open shop offered to motion picture producers in the form of lower wages and an abundant supply of nonunion workers. Since the 1890s, Harrison Gray Otis, publisher of the *Los Angeles Times*, had united with business owners in the city to suppress organized labor. While Otis used the *Times* to turn public opinion against unions, the Merchants and Manufacturers Association (M&M) earned the title "militant champion of the open shop" by using black lists, lockouts, and the importation of unorganized Mexican and African American workers. The M&M's hostility to labor organizations was clearly elucidated in its "Declaration of Principles," wherein the association asserted the right of employers and employees to be free from "unwarranted picketing and boycotts, the closed shop, the check-off, and any other restriction which constitutes unjust interference with their industry."[12]

The *Times* and the M&M honed their anti-union techniques during the first decades of the twentieth century, so that by the dawn of the twenties Los Angeles boasted some of the lowest wage rates in the country and subsequently became a model for the national campaign to establish the open

Figure 14.1. The Selig Mission Studio, c. 1911. *Academy of Motion Picture Arts and Sciences*

shop. "It should be a matter of great pride to the members of their association," M&M President I. W. Rice trumpeted in his annual report for 1920, "that the cause for which we have worked and fought during a quarter of a century is now so entirely justified by public opinion throughout our country." In a perverse interpretation of the freedom and opportunity which the West offered, Rice characterized M&M members as "pioneers in the struggle for industrial freedom and law and order," while the Los Angeles Chamber of Commerce proclaimed that the "red-blooded, energetic American has turned his face Westward and in ever increasing numbers is moving to the land of his dreams—Southern California, the land of opportunity—where individual initiative under the open shop is still an asset." Later in the decade, former Chamber of Commerce President R. W. Pridham would explain the import of the open shop to the city's development. The open shop, Pridham declared, "is worth more to Los Angeles than anything else the community possesses, and should be maintained perpetually at any cost." Striking a high point in hyperbole, Pridham went on to assert that the principles of the open shop "should be taught at mother's knee, and around the fireside, so that future generations will practice it with vigor and determination."[13]

By the time the leading motion picture producers had established large studios in the city, the open shop policy was the labor law of Los Angeles. Eager to replicate the profitable labor-management policies of the city's business leaders, the most powerful motion picture producers eschewed the personal, paternalistic method they used to control the growing number of big-salary star players in their studios and instead opted for a less personal,

joint coalition to assert control over craft and service workers in the industry. As early as 1917, producers established the Motion Picture Producers
Association (MPPA), which was composed of seventeen of the largest studios on the West Coast, including Famous Players–Lasky (later Paramount),
Fox, and Universal. As a class-based organization, the MPPA set uniform
labor policies for its members as producers worked together to combat
unionization and to keep wages low. Ever vigilant, MPPA Secretary W. J. Reynolds played the role of sentinel, responsible for keeping watch over the
open shop in Hollywood. Reynolds's written warning to studio producers
in the spring of 1920 regarding the possible infiltration of studio labor by
members of the Industrial Workers of the World (IWW) provides just one
example of such vigilance. Although the MPPA was replaced by the Association of Motion Picture Producers (AMPP) in 1924, the latter organization
was also grounded on the principles of the open shop, and producers maintained a steadfast commitment to this labor policy through the decade of
the twenties.[14]

Unfortunately for studio workers, while Los Angeles business leaders and
Hollywood producers were united as a class in their opposition to unionization, the growing number of men and women who reported to the studios
to work each day failed to coalesce in a similar fashion. In part, this lack
of unity was the natural by-product of the wide variety of jobs held by studio workers. By 1920, there were over six thousand men and women who
worked in the studios in jobs as varied as carpentry and costuming. By the
end of the decade, the number of workers in Hollywood surpassed ten thousand, and jobs were increasingly specialized.[15] "The employees of this big
studio number 700," noted one reporter of the Goldwyn facility in 1920.
As impressed with the diversity of jobs as with the size of the workforce, the
reporter also noted that "practically every branch of industrial activity is
represented."[16]

In addition to divisions which stemmed from the diversity of jobs performed in the studios, workers were significantly divided by union affiliation
as well. Although producers worked hard to prevent any unionization in
Hollywood, a small number of workers began to organize during the mid
1910s. In the studios, unionized workers belonged to one of two very different types of organizations, both of which were affiliated with the American Federation of Labor (AFL). The first type of union organization consisted of the building trades unions, namely, the United Brotherhood of
Carpenters and Joiners (Carpenters) or the International Brotherhood of
Electrical Workers (Electricians), which were organized along traditional
craft lines. In marked contrast, the International Alliance of Theatrical and
Stage Employees (IATSE) was established in 1893 as an industrial union,
designed to organize all workers in the live theater industry and, later, in
the motion picture industry.[17]

Figure 14.2. Men working in studio property room. *Academy of Motion Picture Arts and Sciences*

While the presence of distinct and separate building trades unions such as the Carpenters and Electricians was enough to problematize the development of a general sense of worker consciousness, the added presence of IATSE, which claimed jurisdiction over all workers in the motion picture industry—including carpenters and electricians—led to explicitly oppositional relations among unionized workers in Hollywood. For example, the first strikes in Hollywood, staged by IATSE members seeking higher wages and union recognition in 1918 and 1919, revealed the deep divisions among studio workers: during both conflicts members of the building trades unions crossed the picket lines and filled striking IATSE members' jobs. Clearly, by competing against each other to establish jurisdiction in the motion picture industry, leaders of IATSE and the building trades unions had created a divisive climate among the studio workforce which prevented the development of a collective consciousness and seriously undercut the effectiveness of labor activism in Hollywood.[18]

Divisions among workers which resulted from diverse crafts and competing union organizations were reinforced by the strictly defined gendered division of labor that existed in Hollywood. In the studios, men performed jobs associated with traditional masculine aptitudes such as craftsmanship and mechanical and technical skills. They worked in property rooms, machine shops, carpenter shops, camera departments, and projection rooms. In contrast, women worked in the few jobs traditionally associated with the female sphere, including costuming, office, and wardrobe work. In addition, women were employed in the film laboratories, where they worked in printing and editing, performing tasks that required such presumed feminine traits as dexterity and patience. Contemporaneous descriptions of women laboratory workers were loaded with such gendered assumptions. For example, a reporter for *The Film Index,* James E. McQuade, noted that in the finishing room, film "is first wiped with cloths by nimble fingered girls," while *Motography*'s Eugene Dengler reported that in the film labs, machines were all "tended by deft-fingered girls."[19] Socially constructed ideals of feminine traits were used not only to explain women's presence in certain jobs but also to justify their exclusion from other workplace opportunities in the motion picture industry. In consequence, during the twenties, women made up only about 12 percent of the studio workforce.[20]

A sense of difference between men and women workers which was based upon the division of labor was reinforced with corresponding gendered pay differentials. For example, in costume departments, where men worked as tailors and women worked as seamstresses and milliners, 63 percent of the men earned the highest wages in the department while only 9 percent of the women earned such high wages. Conversely, only 17 percent of male workers were in the lowest wage bracket while 79 percent of women earned the lowest wages paid to those employed in the costume departments. The same wage differentials existed in office work; the majority of men earned the highest wages paid while almost half of the women earned the lowest wages paid to studio office workers.[21]

In the studios, conceptions of gender difference meant not only that women were restricted to a few poorly paid jobs associated with traditional constructions of femininity, but that they were also excluded from union organization. Although women were not officially barred from membership

Figure 14.3. Women working in film processing. *Academy of Motion Picture Arts and Sciences*

in IATSE, local unions had the power of discretion—or more to the point, the power of discrimination—regarding admission. As a result, while IATSE leaders worked aggressively to organize male workers, female workers under IATSE's jurisdiction remained unorganized until 1929. Similarly, the building trades unions were notorious for their exclusion of women. Wedded to concepts of the family wage and the male breadwinner, the local studio craft unions in their admissions practices reflected the AFL view that women who worked in the trades were "invading" men's terrain and subverting men's ability to provide for their families.[22] Absent separate union organizations for traditionally female jobs such as seamstress work in costume shops, women workers generally remained unorganized and marginalized by both male workers and male producers in Hollywood's studios during the period. And despite the relatively small numbers of women, their exclusion from union organizations further impeded the establishment of any sense of worker consciousness in the studios.

By 1920, the absence of a collective identity among studio workers, coupled with the anti-union coalition which studio producers had established, meant that owners exerted tight control over their employees. Cradled in the comfortable environs of open shop Los Angeles, producers paid studio workers, with their special expertise and training, the same low wage rates paid to other workers in the city. In Hollywood, low wages were compounded by poor working conditions for many studio employees. Laboratory technicians, for example, were compelled to work long hours in an unhealthy environment. "Conditions were bad," noted one labor paper of work in the laboratories during the period. "Dark-room denizens had to have the protection of heavy boots, sloppy clothes, rubber gloves, and aprons. The work," the paper concluded, "was physically hard." But largely unorganized and lacking any sense of collective consciousness, workers could do little to improve their lot.[23]

Yet while in 1920 producers could survey with great satisfaction the nature of labor-management relations in the studios, by the summer of 1921 union workers would mount a significant challenge to producer control in Hollywood. Angered by wage reductions and the lengthening of their work day, union men walked off their jobs and instituted the largest and most significant strike action to date in the studios. With producers united in their will to crush the strike and workers demonstrating a burgeoning sense of collective consciousness, the stage was set for conflicts of unprecedented proportions. And for studio employees, the outcome of the strike would be momentous, largely determining the conditions under which they would work during the decade of the twenties.

In early 1921, it was readily apparent that the excesses of the building frenzy on the West Coast were beginning to catch up with studio producers. Over-extending themselves in the construction of elaborate studios as well as in the production of increasingly lavish feature films, producers were beginning to experience serious financial problems.[24] According to Jesse L. Lasky, first vice president of Famous Players–Lasky Corporation, the current situation was "the inevitable outcome of the mistaken assumption on the part of many engaged in the making of pictures that the bonanza period would last indefinitely."[25] Or, as one reporter succinctly explained, the current fiscal crisis was the result of "the running wild of all the big film producers."[26] In order to stave off financial ruin, "retrenchment" became the buzzword among producers during the first six months of 1921. At individual studios, expenses were reduced through ad hoc salary cuts among both "big-salaried players" and the "mechanical staffs." Numerous studios also cut costs during the spring through worker layoffs. Yet despite these efforts, by early summer conditions in the studios had not improved, and unemployment rates remained high. *Variety* reported, "the studios are haunted each day by hundreds looking for work, and [for] every [studio] job that there is within Los Angeles there are ninety applicants."[27]

While conditions appeared bleak for studio workers, they were about to grow considerably worse. To this point, individual studios had been instituting wage cuts and layoffs on a sporadic basis. But in July, Lasky spoke unofficially for West Coast producers when he proclaimed: "The day of a complete showdown in the picture industry has arrived.... We must regard the present moment as the most critical that the film industry has faced during its existence."[28] In light of his notoriously anti-union stance, Lasky's reference to a showdown should have given workers pause; for producers it was the signal for an organized, industrywide institution of a 12 percent daily wage decrease and a shift from an eight-hour to a ten-hour day.[29]

Such drastic wage cuts, accompanied by mandates for longer hours, demonstrated not only the severity of the financial crisis for the motion picture industry in Hollywood but also producers' arrogance and power. Cognizant of deep divisions among Hollywood unions and confident of the control they exercised over all employees, producers anticipated neither the revolt of workers nor their unity in action. But by establishing uniform wage cuts that impacted all workers, regardless of craft or union affiliation, producers had unwittingly provoked a unified response from the leaders of both the building trades unions and IATSE. United in their refusal to accept workplace changes, 800 union men walked out of Goldwyn, Lasky, Metro, Fox, Realart, Hal Roach, Hamilton White, and Buster Keaton studios during the third week of July.[30] Within a few days, the conflict grew to include over 1,200 men when workers walked out of Universal, Brunton, Ince, and Christie studios. Describing the commitment of all strikers, Vern Ostendorf, secretary of the Studio Strike Committee, proclaimed: "We intend to stay out. We will not consider the ten-hour day or the $1 cut."[31]

In their firm and unified response, members of IATSE and the building trades unions caught the producers off guard. "The strength of the strike," *Variety* reported, "is in the fact that one of the assistants that . . . [the producers] had counted on, the Building Trade Council, has not responded. The latter is standing by the International Alliance of Theatrical and Stage Employees."[32] Such unity among formerly rival unions was also facilitated by a very recent jurisdictional settlement. In an effort to establish union peace in the studios, the AFL executive council in early 1921 had ordered IATSE to divest itself of studio craft workers such as carpenters and electricians. Forced into compliance by the threat of expulsion, IATSE leaders acquiesced to some sharing of studio jurisdiction in July, and a tenuous jurisdictional peace among union leaders was officially established in Hollywood.[33]

Yet while the leaders and members of formerly rival unions appeared to be overcoming their divisions, no evidence suggests that the 1921 strike

provoked a more inclusive labor action in terms of gender. Rather, the 1921
strike was primarily a dispute between male studio producers and male
unionists, and both groups ignored the needs of women workers, who continued to experience low wages and limited employment opportunities. In
consequence, as a labor action designed to empower workers in the studios,
the 1921 strike was fundamentally flawed by the perpetuation of male privilege and the marginalization of women workers in Hollywood.[34]

Nonetheless, the coalition among formerly rival male union groups during the early days of the strike demonstrated that a united workforce could
mount significant challenges to producer dominance in the studios. Without skilled craftsmen and mechanics, studios struggled to maintain production schedules. While MPPA Secretary W. J. Reynolds issued daily statements
claiming that the strike was not hampering the studios, one reporter noted
that "a general survey of the situation . . . shows [these] statements are in
error."[35] Indeed, contrary to Reynolds's assertions, several studios were
completely shut down for a protracted period of time by the strike while
production schedules at most studios were significantly disrupted. "It was
impossible to discover a single plant," *Variety* reported during the first week
of the strike, "that was running on full time."[36]

The power of a united workforce was also demonstrated in the broader
economic actions of workers. Unionists, according to one labor paper, were
determined to "take as many dollars . . . out of the coffers of the producers
and see how they like it."[37] The main thrust of economic sanctions was
directed at supporting the growing national movement to close theaters
on Sundays. Strikers planned to join forces with various church groups in
the city and began to circulate petitions and gather signatures in support
of the proposed blue law. Although workers had previously opposed the
Sunday closing movement, according to Vern Ostendorf, strikers were now
"100 percent" in support of the blue-law campaign. The unions, the labor
paper *Los Angeles Citizen* noted, believed in "fighting the devil with fire."[38]

Efforts to empty producers' coffers also included organizing a nationwide
boycott of any theater showing "the pictures of wage-cutters." And while
economically motivated, the decision to launch a national boycott demonstrated strikers' increasing appreciation of worker unity. As labor leaders
explained, the boycott of pictures made with "scab workmanship" would be
successful because "when the working people, who are the great majority
who attend picture shows, refuse to view these scab-made pictures the natural result will be no sales of these unfair products." If workers throughout
the country united in an economic action against the producers, they would
no longer be able to sell their films. Then, the *Citizen* queried, "what will be
the use of making them?" To advertise their boycott and explain the nature
of the conflict in the studios, strikers sent out tens of thousands of circular
letters imploring other workers to stay away from unfair films. "Every city,

town, and village in the United States and Canada . . . in which there is a Labor organization is to be furnished with a list of the Los Angeles autocrats,"
the *Citizen* reported.[39] Summarizing strikers' diverse activities, *Variety* noted
that "the strike committee . . . is going to leave no stone unturned to gain
victory for the labor side."[40] More to the point, by expanding the conflict to
workers throughout the nation, strikers were demonstrating a burgeoning
sense of (male) worker collective consciousness.

Realizing that a united workforce could significantly impact power relations in the studios, producers went on the offensive. Viewing the strike as
an opportunity to rid the studios of unions, they turned the walkout into
a lockout and refused to negotiate with the Strike Committee over wages.
"It is a question of making [pictures] at a lower cost or not making them at
all," Samuel Goldwyn blustered. "In other departments there have been reductions and labor should be just as willing to do its share as others have
been."[41] Producer recalcitrance meant they not only refused to negotiate
with union leaders, but also declined even to meet with federal arbitrator
Charles T. Connell, stating abruptly that "there is nothing to mediate."[42]

Producers believed they could weather the strike and cobble their way
through the summer production season without union workers for several
reasons. First, a seasonal decline in box office receipts had resulted in a
backlog of inventory and therefore generally low production demands. But
more important, high unemployment in the industry, combined with a
large supply of nonunion workers in the city of Los Angeles, led producers
to believe they could use strikebreakers to fill their minimal production
needs. This assessment proved accurate, and within a relatively short period
of time studios had resumed necessary production through the aggressive
recruitment of strikebreakers. "Strikers' places," the *Motion Picture News* reported during the second week of the strike, "were promptly taken by nonunion men."[43]

In their battle to break both the strike and the unions, producers also
called upon the Los Angeles business community for support. Eager to assist, the M&M passed a resolution opposing Sunday closings in an effort
to counter strikers' blue-law petitions. The resolution also "requested"
that the tens of thousands of individuals employed by M&M companies "refrain from lending their signatures."[44] A month later, M&M leaders would
actively lobby the Los Angeles City Council, arguing that Sunday closings
were an undue restraint on a business important to the city. "The motion-
picture industry has for years," M&M leaders asserted, "been one of the
main sources of our prosperity and to harass this industry by legislation . . .
would react upon the entire community and produce disastrous results."[45]

The M&M's support was augmented by the *Times,* whose editors viewed
the strike as a dangerous assault on business owners. Depicting studio labor
leaders as un-American, the *Times* charged that in a mass strikers' meeting,

labor leader John S. Horn had attacked the American Legion. Reportedly, Horn stated that American Legion members were being used as potential strikebreakers by producers, and called for "every man in the hall that has a Legion button on to take it off and destroy it."[46] Although the *Citizen* accused the *Times* of printing "a premeditated lie" and the story was later refuted when a member of the local Legion investigated, the smear of un-Americanism could not easily be wiped clean. Summarizing the role of the *Times* in the conflict, the *Citizen* charged that "the 'rat' *Times* . . . always rushe[s] to the aid of the employer in every industrial struggle."[47]

Locked out of studios that had resumed production with the use of strikebreakers, unable to negotiate with recalcitrant producers, and facing a hostile business community and press, strikers found themselves in a precarious position by early August. Their newfound unity buckled, and divisions among formerly rival union groups began to reemerge. Thus, although united in action during the early stages of the strike, IATSE members were soon chafing under the direction of the Strike Committee, which was dominated by members of the building trades unions. Cognizant of past jurisdictional squabbles and the fragile unity among strikers, producers began to apply pressure on IATSE in an attempt to reignite the smoldering disagreements among the striking unions. According to historian Steven J. Ross, producers may have gone so far as to bribe IATSE leaders to return to the studios. As Ross notes, during the second week of August, IATSE leaders suddenly held a highly suspicious meeting and voted to end the strike.[48] Contemporaneous assessments of the relationship between IATSE and the producers support Ross's conclusions. As one reporter for *Variety* wrote shortly before IATSE's decision to return to the studios: "The statement is freely made that had the proposition been one that was entirely up to the I.A.[TSE] the difficulty would have been settled weeks ago."[49]

The break in unity among studio unions meant immediate defeat for the strikers. Publicly citing mismanagement of the strike, IATSE members returned to the studios and scrambled to regain their jobs during the third week of August.[50] While carpenters and other building trades workers remained outside the studios, willing to "fight it out if it should take a year," their determination would go for naught. "As far as we are concerned," W. J. Reynolds of the Motion Picture Producers Association triumphantly crowed following IATSE's return to the studios, "the strike is over."[51]

Disunity among union members and the continued coalition of producers during the 1921 strike had a decided impact on labor-management relations in the motion picture industry through the decade of the 1920s. Although the business outlook improved significantly for the studios by early 1922, benefits were not passed on to workers. Instead, during the decade, producers were able to keep the wages of studio workers, with their special training and experience, comparable to the wage rates paid to other workers in Los Angeles. The city's wage rates were already well below the national average; for example, building trades workers' wages in Los Angeles were 33 percent lower than those in twenty other American cities. For women, the impact of the strike—from which they had been excluded—was equally significant. The continuation of low wage rates, compounded by gendered pay differentials, meant that women's earnings remained pitifully small.[52]

In addition to low wage rates, men and women in the studios also had to contend with high rates of unemployment during the 1920s. After compiling extensive data for the sixteen largest studios in Los Angeles during 1923, 1924, and 1925, the California Bureau of Labor reported that the "most interesting and important fact revealed by the Bureau's study of employment conditions in the motion picture industry is [its] irregularity." Variations in employment, the study contended, led to the problem of "broken earnings by the workers engaged in the industry."[53] While such unstable employment had a seriously negative effect on studio workers, producers remained unresponsive. In fact, unstable employment was not only the by-product of irregular production schedules but also the result of purposeful machinations of producers, who set up a "placement bureau" following the strike. Replicating the model created earlier by the M&M for the city of Los Angeles, producers established a hiring hall that was designed to keep a surplus of nonunion workers in the studios. The effectiveness of the hall was documented by the *Citizen,* which reported in 1926 that "refusing to hire [union] members" was a common producer tactic following the strike.[54]

Producers' discrimination against union men in the wake of the 1921 strike also included the outright firing of workers who either were union members or were attempting to organize the studios. For example, Herbert Sorrell, a painter who began work at Universal Studios in 1923, remembered being fired numerous times during the mid 1920s for belonging to the union. According to Sorrell, job foremen would periodically ask workers in the studios if they had union cards. Answering in the affirmative during the 1920s generally led to termination.[55] Similarly, Bill Edwards, a costumer at Paramount studio, remembered the necessity of meeting in secret, in a moth-proof fur room, to discuss the unionization of costumers. "In those days," Edwards noted, "one had to hide all involved in this sort of activity or you may be subject to immediate dismissal."[56] The labor paper *Flashes* later described the aftermath of a secret organizational meeting among laboratory workers during the early 1920s: "The next morning and during the day [organizers were] routed. Blasted from existence." Producers "knew all," the paper explained, because a "spy somewhere had peached on them."[57]

Through the better part of the decade, low wages, unstable employment, and overt discrimination against unionized workers reflected the iron-fisted control that producers maintained over their employees. And the virtually unchecked power producers exercised in the studios demonstrated not only the strength of their coalition, but the efficacy of the open shop in Los Angeles. Conversely, the divisions among the workforce which had emerged with the industry's establishment in the West helped ensure the continuing impotence of Hollywood workers and their unions.[58]

The consequences of such hostile labor relations extended far beyond the 1920s. When studio workers—both male and female—began to organize in greater numbers in response to the passage of the National Labor Relations Act (1935), producers and Los Angeles business leaders continued to hold an antagonistic posture toward unions and their members. But despite their best efforts, the era of the open shop was going into eclipse in both the city of Los Angeles and the studios. In consequence, as workers continued to fight for the right to unionize, Hollywood was engulfed by bitter, often violent strikes during the 1930s and 1940s. In light of their historic hostility to unions, producers' decision to use strikebreakers, studio police, tear gas, and fire hoses to break the picket lines during some of these conflicts comes as no surprise. Equally predictable were the numerous jurisdictional squabbles among rival unions which plagued the studios during these decades and which continued to undercut the effectiveness of labor activists. Finally, as strikers themselves noted in a handbill they circulated during the 1945 studio strike, the M&M and the *Los Angeles Times* were continuing to do their share in this extended war against organized labor. In hindsight from the scenes of these violent labor battles, the 1921 strike and its aftermath appear determining. And western myths to the contrary, for the thousands of motion picture workers who labored in the studios—whether during the 1920s or 1940s—Bronco Billy was proving to be an illusive character indeed.

NOTES

1. Kalton C. Lahue, *Winners of the West: The Sagebrush Heroes of the Silent Screen* (New York: A. S. Barnes, 1970), 25–30; Eileen Bowser, *The Transformation of Cinema, 1907–1915* (Berkeley and Los Angeles: University of California Press, 1990), 151–52; Benjamin B. Hampton, *A History of the Movies* (New York: Covici/Friede, 1931), 35.

2. For a full discussion of the association of western myths with the motion picture industry, see Lary May, "The New Frontier: Hollywood 1914–1920," in May, *Screening Out the Past: The Birth of Mass Culture and the Motion Picture Industry* (Chicago: University of Chicago Press, 1980). For more on early western films, see Lahue, *Winners of the West,* and Bowser, *The Transformation of Cinema.*

3. For more on the early history of Los Angeles labor, see Grace Heilman Stimson, *Rise of the Labor Movement in Los Angeles* (Berkeley and Los Angeles: University of California Press, 1955), and Louis B. Perry and Richard S. Perry, A *History of the*

Los Angeles Labor Movement, 1911–1941 (Berkeley and Los Angeles: University of California Press, 1963). To date, relatively few works have been published on Hollywood labor history. For works that include brief sections on the 1920s, see Murray Ross, *Stars and Strikes: Unionization of Hollywood* (New York: Columbia University Press, 1941), and Perry and Perry, *History of the Los Angeles Labor Movement*. For an exhaustive, unpublished account of Hollywood labor history, see Michael Nielsen, "Motion Picture Craft Workers and Craft Unions in Hollywood: The Studio Era, 1912–1948" (Ph.D. dissertation, University of Illinois at Urbana-Champaign, 1985). For recent published work on Hollywood labor during the 1930s and 1940s, see Mike Nielsen and Gene Mailes, *Hollywood's Other Blacklist: Union Struggles in the Studio System* (London: British Film Institute, 1995), and Laurie Pintar, "Herbert K. Sorrell as the Grade-B Hero: Militancy and Masculinity in the Studios," *Labor History* 37 (Summer 1996): 392–416.

4. For a full description of opening night at Koster & Bial's, see Charles Musser, *The Emergence of Cinema: The American Screen to 1907* (Berkeley and Los Angeles: University of California Press, 1990), 118–19. For general works on the history of the early film industry, see Bowser, *The Transformation of Cinema;* Thomas Cripps, *Hollywood's High Noon: Moviemaking and Society before Television* (Baltimore: Johns Hopkins University Press, 1997); Richard Koszarski, *An Evening's Entertainment: The Age of the Silent Feature Picture, 1915–1928* (Berkeley and Los Angeles: University of California Press, 1990); Robert Sklar, *Movie-Made America* (New York: Random House, 1976).

5. George Blaisdell, "Mecca of the Motion Picture," *The Moving Picture World,* July 10, 1915, 215–55.

6. Robert M. Henderson, *D. W. Griffith: His Life and Work* (New York: Oxford University Press, 1972), 42, 97.

7. Blaisdell, "Mecca of the Motion Picture."

8. Bowser, *The Transformation of Cinema,* 151–52; James E. McQuade, "Making Selig Pictures," *The Film Index,* November 20, 1909, 416, from Kalton C. Lahue, ed., *Motion Picture Pioneer: The Selig Polyscope Company* (New York: A. S. Barnes, 1973).

9. Blaisdell, "Mecca of the Motion Picture." For more on Universal Studio's early development, see I. G. Edmonds, *Big U: Universal in the Silent Days* (New York: A. S. Barnes, 1977).

10. Jack Neville, "Louis B. Mayer Studio Model Plant," 59; "Goldwyn Studios Now Cover 50 Acres," 58–59; Rene R. Riviere, "The Brunton Studios," 53; "The Metro Studios," 71, all in *Exhibitors Herald,* July 3, 1920.

11. James Clifford Findley, "The Economic Boom of the Twenties in Los Angeles" (Ph.D. dissertation, Claremont Graduate School, 1958), 400. For more on the business development of the industry, see, for example, Tino Balio, ed., *The American Film Industry* (Madison: University of Wisconsin Press, 1985), and Mae D. Huettig's classic *Economic Control of the Motion Picture Industry: A Study in Industrial Organization* (Philadelphia: University of Pennsylvania Press, 1944).

12. Merchants and Manufacturers Association, "Fifty Years of Service," *Fiftieth Annual Report,* 1946, 22–24.

13. Findley, "Economic Boom," 244, 257–58; R. W. Pridham, "Good Business and the Open Shop," *Southern California Business,* 6 (June 1927): 18, quoted in Findley, 246.

14. For more on studio producers, see, for example, Neal Gabler, *An Empire of Their Own: How the Jews Invented Hollywood* (New York: Anchor Books, 1988). For more on producers and early labor policy, see Steven J. Ross, *Working-Class Hollywood: Silent Film and the Shaping of Class in America* (Princeton: Princeton University Press, 1998); W. J. Reynolds to Hal Roach, March 5, 1920, Hal Roach Collection, Special Collections, University of Southern California (hereafter cited as Hal Roach Collection). AMPP continues to exist today but is now the Association of Motion Picture and Television Producers. "Summary of Activities of the Association of Motion Picture Producers, 1938–1944," 1, Academy of Motion Picture Arts and Sciences Clipping Files; "History of AMPTP," released by AMPTP, Los Angeles; MPPDA By-Laws, April 7, 1922, Hal Roach Collection.

15. California, Bureau of Labor Statistics, *Twenty-Second Biennial Report 1925–26* (Sacramento, 1926), 133; California, Bureau of Labor Statistics, *Twenty-Third Biennial Report 1927–28* (Sacramento, 1928), 234; *Motion Picture Herald,* December 20, 1941.

16. *Exhibitors Herald,* July 3, 1920. For a full discussion of the process of systematizing production techniques in the early studios, see Janet Staiger's work in David Bordwell, Janet Staiger, and Kristin Thompson, *The Classic Hollywood Cinema: Film Style and Mode of Production to 1960* (New York: Columbia University Press, 1985).

17. Perry and Perry, *History of the Los Angeles Labor Movement,* 321–24. For a work that focuses on the early years of IATSE, see Robert Osborne Baker, *The International Alliance of Theatrical and Stage Employees and Moving Picture Machine Operators of the United States and Canada* (Lawrence, Kans.: published by the author, 1933). Unpublished accounts include John Russell Cauble, "A Study of the International Alliance of Theatrical and Stage Employees and Moving Picture Operators of the United States and Canada" (M.A. thesis, UCLA, 1964), and Nielsen, "Motion Picture Craft Workers."

18. Perry and Perry, *History of the Los Angeles Labor Movement,* 322–24; Nielsen, "Motion Picture Craft Workers," 80–81, 88–90. For labor accounts of the 1918 strike, see *Los Angeles Citizen,* August 30 and December 6, 1918. For producer records of the 1918 and 1919 contract settlements, see Hal Roach Collection.

19. James E. McQuade, "Making 'Selig' Pictures," *The Film Index,* November 20, 1909, 4–6, from Lahue, *Motion Picture Pioneer;* Eugene Dengler, "Wonders of the Diamond-S Plant," *Motography,* 6, no. 1 (July 1911), from Lahue, *Motion Picture Pioneer;* A. L. Parker, "The Dark Stars of the Industry," *Exhibitors Herald,* July 3, 1920, 67. For more on the gendered division of labor in early film processing, see Karen Ward Mahar, "Women, Gender, and the Rise of the American Film Industry, 1896–1928" (Ph.D. dissertation, University of Southern California, 1995).

20. California, Bureau of Labor Statistics, *Twenty-First Biennial Report 1923–24* (Sacramento, 1925), 304, and *Twenty-Second Biennial Report, 1925–26, 113.*

21. California, Bureau of Labor Statistics, *Twenty-Second Biennial Report,* 145.

22. For more on the admissions practices of IATSE, see Baker, *The International Alliance.* For a classic statement on women's intrusion into men's craft work, see Edward O'Donnell, "Women as Bread Winners—the Error of the Age," *American Federationist* 4 (October 1897), in Eileen Boris and Nelson Lichtenstein, eds., *Major Problems in the History of American Workers* (New York: D. C. Heath, 1991), 232–34.

23. Herbert K. Sorrell, Oral History, interviewed by Elizabeth J. Dixon, 1963, UCLA Special Collections, UCLA. For wage rates in the industry, see the following items located in the Hal Roach Collection: W. J. Reynolds to Hal Roach, September 23, 1918; "Bulletin" from W. J. Reynolds, September 16, 1919; Carpenters' District Council of Los Angeles County, Open letter regarding Wages, August 4, 1919; IATSE Wage Scales for the period between September 1, 1919, and June 1, 1920; "Memorandum of Wage Scale and Working Conditions to Remain in Force and Effect Until Sept. 15, 1920," *Flashes: The Voice of the Membership,* September 1939.

24. *Variety,* January 28, February 11, April 29, June 10, July 1, and July 22, 1921; *Exhibitor's Herald,* July 2, 1921.

25. *Motion Picture News,* July 9, 1921.

26. *Variety,* February 11, 1921.

27. *Variety,* July 1, 1921.

28. *Exhibitors Herald,* July 2, 1921; *Variety,* July 1, 1921; July 8, 1921; *Motion Picture News,* July 9, 1921.

29. *Variety,* January 28, July 8, and July 22, 1921; *Los Angeles Citizen,* July 22, 1921.

30. *Los Angeles Citizen,* July 15, 1921. The list of worker groups on strike included IATSE, United Brotherhood of Carpenters, International Brotherhood of Electrical Workers, Bridge, Ornamental and Structural Workers, Painters, Decorators, and Paper Hangers of America, International Machinists, International Plasterers' Union, Bricklayers, Billposters, American Federation of Musicians, Actors and Artists Association of America, Hod Carriers and Common Laborers' Union, Plumbers and Pipe Fitters, Sign, Scene, and Pictorial Painters, and the Motion Picture Machine Operators.

31. *Los Angeles Times,* July 26, 1921.

32. *Variety,* July 22 and 29, 1921; *Los Angeles Times,* July 22, 1921.

33. Perry and Perry, *History of the Los Angeles Labor Movement,* 322–24; Nielsen, "Motion Picture Craft Workers," 80–81, 88–90; United States Congress, House, Committee on Education and Labor, *Jurisdictional Disputes in the Motion Picture Industry, Hearings Before a Special Subcommittee of Education and Labor on H.R. 111,* 80th Congress, 1st Session, 1948, 1030.

34. While the *Citizen* referred in two editions to "men and women" workers who were locked out of the studios, no further evidence suggests that women workers were involved in a central way in the strike. More likely, the reference to women was part of an effort by the paper to engage public sympathy for striking workers, the overwhelming majority of whom were male.

35. *Variety,* July 22, 1921.

36. *Variety,* July 22, July 29, and August 5, 1921.

37. *Los Angeles Citizen,* July 29, 1921.

38. *Los Angeles Times,* July 26, 1921; *Los Angeles Citizen,* July 29, 1921.

39. *Los Angeles Citizen,* August 12 and September 16, 1921.

40. Sunday closing was a serious issue for the producers. Just a few months earlier, in April, Pomona residents had voted to close all amusements, including movie houses, on Sundays, thereby providing the national movement to close theaters on Sundays with new life. *Variety* April 8, July 22, and July 29, 1921.

41. *Variety,* July 22, 1921.

42. *Los Angeles Citizen,* August 12, 1921; *Variety,* July 22 and 29, 1921; Perry and Perry, *History of the Los Angeles Labor Movement,* 324.

43. *Motion Picture News,* August 6, 1921.

44. *Variety,* August 5, 1921.

45. Los Angeles City Council Records, vol. 124, 423, from Findley, "Economic Boom," 393.

46. *Variety,* August 5, 1921.

47. *Los Angeles Citizen,* July 22, 1921; *Variety,* July 29, 1921.

48. Ross, *Working-Class Hollywood,* 131–33; see also Nielsen's discussion of charges during the late teens that IATSE was a "sweetheart" union of the producers.

49. *Variety,* August 19, 1921.

50. *Variety,* August 19 and 26, 1921.

51. *Variety,* August 26, 1921; *Exhibitors Herald,* August 27, 1921; Nielsen, "Motion Picture Craft Workers," 96; Perry and Perry, *History of the Los Angeles Labor Movement,* 324.

52. California, Bureau of Labor Statistics, *Twenty-Second Biennial Report, 1925–26;* "Wage Rates for Studio Workers," Hal Roach Collection. Only Atlanta and Richmond boasted lower wage rates. National Industrial Conference Board, *Wages in the United States, 1914–1929* (New York: National Industrial Conference Board, 1930), 162, from Findley, "Economic Boom," 247.

53. California, Bureau of Labor Statistics, *Twenty-Second Biennial Report 1925–26,* 133.

54. *Los Angeles Citizen,* November 19, 1926; Findley, "Economic Boom," 245.

55. Sorrell, Oral History, 17–18.

56. Bill Edwards, oral interview, interviewed by Steven J. Ross, May 31, 1989, Los Angeles; audiocassette in possession of Steven J. Ross.

57. *Flashes,* September 1939.

58. Perry and Perry, *History of the Los Angeles Labor Movement,* 321. The only notable change in Hollywood labor relations during the decade was the establishment of the Studio Basic Agreement (SBA), which went into effect in 1927. While the SBA recognized several unions, it was based on adherence to the open shop and precluded democratic, rank-and-file unionism. Ultimately, the SBA served the needs of producers rather than studio workers.

PART FIVE

The End: Metropolitan Finale

BECAUSE IT ACTED as a magnet for tubercular patients and other health-seekers, Los Angeles had long been a place where people went to get well or die trying. But where else could a cemetery be elevated to the status of cultural, even environmental, icon? In the concluding essay, David Charles Sloane analyzes the intersection of death and real estate in 1920s Los Angeles that was Forest Lawn.

CHAPTER FIFTEEN

Selling Eternity in 1920s Los Angeles

David Charles Sloane

In 1928, when *Harpers Magazine* writer Sarah Comstock tried to describe Los Angeles, she was immediately taken by its hustle-bustle. First, she tried to cross a street, and found instead, "I quiver, cower, make a dart, halt in panic."[1] If the arrival of the car in addition to the street railway made the city's streets as congested and dangerous as any in America, then electricity illuminated its street life: "Lights, lights, lights. Along Spring Street and Broadway and Hill, throughout the downtown cross streets, they focus in fierce incandescence." Welcome to the big city. In the city that so many current commentators believe has never had a downtown, she not only found one, she was overwhelmed by it. The neon billboards were so plentiful, so bright, "you long to hush them, to be rid of their blinding clamor, their deafening glare." Surrounded by "the jamming throng," she described a metropolis in the middle of a great boom.

Comstock attempts throughout her article to define the city. The bustle is one way, as are the many midwestern migrants, but she eventually decides that the hustle is more accurate: "Selling is Los Angeles' all-absorbing business." She tries to visit an old friend whom she has not seen in years, and is rebuffed with an abrupt, "Sorry, but I am *not* buying any real estate." Bang, the door closes. No friendly suburban manners here. Comstock is fascinated with the selling, sales, and door-to-door marketing. Finally, she demonstrates the extreme to which selling is the city's business by relating another friend's frustration:

> I had been as patient as possible. I had been offered every kind of real estate, gotten fallen arches from running downstairs and up, and still I had preserved my manners. But I've slammed the door in somebody's face at last. That woman tried to sell me a cemetery lot!

Comstock's friend's disturbing experience represented an important change in American life. The modern cemetery was no eighteenth-century church-yard with a preordained community, nor a nineteenth-century voluntary association of local residents serving the needs of their neighbors. Now the cemetery was a modern business searching for a market. Burial of the dead was no longer a family matter, but a professional service provided in as efficient a manner as possible for a price. Just as the city of Los Angeles was being defined by its mania for selling, the burial place was being redefined by its need to sell itself to survive.

Such a change was only slowly and grudgingly accepted by Americans torn between their love of the new, exciting consumer culture and their fears about the loss of civic and personal virtue. In Los Angeles, Hubert Eaton reshaped the conventional cemetery to reflect that new culture, those new circumstances. His creation, Forest Lawn Memorial Park, not only proved to be a durable model imitated countless times nationwide; it also became a tourist destination with a worldwide reputation. A century earlier, American cemeteries such as Mount Auburn outside of Boston or Greenwood in Brooklyn had been mandatory tourist stops in cities bereft of museums, parks, and public spaces. By the end of the nineteenth century, cemeteries "were visited by people mainly from a sense of duty."[2] Forest Lawn recaptured the attention of commentators and the public alike by us-ing the modern tools and ideas of business to sell a traditional set of values sculpted into a unique landscape.

REINVENTING THE CEMETERY

Forest Lawn Cemetery was established in 1906 just outside of Glendale, Cal-ifornia, on the site of a failed real estate development.[3] The cemetery strug-gled until 1917, when Hubert Eaton reinvented it. Eaton was from Missouri, the son and grandson of educators. He was trained as an engineer. Around 1910 the mine he owned failed. Friends suggested that he leave engineer-ing and move into sales, a choice that eventually led him into the cemetery business. In 1913 he came to Forest Lawn. Three years later he deftly took control of the institution, assuming the position of general manager but also being part of the ownership group, the American Security and Fidelity Company, which controlled the land and development of the burial place. Eaton had watched as Forest Lawn struggled financially, and he certainly knew that other cemeteries of the same generation were failing regularly throughout the United States. Managed as private corporations for the first time in American history, these new burial associations were facing the same vagaries of the market as other commercial enterprises. Eternal life had a dual importance as Eaton tried to develop a landscape that would withstand financial and other possible troubles. He knew how he wanted to reinvent the cemetery as a memorial park, and within a decade Forest Lawn had become the cultural icon that would attract satires from Evelyn Waugh and Aldous Huxley and a scathing exposé from Jessica Mitford.[4]

According to Eaton, the first time he saw Forest Lawn Cemetery, only ten of fifty-five acres were developed as burial sections, and it had "no buildings, no improvements, with the exception of a grove of olive trees and a few scattering [*sic*] headstones." Sixteen years later, Forest Lawn consisted of 200 acres, had interred over 28,000 people, averaged over $1 million a year in sales, and had assets of $10 million. Its Great Mausoleum had accumulated sales of over $3 million. In 1929, 400 employees orchestrated 3,600 interments and 900 weddings before 525,000 visitors. An architectural department of 12 architects and 12 engineers oversaw the landscape's development. People thronged to the Easter sunrise services, listened to the Forest Lawn hour on the radio, and read its booklets on culture and history.[5]

Eaton had completed the reinvention of Forest Lawn by installing the "memorial park" concept. The memorial park differed from the conventional cemetery in three ways. First, all individual earth-burials, instead of being marked by individual and family monuments purchased from monument dealers unconnected to Forest Lawn, were memorialized by a flush-to-the-ground bronze plaque. Families could on rare occasions purchase a piece of statuary from Forest Lawn to memorialize their lot, but the vast majority of graves were marked by the simple plaque. Second, Forest Lawn installed thematic features throughout the grounds to identify the various burial sections and to present a unified appearance to the public. The features ranged from copies of Michelangelo's greatest works to chapels constructed on the plans of famous European churches. Third, the memorial park gradually expanded its business to include activities previously separate from the cemetery. Most significant was the opening of Forest Lawn's own mortuary in the early 1930s. The purpose of these three departures was to provide management with the institutional structure to control, and thus profit from, more of the steps in the burial process and to allow it to present as unified a landscape as possible to the public.

The "memorial park" that mourners and other people visited in 1929 was entered through the world's largest wrought iron gates. A "sweeping drive" took the visitor past a pond in which Edna Parsons's *Duck Baby*, one of the successes of the 1915 San Francisco Exposition and Forest Lawn's first feature, sat on a pedestal, up toward the Elizabethan-styled Administration Building. From there, one could go to the top of Mount Forest Lawn, where the Tower of Legends served as the ornamental mask of the burial place's water tower. Here, on the steps, the choir would stand in front of as many

Figure 15.1. The *Last Supper* window was dedicated in 1931 in Forest Lawn's Memorial Court of Honor in the Great Mausoleum in Glendale. *Forest Lawn Memorial Parks & Mortuaries*

Figure 15.2. Forest Lawn took delivery of an exact reproduction in white Carrara marble of Michelangelo's *Moses* in the mid 1920s. *Forest Lawn Memorial Parks & Mortuaries*

as fifteen thousand people for the annual Easter sunrise service. Or visitors could round a bend from the Administration Building and see the chapel modeled on the Wee Kirk O' The Heather, "an exact reconstruction of Annie Laurie's church at Glencairn, Scotland."[6] In this, the second of Forest Lawn's chapels, burial services alternated with weddings.

Further along came the Great Mausoleum, with its double-concrete and granite walls rising in four (of an eventual eight) giant tiers up the hillside. Preparations were being made at the mausoleum for the installation of Rosa Morelli's stained glass copy of Da Vinci's *Last Supper,* prepared from original drawings borrowed from European government collections. Amid a large collection of both original and copied sculpture was a full-sized copy of Michelangelo's *Moses,* a recent addition. While *Moses* sat in the Great Mausoleum, other sculptures dotted the burial sections. They were particularly noticeable since the graves were all marked only by flush-to-the-ground bronze markers. Below the mausoleum stood the Little Church of the Flowers, with a copy of Bertel Thorvaldsen's *Christus* nearby.[7] Forest Lawn provided both a comprehensive set of services for the dead and an attractive group of sights for the living.

A CHILD OF LOS ANGELES

Forest Lawn was probably not possible anywhere but Los Angeles. The city was unburdened with a long institutional history; it was open to new people and new ideas, especially when they reinforced the cultural values of the emerging Anglo majority. John William Mitchell wrote in 1910, "Los Angeles, less than two decades ago, was an adobe pueblo. Today it is a metropolis." The foundation of this growth was a remarkable midwestern migration between 1880 and 1930.[8] The region grew by two million people, the vast majority of them from the American Midwest. As Sarah Comstock observed, you were as likely to see a "toil-worn old woman [clinging] to a marital arm" on the downtown streets, as you were the "go-getters." "Surely a strange street rabble, yokels rubbing elbows with cheap sophistication. Ah, now you recall a name often heard—'Paradise of the Corn Belt.'"[9] Thousands moved into the city of Los Angeles, but small settlements such as Pasadena, Santa Monica, and Hollywood also grew into regional centers. Forest Lawn's hometown of Glendale expanded from 2,700 people in 1910 to 60,000 by 1930.

Forest Lawn succeeded in drawing thousands of these new residents into contracts for burial spaces by developing a landscape which mirrored their belief that Los Angeles was a new city with new ways of doing things and quieted their fears that everything, including their burial space, would be transitory in this rapidly expanding metropolis. Recall that Hubert Eaton, consummate salesman, was a midwesterner himself. At least part of Forest Lawn's success came from Eaton's ability to translate his own values, shaped in the house of his father's ministry, and his own distrust of industrial America, rising out of his failed career as a mining engineer, into a carefully constructed space attractive to exactly those people pouring into Southern California.

Eaton proclaimed his vision for Forest Lawn in a remarkable document, "The Builder's Creed." The Creed, which Eaton wrote in 1917, is now immortalized in granite outside the entrance to the Great Mausoleum. It spoke directly to the migrants, drawing a striking contrast between the old midwestern industrial cities and the golden light of the City of the Angels.

> I therefore prayerfully resolve . . . that I shall endeavor to build Forest Lawn as different, as unlike cemeteries as sunshine is unlike darkness, as Eternal Life is unlike Death. I shall try to build at Forest Lawn a great park, devoid of mis-shapen monuments and other customary signs of earthly Death, but filled with towering trees, sweeping lawns, splashing fountains, singing birds, beautiful statuary, cheerful flowers; noble memorial architecture, with interiors filled with light and color, and redolent of the world's best history and romances.

Many of the migrants had witnessed grave sites being disturbed during urban expansion or obliterated by rural neglect. Even when they survived, the continuous additions of memorials had turned many cemeteries into forests of stone monuments. Individually, the monuments might be wonderful, but collectively, little sense of community heritage remained.

Forest Lawn's decision to prohibit individual and family monuments not purchased from the memorial park was intended to counter this trend. The purpose of mandating that individual graves be marked with bronze plaques was to ensure that the "ordinary tombstone," which is "not a thing of beauty," would not mar the appearance of the memorial park. The simpler lawnscape would be easier and more efficient to maintain. The memorial park could more easily assure the public that their fears of neglect were unnecessary with this environment. It had the additional quality of democratizing the landscape, since only a very few people would have visible monuments. The majority of graves would be marked equally. The combination of "Art and nature's beauty" joined with "modern facilities" gave the lot-holder the best of both worlds.

Prohibiting monuments produced a landscape of lawns. The cluttered appearance of the old cemetery was impossible. Instead, wide roads swept around the large burial sections, giving the visitor a sense of passing through a carefully maintained park. In a few places statues dotted the green rolling hills, much as they might have on a nineteenth-century English estate. Most of the grounds, though, appeared untouched save for the glint of the bronze when the sun sat at the right angle to highlight the markers. Nature is clearly tamed in this lawnscape, but captive elements, such as song birds and ornamental flowers, were allowed to flourish. Just as Southern California would become famous for its residential gardens, Forest Lawn would cultivate its image as a garden of culture.

For on the velvet green acres, Eaton inserted attractions that would entice the public and please lot-holders (or was it the opposite—entice lot-holders and please the public?). The placement and symbolic values of such features had to be carefully considered by the memorial park's management. Earlier cemeteries had attracted people through magnificent monuments gracing individual family lots, graves of historically important persons, or the resting places of those connected with tragic stories. Some cemeteries, such as Père Lachaise in Paris, had reburied important cultural figures, such as the tragic lovers Héloise and Abelard, as a way to gain credibility and stature.[10] Mostly, though, such attractions had not been planned, but had accrued as the cemetery evolved with the community.

Like so many Los Angeles entrepreneurs, Eaton was not willing to wait. Forest Lawn eventually would become a favorite resting place for Hollywood icons, such as Walt Disney and Humphrey Bogart. However, Eaton wanted his attractions to transcend individuals and proclaim a small set of important cultural values he associated with the community he hoped to convince to purchase space in Forest Lawn. If these values were appropriately and effectively introduced into the landscape, the artifacts would embellish the visitors' experience and provide a justification for the burial place long after its graves and crypts were filled.

THE BUILDER'S CREED

Central to Eaton's concept of the "memorial park" in contrast to the cemetery was his vision of a Christian life and death. The Builder's Creed begins with the declaration, "I believe in a happy Eternal Life." Eaton firmly placed himself among the growing chorus of early twentieth-century believers proclaiming the joyousness of religion and its importance to secular life. Both Aimee Semple McPherson and Bruce Barton, symbols of religion's influence on society in the 1920s, supported Eaton's establishment. McPherson, Los Angeles's saleswoman of enthusiastic evangelicalism, is buried above the Great Mausoleum along Sunrise Slope.[11] Her carefully scripted services were, to Sarah Comstock, "a complete vaudeville program" where every act heightened the sense of the spectacle.[12] Barton, the famed advertising pioneer and author of *The Man Nobody Knows* (1925), his best-selling description of Jesus Christ as the founder of modern business, wrote several articles on the cemetery, culminating in 1937 with a *Reader's Digest* article entitled "A Cemetery without Gloom."[13] Both these symbols of 1920s exultant Christianity embraced Forest Lawn as a welcome innovation.

Eaton was a vigorous proponent of a new, invigorated, humanized Christianity. His biographers tell of his vain search for a "smiling Christ" in painting or sculpture. Barton used Christ to exemplify the modern world of business, merging faith and business into a single entity. Eaton adapted Christ to his thematic landscape. If Barton's Christ was "the most popular dinner guest in Jerusalem," Eaton's was a modern family man who smiled "when a child clambered on His knee." In keeping with 1920s optimism, Eaton could only ask: ". . . if He had never smiled, would they have surrounded Him as they did?"[14] Not incidentally, such a religious stance not only fit with contemporary attitudes, it also implied that the burial place need not be so somber and serious.

While American cemetery sections had been dotted with statues of Christ, the Virgin Mary, and other icons of Christian writings since the introduction of three-dimensional monuments in the 1820s and 1830s, these were family monuments owned and maintained by individuals. In the thematic environment of Forest Lawn, the hypothetical smiling Christ was intended as a collective memorial, appropriately placed in the landscape.

Although Eaton never found his smiling Christ, he purchased a copy of Thorvaldsen's 1821 *Christus*. He first placed the statue near the Little Church of Flowers, eventually moving it in 1947 to a newly designed Garden of Christus.

Such religious sentiments reflected changes in American social attitudes toward death. The Victorians had reveled in death as a part of life. The elaborate rituals of death had produced dozens of guidebooks as to how one should act and what a family was expected to do after a death. These conventions were reinforced by community standards. However, twentieth-century urban Americans, particularly in the middle class, were less and less willing to maintain those standards and hold to the long, harsh conventions surrounding mourning. They appeared to be looking for an alternative vision of eternity. Barton and Eaton, among others, responded.

The synergy between Eaton and Barton was complete when, in 1927, Barton wrote an introduction to Forest Lawn's guide to its art. In "A First Step Up Toward Heaven," Barton equated Forest Lawn with his vision of a gladsome religion. He began with the startling line, "Nothing in Los Angeles gives me a finer thrill than Forest Lawn." We associate "thrill" with roller coasters, not burial places. He found Forest Lawn thrilling because "pagan and pessimistic" symbols of "men's utter hopelessness in the face of death" were not allowed. Instead, "every tree and shrub and flower proclaims that 'Life is Ever Lord of Death, and Love Can Never Lose Its Own.'" Noting the weddings, the statues, and the visitors, Barton concluded, "The followers of a triumphant Master should sleep in grounds more lovely than those where they have lived—a park so beautiful that it seems a bit above the level of this world, a first step up towards heaven."[15] The submission of death to a landscape of life shelters the visitor from the horrors of death and reinforces the secularization of religion. Selling eternity becomes a natural extension of a persuasive argument for a landscape void of death and ornaments directly related to the dead.

The connection between Eaton and Barton seems a marvelous coincidence of history. Barton not only mirrored Eaton's religious beliefs, he articulated the advertising credo that helped catapult Forest Lawn from obscurity. In 1927, Barton, one of the founders of the legendary advertising firm BBD&O, wrote his famous "Creed of an Advertising Man." This statement exalts the new field of advertising as the "voice of business." It continues by justifying advertising as a service, "a creative force that has generated jobs, new ideas, has expanded our economy and has helped give us the highest standard of living in the world." In case readers did not understand the importance and genuineness of such a mission, Barton added that "in the larger development of business and the gradual evolution of its ideas lies the best hope of the world." Eaton's earlier rejection of the past as encapsulated in the Builder's Creed laid out a vision of the new memorial park, whose essence was its ability to sell itself to a community its landscape embodied.

American cemeteries had advertised their services since before the Civil War. For most of the nineteenth century, "advertisements" consisted of small notices in the newspaper supplemented by guidebooks illustrated first with lithographs, then photographs, of prominent sights within the grounds. Forest Lawn pioneered a broader kind of advertising. Harry Earnshaw, the memorial park's advertising consultant, wrote that while most people found "something incongruous at first in the idea of a cemetery advertising for business," his attitude was if you have "something worthy for the people, you must tell them if you want to sell them."[16] He proudly proclaimed the difference between Forest Lawn and earlier cemeteries when he asserted that Forest Lawn "boldly tells the public its story, in its own way. It uses for that purpose, practically every legitimate medium of advertising—radio, newspapers, billboards, theatre programs, direct advertising through the mail, printed literature and publicity." From the door-to-door salespeople that startled Sarah Comstock's friend to the elaborate billboards Southern California has come to take for granted, Forest Lawn was at the forefront of commodifying the grave.

According to Harry Earnshaw, radio was the key in the 1920s. Forest Lawn came of age with modern radio. By 1929, over ten million families owned radios, Americans spent $850 million annually on radio equipment, and NBC was already charging as much as $10,000 an hour to sponsors. Aimee Semple McPherson started her own station, KFSG, as did others throughout the nation. In 1928, Forest Lawn sponsored an hour of music built around such themes as "Song of the Sea," "Love Songs of the World," and "Music of Devotion." The advertising message emphasized "the cultural and aesthetic features" of the burial place while always including an invitation to visit "one of the best known places of interest in Southern California." Earnshaw realized that radio was a new advertising medium—"a new and curious combination of art and showmanship and advertising"—where simple messages had to be crafted or the advertiser would "demonstrate how little he knows what the public wants."[17]

On the billboards that Forest Lawn also used to advertise the cemetery, the same sentimental messages were substituted for direct statements about death and burial. One billboard had a simple painting of the sea, without land or any other objects, and the inscription: "Eternal—as the sea." Naive by modern commercial and cultural standards, these ads were nonetheless effective in representing the message Forest Lawn's management wanted the reader to grasp. Eaton's happy eternal life was thus associated with Forest Lawn's eternally continuing business.

BRINGING MICHELANGELO TO LOS ANGELES

The second principle of the Forest Lawn landscape was that its aesthetics started with the Renaissance and ended with American academic art of the late nineteenth century. In the beautifully produced Art Guide which the memorial park published from the late 1920s to the early 1960s, and the earlier souvenir booklet "The Chimes," the "collection" was lovingly described and illustrated. Partly the Guide bolstered management's attempt to convince people that it had a significant art collection when in reality most sculptures were copies. Also, the art drew attention to Forest Lawn in a way that little else could have in 1920s America. Just as important, the Guide and the advertising reinforced the impression that in this boom city, in this transitory and dangerous age, Forest Lawn would last because it championed art that had survived for ages.

The collection began in 1915, when Eaton traveled to San Francisco's Panama Pacific International Exposition. The exposition was an impressive experience with a wide range of attractions. Among the most popular exhibits were an unlikely pair, *The Tower of Jewels,* a monumental rococo architectural confection festooned with cut-glass pendants, and Edna Parsons's *Duck Baby,* a diminutive bronze statue of an impish child holding two baby ducks. The *Tower of Jewels* was not for sale (although Forest Lawn's Tower of Legends was clearly modeled upon it), but Hubert Eaton was able to purchase *Duck Baby* (for $886) as the foundation stone for his reinvented memorial park. It was when his board of directors disagreed with the purchase that Eaton established a new company and assumed control of the entire development.[18]

Duck Baby and the many art features that followed it were essential to his vision of a successful modern cemetery. Eaton wrote repeatedly about "the memorial instinct." He reminded readers that many of the world's great art and architectural achievements had been completed because of the "memorial idea." The Pyramids, the Taj Mahal, Westminister Abbey, and countless sculptures and paintings memorialized gods or humans. Eaton hyperbolically claimed that everything "passes except that generated by this memorial idea." However, the standardization and commercialization of monuments meant everyone was memorialized, but few monuments were inspirational. Indeed, the lack of distinguished monuments had spurred a nationwide conversation in the immediate aftermath of World War I as to whether communities should not raise another "doughboy" statue, but rather should build memorial stadiums, parks, or other venues. Such sentiment threatened the cemetery as an institution. Increasingly, cemetery sections were filled with standardized monuments and markers, suggesting a problem similar to that posed by the ubiquitous doughboys in the arena of civic art. A lack of distinctive monuments might well cause people to question the value of the cemetery. The midwestern migrants had left cities with conventional cemeteries and traditional public art to come to Los Angeles. *Duck Baby* seems an unlikely antidote to such concerns, but for Eaton it was the perfect beginning.[19]

Parsons's sculpture served multiple purposes. First, it tied the nondescript Glendale burial place to one of California's most glorious recent events, the San Francisco Panama Pacific Exposition. In one stroke, Eaton had acquired a trophy of that success, which was still fresh in people's minds. Further, *Duck Baby* represented an accessible, popular art, not involved in the increasing contention about the place of art in American society. Only a few years before, in 1913, New York had been rocked by the Armory Show, with its very controversial showing of the cubists and other avant-garde modernist paintings. Parsons's sculpture was both sentimental, appropriate for a burial place, and honored, if by an older generation of academician artists. Finally, the sculpture was not standard operating procedure. It signaled a new beginning, as promised in the Builder's Creed. Unable to purchase the *The Tower of Jewels,* Eaton was quick to promise a grandiose mausoleum and manicured grounds filled with art works that people would admire.

Quite quickly, Eaton became much more aggressive and grandiose in his intentions. He traveled extensively in war-exhausted Europe, buying dozens of statues and making friends in many capitals. In 1926, Forest Lawn announced the arrival of a replica of *Moses.* Unlike other copies, this statue had been cast from the original in St. Peter's Church in Rome. Even the marble, from the quarries at Carrara, was the same as that used by Michelangelo. While the inauthenticity of the replica grates on our "modern" sensibilities, Forest Lawn's management reveled in its ability to bring to the boomtown of Los Angeles this great piece of art. At the public ceremony accompanying its arrival, speakers from the University of Southern California, the California Federation of Women's Clubs, the Tuesday Afternoon Club of Glendale, and the Italian Embassy preceded the California poet laureate and author of the "Mission Play," John Steven McGroarty.[20]

CEMETERY AS STAGED SPECTACLE

Moses was just one of a long line of copies that shaped the landscape of Forest Lawn. Most notable during the 1920s was the decision to build chapels modeled on famous European sacred spots. The first was the Little Church of the Flowers, "an exact replica of the village church at Stoke Poges, where Gray's 'Elegy' was written." The planners allowed themselves to make slight alterations, such as adding observatories adjacent to the pews. The observatories were filled with flowers and singing birds in the continuing attempt

Figure 15.3. Pearl Keller dancers at the newly landscaped entrance pond at Forest Lawn. *Forest Lawn Memorial Parks & Mortuaries*

to "depict life, and not death."[21] Later, in 1929, Annie Laurie's ruined church at Glencairn would be reconstructed as Wee Kirk O' The Heather, and long after the 1920s, the cemetery would add the Church of the Recessional, modeled on a twelfth-century church where Rudyard Kipling worshiped.

Again, the churches served a dual purpose. Each was associated with a well-known figure in American popular culture, especially late Victorian popular culture. Gray's "Elegy" was memorized by many schoolchildren, and Robert Burns's sentimental story of Annie Laurie by many others. Beyond these associations, though, the chapels served as working churches bringing services into the cemetery and away from the funeral home and other religious institutions. As Eaton stated, "This church [Little Church of the Flowers] . . . was thrown open for sermons, funerals, weddings, christenings, etc." And, people came.

The decision by Forest Lawn to offer the chapels for weddings, christenings, and other such events was a logical extension of the Builder's Creed, whereby the burial site becomes a place of life, not death. However, the public's willingness to accede to this philosophy shows a startling change from previous attitudes. The cemetery had been a solemn, sacred ground dedicated to the preservation of the memory of the dead. Now, the living claimed a place previously unacceptable in urban American cemeteries. People have used burial places for picnics, relaxing walks, even sexual trysts, but the notion of going to the cemetery for a joyous event surprised many people, as it would today. As Eaton's biographer wrote about the first wedding in 1923: "Friends were aghast and agog. People got married on flag poles, in submarines, at Coney Island, but not in a cemetery."[22] Eaton was reportedly ecstatic, believing that he had finally convinced people to treat Forest Lawn differently than they would have other cemeteries, not to mention that all those celebrants were being introduced to Forest Lawn's services.

The idea was to attract the public for more than passive participation in the mourning ritual. At almost every level, Forest Lawn's management wanted the new landscape to be a place of spectacles where spectators could learn about the past (their past as defined by management) and where they could enjoy themselves doing it. All the replica churches and statues, singing birds and splashing fountains, served this aim. But it was in the Great Mausoleum that Eaton first experimented with developing an artistic highlight that would reinforce his Builder's Creed while startling the viewer.

The Great Mausoleum was itself a replica, modeled roughly on the Campo Santo, Italy's most renowned burial space. Modern construction and modern needs for a larger number of crypts forced alterations to the original pattern, but both are imposing buildings. Eaton's determined attack on previous concepts of the cemetery was evident here: "Here again we planned to eradicate gloom and depression, substituting cheer, bright colors, depicting galleries of art rather than halls of death."[23] *Moses* was placed in a central corridor of the mausoleum, and other art works were scattered around it. In his travels, Eaton had collected a large selection of statues, and they were put to use to break up the long corridors of the mausoleum.

The central exhibit, though, was an original replica. In 1924, Eaton sailed for Europe on the trip that would eventually produce not only *Moses* but also Rosa Moretti's reproduction of *The Last Supper*. The Morettis had been making stained glass in Perugia for generations, according to all accounts. The task of firing the reproduction took six years. The completed product was placed in a specially built theater where it was opened for daily viewing. However, unlike the other art works, this display was not at the viewer's discretion; Forest Lawn presented *The Last Supper* in a dramatic fashion. The showings occurred at scheduled times, when visitors were admitted to rows of cathedral chairs. At first, only a curtain was visible; then the lights were dimmed and a prerecorded "radio voice" told the history of the window. At the end of the story, accompanied by music, the curtain parted, revealing the window. Shutters, which sheltered the window from sunlight damage, were then slowly opened so the viewers could see what the window would look like at various times of the day.[24]

The installation of *The Last Supper* signaled an important step in achieving Eaton's vision for Forest Lawn. In the years that followed, Jan Styka's *The Crucifixion,* originally painted for the St. Louis Exposition in 1904, would be installed in a new Hall of the Crucifixion, constructed on the site of the earlier Tower of Legends, Robert Clark's *The Resurrection* would be added to the Hall after a competition sponsored by Forest Lawn, and a second theatrical viewing would be scheduled for these two massive paintings, with visitors exiting directly into the new Forest Lawn Museum and gift shop. While all these changes were ahead, the installation of the Moretti window, and its success with visitors, demonstrated the ability of Forest Lawn to draw viewers to the attractions.

Barbara Rubin and her co-authors have persuasively argued that *The Last Supper, The Crucifixion,* and *The Resurrection* "delineate in an especially powerful way the overarching and unifying strategy of Eaton's Grand Plan." Each serves as a lesson in a story sequence that is an analogue for the services the memorial park provides its clients. For instance, *The Last Supper* "establishes the importance of rational, calm planning to meet the profound crisis death represents." After all, what is the last supper but a meeting in which a group of friends work out the issues surrounding the impending death of one of their fellows? The other members of the trilogy of attractions serve as depictions of loss and renewal. Eaton's lifelong search for a "smiling Christ" was an implicit quest for a belief in eternity, and, had he been successful, such an art work would have embodied that belief at Forest Lawn.

However, the trilogy also serve as reminders of the changing nature of popular culture in twentieth-century America. Static exhibits of sculpture and paintings were increasingly difficult to sell in competition with the radio and, especially, movies. Content to sanctify premodern artifacts rather than chance the dangers of abstraction and nonrepresentational art, the managers of Forest Lawn were still intrigued by the selling power of theater. Each staged show created a captive audience to which the managers could send a message about Forest Lawn's services and programs. Each also provided further vindication for expanding the business's services and for its overall strategy to sell eternity.

As the 1920s ended, Hubert Eaton was on the verge of taking a further radical step toward making Forest Lawn a prototype of the modern cemetery corporation. The allied businesses providing Americans with services made necessary by the death of their loved ones had traditionally not been in competition. The cemetery sold lots and maintained them. The monument dealers sold and erected memorials. The florists sold flowers. And the funeral directors oversaw the burial process and provided specific services such as embalming. While these sharp distinctions had blurred in some states, where some funeral directors also sold monuments, these professional divisions largely continued through the 1920s. Forest Lawn simply obliterated them.

First, as part of the decision to implement the "memorial park" concept, Forest Lawn began selling bronze markers for individual and family monuments. Then, next to their Elizabethan Administration Building, Forest Lawn opened a flower shop. Finally, in the early 1930s, Eaton opened the state's first cemetery-owned mortuary. In keeping with the centralizing trend of the American consumer culture, Forest Lawn now represented a one-stop-shopping place for those in need or considering their future needs. Opening the mortuary, however, produced a counterattack from outraged funeral directors, who were essentially eliminated from the burial process at Forest Lawn. They attempted to stop this development through legislative action. Ultimately they failed.

THE CRITICS

Evelyn Waugh and Lewis Mumford, among many other critics, believed it was Forest Lawn that had failed. The English Catholic Waugh imagined Forest Lawn as the ironic symbol of a bankrupt American culture. Writing to his friend Cyril Connolly in 1928, Waugh argued, "There is no such thing as an 'American.' They are all exiles uprooted, transplanted & doomed to sterility." Forest Lawn was representative of that sterility—not an authentic culture, but a mere imitation.[25] From the copies of European masterpieces to the ostentatiousness of the Great Mausoleum, the landscape turned art into a comical spectacle. And, the art was not in its context, not responding to its intended audience. Instead, even the good pieces were isolated objects serving as a commercial stage.

American critics were no less harsh. As Frank MacShane would write in 1961, such commercial superficiality from a California institution should not surprise us. "In a sense it is hard to know whether to laugh or cry when one visits Forest Lawn—to curse its bogus view of Christianity and the saccharine picture of life it represents—or to laugh it off as merely another Californian monument to bad taste."[26] Forest Lawn quickly came to represent many of the things American commentators found wanting in Southern California. It was too superficial, too happy, too serene, and ultimately inauthentic. With the victory of modernist values among cultural critics nationwide, Forest Lawn was bound to become an object of satire; Waugh's decision to lambast it could have easily been made by other, less talented, writers.

However, Jessica Mitford's exposé in her *American Way of Death* demonstrates it was not only aesthetic concerns that raised the hackles of critics. Forest Lawn might have looked backward for its values, but it looked forward with its innovative use of advertising, its profitable corporate structure, and its centralization of all services within its grounds. As the services for the dead were increasingly professionalized during the first half of the twentieth century, considerable social tension surrounded the family's loss of control over the process of death and interment. Mitford's attack codified the concerns of many commentators, while expressing the fears of millions of Americans.

Others might have raised questions about the "community" for which Forest Lawn was created. The memorial park followed the Southern California pattern of discriminating on the basis of race and ethnicity. Just as the burial sections were dotted with sculptures out of the European heritage, only people of Caucasian descent were welcome to purchase lots. Such discrimination mirrored the covenants attached to land deeds in many Los Angeles subdivisions, and throughout the nation by the early twentieth century. Forest Lawn would vigorously defend its right to limit its burials to Caucasians until legal action overthrew the entire system of covenants.[27]

The architectural and urban critic Lewis Mumford apparently never commented directly on Forest Lawn. However, his general thrust was clearly opposed to Eaton's use of the European past as a substitute for an American reality. As Miles Orvell has demonstrated, Mumford was appalled by exactly the cultural model that Forest Lawn proposed: "It was the mechanical reproduction, the mere imitation, of past models (especially European) that would stultify American culture and that must be avoided."[28] Such imitation consisted of half-baked history crafted to suit the commercial needs of those developing the artistic collection. It was modern culture at its worst.

GREAT AMERICAN MIRROR

Architectural scholars David Gebhard and Harriette von Breton have turned Mumford's criticism on its head, arguing that what makes Los Angeles unique is its role as a mirror of America's ideas: "Los Angeles was not the instigator of major innovations, but rather a mirror or reflection of middle class taste. Los Angeles' role from the mid 19th century to the present has been one of taking up ideas which have originated elsewhere, then expanding them in ways never conceived before."[29] They could have been writing of Hubert Eaton and the idea of Forest Lawn. Virtually all the elements that Eaton welded into a single landscape at Forest Lawn had been tried in other cities, but no one imagined them as a unit, as a vision. Eaton did imagine it, and had the venue that made it possible.

In her *Harpers* article, Sarah Comstock asks, "What can we make of it all—this extraordinary assemblage of contrasts, this unique conglomeration of sense and nonsense, culture and vulgar ignorance, restrained beauty and tawdry clap-trap?" She meant Los Angeles, but she also could have been writing about Forest Lawn. The new memorial park flouted the aesthetic conventions of the emerging modernist culture by extolling the inauthentic, applauding traditional values, and rejecting the abstract for the representational. Further, Eaton and his managers manipulated the public through sophisticated applications of modern advertising; their intent was to sell the burial place as a museum, a cultural sanctuary. Such attempts grate on the twenty-first-century cultural critic and scholar. The "smiling Christ" and the naive celebration of the heterosexual family seem Victorian, out of step, and exploitative.

However, along with Gebhard and von Breton, Comstock can help us better understand Forest Lawn's origins, and its relationship to the city it served. She also sees Los Angeles as a reflection of American experiences, as the Great American Mirror. She answers her own question by arguing that Los Angeles "is unique by virtue of her very universality." Los Angeles "represents our American muddle to a degree that no other city does, she becomes a composite portrait of the whole of us, and as such stands alone." Comstock recognized the city as a fascinating study of rapid growth amid the emerging consumer culture. While cultural critics applauded the emergence of modernism during these very years, urban and suburban culture was a complex mixture of new concepts and old ideas. Hubert Eaton exploited some of those new ideas—in advertising, finances, marketing, technology, and communications—to reinforce and, for Los Angeles residents, reassert the artistic sentiments and cultural values of his clientele.

Duck Baby, the Little Church of the Flowers, *Christus,* and the Tower of Legends were intended to signal to those Americans who had come to Los Angeles to escape from older industrial cities and towns that even in death they would inhabit a new city. No stoneyards, no disturbed graves. They would not be buried in a "civic liability" but in a burial place that reflected their vision of Los Angeles. Comstock argued that America had "strangely merged in this one astounding city." The American ability to "rush and roar and glitter," "splurge and boast," and place "good breeding, good taste, and intellect at the summit" had produced Los Angeles as the Great American Mirror. Forest Lawn mirrored the tensions embedded in the nation and in the city, with its racial covenants, valorization of a Victorian aesthetic, embracing of modern business techniques, and classic mixture (in Warren Susman's words) of "piety, profits, and play." The combination of gladsome religion, European heritage, and aggressive advertising made Forest Lawn a product both of the new consumer culture and of the older, staid Victorian culture. By combining them, Eaton was able to sell eternity to generations of residents of Los Angeles.

NOTES

1. Sarah Comstock, "The Great American Mirror: Reflections from Los Angeles," *Harpers Monthly Magazine,* May 1928: 715–23. On Los Angeles in the 1920s, also see Kevin Starr, *Material Dreams: Southern California through the 1920s* (New York: Oxford University Press, 1990).

2. Hubert Eaton, "Creation of Forest Lawn," an address before the American Association of Cemetery Superintendents conference, reported in *Park and Cemetery* 39 (September 1929): 209.

3. Basic information on Forest Lawn is taken primarily from its promotional literature, especially Forest Lawn, "Art Guide and Interpretations" (1936), and "Pictorial Forest Lawn" (1932). Also see Ralph Hancock, *The Forest Lawn Story* (Los Angeles: Angelus Press, 1964); Adela Rogers St. Johns, *First Step Up Towards Heaven: Hubert Eaton and Forest Lawn* (Englewood Cliffs, N.J: Prentice-Hall, Inc, 1959); and Barbara Rubin, Robert Carlton, and Arnold Rubin, *L.A. in Installments: Forest Lawn* (Santa Monica: Westside, 1979). For my earlier consideration of Forest Lawn as a model for the twentieth-century American burial place, see David Charles Sloane, *The Last Great Necessity: Cemeteries in American History* (Baltimore: Johns Hopkins University Press, 1991), 159–90.

4. Aldous Huxley, *After Many a Summer Dies the Swan* (New York: Harpers, 1939); Evelyn Waugh, *The Loved One* (Boston: Little, Brown, 1948); Jessica Mitford, *The American Way of Death* (New York: Simon and Schuster, 1963).

5. The numbers come from Eaton, "Creation of Forest Lawn," 209–11; the comments on the sunrise service and radio from Harry Earnshaw, "Advertising a Cemetery," *Park and Cemetery* 39 (September 1929): 212–15.

6. Eaton, "Creation of Forest Lawn," 210.

7. The description is taken from Leslie S. Hoagland, "Making a Cemetery a Civic Asset Instead of a Civic Liability," *The American City* 35 (July 1926): 66–68.

8. Robert Fogelson, *The Fragmented Metropolis: Los Angeles, 1850–1930,* rpt. ed. (Berkeley and Los Angeles: University of California Press, 1993), is the source for the information on Los Angeles; Comstock, "The Great American Mirror," 716.

9. Comstock, "The Great American Mirror," 716.

10. Sloane, *The Last Great Necessity,* 81.

11. Her grave is noted in J. Culbertson and T. Randall, *Permanent Californians: An Illustrated Guide to the Cemeteries of California* (Chelsea, Vt.: Chelsea Green, 1989). Sarah Comstock wrote an evocative portrait of McPherson just months before her piece on Forest Lawn; the similarities of spectacle are quite striking. See "Aimee Semple McPherson: Prima Donna of Revivalism," *Harpers Magazine,* December 1927: 11–19.

12. Comstock, "Aimee Semple McPherson," 12.

13. Barton, "Cemetery without Gloom," *Reader's Digest,* August 1937: 73–76. Barton is discussed by Warren Susman, "Culture Heroes: Ford, Barton, Ruth," in his *Culture as History: The Transformation of American Society in the Twentieth Century* (New York: Pantheon, 1972), 122–31.

14. Warren Susman, "Piety, Profits and Play: The 1920s," in H. H. Quint and M. Cantor, eds., *Men, Women, and Issues in American History: Volume II* (Homewood,

Ill.: The Dorsey Press, 1975), 208–10; "smiled" quote from St. Johns, *First Step Up Towards Heaven*, 278.

15. Barton, "A First Step Up Toward Heaven," as introduction to "Pictorial Forest Lawn" (published by Forest Lawn, 1944). Barton's introduction was used in a variety of Forest Lawn publications starting in 1927.

16. Earnshaw, "Advertising a Cemetery," 213.

17. The statistics come from Mary Beth Norton et al., *A People and a Nation: A History of the United States, Volume II: Since 1865* (Boston: Houghton Mifflin, 1990), 704; the description of Forest Lawn advertising from Earnshaw, "Advertising the Cemetery," 213–14. Comstock, "Aimee Semple McPherson," 16, notes the importance of radio to McPherson's performance and success. For further discussion of these issues, see Lynn Dumenil, *Modern Temper: American Culture and Society in the 1920s* (New York: Hill and Wang, 1995), especially 194–96.

18. Rubin, Carlton, and Rubin, *L.A. in Installments*, 16–18. For information on the exposition, see Robert W. Rydell, *All the World's a Fair: Visions of Empire at American International Expositions, 1876–1916* (Chicago: University of Chicago Press, 1984), 212–33.

19. Eaton would eventually gather together his thoughts on the "memorial idea" into a pamphlet, "The Co-Memorial," published by Forest Lawn Memorial Park in 1954.

20. The description of the ceremony appeared in the *Los Angeles Times* on April 19, 1926, pt. II, 2, while the description of John Steven McGroarty comes from St. Johns, *First Step Up Towards Heaven*, 206.

21. Eaton, "Creation of Forest Lawn," 210.

22. St. Johns, *First Step Up Towards Heaven*, 175.

23. Eaton, "Creation of Forest Lawn," 210.

24. Frank MacShane, "Forest Lawn," *Prairie Schooner* 35 (Summer 1961): 142.

25. Evelyn Waugh to Cyril Connolly, January 2, 1928, *The Letters of Evelyn Waugh*, ed. Mark Anthony (New Haven: Yale University Press, 1980), 259–60.

26. MacShane, "Forest Lawn," 148.

27. See my discussion of this issue in *The Last Great Necessity*, 187–88.

28. Miles Orvell, *The Real Thing: Imitation and Authenticity in American Culture, 1880–1940* (Chapel Hill: University of North Carolina Press, 1989), 169.

29. Quoted in Gordon DeMarco, *A Short History of Los Angeles* (San Francisco: Lexikos, 1988), 120.

CONTRIBUTORS

CLARK DAVIS, an assistant professor of history at California State University, Fullerton, is author *of Company Men: White Collar Life and Corporate Cultures in Los Angeles, 1892–1941* (Johns Hopkins University Press, 2000). He is currently writing a book about the history of career success ideals in postwar America.

MIKE DAVIS is the author of *Magical Urbanism: Latinos Reinvent the U.S. Big City* (Verso, 2000). He lives in Papaaloa, Hawaii, and teaches at the State University of New York, Stony Brook.

WILLIAM DEVERELL is an associate professor of history at the California Institute of Technology. He teaches and writes on the history of the nineteenth- and twentieth-century American West. With Greg Hise he is editing an environmental history of Southern California.

MICHAEL E. ENGH, S.J., is an associate professor of history at Loyola Marymount University, where he serves on the executive committee of the Center for the Study of Los Angeles. His most recent work is a volume of edited primary sources, *Frontiers and American Catholic Identities* (Orbis Press, 1999), and his present research focuses on social reform movements in Los Angeles, 1890–1950.

DOUGLAS FLAMMING is an associate professor of history at the Georgia Institute of Technology, where he is also Director of the Center for Society and Industry in the Modern South. He is currently writing a book entitled "A World to Gain: African Americans and the Making of Los Angeles, 1890–1940."

PHILIP GOFF is associate professor of religious studies and Director of the Center for the Study of Religion and American Culture at Indiana University–Purdue University at Indianapolis. He is editor of the journal *Religion and American Culture* and co-editor of the forthcoming *Themes in American Religion and Culture* (University of California Press, 2001). He is currently at work on a book entitled "Heavenly Sunshine: Charles E. Fuller, Religious Radio, and the Rise of Modern Evangelicalism."

GREG HISE is an associate professor of urban history in the School of Policy, Planning, and Development at the University of Southern California. He is the author of *Magnetic Los Angeles: Planning the Twentieth-Century Metropolis* (Johns Hopkins University Press, 1997) and co-author, with William Deverell, of *Eden by Design: The 1930 Olmsted-Bartholomew Plan for the Los Angeles Region* (University of California Press, 2000). Currently he is writing a landscape history of nineteenth-century Los Angeles and editing an environmental history of Southern California.

DOUGLAS MONROY is a professor of history at Colorado College. He is the author of *Thrown among Strangers: The Making of Mexican Culture in Frontier California* (1990), winner of the James Rawley Prize of the Organization of American Historians, and *Rebirth: Mexican Los Angeles from the Great Migration to the Great Depression* (1999), both from the University of California Press.

BECKY M. NICOLAIDES is an assistant professor of history and urban studies and planning at the University of California, San Diego. She is completing a book on the history of working-class suburbia in Los Angeles.

LAURIE PINTAR received her Ph.D. from the University of Southern California and teaches in the History Department at Loyola Marymount University. Her current project is a study of labor and gender in Hollywood's studios during the 1930s and 1940s.

NANCY QUAM-WICKHAM is associate professor of history at California State University, Long Beach. Her book *The Power of Oil* is forthcoming from University of California Press.

STEVEN J. ROSS is a professor of history at the University of Southern California, where he teaches courses in American social history and popular culture. He is the author of *Working-Class Hollywood: Silent Film and the Shaping of Class in America* (Princeton University Press, 1998) and *Workers on the Edge: Work, Leisure, and Politics in Industrializing Cincinnati* (Columbia University Press, 1985).

MATTHEW W. ROTH was founding curator of the Petersen Automotive Museum in Los Angeles and now directs the archives for the Automobile Club of Southern California. He is also a Ph.D. candidate in history at the University of Southern California, and his dissertation examines road and freeway development in Los Angeles.

TOM SITTON is a curator of American history at the Natural History Museum of Los Angeles County. He is working on a book examining Los Angeles political history during the 1938–53 administration of Mayor Fletcher Bowron.

DAVID C. SLOANE is an associate professor in the School of Policy, Planning, and Development at the University of Southern California. He is co-author, with Beverlie Conant Sloane, of *Medicine Moves to the Mall: The Evolving Architecture of Health Care* (Johns Hopkins University Press, forthcoming 2002). His chapter on Forest Lawn is an extension of a broader discussion of the cultural history of burial places in *The Last Great Necessity: Cemeteries in American History* (Johns Hopkins University Press, 1991).

JULES TYGIEL is a professor of history at San Francisco State University. He is the author of *The Great Los Angeles Swindle: Oil, Stocks, and Scandal during the Roaring Twenties* (Oxford University Press, 1994) and *Past Time: Baseball as History* (Oxford University Press, 2000).

INDEX

Compositor:	G&S Typesetters
Text:	10/12 Baskerville
Display:	Baskerville
Printer and Binder:	Sheridan Books, Inc.